IN GOOD CONSCIENCE

KANSHA
PROJECT

By
Military Intelligence Service
Association of Northern California

感謝

KANSHA PROJECT

In Good Conscience
Supporting Japanese Americans During the Internment

Shizue Seigel

AACP, Inc.
San Mateo, California

A Project of the Military Intelligence Service Association of Northern California

AACP, Inc.
P.O. Box 1587, San Mateo, CA 94401
800-874-2242
www.asianamericanbooks.com

ISBN (cloth): 0-934609-18-7
ISBN (paper): 0-934609-19-5
Major funding for this publication provided by the California State Library's Civil Liberties Public Education Program, and by the donors listed in the acknowledgments.

Library of Congress Control Number: 2005932362

KANSHA
PROJECT

This book is made possible by the feeling of *kansha*. The English translation is "appreciation,"

but *kansha* has a profoundly soulful dimension, with shadings that cannot be adequately conveyed in translation.

When a great favor is conferred, it awakens a gratitude so profound

as to be endless, an energy inspired by the goodness and connection that is at the root of life, an energy that must be honored and kept alive

by passing it, not only back to the benefactor, but onward and outward to others in expanding ripples.

A single candle glimmering in the night is more deeply appreciated than a hundred in daylight.

For many Japanese Americans during the internment, wartime kindnesses, large and small, kindled hope and reasserted humanity

in the darkest of times. That flame still burns today.

Kansha puts focus, not merely on what happened to Japanese Americans in the past,

but on the rights and responsibilities of all Americans.

It focuses not on bitterness or self-pity, but on what each of us can do today

to prevent such injustice from happening ever again to any group.

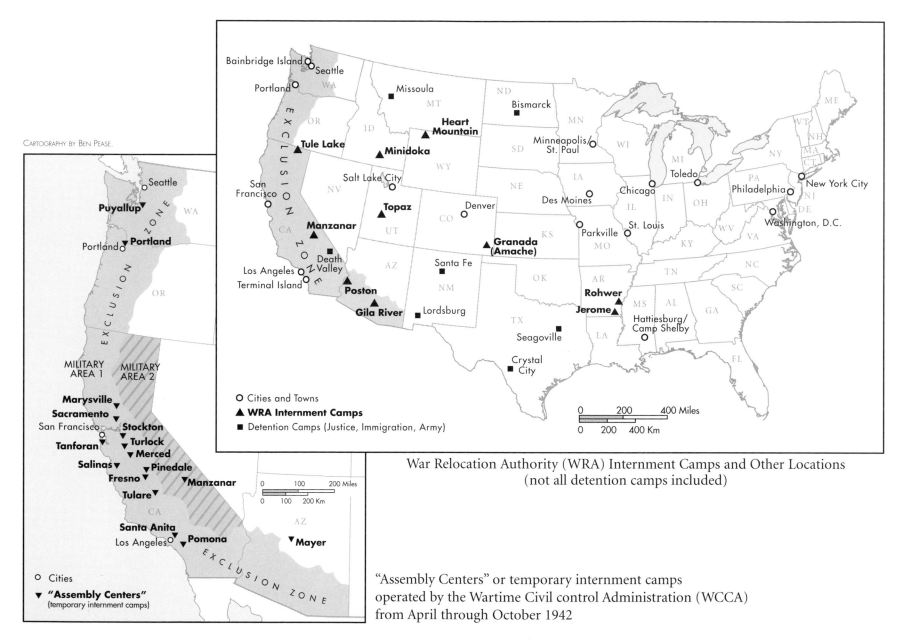

CARTOGRAPHY BY BEN PEASE.

Bainbridge Island
Seattle
Portland

WA
OR
ID
MT
ND
MN
WI
MI
ME
VT
NH
MA
CT
NY
PA
NJ
DE
MD

Missoula
Bismarck

Heart Mountain

Tule Lake
Minidoka

Salt Lake City

NV
CA
UT
WY
SD
NE
IA

Minneapolis/ St. Paul
Toledo
Chicago
IN
OH

New York City
Philadelphia
Washington, D.C.
WV
VA

Topaz
Denver
CO

San Francisco

Manzanar

Death Valley

Los Angeles
Terminal Island

Poston
Gila River

AZ
NM

Santa Fe

Lordsburg

Granada (Amache)
KS
MO
Parkville
St. Louis
KY

Des Moines
IL

Rohwer
Jerome
AR
MS
AL
GA
TN
NC
SC

Hattiesburg/ Camp Shelby

TX
OK
LA

Seagoville

Crystal City

FL

○ Cities and Towns
▲ WRA Internment Camps
■ Detention Camps (Justice, Immigration, Army)

0   200   400 Miles
0   200   400 Km

War Relocation Authority (WRA) Internment Camps and Other Locations
(not all detention camps included)

Seattle
WA

Puyallup

Portland
Portland

EXCLUSION ZONE

OR

MILITARY AREA 1
MILITARY AREA 2

Marysville
Sacramento
San Francisco
Stockton
Tanforan
Turlock
Merced
Salinas
Pinedale
Fresno
Manzanar
Tulare

CA

Santa Anita
Los Angeles
Pomona
Mayer

AZ

EXCLUSION ZONE

0   100   200 Miles
0   100   200 Km

○ Cities
▼ "Assembly Centers"
(temporary internment camps)

"Assembly Centers" or temporary internment camps
operated by the Wartime Civil control Administration (WCCA)
from April through October 1942

Contents

PREFACE

This book is about ordinary people who became extraordinary by acting when others did not. After Japan attacked Pearl Harbor, the general public sanctioned the forced eviction and mass incarceration of 120,000 Japanese Americans—U.S. citizens as well as noncitizens—for no reason other than their Japanese ancestry. During an era when fear, anger and racial prejudice gripped the nation, only a relative handful recognized that the United States government was committing a great wrong, and even fewer went out of their way to assist the victims. These courageous and compassionate few saw clearly what Congress did not acknowledge until the Civil Liberties Act of 1988 (Redress Bill)—that the act of internment was "a grave injustice...without adequate security reasons and...motivated largely by racial prejudice, wartime hysteria, and a failure of political leadership."

In today's post-9/11 world, as a largely apathetic public once again ignores the erosion of civil liberties, we have much to learn from the courageous few who supported Japanese Americans during World War II.

We could only record a sampling of the many individuals who deserve to be acknowledged, and we hope that others will carry on the task. We feel sure that you will find these stories of ordinary people acting in good conscience as inspiring as we did. Every act of compassion, no matter how small, is an act of courage with far-reaching consequences. *(For an overview of decisions leading to the internment, see "Why the Mainland and Not Hawaii: Decisions Leading to Mass Incarceration. For more on methodology, please see "Conclusion: How We Chose the Stories and What We Learned.")*

NOTES ON TERMINOLOGY: During the internment era, both Japanese immigrants and their U.S.-born children were referred to rather clinically as *persons of Japanese ancestry*. The term *Japanese American* was not in wide use at the time. Immigrants in general were commonly identified by their countries of origin: the *Irish*, the *Italians*, and so forth, with no distinction made between permanent residents, naturalized citizens and American-born citizens. With the onset of World War II, unnaturalized immigrants from the Axis countries were automatically designated as *enemy aliens*.

An additional problem faced immigrants from Japan because, unlike their counterparts from Europe, Asian immigrants were barred from naturalized citizenship because of race, even if they had lived in the United States for fifty years or more. A 1790 immigration law limited naturalized citizenship to "free white persons." Congress extended the right of naturalized citizenship to persons of African descent in 1870, but not to Japanese immigrants until the Walter-McCarran Act of 1952.

This book uses the term *Japanese American* to refer to both citizens and noncitizens of Japanese ancestry. The immigrant generation are the *Issei*—the Japanese word for "first generation." Their children, born on U.S. soil and American citizens by right of birth, are the *Nisei*, or "second generation," and their grandchildren are the *Sansei*, or "third generation." The *Kibei* were born in the United States and educated in Japan but later returned to live in the United States. The term *Nikkei* refers to both emigrants from Japan and to their descendants living anywhere outside Japan.

Prior to and during World War II, government officials, including Pres. Franklin D. Roosevelt, occasionally used the term *concentration camp*, in regard to the mass incarceration of Japanese Americans, but wider use was made of such euphemisms as the *Evacuation*, *evacuee*, *assembly center* and *relocation center*. Today these terms are generally avoided except when quoting from contemporary sources.

Recently, an increasing number of scholars maintain that technically only foreign nationals can be "interned," and therefore, *internment* and related words should not be applied to U.S. citizens. Instead, they favor terms like *incarceration*, *incarcerees* or *inmates*, *temporary detention camp*, and *concentration camp* or *prison camp*.

The debate is ongoing, and a survey of recent books reveals wide variance in terminology. We deliberated long and hard before choosing the following terminology for this book. We refer to the *Evacuation* as the *eviction* (in the early stages) and the *internment* (in later stages.) In the spring of 1942, *evictees* were forced from their homes on the West Coast *exclusion area*, and *interned* or *incarcerated* in *temporary internment camps* or "assembly centers" (in quotes) operated by the Wartime Civil Control Administration (WCCA). Later, *internees* were sent to more permanent *internment camps*. Some scholars advocate the use of *internee* and *internment camp* only for the camps for "dangerous enemy aliens" administered by the Department of Justice, the U.S. Army or the Department of Immigration. We have chosen to refer to these camps collectively as *detention camps* to avoid confusion with the ten "relocation centers" administered by the War Relocation Authority (WRA). Although we do not dispute the fact that the WRA camps were concentration camps in the sense generally understood in 1942, we have chosen to use the term sparingly because its meaning has been overwhelmingly colored by what we now know about the Nazi death camps.

A PROJECT OF THE MILITARY INTELLIGENCE SERVICE ASSOCIATION OF NORTHERN CALIFORNIA

The Military Intelligence Service Association of Northern California undertook to sponsor *In Good Conscience* because many of us Nisei who served as military intelligence specialists during World War II volunteered from the very internment camps where we were unjustly incarcerated. We dedicate the book to those who extended kindness to us and our families when we needed it most.

This book would not have been possible without financial grants from the California State Library's Civil Liberties Public Education Program and donations from the many friends of the Military Intelligence Service Association of Northern California (MIS NorCal). We are thankful to all those who contributed so generously. We are also indebted to those who nominated the people described in this book, or provided invaluable leads, information or other assistance. *(See Acknowledgments.)*

The Kansha Project was most fortunate to have the authorship and graphic design of our talented and hardworking Shizue Seigel. We also give many thanks to the following volunteers for their comments and advice: advisory committee members Brenda Wong Aoki, Stephen Fugita, Wendy Hanamura, Jeanne Wakatsuki Houston, Chizu Iiyama, Ken Kashiwahara, Ben Kobashigawa, Yuri Kochiyama, Wayne Maeda, Charles T. Morrissey, Gary M. Mukai, Rev. Paul M. Nagano, Jerrold Takahashi and Stephen Yale; readers Eric Chang, Warren Mar, Li Miao, Ben Pease, Diane Rigda and Emily Zimmerman; and proofreader Robert A. Pease.

Furthermore, this project would not have been possible without the personal interest and cooperative endeavor of my advisory team members: fiscal manager Sukeo Oji and advisory associates Fred Kitajima and Walter Tanaka. We are also grateful for the capable and patient administrative assistance of Susie Takeda; for the early encouragement and support of Eric Saul, the father of the Kansha Project; and for the extensive contributions of Harry K. Honda, Ted Tsukiyama; Rev. Paul M. Nagano; Allen H. Meyer; Hisaji Q. Sakai, MD, and Ted M. Hopes; Stephen McNeil; Richard Potashin; Paul Ohtaki; Glenn Kumekawa; Marie Masumoto; and Marion Kanemoto and Joanne Iritani.

We thank Paul Osaki of the Japanese Cultural and Community Center of Northern California for providing us with office space and facilities in San Francisco; Florence Hongo of AACP, Inc., for acting as publisher; George Hinoki, Don Tamaki and Jeff Woo for legal advice, and cartographer Ben Pease for maps.

To all those who contributed to the successful completion of this book, many thanks.

— Col. Harry Fukuhara (U.S. Army, retired)
Kansha Project Director

LEFT: MILDRED AND WALTER WOODWARD COEDITED AND PUBLISHED *THE BAINBRIDGE REVIEW.* COURTESY OF MARY CALISTA WOODWARD PRATT AND PAUL OHTAKI. *BELOW:* THE DECEMBER 8 "WAR EXTRA." COURTESY OF *THE BAINBRIDGE REVIEW* AND PAUL OHTAKI.

WALT AND MILLY WOODWARD:
"OUR CONSTITUTION MUST NOT BE TOSSED ASIDE"

In Puget Sound in northwestern Washington, on the night of December 7, 1941, the lights burned unusually late at the office of Bainbridge Island's tiny community newspaper, *The Bainbridge Review.* A civil defense warden rapped on the door. When publisher Walter Woodward cracked it open, the warden scolded him. "Don't you know they bombed Pearl Harbor this morning? Put out those lights now, or I'll shoot 'em out!"[1]

Woodward and his wife, Milly, hurriedly plastered their windows with a thick layer of newspapers and worked through the night. They were printing a special edition of their weekly paper—a one-page "War Extra." The Woodwards were fully aware that strategic installations around Bainbridge Island made a tempting military target, but they were even more concerned that mounting anger and hysteria might be aimed at their Japanese American neighbors. They felt a pressing responsibility to raise a moderating voice.

The next morning, Bainbridge Islanders opened *The Review* to news items about air-raid warnings and blackouts and to a carefully considered editorial titled "Plain Talk." Walt Woodward wrote:

> There are on this Island some 300 members of 50 families whose blood ties lie with a nation which, yesterday, committed an atrocity against all that is decent....

> [T]here is the danger of a blind, wild hysterical hatred of all persons who can trace ancestry to Japan. That some of those persons happen to be American citizens, happen to be loyal to this country and happen to have no longer a binding tie with the fatherland are factors which easily could be swept aside by mob hysteria....

> Island Japanese, as never before, must prove their mettle as loyal Americans. They must realize that they will be the objects of intense scrutiny. They must not resent this. They must welcome it. They must do everything in their power to ferret out those among their number—if any there be—who do not have an abiding love and loyalty for this America of ours.

> To other Islanders, *The Review* says this: These Japanese-Americans of ours haven't bombed anybody. In the past they have given every indication of loyalty to this nation. They have sent, along with our boys, their own sons...into the United States Army....

> Let us so live in this trying time so that when it is all over, loyal Americans can look loyal Americans in the eye with the knowledge that, together, they kept the Stars and Stripes flying high.[2]

According to Woodward, his was the only newspaper in western Washington to oppose the internment.

◆   ◆   ◆

THE BAINBRIDGE REVIEW'S LOGO. COURTESY OF THE BAINBRIDGE REVIEW.

In Woodward's family, a sense of social justice stretched back to a grandfather who sheltered runaway slaves in a Vermont outpost of the Underground Railroad. As a young man, however, Walt showed far more interest in sports. Born in Seattle in 1910 to a prominent physician, the young collegian volunteered as an unpaid sports writer for *The Seattle Times* while studying pre-med at the University of Washington. After college, he landed a cub reporter's job at the *Juneau Daily Empire*. Within a month of his arrival in Alaska, he fell for a vivacious, redheaded schoolteacher, Mildred Logg. Soon after they married in 1935, Woodward was offered a job at *The Seattle Times*.

After a year in Seattle, Milly persuaded Walt to move to Bainbridge Island. He commuted to work at *The Seattle Times* while Milly taught at Bainbridge High School.

Milly had been born on the Island. Her family had summered there for generations, and its fir-cloaked hills and small stony beaches were in her blood. The 4-by-10-mile island was only thirty minutes west of Seattle by ferry, but it felt a world away. Most of the Island's residents lived on farms and cabins frequently shrouded by rain and fog, and only loosely connected by rugged dirt roads.

Bainbridge Island had first been settled in the mid-19th century. In the late 1800s it had boasted the world's largest sawmill, which spawned colonies of millworkers from Japan, Hawaii and the Philippines. Many of them remained after the mill closed. In 1940, the Island's population of 3500 included 274 Japanese Americans among its eclectic mix of rugged backwoodsmen, well-to-do summer folk, shipyard workers and farmers.

In 1940, the Woodwards purchased *The Bainbridge Review,* in partnership with local attorney Laurance Peters and his wife, Claire. At first, Woodward kept his day job and devoted his evenings to *The Review.*

In late 1941, Walt quit *The Times* and committed himself full time to his little paper. The Woodwards bought out their partners and moved into the little wooden *Review* building in Pleasant Beach, a tiny village on the Island's secluded south side. Walt and Milly and their small daughter lived in one half of the building; the newspaper took up the other half.

WALT WOODWARD
CUT A DASHING FIGURE
AS A JOURNALIST FOR
THE SEATTLE TIMES IN
1938. COURTESY OF MARY
CALISTA WOODWARD PRATT AND PAUL
OHTAKI.

The young couple plunged into the endless business of running a small-town paper, spending most of their waking hours as "newspaper owners, publishers, editors, reporters, advertising salesmen, business managers, typesetters, stereotypers, printers, pressmen, mailers and janitors."[3] Walt did most of the writing, but Milly was a full partner in every decision. "If she didn't approve, it didn't get in the paper," he claimed.

The Review achieved national recognition when the Associated Press picked up the little paper's story about the British warship *Warspite.* The battle-scarred vessel, with blood still on its decks, had limped its way from the Mediterranean to the Bremerton Naval Shipyard in Puget Sound, where it was undergoing repairs. Its presence was an open secret to Bainbridge Islanders, but *The Review,* in a "solemn duty to our readers," was the first newspaper to report this breach of U.S. neutrality. *Time* magazine praised the "suburban weekly, brightly edited by young Seattleites," for its courage.[4]

But it was the outbreak of war and subsequent violations of Japanese American civil liberties that brought forth the Woodwards's true courage. At a time when the term *Japanese American* was not in common usage, the Woodwards used the paper throughout the war to remind Bainbridge Islanders that "Island Japanese" were not the enemy overseas but schoolmates and neighbors with the same constitutional rights as all Americans. In *The Review*'s War Extra, prominent articles about the loyalty of Japanese Americans overshadowed items about air raids and blackouts. In an article headlined "Japanese Leaders Here Pledge Loyalty to America," Woodward interviewed Issei strawberry grower H. O. Koura of the Japanese Chamber of Commerce, who said, "My sole purpose is to raise [my six] children to be good members of American society.... I am positive every Japanese family on the Island has an intense loyalty for the United States of America and stands ready to defend it."

Koura's son Art, a member of the fledgling local chapter of the Japanese American Citizens League (JACL), added, "Every Japanese, first or second generation, will do everything he can to protect this nation's flag. If there is any sign of sabotage or spies, we will be the first ones to report it to the authorities." The young Nisei then lapsed into all-American slang: "I think Japan is 'nutty' to try this."

MILLY AND WALT WOODWARD, 1941. COURTESY OF MARY CALISTA WOODWARD PRATT AND PAUL OHTAKI.

Also prominent in the War Extra was an article about the death of Anna Osgood, a local Congregational minister's wife: "[L]ong a friend and patron of Island Japanese, [she] did not live to learn of Japan's hostilities against the United States." Woodward pointedly added that Mrs. Osgood had taught English to the Issei and "a little about the American values, ideals and lifestyle that their children were exposed to in the public schools."

Ironically, at the outbreak of the war, the Woodwards themselves had only a nodding acquaintance with Japanese Americans except for Paul Ohtaki, a shy, quiet high school senior who had been working for them for about a year as a part-time janitor. "[T]he Japanese community kept to itself," Woodward recalled later.[5] "There was no integration [but if] there was animosity, it wasn't apparent to Milly and me.... They went their way and we went ours." Paul, like most of the Japanese Americans, lived in Winslow, the Island's biggest town. He drove his father's battered Model A out to Pleasant Beach once a week to clean *The Review*'s paper-littered floor after a pressrun. "It's a ten-minute drive nowadays," he says, "but in those days, on the Island's narrow dirt roads, it seemed like an awfully long drive."[6]

According to Paul, the War Extra "set the pace for the Bainbridge Island community" and paved the way for others to show support for the Japanese Americans. The Woodwards were not alone (*see box: Bainbridge High School*) but they were the most visible. On the afternoon of December 8, a group of young Nisei crowded into Woodward's office to ask his advice. He counseled them to avoid suspicion by not gathering in large numbers. They should close the Japanese-language school. They should be prepared to prove their loyalty by joining the armed forces, and giving their lives if necessary.

The following months were filled with tension. Rumors flew that there were Japanese submarines off the coast, that hidden radio transmitters were being used for espionage, that Japanese spies had been caught photographing the navy yard. Bainbridge Islanders felt particularly vulnerable because of strategic targets nearby. The Bremerton Naval Shipyard was two miles to the southwest across a narrow strait; the Boeing Aircraft plant, a large Seattle shipyard, the Keyport Torpedo Station and a navy fuel depot were located within a ten-mile radius. On the Island itself, a top-secret navy radio communications station was located at Fort Ward, and minesweepers were outfitted at the Winslow shipyard. When a transformer exploded at Winslow, many residents were sure the huge blast signaled a Japanese invasion.

Woodward recalled, "We were very frightened...the whole Puget Sound country was.... We were positive that the rotten Japs were lousy marksmen and would aim for Boeing or the Naval Shipyard and...hit us."[7] Even today, more than sixty years later, some residents still insist that the terror they felt justified interning all the Japanese Americans. They were sure they were fighting for their very existence.

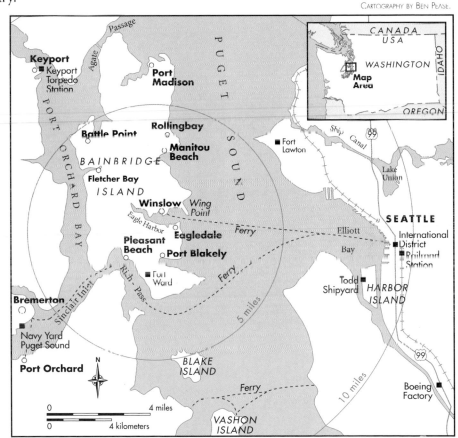

CARTOGRAPHY BY BEN PEASE.

While the Caucasians scanned the skies for invading bombers, the Island's Japanese Americans wondered what would happen to them. Even before Pearl Harbor, they had felt themselves to be second-class citizens in many ways. They were denied work at the navy yard or at Boeing, and were barred from many unions. Now they were being stared at with increasing suspicion. Nevertheless, many were not worried at first. Their ancestry might be Japanese, but most Nisei felt thoroughly Americanized. Their Issei parents had been living in the United States since at least 1924, when the United States cut off immigration from Japan. The immigrants may have had emotional ties to their homeland, but they had cast their lot firmly with their adopted country.

The majority were strawberry farmers. Bainbridge berries commanded premium prices ever since they were served to the Queen of England on her visit to Vancouver Island in the 1930s. The succulent red berries that symbolized luxury to the end-consumer were the fruits of painstaking labor.

The Island's moist climate was ideal for berries, but the soil was rocky and hilly and hard to irrigate. The densely forested land had to be cleared foot-by-foot of towering Douglas fir and cedar, and the stumps blasted out with dynamite. Then came the laborious work of plowing and ditch-digging. After the plants were set, they needed to be kept weed-free and healthy for two years, until they were mature enough to bear fruit. By the time the first good harvest came in, most farmers were deeply in debt for fertilizer and supplies.

Most Issei farmers had barely scraped out a living during the Depression. Just prior to the war they had finally begun to look forward to better times. The economy was picking up. Their sons were finishing high school and getting old enough to help out full time. With the extra manpower, some families were finally able to buy their own land instead of renting, and a few were beginning to replace their horse-drawn equipment with tractors.

◆ ◆ ◆

The days that followed Pearl Harbor escalated in tension. The local sheriff began to pay regular visits to each of the fifty Japanese American families scattered throughout the Island. Bank accounts were frozen and radios confiscated. Then the FBI arrived and set up headquarters at Fort Ward. They visited each house in turn, searching every room and poring over the books. Nervous families burned or buried possessions associated with their Japanese roots: treasured books, phonograph records and family heirlooms. They buried the guns they used for hunting and for scaring crows out of the fields, got rid of bird-watching binoculars, and destroyed their cameras and any photographs that happened to include U.S. Navy ships. In spite of their precautions, H. O. Koura and many of the Island's other Issei men were taken away by the FBI.

"Most of the older Issei were arrested and sent to a Department of Justice camp," recalled Paul. Paul's parents feared the day the FBI would come for them, because in addition to growing berries, they operated the Island's only Japanese-language school. "They were arresting anybody who was a teacher or a leader in the community," said Paul. "They took my father away, but they didn't keep him. We were surprised and relieved when he came home."[9]

To this day, Paul puzzles over why his parents were spared. "Most of the farmers had dynamite for blasting stumps and shotguns for scaring crows out of the fields. We didn't have any dynamite because we were renting land that had already been cleared," he muses. "And our place was pretty small. Some of the others who had big properties were kind of isolated geographically, so their neighbors got suspicious that they might be up to something. Or maybe it was because my parents were Christians and not Buddhists like most other Issei. I think our neighbors thought we were running a Christian after-school program."

HIGH SCHOOL STUDENT PAUL OHTAKI WORKED AS A JANITOR FOR *THE BAINBRIDGE REVIEW.* COURTESY OF PAUL OHTAKI

Nobody was quite sure where the arrested men had been sent or when they would come back. Tensions continued to rise. On February 19, 1942, President Franklin D. Roosevelt signed Executive Order 9066 authorizing the exclusion of all persons of Japanese ancestry from the West Coast. Later that month, the government forced Japanese Americans off of Terminal Island, located just south of Los Angeles, without providing them with a place to go. *(See chapter: Virginia Swanson Yamamoto.)*

In late March, Bainbridge Islanders became the first Japanese Americans to be incarcerated en masse. On March 24, a detachment of soldiers arrived from Seattle, rifles at the ready. Fanning across the Island, they nailed up copies of Civilian Exclusion Order #1, ordering all persons of Japanese ancestry to leave Bainbridge Island by March 30, 1942.

Woodward was furious. He editorialized, "Where, in the face of their fine record since December 7, in the face of their rights of citizenship...in the face of American decency, is there any excuse for this high-handed, much too-short evacuation order?"[10] It was the beginning of "an editorial tirade which didn't cease until the war was over," Woodward said later. "We said over and over and over again this is an outrage, this is a blatant violation of...those rights being guaranteed by the Bill of Rights.... We really didn't do it for any great love of [Japanese Americans]. We did it because if it could happen to them, it could happen to German Americans, to Chinese Americans, to fat Americans, to Rotary Club Americans, to any kind of Americans."[11]

Not everyone agreed with Woodward. Only one or two businesses withdrew their advertising, but "a frightening number" of readers canceled subscriptions. The Woodwards feared for the future of their paper until the local drugstore called to double its regular order. "We suddenly felt much better," said Woodward. "We realized [our readers] wouldn't give us the honor of their names on our subscription rolls, but by God, they still were reading it."[12]

The eviction order was "brutal," Woodward declared.

> It gave those Japanese American citizens only a very few days to arrange their businesses, their home, their animals, and their strawberry farms, then only three months away from a potential profitable harvest. They could take with them only those possessions that they could carry. The financial losses suffered...must have been monstrous.[13]

The evicted farmers were forced to abandon a strawberry crop potentially worth $250,000 at harvest time. Although some were lucky enough to have neighbors and friends who offered to look after property or store belongings, most had to abandon everything.

On Paul Ohtaki's last day of work at *The Review*, Woodward promoted him. He offered Paul a stipend of $5.50 a week to write a weekly column from the internment camp. Woodward wanted a report of the "births, deaths, who got married, who is playing first base on the baseball team...[t]he usual news of a small community. We told Paul we would publish it under a standard paragraph which would say, 'This is news about Japanese American neighbors of ours who at the moment are away from the Island, but are going to come back.'"[14]

Paul tried to refuse, thinking his vocabulary limited and his grammar shaky. Woodward reassured him. "Just write everything as if you were talking to us right now," he said. "We can fix it up."[15]

On the morning of March 30, the evictees were picked up from their homes by large army trucks and taken to the Eagledale dock, where they were loaded onto a government-chartered ferry. High-school students skipped classes to witness the scene; friends and neighbors came to bid farewell. Some soldiers had to blink back tears as they helped the evictees with their luggage and soothed fussing children. During their short stay on the Island, the tough New Jersey GIs had had their hearts touched by the evictees. An officer told Woodward:

ON WOODWARD'S ADVICE, YOUNG NISEI DEMONSTRATED THEIR AMERICANISM BY HELPING SOLDIERS POST EXCLUSION ORDERS AT THE ISLAND'S MOST VISIBLE LOCATIONS, MARCH 25, 1942.
COURTESY OF THE *SEATTLE POST-INTELLIGENCER* COLLECTION, MUSEUM OF HISTORY & INDUSTRY, PI-28038.

Why, these people have completely won us over. Do you know what they did the first day we arrived? They sent four or five of their young people down to help us get acquainted with the Island. They actually helped the men post the evacuation notices. Having to move these people was one of the toughest things this outfit has ever been told to do.[16]

Not all who went to see the evictees off wished them well, however. Some went out of curiosity and others out of spite. The long trudge onto the ferry, one Nisei later recalled, was the most humiliating moment of his life.

In keeping with a cultural upbringing that valued cooperation and frowned on public displays of emotion, most evictees put brave and smiling faces on their misery, prompting a *Seattle Times* editorial to state:

> Japanese departed their homes cheerfully, knowing full well...that the measure was designed to help preserve the precious, kindly camaraderie among divergent races which is one of this country's great contributions to humanity.[17]

Woodward was "nauseated" by this "puerile" statement. To him, it was clear that the evictees' outward calm masked heartbreak and terror.

The evictees had no idea where they were being taken or for how long. Many assumed that Bainbridge Island was a special case, because of its proximity to military targets, and that they would be able to return home within a few weeks or months. Only later would they realize that they were the first of 120,000 Japanese Americans to be put in American concentration camps.

Woodward instructed Paul to write a fifty-word article about the journey: "What did you do, how did the soldiers treat you, how did the older folks make out, anyone get sick on the way down..."[18] He instructed his new cub reporter to pass the article to a certain soldier when the evictees arrived at their destination. Woodward had asked the soldier to forward it to *The Review* via AP wire.

The ferry took the evictees across Puget Sound to Seattle. At the rail line fronting the docks, they boarded a waiting train. As the train rolled out, Paul was surprised to see some of his high school classmates running along Railroad Avenue, waving a final good-bye. The young people had hopped onto the commercial ferry and raced to the railroad tracks to give them a

AT THE EAGLEDALE DOCK, EVICTEES PREPARE TO BOARD A FERRY TO SEATTLE EN ROUTE TO AN UNDISCLOSED INTERNMENT CAMP. COURTESY OF THE *SEATTLE POST-INTELLIGENCER COLLECTION,* MUSEUM OF HISTORY & INDUSTRY, PI-28055

final send-off. On the train, one Nisei finally had time to catch his breath and write a letter, which was published in *The Review*.

> ...I would like to make it clear that there are none among us who are bitter about having to go.... [T]o the people on the Island I would like to say good-bye and I hope to see you all soon...many of us will never forget the friends we have on the Island.

> It's rather hard to write a letter under conditions such as they are now, Woodward, but...[y]ou were one person who had faith in us and I hope that we will never give you cause to lose that faith....[19]

After two days on the train with blinds drawn, the evictees arrived in the dusty town of Independence, California, on the east side of the Sierra Nevada. They were transferred onto buses, which drove ten miles north. "All we could see was sand, with sagebrush and tumbleweed blowing in the wind on both sides," recalled Paul.[20] Just after noon on April Fools' Day 1942, the Bainbridge Islanders became the first group to be interned at the Manzanar internment camp. They were joined later that afternoon by a group from Terminal Island.

At the sight of the camp, Paul remembered:

A MOTHER AND HER CHILDREN WAIT TO LEAVE BAINBRIDGE ISLAND. COURTESY OF THE DENSHO PROJECT, THE JAPANESE AMERICAN LEGACY PROJECT, THE BAINBRIDGE ISLAND JAPANESE AMERICAN COMMUNITY COLLECTION, AND THE KITAMOTO FAMILY COLLECTION.

> Our hearts sank to a new low. Even some of the soldiers who escorted us down couldn't believe what they saw. [S]ome had tears in their eyes as they left us.[21]

The Islanders' new home was situated in an arid valley walled by towering mountains. The camp's perimeter was surrounded by two rows of barbed wire enclosing a 10-foot-wide no-man's land. Army sentries manned the gates, and the machine guns in the tall guard towers pointed inward.

In his first dispatch to *The Review*, however, Paul accentuated the positive. The Bainbridge Islanders had arrived at Manzanar "well and cheerful" at 12:30 p.m. "Everyone enjoyed the trip," he continued, "but missed his Island friends. On the train there was group singing, card playing and 'chatting' with the soldiers who accompanied the evacuees. Islanders were treated 'swell' by the Army and in return, cooperated fully because the soldiers were so courteous."[22]

Decades later, Paul recorded some of the less pleasant realities that he had omitted from his reports to *The Review*.

> We were the guinea pigs, the first ones to be evacuated. A lot of us thought we would be held for a few weeks and then allowed to come home. But when we saw that barbed wire....[23]

> We suddenly realized that tar-papered barracks divided into 20 x 20 ft. rooms were supposed to be our new homes. They were just being put up.... [T]he floors were laid with wet green lumber, so as it dried out, the cracks in the floor became wider each day. In the evening, the winds would churn up [and] blow fine sand all over the room and all over our bodies.

> Immediately upon our arrival, our very first assignment was to put straw into canvas ticks to make mattresses, which we placed over our wired spring cots. We were issued old olive-drab Army blankets. Each compartment had a small Coleman oil heater to take the chill out of the evenings.

> Our first lunch was horrendous. We had canned spinach...the same dark-green color as the Army trucks.... But worse...we got sick on our first meal. Many suffered from diarrhea. Some thought we were being poisoned. What had happened was that the kitchen crew...were new on the job. [They] had washed the dishes for the first time with strong detergent, which they hadn't rinsed off very well.

> The latrines were not completed. The stools and wash basins were not working, stall partitions were not set up, and there was a long line of people with upset stomachs waiting their turn. What a mess on the first day.

> But as the months went by, things settled down. Linoleum was laid on the floors, the walls that divided the compartments were extended up to the roof, so the inhabitants could no longer hear every word uttered by their neighbors. The wash basins were hooked up, showers installed, and stalls partitioned. Things settled down to a somewhat normal routine.[24]

Paul was neither a trained journalist nor a natural writer, and as the weeks went by, he struggled to find items to send to *The Review*. After missing several deadlines, he sent Woodward a copy of the camp newspaper, *The Manzanar Free Press*, in lieu of a dispatch. He received a scolding by return mail:

THE INTERNMENT CAMP AT MANZANAR UNDER CONSTRUCTION WITH THE SIERRA NEVADA IN THE DISTANCE. COURTESY OF THE BANCROFT LIBRARY, UNIVERSITY OF CALIFORNIA, BERKELEY. WRA PHOTOGRAPHS.

BAINBRIDGE HIGH SCHOOL

Many staff and students in the Bainbridge Island school system took their civics lessons to heart by extending help and sympathy to the Japanese American students. The morning after Pearl Harbor, Island school superintendent Phil Ruidl joined high school principal Roy Dennis for a special assembly held at Bainbridge High School. They and several teachers pleaded for calm and understanding, urging the students not to give in to war hysteria.

In March 1942, just before all Japanese Americans were removed from the Island, the high school baseball season began. For the season opener, Coach Walter "Pop" Miller started all six Nisei players, even the backbenchers. Walt Woodward reported: "[I]t was their last appearance before being evacuated. How they wanted to leave with a victory! And how their fellow teammates wanted to win for them." Pop kept the Nisei players in the game in spite of disastrous hitting and pitching and numerous errors. "Coach Miller didn't care about the score," recalled Paul Ohtaki fondly. "He just wanted all of the Japanese Americans to play their last game for Bainbridge and enjoy themselves. We lost 15–2, but Pop Miller's kindness will be remembered."

After the game, Woodward happened on a poignant scene that captured the pain that many Islanders were feeling. "[I]n the dejection of defeat," he recalled, "the Bainbridge Nisei catcher, still wearing his bulky chest protector and dragging his mitt and mask, came clumping down the corridor to the locker room. Suddenly, from somewhere, a beautiful blonde appeared and ran after him. Her face glistening with tears, she caught up to him, threw her arms around his sweaty bulk, kissed him, and ran off, sobbing."[8]

Bainbridge's Japanese American students were forced to leave their classrooms a mere seven weeks before the end of the semester. Wanting the seniors to receive their diplomas on time, Superintendent Ruidl and Principal Dennis quickly assembled books and lesson plans and sent them to Manzanar so that the interned seniors could complete their studies by correspondence. On May 20, Bainbridge High's graduation list included thirteen graduates "in absentia." The Nisei graduates improvised a senior banquet and dance at Manzanar. Three weeks later, they held commencement exercises featuring diplomas, commencement programs and speeches mailed to them by Ruidl and Dennis. The package included a heartwarming surprise: copies of the school yearbook, autographed by the classmates they had left behind.

During the summer break, Ruidl hired former Island teacher Kathryn Stanford to prepare lesson plans so that seventh graders through juniors could also complete their interrupted studies. The necessary materials were shipped to Manzanar in late August. At the time, Manzanar's school buildings had not yet been constructed, but Island students began their own impromptu makeup classes as soon as their books arrived, studying three nights a week with the help of Nisei volunteers. When Manzanar's school finally opened in mid-October, Island students received credit for their correspondence work.

Dear Lazybones,

Come, come, my good man, I find the *Manzanar Free Press* to be very fine reading...but where in the hell has my Manzanar correspondent gone?

Seriously, butch, you'll be doing your own people a great harm if you quit sending us all the local gossip down there.... When this mess is all over, you people are going to want to come home. You'll be welcomed with open arms by the vast majority of us. But those who don't or won't understand will not feel that way. They may actually try to stir up trouble.

But they'll have a hell of a hard time of it, if, in the meantime, you've been creating the impression every week and every week that the Japanese are just down there for a short while, and that—by being in *The Review* every week—they still consider the Island as their home. Any and every scrap of stuff you can gather about how they miss the Island is fuel for the fire. See what I mean?

So...enough of this lazy man's reporting. Let's have Ohtaki back on the firing line.[25]

Woodward's letter gave Paul his first clear notion of the purpose of those weekly columns.

It is hard to believe the foresight Walt and Mildred Woodward had....While we were making our plans for the evacuation...the Woodwards were...making plans to smooth our return home.... [After this] I took this matter of reporting the news more seriously.[26]

Faithfully, *The Review* printed weekly items on who had the chicken pox, whose foot was crushed in an accident, and who got pneumonia. For Island residents, it published instructions on how to address "highly-prized letters from 'home'" and how to apply for a visitor's pass to Manzanar. H. O. Koura's father, Nobuzo Koura, died of pneumonia. On a lighter note, Sachiko, H. O.'s daughter, placed third in a Fourth of July beauty contest and the Comets, an all-Island softball team, was tied for the camp's league lead. *The Review* also described how a bath-loving Issei dealt with a ban against using the laundry sinks as bathtubs. He lugged his own private washtub to the showers each day, filled it up under the showerhead, and then climbed in for a scrub-down.

In June, Woodward asked Paul about the strawberry crop. In a normal year, the

NEWLY ARRIVED INTERNEES STUFF STRAW INTO CANVAS BAGS TO MAKE MATTRESSES.
COURTESY OF THE BANCROFT LIBRARY, UNIVERSITY OF CALIFORNIA, BERKELEY, WRA PHOTOGRAPHS.

harvest would have been well under way. Picking strawberries was painstaking work. Pickers had to walk on their knees alongside the low-growing plants and pick the berries carefully so as not to bruise them. If it rained, the berries had to be harvested immediately or they would rot.

But 1942 was not a normal year. Although some of the farmers had arranged for others to care for the crop, many of the caretakers were not good managers. Furthermore, the defense industries were booming, and a lot more money could be made working at the shipyard than in the fields.

In a letter to Paul, Woodward wrote:

> The berry crop is the nuts this year. Rain all the time except for one or two good, hot days. No pickers, or very few.... Islanders (including a lot of gents you know) just won't turn out and try to save the crop.... This...might be [a] story for you to work up. What are Japanese berry farm owners instructing their Island managers to do about next year's crop in the face of semi-failure or near complete failure this year?[27]

FILIPINO WORKERS TENDING A STRAWBERRY FIELD ON BAINBRIDGE ISLAND FOR AN INTERNED JAPANESE AMERICAN FARMER.
COURTESY OF THE *SEATTLE POST-INTELLIGENCER* COLLECTION, MUSEUM OF HISTORY & INDUSTRY, PI-22567.

Most of the interned farmers told Paul they were giving up on strawberries for the next season. Instead, they planned to rent out the fields for less labor-intensive crops.

Ironically, a few months later, Paul and hundreds of other internees were instrumental in saving another harvest for Caucasian farmers when the sugar-beet harvest in Montana and Idaho was imperiled by a labor shortage. Internees from several camps were released to help with the harvest. Paul spent two months in the sugar-beet fields. In his absence, Sadayoshi "Sada" Omoto took over the weekly dispatches to *The Review.*

◆　◆　◆

Many Bainbridge Nisei still subscribed to *The Review.* It provided them with a connection with home and a sympathetic ear. Around Thanksgiving, a Nisei on temporary leave from camp wrote to *The Review:* "It sure felt good to roam into a city, shop, see a movie, eat at a cafe, and feel free again. Going around town, seeing the decorations for the coming Christmas sometimes made my tears run, with the world as it is...."[28] Woodward ran the letter with the comment, "We...don't think those are the words of an enemy of this nation."

His overriding concern was for the long term, and he counseled the young Nisei to demonstrate their loyalty and avoid unfavorable publicity. "[T]he press services will pick up anything that indicates disloyalty.... The Nisei should watch their every act, so that the nation will get a true picture of their attitude."

His concern was heightened less than two weeks later, when a Pearl Harbor Day riot erupted at Manzanar. *(See chapter: Helen Ely Brill.)* The news services reported that an internee had been killed and nine others injured. For days, Woodward fretted, unable to contact his internee reporters because the entire camp had been placed under a communications embargo. He finally learned that none of the Bainbridge Islanders had been involved in the trouble. The Islanders kept to themselves and posted a large Bainbridge Island sign outside their block. He editorialized that the Islanders didn't belong at Manzanar. Interning them with the Californians was like packing a "Washington State Apple in a crate of California lemons," Woodward declared.[29] He launched a campaign for them to be transferred to the Minidoka internment camp in Hunt, Idaho, where most of the Japanese Americans from the Northwest had been sent.

Less than two months after Woodward wrote "strongly-worded letters" to WRA officials, the deputy director wrote him to say that the Islanders would be transferred to Minidoka "as soon as possible."

As the Bainbridge Islanders prepared to move to Minidoka, a *Review* editorial celebrated the announcement that Hawaiian Nisei would be allowed to volunteer for Army combat units.

> *The Review* always has believed that the Nisei were loyal to America.... They, perhaps more than any other group in this nation, are "on the spot" as the result of Japan's unprovoked assault on us. They, more than anyone else, should have an impelling desire to smash Japan.[30]

Nine Island Nisei soon volunteered for the army. Throughout 1943, *The Review*'s Japanese American column reported more and more departures from camp. Some joined the army; others went to college or found work outside the exclusion zone. In July 1943, Paul Ohtaki obtained leave clearance to go to Chicago to work. Tony Koura, a senior at the internment camp's Hunt High School, volunteered to take over reporting duties. In March 1944, Tony left Minidoka to attend school in Chicago. He was replaced

THE REVIEW'S SECOND NISEI CORRESPONDENT WAS BAINBRIDGE HIGH SCHOOL CLASS PRESIDENT SADA OMOTO.

by his sister, Sachiko "Sa" Koura. When Sa got a job in Twin Falls, about fifteen miles away from Minidoka, she tried to resign her reporter's post. Woodward wrote back:

> No, let's not let the column drop.... *The Review* has stuck out its neck good and proper for you people not because you are "you people" but because you are Americans and temporarily have lost the citizenship right this nation guarantees to every citizen. The news from [Minidoka]...is a torch held high in the name of good American citizenship.... It is a torch which has burned steadily since a very bad day in December 1941. Don't let its light go out—even temporarily.[31]

Properly chastened, Sa traveled to Minidoka every week to gather news to send to *The Review*. Sa's reports frequently included enlistments, furloughs and promotions. By early 1945, forty-four of the Island's 191 Nisei were in military service, including six boys from the Sakuma family, five Okazakis and four Omotos.

Sa's brother Art Koura was fighting in France with the all-Nisei 442nd Regimental Combat Team. A letter he wrote to a friend was printed in *The Review* in August:

> [T]he type of combat we have been engaged in during our whole month of combat is about the hardest there is: attack, rout the enemy, advance and go through the same thing again and again, day after day. We never stay in one place long enough to wash, shave, bathe or anything.... [W]e must have a crack outfit because already our combat unit has received high praise—we've acted as a spearhead unit a number of times and always accomplished our mission. However, we've paid dearly in casualties and lives, same as any other front-line outfit. There's many of our friends we will never see again —they gave their lives for what they believed in, and so we can live a fuller life in America. Yes, no one can say that they died in vain.
>
> I've had many exciting experiences.... I've had a Jerry fall dead just six feet from me; have used hand grenades; have shot and injured or killed an enemy at close range, etc. And boy, I ain't kidding when I say I was scared a number of times.[32]

Two months later, Art; Sa's fiancé, Momoichi "Mo" Nakata; and a neighbor became the first Island Nisei to be wounded in battle. They were among the 800 Nisei killed or wounded in France during the 442nd's four-day effort to rescue a "Lost Battalion" of 211 Texans. Woodward's letter to Sa didn't waste time on personal sympathies; it was firmly fixed on the big picture:

> Nice going on the casualty coverage.... I told about 20 of your...friends...before that little train ride to Manzanar so long ago that about the only way youse guys and gals could punch some sense into us all-American patriots was for some of you to go out and stop some enemy bullets.... Sachiko, gal, don't you miss one damn casualty or death. Let's be sure— you and I—that our Island boys' sacrifices are not in vain.[33]

TONY KOURA, *THE REVIEW*'S THIRD NISEI REPORTER, ATTENDED HUNT HIGH SCHOOL WHILE INTERNED AT MINIDOKA.
COURTESY OF PAUL OHTAKI AND TONY KOURA.

By that time, Woodward was running into some heavy verbal flak on the Island. In the fall of 1944, as discussion increased about allowing Japanese Americans to return to the West Coast, Island resident Lambert Schuyler called for a mass meeting. Although his ancestors had been in the country for 200 years, Schuyler had changed his name from "Sternberg" to "Schuyler," in the belief that a German surname would hurt sales of his book, *Think Fast, America*. He had declared his views in a February 1944 letter to *The Review*:

> In the face of their barbaric treatment of our men in Bataan, we don't want any Japs back here ever.... You would not have your daughter marry one.... And because they are unassimilable as well as despised...they will be unhappy, resentful, vengeful.... Could we ever trust a Jap again?[34]

On the day of the meeting, Walt was coming down with the flu so Milly covered the gathering. Two hundred people met to listen to Schuyler's proposal to send all Japanese Americans, along with their "Jap-loving" supporters, to a nameless Pacific island. The Woodwards were not mentioned by name, but Milly was sure they topped the list of "Jap-lovers."

In the following weeks, *The Review* received a steady stream of letters, pro and con. Woodward printed them all, except for the anonymous hate letters. Major M. J. Hopkins, retired, US Army Corps of Engineers, and Chairman of the WW II Bainbridge Island

TONY KOURA'S SISTER SACHIKO WAS *THE REVIEW'S* FOURTH AND LAST CAMP COLUMNIST. COURTESY OF PAUL OHTAKI.

Civil Defense Committee, declared that "the traditions, the ways of thought and the customs of the Japanese, including the American-born, are so different from ours that it would take at least fifty years to assimilate them successfully."[35]

Paul Ohtaki's friend and neighbor, Mildred Cumle, quickly retorted:

> Many more Japanese would be "assimilated" if they were given a chance.... Mr. Hopkins has dishonored the office which he holds in the Boy Scout organization.... Here at home some folks sit comfortably by their fireplaces...attending race-hatred

MEMBERS OF THE 442ND TRAINING AT FORT SHELBY. COURTESY OF THE BANCROFT LIBRARY, UNIVERSITY OF CALIFORNIA, BERKELEY, WRA PHOTOGRAPHS.

meetings, loudly proclaiming their Americanism [while denying] the rights of citizenship to the boys that live in fox-holes.[36]

Another reader submitted a full page of quotes from federal and local officials affirming the loyalty of Japanese Americans, while a local real estate agent advised the internees to sell their Island properties and settle in areas where "there is not the height of feeling against them."[37] An Eagledale woman who said she had grown up with Japanese Americans complained:

> I saw them learn all they could from us—how we dressed, wore our hair, ate, built our homes and played our games, yet I can truthfully say that I [have] never learned one single thing about anything from a Jap.... The Japs came to absorb and ape, not to share.... I, like Major Hopkins, do not want them as my neighbors.[38]

Schuyler held a follow-up meeting on November 24. Only thirty-four people showed up, including Walt Woodward. Due to the low turnout, Schuyler tabled plans to sign up members for his anti-Japanese "Live and Let Live Legion." He accused Woodward of lowering attendance by circulating rumors that he was a Nazi.

Woodward sat silent, scribbling notes as he was attacked by one speaker after another. The speakers' words were their own indictment, and he reported the meeting in detail in *The Review*. Schuyler declared:

> When the authors [of the Declaration of Independence] wrote that "all men are created equal," they meant all white people are created equal.... [W]e're nuts if we think we can get all people to live together without some of them being unsexed.... [Japanese Americans] deserve better than to come back where they will be despised. If they were put out on those islands [in the middle of the Pacific], they would be by themselves. They would be happy Japs.[39]

One man proposed that Congress banish the internees to Indian-style reservations. Another told Woodward that *The Review* should not claim to speak for the majority. "I don't want my kids to go to school with [the Japanese Americans]. My wife doesn't want to rub elbows in the stores with them." Only one speaker challenged these views—Winslow shipyard worker Louise Gregg, who was promptly labeled a Communist.

Schuyler's group never held any further meetings, but as Woodward's article on the proceedings was passed from hand to hand, *The Review* received many letters. The most compelling came from GIs, both Japanese American and Caucasian. From Fort Snelling, Minnesota, former Bainbridge High School class president Sada Omoto reminisced about the "happier days we knew 'back home'":

A BAINBRIDGE ISLANDER
AND HIS INFANT IN
FRONT OF THEIR
MINIDOKA BARRACK.
COURTESY OF THE DENSHO PROJECT, THE
JAPANESE AMERICAN LEGACY PROJECT, THE
BAINBRIDGE ISLAND JAPANESE AMERICAN
COMMUNITY COLLECTION, AND THE
KITAMOTO FAMILY COLLECTION.

[W]e freely and eagerly took in athletics and school activities along with your Johns and Janes.... To me this life at school was a hint of what life could be like, with its friendly and cheerful atmosphere.... But life has changed, and we all like to feel that we are in this fight for the preservation of your America and ours, and its ideals we have been taught.[40]

From the U.S. Pacific Fleet, a Caucasian friend of Sada's lamented:

What is coming of the people back there [on Bainbridge Island]? It makes me shake all over to think of it. To think that those narrow-minded self-centered hypocrites are going to be my neighbors.[41]

A Caucasian tech sergeant also stuck up for his former classmates:

They are a lot better citizens than the majority of those who object to their return.... I'd fight Tojo's Nips from h--- until breakfast, but our Japanese Americans deserve the same consideration as any other American-born [children of] immigrants.[42]

A GROUP OF CHILDREN PREPARE TO LEAVE MINIDOKA AND RETURN TO BAINBRIDGE ISLAND. COURTESY OF THE DENSHO PROJECT, THE JAPANESE AMERICAN LEGACY PROJECT, THE BAINBRIDGE ISLAND JAPANESE AMERICAN COMMUNITY COLLECTION, AND THE KIIAMOTO FAMILY COLLECTION.

In December, the army announced that Japanese Americans would be allowed to return to the West Coast as of January 2, 1945, but it was not until late April that the first Japanese American family returned permanently to Bainbridge Island. Issei Saichi Takemoto and his family were the first to come home—to overgrown strawberry fields, shattered windows, and missing possessions. After a night huddled under their overcoats, they received emergency bedding and other household goods from the Congregational Church and other donors. A month later, Floyd Schmoe organized an American Friends Service Committee (AFSC) work party to help clear land and set new strawberry plants.

Gradually, former Island residents trickled back without incident, but about half the population never returned. Only 150 of the Island's acres had been owned by Japanese Americans before the eviction, so many former Islanders had nothing to come back to. Of *The Review*'s four Nisei correspondents, only Sa returned.

After the war ended, *The Review* turned its attention to campaigns for a new library, new schools and a bridge to the Kitsap mainland. In the late 1940s, Woodward worked briefly for the Republican National Committee in Washington, D.C. The Woodwards then returned to Bainbridge and edited *The Review* until 1963, when they passed on the job to Dave and Verda Averill. In 1988, they sold their remaining interest in the paper to the Averills.

Woodward maintained a strong commitment to civil liberties. He joined a speakers' bureau formed by Sa and other Japanese Americans to educate others on the lessons of the internment. He testified at the Seattle hearings of the Commission on Wartime Relocation and Internment of Civilians in 1981, stating, "God willing there will never be a 'next time.'"[43]

The Woodwards considered *The Review*'s consistent stand against the internment to be their finest hour. In their later years, they were honored many times over for their farsighted and steadfast courage. They were featured in the PBS documentary *Visible Target*, and the Island's middle school was named after them. The character of a fearless newspaper editor in the best-selling novel *Snow Falling on Cedars* was modeled on Walt, and he was inducted into the Washington State Centennial Hall of Honor.

After a lifetime of doing the right thing, Mildred Woodward died in 1989. Walter died in 2001 at the age of 91. They would have been pleased to learn that in 2003, an Island school received a state grant to develop a curriculum for its sixth graders about the internment and its current implications. They would have been less pleased, but probably not surprised, by the result.

A small but vocal group of parents objected to the two-week lesson plan.[44] Where was the balance, they wanted to know, in teaching students that the internment was wrong? Citing the need for security in the wake of 9/11, the protesters brandished widely discredited books written by right-wingers Lillian Baker and Michelle Malkin to justify the internment. One can imagine Walt Woodward chuckling at the irony. It was in the sixth grade that he himself had learned, so many years ago, to champion civil rights. "[T]here was a wonderful teacher named Ms. Breen," he recalled, "and she pounded into my thick head that there was such a thing as a Bill of Rights.... I had to read it and remember it and I did."[45]

Perhaps Woodward would have defended the parents' right to free speech while suggesting that they read the Civil Liberties Act of 1988, or Redress Bill, which reads in part:

> The Congress recognizes that...a grave injustice was done to both citizens and permanent residents of Japanese ancestry by the...internment of civilians during World War II.... [T]hese actions were carried out without adequate security reasons and without any acts of espionage or sabotage documented...and were motivated largely by racial prejudice, wartime hysteria, and a failure of political leadership.... For these fundamental violations of the basic civil liberties and constitutional rights of these individuals of Japanese ancestry, the Congress apologizes on behalf of the Nation.[46]

VIRGINIA SWANSON (YAMAMOTO):
EVICTION FROM TERMINAL ISLAND

On February 28, 1942, Virginia Swanson looked over the Japanese Baptist church on Terminal Island. For forty-eight hours, the tall blond Baptist missionary had worked nonstop, but now she paused for a last look at the place she loved so well.

> It was a solemn moment, knowing that within a few minutes we would leave our church forever. As we stood there, we thought of the wonderful days God had given us on the island. How beautiful the building looked with its patio of green grass, the fine chapel, and the young people's parlor. We thought of the three or four hundred children who had attended our Sunday school and [fear] flashed in my mind...what about the children? I would always remember them singing with all their hearts while Hazel (Takii) Morikawa played the piano. What would happen to them?

VIRGINIA SWANSON, 1986. COURTESY OF MIMI YAMAMOTO SIEGEL.

> Our work now finished, it was time to leave. The days of the Terminal Island church had come to the end, though the memory of it will live in our hearts always. I turned out the lights, put my key on the table, and left the door open for the army, which occupied the building within days.[1]

On that grim February day, residents of Terminal Island became the first Japanese Americans to be evicted en masse from their homes simply because of their race. Nearly 3,000 of them were crammed into the southeast portion of the island, also known as East San Pedro. In the isolated community about twenty-five miles south of Los Angeles, the men fished for sardines, mackerel, skipjack

21

and tuna in coastal waters, and the women worked in the nearby fish canneries. They lived in densely packed company housing on unpaved streets named Wharf and Cannery, or Tuna, Albacore, Sardine and Pilchard. Terminal Island was an earthy, homogeneous community where it was often possible for the Issei to forget they had left Japan at all. The tight-knit group developed many community organizations and services, including active Buddhist and Baptist churches.

Virginia Swanson had first arrived on Terminal Island as a missionary in 1932. Little did she know as a child growing up in Minneapolis that her entire adult life would be devoted to the physical and spiritual welfare of Japanese Americans. In high school, when she studied Japanese immigrants for a social studies project, she was horrified to learn about the long succession of laws that prohibited Asian immigrants from becoming citizens or owning land. She was deeply moved by the injustices inflicted on the Japanese farmers and fishermen by powerful economic and political interests.

A few years later, when Miss Swanson decided to become a missionary, the Women's Baptist Home Mission Board offered her a choice of positions. "When the Japanese [Americans]...were mentioned," she recalled, "I knew that they were the people with whom I wanted to share part of my life."[2]

After a short stint in Sacramento, Miss Swanson was assigned to Terminal Island to work with Rev. Eric Kichitaro Yamamoto and two other Caucasian missionaries: Mildred Cummings and Hetty Evans. After Reverend Yamamoto was transferred in 1940, Rev. Harold K. Tsuchiya and Canadian Nisei Jitsuo Morikawa offered services in Japanese and English. By 1941, there were 400 students in the Sunday school and about 1,000 more in the Young People's Union.[3] The church offered practical as well as spiritual support through clubs and story hours for girls and boys, a ladies' organization, an English class, a Japanese-language school, a nursery school and a welfare program for troubled families.

The young Nisei girls took to the blue-eyed blond missionary immediately, according to Teruko Miyoshi Okimoto. Miss Swanson introduced a "bit of glamour" to the working-class community and served as "a role model for us to emulate with her grace and elegance."[4]

The boys were less impressed. "I was one of the first guys to be baptized," claimed Charlie

JAPANESE AMERICAN BUSINESSES ON TERMINAL ISLAND.
COURTESY OF THE BANCROFT LIBRARY, UNIVERSITY OF CALIFORNIA, BERKELEY, WRA PHOTOGRAPHS.

O. Hamasaki. "I volunteered 'cause I feel sorry for Miss Swanson. They wanted to baptize a lot of guys but they say, 'I don't want to take a bath.'"[5]

Youth activities for the boys got a boost when Miss Swanson persuaded her family to come out from Minneapolis. While Miss Swanson worked at the church full time, her widowed mother taught Sunday school and "kept the door of our house open to welcome our Japanese friends."[6] And brother John, better known as Bud, was a huge hit with the boys. Yutaka Dave Nakagawa, who grew up to become a youth counselor himself, recalled:

> Virginia Swanson...realized that she had difficulty reaching the boys in the island so she recruited her brother Buddy Swanson to come and help her.... I can still vividly recall the day Buddy strode into the room filled with curious, hyperactive kids and instantly commanded attention by his booming voice of welcome. He caught our immediate fancy not by his talk but by his action. First thing he did was line us up in several rows and taught us how to walk with our hands upside-down! Pretty soon we were hand-standing all over the place and loving every moment of it. Buddy...would recruit some of his friends to take us on field trips like the slaughterhouse and meat processing plants where we ate wieners and had a ball. He showed us how to make Indian drums out of stretched dried cowhides and showed us competitive games with each other. I watched with awe and fascination as he converted us from lackadaisical kids to ones of achievement and self worth. A seed was born within me that day and I vowed someday to be just like Buddy Swanson—a friend of boys.[7]

Throughout the 1930s, the Baptist church was a vital part of the Terminal Island community. A revival meeting by Dr. Ralph Mayberry inspired seventy-two young people to "come forward for Christ." A few years later, a weeklong crusade garnered 125 souls. Miss Swanson thought of her early years at Terminal Island as "among the happiest" of her life. Then, not long after her dearly loved mother died, came Pearl Harbor.

Fusaye Hashimoto remembered the day well.

> It was a very clear day—so clear that the ocean breakwater seemed as if it was near enough for even me to swim across.... We were all going about our everyday work in the usual manner when the telephone rang. I immediately ran to the phone and held up the receiver. It was

DR. RALPH L. MAYBERRY
As executive secretary of the Los Angeles Baptist City Mission Society, Dr. Mayberry supervised six Japanese American Baptist missions in the Los Angeles area before and after World War II. During the internment, he continued to support the Baptists in any way he could. Mayberry was an able administrator who took his faith and his job to heart. His outspoken honesty and his passionate opposition to injustice made him an enduring advocate for the Japanese American Baptists.[8]

DR. JOHN WILLIAM THOMAS
As secretary of the Department of Cities of the American Baptist Home Missions Society, Dr. Thomas oversaw the national Baptist ministry with Japanese Americans during the internment. While some Protestant agencies focused on nurturing interdenominational Christian churches in the camps, Thomas worked with Quakers, the Mennonites and the Church of the Brethren to develop resettlement programs serving all internees regardless of religious affiliation. He is fondly remembered by many Nisei because he expressed his warm and abiding personal interest in their welfare through letters of recommendation, personal letters and visits, and invitations to stay at his home while in transit.[9]

Mrs. K—. She exclaimed, "Japan and United States are at WAR!" It all sounded very silly to me, so I just laughed and told her, "Stop kidding around when I'm so busy with my washing." However, something struck me that all was not well by the way her voice sounded over the phone. Her voice was shaking, but yet, it sounded frantic, as if something in her throat would tighten at every word she tried to utter.... Then I knew—I knew—it was the most dreadful thing that could ever happen—WAR![10]

Fear transformed the official view of Terminal Island's Japanese American community. The fishing village was a tiny, little-known enclave in an area bristling with strategic targets—shipyards, a naval air base, a naval training facility, a submarine base, rail yards and petroleum storage tanks. Miss Swanson recalled:

> Soldiers fanned across the island. Japanese aliens who were crossing the ferry to return to their homes in the city were temporarily interned. Soon came news that all Japanese who were trying to take the ferry were in an enclosure and guarded by soldiers. I rushed down there and found them caged and terrified, some of the soldiers were near drunk to ease the pain of the realization of war. Older Japanese were herded into big army trucks and taken to the federal prison and immigration building. Little children were not allowed to go home until late in the evening, when a high official came to issue an order.[11]

In the middle of the night, community leaders, priests, and language teachers were arrested by the FBI. Fusaye Hashimoto's father was one of them.

IN THE PANIC FOLLOW-ING THE ATTACK ON PEARL HARBOR, JAPANESE AMERICANS DISEMBARKING FROM THE TERMINAL ISLAND FERRY WERE HELD "CAGED AND TERRIFIED" IN A WIRE ENCLOSURE. COURTESY OF THE UNIVERSITY OF SOUTHERN CALIFORNIA, ON BEHALF OF THE USC SPECIALIZED LIBRARIES AND ARCHIVAL COLLECTIONS.

> [A]round twelve o'clock midnight [m]y younger sister and I were in bed, unable to sleep.... Suddenly—Bang! Bang! Bang!—somebody was banging our door so hard that it frightened us terribly.... It was two FBI men who wanted to take Dad away for questioning. My brother pleaded with them to take him in place of Dad because Dad is so old! The pleading was useless. Before Dad took his final step at his home, which he had struggled so hard to build up, he said cheerfully that he would be right back, knowing all the time that he might never come back again. After he left, we heard more banging at the neighbor's door. We heard crashing of glass. We heard voices yelling, "We'll break the door down if you don't open it![12]

Terminal Island was soon transformed into what felt like an enemy enclave: the harbor was patrolled twenty-four hours a day, a curfew was imposed, and sentries monitored the two entrances to the island. Miss Swanson recalled:

> People flocked to church, hoping to find comfort. That week was a dark one. The

phone was dead, and food was hard to come by. Lights were blacked out in the evening, and it rained torrents. Wednesday evening, we had our prayer meeting in the dark.[13]

The bad news kept coming. Immediately after Pearl Harbor, all U.S. branches of Japanese banks were closed and outstanding loans called in. Bank deposits of both citizens and aliens who had been doing business with Japan were frozen. Japanese fishermen were barred from leaving the harbor to fish. The biggest canneries fired all employees of Japanese heritage. So many people were thrown out of work that a survey was taken in late December to assess the economic consequences. Of 561 families, almost half reported that they would be destitute within three months. The Japanese American Citizens League (JACL) gave Miss Swanson $700, and asked her to provide food and cash to the neediest families.

On February 9, 1942, the FBI swept across the island arresting all Issei with commercial fishing licenses. Between 400 and 500 men were taken to a nearby Immigration Service detention facility. Many would spend months or years in a series of Department of Justice detention centers.

Miss Swanson did her best to publicize the plight of the families who were left to fend for themselves. *Los Angeles Daily News* reporter Earl O'Day was one of the few with the courage to write a sympathetic account. The day after the FBI raid, he wrote:

Rumors that all Japanese are to be lined up and machine-gunned have led more than 55 families...to flee the island.

Heads of families now interned have left their relatives destitute with no prospect of incomes.

Unscrupulous second-hand dealers whisper warnings and buy treasured household furnishings dirt cheap from racial families who traditionally resist aid or charity in any form.

Among those families [is]...Mrs. Kazuye Hatashita.... Her husband is president of the Japanese Fishermen's association. He is in an inland federal detention camp. There are nine children of which the oldest is Kimio, 22. Kimio is a corporal in Uncle Sam's army, now stationed somewhere down in the south Pacific waiting to take a crack at Japanese soldiers. A service flag adorns the house where the Hatashitas live. They do not complain, but they are worried about funds.

Women and children are beginning to present a serious relief problem. Children are going to school without lunches. More than 365 families have been broken up.

In spite of all this, the JACL (Japanese American Citizens League) president, Kiyoshi

Higashi, insists the Japanese "have their chins up." They have pitched in to serve as interpreters for government agencies, they are making sweaters and blankets for the Red Cross, and for brothers in the army.

Nearly all windows bear the stickers of Red Cross and Community Chest drives.

Into this state of affairs has stepped one Caucasian agency, represented by Virginia Swanson, Japanese Baptist church missionary who has worked on the island for nine years. Miss Swanson was named administrator of the relief fund of $700 voluntarily raised by the JACL.[14]

The O'Day article was a rarity. More typical was Miss Swanson's experience with *Life* magazine, which "omitt[ed] the pictures that were favorable to the Japanese and misrepresent[ed] church attendance and activities." She called the magazine to protest, but the damage had been done.

A newsreel cameraman confided to Miss Swanson that he had little control over what was shown to the public.

Yesterday...I took pictures of the children and the young people. When we showed them [my supervisors] all had the same reaction. They aroused sympathy and that's not what we want in war time. We must stir hatred. These Japanese people are more loyal than I am, but we don't want to put that on the screen. Our pictures must show that the Japanese are a menace.[15]

In the following days, a dizzying succession of rumors and official announcements rained on the dazed inhabitants. On February 15, residents were given a thirty-day notice to clear the island. On February 19, President Roosevelt signed E.O. 9066 authorizing the mass removal of Japanese Americans from the West Coast. A Japanese submarine shelled an oil refinery on the California coast on February 23. The following night a radar echo that later turned out to be a stray weather balloon prompted an antiaircraft barrage of 1400 shells into the empty skies above Los Angeles. A ripple of panic spread through the state and Terminal Island's eviction date was moved up. On February 26, residents were given forty-eight hours to leave the island. The government made no provisions to house or feed the displaced. The evictees were on their own. Miss Swanson described an unbelievably fearsome atmosphere:

WITH THEIR OWNERS INTERNED, TERMINAL ISLAND FISHING BOATS LIE IDLE. COURTESY OF THE BANCROFT LIBRARY, UNIVERSITY OF CALIFORNIA, BERKELEY, WRA PHOTOGRAPHS.

Unethical junk dealers went through the island urging women to sell their furniture while they still could, and household belongings were sold for almost nothing. Soldiers carrying bayonets could be seen everywhere, and small combat cars drove up and down the narrow alleys terrifying people. In this atmosphere, many were fearful of the future.[16]

After the thirty-day notice was issued, a coalition of Baptists, Buddhists and Quakers quickly organized to help the Terminal Islanders through the transition. A survey revealed that over 300 families had no place to go and most were short of cash. There was little housing available; the hotels in Little Tokyo were filled to capacity, and "For Rent" notices were often accompanied by signs reading "No Japs!" or "No children." One family who found a place to live had their furniture-laden truck torched by vandals.[17]

Since most of the husbands and fathers had been arrested, wrenching decisions fell to their wives and children: getting the best prices for their fishing boats and gear, finding places to live, and selling or transporting their household possessions.

The Baptists set about converting two East Los Angeles Japanese-language schools into hostels that could accept about half the homeless. Rev. Julius Goldwater arranged for several Buddhist churches in Los Angeles to take in some people, and the American Friends Service Committee scrambled to find places for the rest.

When the second eviction notice came, Miss Swanson wrote:

> When we heard the rumor that everyone would have to leave in forty-eight hours, I told residents it couldn't be true. However, when I phoned the navy office, the officer said, "This time it's true. Get the people off the island in forty-eight hours." I could hardly respond, for all I saw were the many people who had signed up with us, and I did not know at the time how many hostels were ready. At that moment, a Quaker friend [Herbert Nicholson] came in and, understanding what had happened, said, "Let us pray." All that came to my mind was this. "O God our help in ages past, our hope for years to come."

> We got on the telephone and asked for the volunteer help of Japanese and Caucasians. A number of volunteers came forth: Mr. and Mrs. Herbert Nicholson, who were Quakers, Dr. Alan Hunter [sic] and some Congregational church members, Methodists, a Catholic priest, and a Caucasian Buddhist priest [Julius Goldwater]. But for the most part, most of the helpers came from our church.... All of us worked together to get the residents ready.

> There was much to be done. We typed and mimeographed sheets on which the families were to list their furniture, four blanks for each family. We had to divide the names and place them in the different hostels that we hoped were ready. Children came to church to volunteer, so we sent them from home to home delivering these blank forms, tags, and instructions.

AFTER THE TERMINAL
ISLANDERS WERE
EVICTED, THEIR TINY
HOMES STOOD EMPTY.
COURTESY OF THE BANCROFT LIBRARY,
UNIVERSITY OF CALIFORNIA, BERKELEY,
WRA PHOTOGRAPHS.

All night long, the residents worked. The women packed through the night, but when the trucks came the next morning, some were not done. They would say, "Give me more time; take my neighbor first," but we had to take them, ready or not. In some cases, we had to pull them from their houses crying and rush them off to hostels that were not always ready. In one case, the hostel was not at all prepared for the people who arrived after midnight. The residents had no lights, no gas, no water. But before the forty eight hours were up, so far as I know, every Japanese was off the island with the exception of five who had helped.[18]

◆   ◆   ◆

With her flock scattered, Miss Swanson continued to work tirelessly for the Japanese Americans throughout the war years, visiting the internment camps and assisting resettlers in the Midwest.

I helped in the hostels in various cities and worked on obtaining housing and employment.... I made home visits and also made contact with soldiers at Fort Snelling. With others, I helped establish churches in Detroit, Minneapolis, and St. Paul.[19]

She spoke on behalf of the internees at churches and organizations all over the country. By vividly telling and retelling the story of Terminal Island, she created empathy and understanding for a group that most Easterners and Midwesterners had no experience with. By appealing to people's basic sense of decency and goodwill, she built community support for internees leaving the camps. She wrote appreciatively that:

...some Caucasians spoke out strongly in behalf of the Japanese. Among them were churches, friends, newspapers, and publications. This kind of support continued during the resettlement years.

Support and concern were demonstrated in various ways: money, from churches and individuals, was donated to families in need, offers of assistance were forthcoming. Cleaning and repairing vandalized houses, formerly occupied by Japanese, and chopping down derogatory signs.[20]

After the war, Miss Swanson married Rev. Eric Kichitaro Yamamoto, who had been pastor at the Terminal Island Baptist Church until 1940. They served at Evergreen Baptist Church in Boyle Heights. In 1999, Virginia Swanson Yamamoto passed away at age ninety-two, after a lifetime of service to the Japanese American community.[21]

Tenney Tells Inquiry Goal

Legal Action Will Be Taken Against Roth, Chairman Asserts

"We could probably continue our hearings for more time here, but much of the evidence doubtless would be relative rather than on...

...ared Assemblym... yesterday in... as to when... unittee Inve... activities in... nvene. Thurs... committee... calls it...

Roth Convicted of Contempt

Politician Found Guilty for Refusing to Testify About Alien Broadcasts

Deliberating one hour, a Municipal Court jury yesterday decided George Knox Roth, politician guilty of contempt when he refused to tell a State Assembly committee the names of "Japanese who paid him to broadcast in opposition to the alien evacuation program. Roth faces a possible maximum jail term of six months, a $500 fine, or both, when sentenced next Wednesday.

Roth, called as a witness before the Assembly's committee investigating un-American activities, disclosed he had received about $500 for his radio broadcasts in behalf of the Japanese.

GEORGE KNOX ROTH:
THE PRICE OF INTEGRITY

Few remember George Knox Roth today, but in 1942 he was briefly the most visible Southern California opponent of the internment. For his courage, he may have paid the highest price over the longest period of time.

From mid-February to mid-March 1942, as public opinion swung toward mass internment, Los Angeles listeners tuning to station KMTR in the evenings heard Roth advocate for Japanese Americans.[1] A former college instructor who had recently lost a Los Angeles City Council race by a mere thirty-two votes, Roth took to the airwaves five nights a week from 7:15 to 7:30 p.m. to argue that the Nisei were entitled to the same civil rights as any other American citizen.

Japanese Americans were far from being threats or liabilities, he told listeners. On the contrary, they had made substantial contributions to the larger society, he said.

> At the outbreak of the war, the Japanese community was highly respected for their disciplined work habits, for the high educational qualifications of their Nisei children, and for total self-support, with no indigency, juvenile delinquency or criminal behavior.

> From the outset of the Great Depression in 1930 to December of 1941, Japanese farmers and commission houses gen-

29

erously contributed tens of millions of dollars of surplus foodstuff to Unemployed Cooperatives throughout the Pacific Coast in support of needy veterans and other unemployed.[2]

Roth had extensive knowledge of food relief because he had directed Los Angeles County's Department of Rehabilitation during the 1930s. When World War II broke out, Roth had just started work at the Los Angeles Wholesale Market as a chemist for the State Department of Agriculture. In the course of his job monitoring fruits and vegetables for pesticide residue, Roth ran into an old college friend, Joe Shinoda, whose San Lorenzo Nurseries was the market's largest flower distributor.[3] After Pearl Harbor, Roth volunteered to advise Shinoda and other Nisei members of the JACL's Anti-Axis Committee.

Much of Little Tokyo's established community leadership had already been arrested by the FBI, and young Nisei struggled to step into the void. In a 1977 letter, Masamori Kojima, then executive assistant to the mayor of Los Angeles, recalled:

> I was then a youth of 19 attending UCLA and part of an ad hoc committee in Little Tokyo.... [Most of us were] very young people trying to hold together a sometimes demoralized and leaderless community.... In Los Angeles, only a handful of non-Japanese joined us and were openly vocal in supporting the rights of Japanese Americans.... George Roth was one of that tiny group. He was forthright, courageous and an advisor in what we believed to be the worst of times. He gave us his heart and mind when we needed it most.[4]

By late January and early February 1942, events began to move with frightening speed. The American Legion was calling for the "removal from the Pacific Coast areas of all Japanese, both alien and native born."[5] Seizing an opportunity to eliminate their competition, the Western Growers Protective Association, the Grower-Shipper Vegetable Association and the California Farm Bureau Association were quick to jump on the bandwagon. In Los Angeles, Mayor Fletcher Bowron made a radio speech supporting mass eviction, while the County Board of Supervisors fired all Nisei employees and passed a resolution urging the removal of all Japanese aliens from the West Coast. A *Los Angeles Times* editorial went a step further and urged the removal of American-born Nisei as well, stating, "A viper is nonetheless a viper wherever the egg is hatched...."

To counter the tide of negative publicity, Roth and his friends formed a group called

THE LOS ANGELES PRODUCE MARKET WAS DOMINATED BY JAPANESE AMERICANS BEFORE WORLD WAR II.
COURTESY OF THE BANCROFT LIBRARY, UNIVERSITY OF CALIFORNIA, BERKELEY, WRA PHOTOGRAPHS.

the United Citizens League.[6] The plan was to develop a radio program focusing on positive facts about Japanese Americans. Roth volunteered to host the show and develop the programming. He purchased radio airtime with funds contributed by a group of prosperous Nisei businessmen, including Joe Shinoda, Kay Sugahara of Osage Produce, sporting goods dealer Sam Minami and produce wholesaler Sam Watanabe.

At the time, Roth was 35 years old, with a wife and three young children. A longtime member of the Orange Grove Friends Meeting in Pasadena, he had run twice for the Los Angeles City Council on Fletcher Bowron's reform ticket. He was known and respected by a wide circle of local progressives.

Roth's wife, Irma, recalled, "I wouldn't have had the courage to do what George did, but it was the right thing to do. I just hoped it would work." The Roths were both furious at the idea of mass internment and viewed the broadcasts as a legitimate exercise of free speech. They gave no thought to negative consequences.

Irma Roth recalled, "[George] tried to interview a lot of interesting people. Every night he would have somebody who was opposing the evacuation in hopes that they would have some influence." Few were willing to speak up publicly, however, except for African American leaders, who were quick to condemn the racist character of mass internment. Among Roth's African American guests were local attorneys from both sides of the political spectrum: Norman O. Houston and Hugh MacBeth; Charlotta Bass, editor of the city's largest black newspaper, the *California Eagle*; and Walter White, president of the National Association for the Advancement of Colored People.

George didn't get the help he expected from other quarters, however. Irma recalled:

> George became disenchanted with the Quakers because he didn't think they were doing enough to oppose the internment. They didn't help him with what he was trying to do and he couldn't see any evidence that they were doing anything else. They were just waiting to see what would happen and then they'd move in and facilitate whatever it was. George thought that was a mistake. He thought they ought to oppose the internment rather than just trying to make it easier.[7]

After almost twenty years of membership, Roth quit the Orange Grove Friends Meeting

CAUCASIAN GROWERS AND OTHER GROUPS LOBBIED FIERCELY TO EVICT JAPANESE AMERICANS FROM THE WEST COAST. COURTESY OF THE BANCROFT LIBRARY, UNIVERSITY OF CALIFORNIA, BERKELEY, WRA PHOTOGRAPHS.

and redoubled his own efforts to oppose the internment. Throughout February and March he was frantically busy. In addition to his radio talks, he testified before the Tolan Committee on three points. As a chemist who monitored the safety of produce, he provided meticulous evidence to counter rumors that Japanese American farmers were poisoning Southern California produce. He also warned that the removal of Japanese Americans from the West Coast would cause a $45 million shortfall in farm production. Finally, he said that during his years as a public relief official, he had known of no Japanese Americans who committed crimes or sought public assistance.[8]

In the second week of March, after the federal government notified JACL leadership that mass internment would definitely be implemented, Roth attempted to get a writ of habeas corpus, which would force the government to prove the necessity of internment in court. The legal effort, also funded by his Nisei friends, stalled because no federal judge was willing to issue a writ. A week later, Roth ended his radio series. The last program was a moving farewell from Japanese Americans bound for internment at temporary "assembly centers."

Within days, Roth was subpoenaed to appear before a local hearing of the California state legislature's Joint Fact-Finding Committee on Un-American Activities. The committee was headed by an ambitious state senator named Jack B. Tenney. He was an attorney and a former songwriter best known for the Gene Autry hit "Mexicali Rose." Tenney was originally a Democrat, but after being ousted by Communists from the presidency of the Los Angeles musicians' union, he became rabidly ultraconservative. After three terms in the California assembly, he was determined to make his mark in the state senate.

A genius at self-promotion, Tenney would not reach the full height of his power until the late 1940s and early 1950s, when he earned the well-deserved nickname "California's McCarthy." But in the months following Pearl Harbor, he was flexing his muscle by using the Un-American Activities Committee to hunt a wide variety of "subversives."

When George Roth was called before the Tenney Committee on March 24, 1942, he was outraged but not particularly worried. After all, he was not a member of any subversive organizations; he had not done anything illegal or underhanded. He had even contacted the FBI before his broad-

TOLAN COMMITTEE INVESTIGATOR INTERVIEWS A DISTRAUGHT YOUNG FARMER FACING INTERNMENT.
COURTESY OF THE BANCROFT LIBRARY, UNIVERSITY OF CALIFORNIA, BERKELEY, WRA PHOTOGRAPHS.

casts to disclose who was paying for them and why.

But committee members excelled at employing confusion and innuendo to create the appearance of guilt where none existed. When Roth was asked if the "Japanese" had given him money for the broadcasts, he made a careful distinction between the "Japanese" who were at war with the United States and the Japanese American Nisei who were loyal U.S. citizens. "I have received money from citizens of Japanese origin, most of them college chums whom I have known for at least 10 years," he said, freely admitting that they had put up $510 of the $625 he spent on airtime.[9]

A committee member pointedly ignored Roth's distinction between the enemy and U.S. citizens. He demanded, "What did the *Japs* want for this money?" [author's italics]

"They merely wanted me to tell the truth...regarding the truck-growing situation in Los Angeles County. Mass removal of Japanese American farmers would seriously impact the county's production of garden vegetables," said Roth.

The committee demanded that Roth name his funders, but he refused. Since he had already provided the names to the FBI, he thought the committee was overstepping its bounds. More important, he wanted to protect his Nisei friends from harassment. Grasping at straws to stall for time, he said he needed FBI approval before revealing names. The committee called his bluff. They immediately telephoned FBI officials, who stated they had no objections. Roth was again asked to name names. Again he balked, complaining that the question was too vague.

At that, Assemblyman James Phillips lost patience. "Do you refuse to give us the names, or will you give them to us now?" he demanded.

"At this moment..." began Roth.

Phillips cut him off. "It appears very clearly that the witness has refused to answer the question." He moved that Roth be charged with contempt.

City Councilman Roy Hampton then testified that he had seen Roth taking

TOKUTARO SLOCUM. During his long association with the JACL, Tokutaro Nishimura Slocum's intensity earned him enemies as well as friends. During World War I he served in France as the highest-ranking Asian in the U.S. Army. He lobbied the U.S. Congress for fourteen years to win citizenship for himself and other Asian immigrant vets. After Pearl Harbor, Slocum turned many in the Japanese American community against the JACL by boasting that his "anti-espionage work" for its Anti-Axis Committee had led to the FBI arrests of many Issei. COURTESY OF THE BANCROFT LIBRARY, UNIVERSITY OF CALIFORNIA, BERKELEY, WRA PHOTOGRAPHS.

Reds Accused of Plan to Dupe Mayor

Attempt to Influence City Defense Council Described at Hearing

Background details of an asserted Communist-inspired plan to influence the city's Defense Council through misrepresentations to the Mayor himself . . .

A surprise visit by Councilman Edward L. Thrasher, who told his version of asserted attempts by Japanese to influence the City Council by visiting the City Hall office of Councilman Norris Nelson, "acknowledged representative of the Mayor in the Council" . . .

A reappearance of Robert Noble, accompanied to the hearing by Ellis O. Jones, already convicted for contempt before the investigating committee — with the one-time pension-planner criticizing the draft and making fun of Gen. Douglas MacArthur . . .

More ramifications of acknowledged offers—if not acceptances—of Japanese funds to create propaganda favoring Japanese interests.

FIST FIGHT AVERTED

All of these, plus a threatened fist fight in the audience, were featured yesterday when the Legislature's interim committee, headed by Assemblyman Jack

LURID HEADLINES GENERATED BY THE TENNEY COMMITTEE DAMAGED INNOCENT REPUTATIONS. *Los Angeles Times,* March 27 and April 1, 1943. Reproduced by permission of the *Los Angeles Times.*

money from an "unidentified Japanese." Returning to the stand, Roth identified the man as Tokutaro Slocum, a member of the JACL Anti-Axis Committee. Far from being subversive, the hyper-patriotic Slocum was an active government informant who was suspected of denouncing his personal enemies to the FBI.

Slocum was called before the committee two days later.[10] He denied giving Roth money, but implicated Joe Shinoda. Shinoda admitted to offering Roth $25 for "miscellaneous uses," which he said Roth declined.

The *Los Angeles Times* reported the day's testimony under a headline blaring, "Reds Accused of Plan to Dupe Mayor."[11] A careful reading of the article reveals no link between Roth and Communists, nor a proven attempt by any Communist to subvert anything—just plenty of vague associations intended to smear the reputations of both Roth and his former boss, civic reformer Clifford Clinton. *(See box: Clifford Clinton and CIVIC.)* The article linked Roth with sinister-sounding "attempts by Japanese to influence the city council." The innocent truth was that Roth had accompanied a group of Japanese Americans to a meeting with City Councilman Norris Nelson. The city employees had been fired en masse because of their ethnicity and were seeking reinstatement.

After less then a week of inconclusive testimony on a variety of subjects, the hearings were adjourned. It would have been much ado about nothing, except that Jack Tenney confirmed that Roth would be prosecuted for contempt of the committee for his refusal to name his Nisei funders.[12]

When George was arrested, Irma was thrust into action. The young mother had been so busy with children and family matters that she hadn't even had time to listen to her husband's radio programs. George's widowed mother put up her house as collateral for his bail, while Irma went to the ACLU seeking legal assistance. She recalled:

I went down personally to talk to the man in charge of the Los Angeles office [Dr. Clinton J. Taft, a Methodist minister] and begged him to provide an attorney for George, because...the only alternative...was the public defender, who was dependent on the prosecuting district attorney for his job—a clear conflict of interest.... Al Wirin was the attorney for the ACLU and he wanted to help George, but the ACLU wouldn't release him to do it. No other attorney would accept the case.[13]

On June 4, the Los Angeles Municipal Court found Roth guilty of contempt of the Un-American Activities Committee.[14] He was sentenced to a thirty-day jail term or a $200 fine.[15] "After George was convicted," Irma remembered, "Al Wirin resigned from the ACLU in order to file George's appeal, which of course got nowhere."

Roth paid the fine, but his troubles were far from over. Although he did not realize the full implications at the time, the Tenney Committee had branded him with a criminal record and a reputation as a subversive. Since many educational institutions did not hire anyone with a criminal record, Roth's future was essentially destroyed. For the rest of his working life, he was forced from job to job as employers declined to renew contracts because of his record.

◆　◆　◆

Until he defied the Tenney Committee, George Knox Roth had made promising strides in life. Of Scots-Irish and German ancestry, son of a barrel maker, he was born March 9, 1907, in Denver, Colorado. He put himself through school, graduating from the University of California, Los Angeles, in 1929 with majors in philosophy and psychology.

In 1933, he captivated Irma Brubaker with his energy and intelligence.

> He seemed so positive about things. His brother-in-law said it was too bad that somebody didn't hire George just to think up ideas. He had more ideas per minute about improving society than anybody we'd ever met. Things that mattered to him, he'd do something about.[16]

Roth displayed his capacity for leadership not long after they met. He was teaching philosophy and psychology at Compton Junior College in March 1933 when the Long Beach earthquake struck. Four banks collapsed near the school, toppling walls of brick into the street. While the college administrators fled for fear of aftershocks, Roth calmly

GEORGE KNOX ROTH MARRIED IRMA BRUBAKER IN 1934.
COURTESY OF IRMA BRUBAKER ROTH.

took charge, securing records for insurance purposes and organizing students to clear the street for emergency vehicles. It was typical of Roth, his wife said, to see what needed to be done, and do it.

About twenty percent of Compton's students were Japanese American. Roth was impressed by the high proportion of "very, very intelligent" Nisei students. In 1934, he went to bat for Isamu Suzukawa, an A student, president of the campus YMCA and editor of the school paper and yearbook. When Suzukawa was passed over for the University of Southern California's annual scholarship in favor of the vice principal's favorite, Roth protested to the USC registrar, who advised Roth take Suzakawa's case to UCLA. He told Roth that that highly qualified student would be able to get a better offer there. As predicted, UCLA offered Suzukawa a stipend as well as a full scholarship.

Roth's faith in Suzukawa was justified. He graduated from UCLA with honors and was studying at the Imperial University in Tokyo when the war broke out. Because of his American ties, he was interned by the Japanese government, but after the war, he went on to become editor of the influential English-language Japanese newspaper *Asahi News*. Roth was proud to have contributed to his success. "Just think how treatment of loyalty to truth makes for loyalty by others to truth," Roth wrote about his relationship with Suzukawa. "Culture and character are transmitted by the very tender loyalties established over the years and not merely by our laws and Constitution."[17]

Roth was not offered tenure by Compton Junior College when his third one-year contract ended. He worked part time and finished his master's degree at USC. His thesis was on the Depression-era co-op movement—self-help groups organized by and for unemployed workers to collect and redistribute food and other resources. In the course of his research, Roth was greatly impressed by the generosity of Japanese American farmers, who donated millions of dollars in surplus crops to the poor.

After earning his master's degree, Roth lobbied the Los Angeles County Board of Supervisors to create a department to coordinate local cooperative self-help efforts. The board created the Department of Rehabilitation in January 1935 and named Roth its administrator. For the next three years, Roth set up programs to organize unemployed workers to glean surplus fruits and vegetables from the fields and collect excess bread from bakeries. Other ventures involved canning, weaving, knitting, baking and housing.

In 1938 Roth was forced out of his job by a county supervisor who wanted to replace him with a relative. Roth went to work for liberal reformer Clifford Clinton as secretary-investigator of CIVIC (Citizens Independent Vice Investigating Committee). The job was a test of moral and physical courage, especially after another investigator was seriously injured by a car bomb.

◆　◆　◆

By the time he agreed to do the radio broadcasts for the Japanese Americans, Roth had amply demonstrated a willingness to stand up for what he thought was right. He had angered some in his quests for justice; he may even have risked a job or two by his uncompromising honesty. But he had always managed to bounce back. He did not expect his appearance before the Un-American Activities Committee to have far-reaching consequences. During the period between his committee appearances and his contempt trial, Roth's main concern was his Nisei friends.

"They took terrible losses when they had to leave," recalled Irma Roth. "One of them had to leave $10,000 worth of celery sitting in the fields with nobody to harvest it."

She recalled that Joe Shinoda and his wife moved to New York. She explained:

INTERNEES ARRIVING AT SANTA ANITA. COURTESY OF THE BANCROFT LIBRARY, UNIVERSITY OF CALIFORNIA, BERKELEY, WRA PHOTOGRAPHS.

> [The Shinodas] didn't go to camp. If you had money, you could [relocate outside the exclusion zone], but the ones that didn't.... I remember these darling Japanese women dressed to the nines, standing in dust up to their ankles. It was just so horrifying! We did some shopping for them. It was so difficult. We had to talk through a screen and the military went through everything to be sure we weren't bringing in a lot of weapons so the Japanese Americans could shoot up the place. The whole thing was a tragedy.[18]

Not long after George's contempt conviction, the Roths were forced to relocate as well. Their landlord evicted them from their house on Mount Washington. Irma knew why:

> He was a retired colonel who wanted to get into the war. They wouldn't take him because he was too old, but he thought it was because he was renting to us, and George had been accused of helping "the Japs." He was sure that we were ruining his life, so we had to move.[19]

Even the Roth children suffered consequences. A half-century later, Mrs. Roth still sighed with indignation at the memory:

> We had neighbors who had a little girl the same age as our son Dana.

CLIFFORD CLINTON.
COURTESY OF DONALD CLINTON.

CLIFFORD CLINTON AND CIVIC
(CITIZENS INDEPENDENT VICE INVESTIGATING COMMITTEE)

In 1937 and 1938, George Knox Roth worked as secretary-investigator for the Citizens Independent Vice Investigating Committee (CIVIC), which had been organized by restaurateur Clifford Clinton and other reformers to expose rampant corruption within the government of Los Angeles mayor Frank Shaw.

It was downright dangerous to work for CIVIC. Clinton's home was bombed in 1937 after he and his allies issued a minority report of the Los Angeles County Grand Jury charging that city officials were engaged in no-bid contracts, kickbacks, bribery and organized vice operations. Then CIVIC's private investigator, Harry Raymond, was severely injured in a car bombing just before he was due to testify about police involvement in prostitution and gambling operations. The *Los Angeles Times*, which had profited in real estate deals with the city, implied that Clinton and Raymond had staged the bombings to generate publicity.

Public opinion turned against the mayor after an L.A. police captain was convicted of the Raymond bombing. In 1938, Shaw became the first U.S. mayor to be recalled from office. Judge Fletcher Bowron was elected to replace him. Clinton encouraged George Roth to run for the Los Angeles City Council on Bowron's reform ticket in 1939 and 1941. He lost the second race by a narrow margin.

Like Roth, Clinton was investigated by the Tenney

CLIFTON'S EXUBERANTLY POLYNESIAN PACIFIC SEAS CAFETERIA WAS ONCE A DOWNTOWN LOS ANGELES HIGHLIGHT.
COURTESY OF DONALD CLINTON.

Committee in March 1942. Foreshadowing McCarthy-era tactics, the committee attempted to link Clinton and the Consumers Council with a Communist plot to "dupe" Mayor Bowron and taint the war effort. After the *L.A. Times* generated lurid headlines implying guilt by association, the matter was dropped.

Far from being a Communist, Clinton was a fervent supporter of social justice and a devout Christian whose family had operated restaurants in California since 1888.[20] Clinton's parents were both former Salvation Army officers, who took their children on two missions to China. The poverty and famine that young Clifford witnessed there sparked a lifelong passion to end hunger.

In the 1930s Clinton operated two thriving restaurants in downtown Los Angeles, naming them after a blend of his first and last names: *Clifford Clinton*, or *Clifton's*. Clifton's Cafeterias provided reasonably priced, wholesome food, and nourished the spirits of the city-bound with on-site chapels. The restaurants themselves were a visual feast, employing waterfalls and foliage, plaster rocks and lush murals to evoke the majesty of the natural world.

Clinton never turned away a customer for lack of funds. During the Depression, his open-handed policy almost bankrupted him before he established a Penny Cafeteria that served two million indigent "guests" during hard times. In 1946 Clinton retired from the restaurant business to found Meals for Millions, an international food relief organization. Today, his descendants continue to "make a friend of every guest" at the last remaining Clifton Cafeteria, which remains a well-run oasis in L.A.'s historic core.

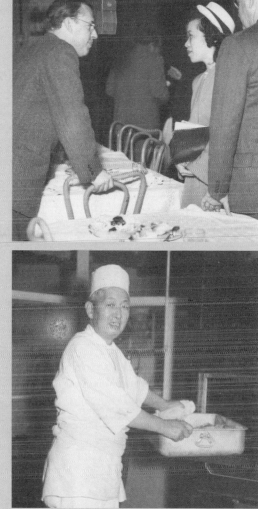

ANOTHER MEMBER OF CLINTON'S PROGRESSIVE CIRCLE WAS AUTHOR CAREY MCWILLIAMS WHO, IN 1944, WROTE *PREJUDICE: JAPANESE AMERICANS, SYMBOL OF RACIAL INTOLERANCE*, THE FIRST SYMPATHETIC ACCOUNT OF THE INTERNMENT. IN THE PHOTO ABOVE, HE GREETS A FORMER INTERNEE AT A MEETING AT CLIFTON'S CAFETERIA SHORTLY AFTER THE BOOK'S PUBLICATION. WRA PHOTOGRAPHER CHARLES MACE'S CAPTION READS, "CLIFFORD CLINTON, THAT OUTSTANDING AND EXTRAORDINARY CITIZEN, IS INTERESTED IN RACIAL FRIENDSHIP AND EMPLOYS NISEI AT THE TWO CAFETERIAS." *BOTTOM:* SHIZUO (JIMMIE) MITSUHATA, WHO WORKED AT CLIFTON'S BEFORE THE WAR, WAS WELCOMED BACK AFTER HIS RELEASE FROM MANZANAR. COURTESY OF THE BANCROFT LIBRARY, UNIVERSITY OF CALIFORNIA, BERKELEY, WRA PHOTOGRAPHS.

He was about six at the time. He was no longer allowed to play with her. Her parents were...college teachers. You would have thought, of all people, they would have had some appreciation or understanding of what was going on. And poor Dana couldn't understand. "What did I do?" he asked me. "You didn't do anything, honey."[21]

Sam Minami's son Dale was born around the same time as the Roths' youngest daughter, Dian. Irma recalled, "Our families were both so poor that I sent him a pair of baby socks and they sent some for my little girl, so we exchanged socks. That's all we could afford at the time." Dale Minami grew up to become part of the legal team that successfully challenged the constitutionality of the internment in the landmark Korematsu case.

At one point, the family was so poor that George was reduced to working in an avocado orchard for "bracero's wages."

He was having trouble finding and keeping teaching jobs. He had already had one strike against him as a registered conscientious objector; now he had a criminal record as well. "If he could get a teaching contract signed before they checked [his records in] Sacramento," Irma explained in a recent intereview, "then he could teach school for a year or so, but if they waited for the verification from Sacramento, why then they would hire somebody else. So he had one-year stands all over the place." For the next few years, George was able to get by only because of the wartime teacher shortage.

In 1948, the Roths thought hard times were over when George was hired to teach at John Muir Junior College in Pasadena. After three years—just as enrollment swollen by the GI Bill began to decline—local papers got wind of Roth's criminal record. When his contract was not renewed, Roth filed suit against the Pasadena Board of Education, but lost. He was forced to take a series of one-year teaching jobs in Whittier, Glendale, Oxnard and the Coachella Valley. A job in San Marino lasted one day, just long enough for the principal to call Sacramento and learn of Roth's criminal record.

Years later, when Roth happened to be in the office of the state superintendent of public instruction, he flipped through a Rolodex file and found his name. Written on his card in red ink were the words "NISEI SYMPATHIZER." Although anti-Japanese sentiment gradually waned after the war, anti-Communist fervor rose sharply. Jack Tenney's Un-American Activities Committee gained fearsome clout. "A lot of people thought George had been convicted of being a Communist, which of course had nothing to do with us at all," recalled Mrs. Roth.

In 1959, Roth decided that he would have more control over his destiny if he went into business for himself. He purchased a business school in Modesto, but was denied accreditation because of his criminal record. He was forced to sell the school at a loss.

For decades, the Roths lived with frustration and financial insecurity. Mrs. Roth recalled:

> George never seemed to get discouraged, although I'm sure at times he was.... But somehow or other, he was clever enough that we never missed a meal, never lost a place to live, never had anything repossessed. We always managed to keep enough income coming in one way or another, partly because of his business school training, and partly because of other things he could do. We always managed to stay afloat, but sometimes I wonder how on earth it ever happened. I look back and think I couldn't do that now.[22]

Finally, in the 1970s, the Roths were eligible for Social Security. "Once I got a steady income, I kind of relaxed," Mrs. Roth said. "I didn't have to worry anymore."

In 1977, she read a statement by U.S. Senator S. I. Hayakawa that the internment had been "the best thing that ever happened to the Japanese Americans." Hayakawa, a conservative Republican, had been born in Canada to Japanese immigrants. Since he was already living in Chicago, Illinois, when the war broke out, he was not personally affected when persons of Japanese ancestry were evicted from the west coasts of the U.S. and Canada. Hayakawa became an internationally renowned semanticist who served as president of San Francisco State College during the late 1960s and early 1970s. He established his conservative credentials through hard-line opposition to student activism, including the ethnic studies movement. He vehemently condemned the redress movement, saying "my flesh crawls with shame and embarrassment" to see "this unconscionable raid on the U.S. treasury" by "a wolf-pack of dissident young Japanese-Americans who weren't even born during World War II."

When Irma Roth read Hayakawa's statements, she recalled:

> I was so angry that I wrote a letter to the JACL in San Diego and said this is absolutely outrageous, especially after all we've been through opposing the internment.... I was so mad at Hayakawa that I just couldn't keep from writing about it.[23]

She sent the letter, without her husband's knowledge or approval, to Henry Sakai, chair of the JACL Pacific Southwest District's Ethnic Concerns Committee.[24] Learning that George's wartime broadcasts had resulted in decades of financial hardship for him and his family, the JACL honored his 70th birthday by setting up a trust fund for the couple's declining years.

By this time, George Roth had indeed become the "man JAs forgot to thank."[25] Joe Shinoda and most of the others who had bankrolled the radio broadcasts had moved away or died, and survivors such as Sam Minami had only vague recollections of the long-ago project. When they learned of Mrs. Roth's letter, Minami; Joe Shinoda's widow, Megumi; and others agreed to help Sakai

SAM MINAMI
WITH IRMA ROTH,
1977. COURTESY OF IRMA
BRUBAKER ROTH.

organize a testimonial dinner scheduled for August 13, 1977. Togo Tanaka, *The Rafu Shimpo*'s prewar English editor, said of Roth, "It took profound dedication to principle and tremendous personal courage to stand against the overwhelming tide.... I've often thought of him as one of the few unsung heroes of those hectic days and weeks."[26] Writer Dwight Chuman interviewed Roth for a sympathetic article published in *The Rafu Shimpo* on July 15.

On the eve of the sold-out dinner, however, Roth came under suspicion once again. Chuman created a controversy by implying in a *Rafu Shimpo* column that the organizers were "myth-making" in order to "rub shoulders with congressmen at fancy testimonial dinners."[27] Charging that "the slate has not been cleared on George Roth," Chuman wrote, "In his book...*Americans Betrayed*, Morton Grodzin wrote off Roth's efforts as 'one of the more bizarre aspects of the opposition to the evacuation.'" Chuman went on to slam Roth for informing the FBI not only about his anti-internment broadcasts but also about postwar contacts with Mao Tse-Tung followers and other groups in the 1950s. Chuman also charged that no written records could be found that Roth had ever been blacklisted, and that state Superintendent of Public Instruction Wilson Riles and the San Marino school administrator had both denied seeing such files.

Testimonial cochair Sakai fired off an indignant response:

> To imply that the committee members...had selfish motives of creating a hero...is totally false.... Mr. Roth stated from the first interview that the FBI was told who paid for the broadcasts in order to stop the rumors that Issei money was involved.... The FBI was against the evacuation because they felt there wasn't any evidence or danger of sabotage [sic] by the Japanese....
>
> Knowing the atmosphere of the 1940's, 50's and even the 60's, it was not unusual for people to be blacklisted and persecuted. It is also understandable that old records have been purged and that anyone involved [in] persecuting Mr. Roth would deny it today.... [I have more faith in] enthusiastic testimony by those who knew Mr. Roth, namely Sam Minami, Pat Okura and Togo Tanaka....[28]

In spite of the last-minute unpleasantness, the testimonial was a success, raising over $10,000 for the Roths. Checks and letters poured in from around the country, often from complete strangers. A San Jose woman wrote:

> You didn't know me during the war hysteria years, yet you stood up to speak for me and all the Japanese Americans.... Many of our Caucasian friends were unsure they would be safe to be our friends and we lost them.... We thank you, Mr. Roth, though we found out so late, that you braved a bitter fight for us Japanese Americans during the most unpopular

and dangerous time.... Our conscience should not rest in peace until all of us say our words and gestures of appreciation to you who did not let his conscience fall asleep when we were being corralled into camps. Thank you, Mr. and Mrs. Roth, for all your sacrifices and the hurts it caused your family.... We can never repay you....[29]

Proceeds from the testimonial helped supplement the Roths' modest income and enabled Roth to continue a study of Buddhism inspired by a Little Tokyo priest, Dr. Nyogen Senzaki.

Both Roths testified at the Los Angeles hearings of the Commission on Wartime Relocation and Internment in August 1981. Irma spoke poignantly of hardships triggered by George's wartime activism:

> The consequences of this conviction were professionally disastrous.... He was finally forced to forgo any hope of teaching.... Unless one has suffered personally from prejudicial treatment, it may be difficult to imagine the self-imposed shame that accompanies such stigma.... Raised eyebrows implied that there must be hidden reasons behind [my husband's] contempt conviction—either he was politically radical or an unfit teacher or temperamentally irresponsible. After all, the Japanese Americans had been re-absorbed into the community and were gaining positions of responsibility and authority, so how could anyone who tried to prevent the evacuation continue to be penalized so long after the fact?[30]

In his own testimony, Roth focused on preventing future injustices. He warned that mass internment remained a very real threat, and alluded to proposals during the Iran hostage crisis to detain Iranians studying in the United States to exchange for American hostages. He urged the creation of special civil liberties courts and commissions in every federal court district to "accelerate decisions guaranteeing to every citizen and alien their constitutional rights in time of emergency."[31]

Throughout his life, George Knox Roth was more concerned about the rights of others than about his own reputation or welfare. By the time he died in 1999 at the age of ninety-two, he had again faded from the memory of the Japanese American community. His widow, Irma, now living in a tiny Pasadena apartment, is one of the few who remember the man who paid so dearly and so long for his integrity.

AT THE JACL EVENT, MR. AND MRS. ROTH WERE PRESENTED WITH A PORTRAIT PAINTED BY FORMER INTERNEE GEORGE AKIMOTO, A PROMINENT POST-WAR ILLUSTRATOR. COURTESY OF IRMA BRUBAKER ROTH.

THE NICHOLSON FAMILY IN JAPAN, 1940.
COURTESY OF SAMUEL NICHOLSON.

REV. HERBERT AND MADELINE NICHOLSON:
"GOD'S SUNSHINE CAME IN TO STAY"

On the morning of Sunday, December 7, 1941, Quaker missionary Rev. Herbert Nicholson and Issei minister Reverend Fujimori held services as usual at the West Los Angeles Japanese Methodist Church. Afterward they sat in Nicholson's car and ate lunch before beginning an afternoon of visits to church members' homes. As they began driving toward their first stop, they saw a church member running toward them, waving frantically and shouting, "*Sensei, sensei* (teacher, teacher), Japan has bombed Pearl Harbor!"[1]

"Oh, it was pathetic," Nicholson recalled later, "to think this terrible thing had happened. [We had all] been afraid something was going to happen, but nothing like that...we were terribly upset."

Quickly, the three men fanned out to call the congregation back to church for an emergency meeting. As he looked out at the church members huddled quietly in the sanctuary, Nicholson's heart went out to them. What would happen to these hardworking Issei gardeners, he wondered? Many of them had young families to support. He suspected that many would be hit by a backlash of hatred against Japan. With impulsive generosity he told them, "Now, you will be losing your jobs...and I don't need any salary anymore, so just forget me. I will keep on coming as long as I can." But the membership was equally concerned that their ministers would soon be out of a job. At Christmas, they gave each of them more than double their monthly salary.

On the afternoon of December 7, no one knew what lay ahead, but some had their suspicions. That night, Nicholson had dinner with eighty-year-old Gisuke Sakamoto, who confided, "I'm on the FBI blacklist because I was in the Japanese army [during the Russo-Japanese War].... We're going to be picked up tonight. I'm sure we are."[2]

"I was quite upset about that," Nicholson recalled. "It was crazy to pick up this innocent old man just because he was in the army back in 1905." But Sakamoto was right. He was arrested in the middle of the night, along with 600 others.

The next morning, Nicholson recalled, "The papers were full of terrible things the Japanese had done in Honolulu. They [said the Japanese Americans] blocked the roads, and...did all sorts of things."[3] He rushed to the FBI office in Los Angeles to protest. "These are a lot of lies they have got in those papers. The Japanese wouldn't do that," he said. The FBI official agreed, saying, "I know.... They're all lies."

WITHIN 24 HOURS OF THE ATTACK ON PEARL HARBOR, OVER 600 "POTENTIALLY DANGEROUS" ENEMY ALIENS WERE ARRESTED. COURTESY OF UNIVERSITY OF SOUTHERN CALIFORNIA, ON BEHALF OF THE USC SPECIALIZED LIBRARIES AND ARCHIVAL COLLECTIONS.

"Then you do something to stop it," the minister urged. "You get news in the paper right away that these reports aren't true.... Emotionally people are upset.... [T]ell them you have already picked up the dangerous Japanese."

The FBI agent shook his head. "We're not in the publicity business. We can't do it."

Next, Nicholson tried Lt. Cmdr. Kenneth Ringle, chief of naval intelligence, whom he had known in Japan. "[A]t least ninety-eight percent of these stories in the papers are lies," Ringle stated, but he refused to say they were all false. When the Quaker urged him to make a pubic statement, he replied, "I can't do anything about it. It's not my job to give publicity." Although the false allegations were quickly investigated and disproved in Hawaii, on the mainland, they were the beginning of a flood of misinformation that turned the public against Japanese Americans. *(See appendix: Overview of the Decision to Incarcerate.)*

Publicity was not Nicholson's job, either; he was simply a temporary minister at the West Los Angeles Japanese Methodist Church. But from that day onward, he waged a one-man public relations campaign for the Japanese Americans. For the next several years, he talked to countless officials and helped hundreds of individual Japanese Americans. His most effective asset was his ability to talk to anyone and everyone with an egalitarian frankness and a homespun logic that was hard to refute. He had an infectious smile and a bottomless faith in the goodness of all humans. Time and again, he tapped into a basic humanity that transcended race and culture and convinced both government bureaucrats and ordinary citizens that the internment was wrong.

◆　◆　◆

Born and raised a Quaker, Herbert Victor Nicholson devoted his entire adult life to serving people of Japanese heritage on either side of the Pacific. He was a warm, direct man with an abiding allegiance to Quaker principles. He wrote in his memoirs:

> Quakers have always been in the forefront of reform and have suffered for it. In the matter of slavery, many Quakers paid fines and were imprisoned for disobeying an unjust law. There is nothing in the Bible against slavery. Even [Saint] Paul took it for granted. But today we are all opposed to human slavery. So, in regard to the death penalty and Christian conscientious objection to war, we believe the tide may turn.[4]

He was born on January 30, 1892, in Rochester, New York, of an Irish immigrant father and a British-born mother. Under the influence of a devout mother and grandmother, he attended Friends meetings and schools and showed an early interest in missionary work. In 1914, after graduating from Haverford, a small Quaker college in Pennsylvania, he experienced a powerful awakening during a nine-week revival meeting led by charismatic evangelist Billy Sunday. "I bowed my head and offered my body, mind and soul to God in a way I had never done before," Nicholson recalled.[5]

NICHOLSON IN PREWAR JAPAN.
COURTESY OF SAMUEL NICHOLSON.

Soon the lanky, bespectacled young man was off to Japan to work as secretary to Gilbert Bowles, a Quaker missionary who headed the Japan Peace Society. Over the next three years, he met with influential Japanese and foreign businessmen and government officials to promote pacifism and oppose Japan's escalating militarism. In 1918, he decided to stay in Japan to devote himself to rural mission work. He married Madeline Waterhouse, a Congregational missionary, in 1920, and two years later they replaced Rev. Gurney Binford and his wife, Elizabeth, who had initiated Quaker activities in the town of Mito, in Ibaraki prefecture.

Among the conservative farmers, it was a slow task to "win folks to Christ."[6] Nicholson focused on the practical needs of the people and slipped in a spiritual word when he could. But even the non-religious could sense that the minister opened himself to God's love and radiated it to everyone around him, as naturally as sunlight. A Japanese-language teacher transliterated his name as *Ni-ko-ru-son,* using ideograms meaning "God's sunshine came in to stay."[7]

For the next seventeen years, the energetic Nicholsons held Quaker meetings for adults and children, taught English, and advised students at the local junior college. When the Friends acquired land on the outskirts of Mito in 1926, the Nicholsons raised funds stateside to build a family home and a student dormitory. Later they added a kindergarten and playground, an "old folks' home" for twenty seniors, a roadside rest house, a lodge for homeless transients, and a goat dairy. When the Friends secured a large lot in Mito, Nicholson borrowed money to construct a building to house a co-op store, a matrimonial bureau, a legal aid service, a Christian sewing school and a nursery school.

Happy and productive years flew by until 1939, when the Friends Mission Board informed Nicholson that they wished to terminate his services because they were low on funds. Nicholson agreed to resign. Since Japan invaded China in 1937, rising militarism had limited his effectiveness anyway:

THE NICHOLSONS AT HIGASHI HARA, THEIR HOME NEAR MITO, JAPAN, 1931.
COURTESY OF SAMUEL NICHOLSON.

> At least once a month, "thought police" called at our home to ask me what I thought of the China incident. The pastors told me not to attend their meetings anymore, as the police always came to ask them what I had talked about. When I visited in the country, plainclothes men always followed me about and returned to every home I visited. So I had to stop calling on friends. Notices were put up saying, "Don't talk to foreigners; they may be spies!"[8]

After teaching for a year at the Canadian Academy in Kobe, the Nicholsons returned to the United States in 1940 and rented a small house in Pasadena, California. The Haddonfield Friends Meeting, which was located near the Nicholson family farm in New Jersey, pledged to send Nicholson a small monthly stipend. He recalled:

> That was our only visible means of support, with three children going to school and living here.... [I]t was a remarkable thing that we never went into debt, and we always had plenty to eat in the house. We never starved. We didn't have any luxuries, but we lived through that period with [only] fifty dollars a month assured income.[9]

GILBERT AND MINNIE BOWLES

After thirty years of service in Japan, Dr. Gilbert Bowles returned to Hawaii with his wife, Minnie, just prior to World War II. The Bowleses are remembered in Hawaii for their social and humanitarian services, particularly to the families of Issei who were arrested and sent to detention camps on the mainland. In 1944, they successfully prevented the military government in Honolulu from dissolving the Buddhist Shinshu Kyokai Mission and confiscating its assets.

GURNEY AND ELIZABETH BINFORD

After decades of Quaker missionary work in Japan, Rev. Gurney Binford and his wife, Elizabeth, retired to the United States shortly before the outbreak of World War II. The Binfords accompanied Herbert Nicholson when he toured Southern California to survey families whose members had been arrested by the FBI. Rev. Binford also coedited with Rev. Allan Hunter *The Sunday Before,* a collection of seven pre-eviction sermons by Issei and Nisei ministers. The pamphlet was widely circulated among church groups to stir compassion for the internees.

Nicholson spread word that he wanted to continue working with the Japanese. In January 1941, he was asked to substitute for Reverend Fujimori of the West Los Angeles Japanese Methodist Church, who had been incapacitated by a stroke. Nicholson was a bit nervous about agreeing to sermonize on schedule because Quakers believed in preaching "when the Spirit moves you,"[10] but he agreed to give it a try. Madeline Nicholson was appointed Sunday school superintendent, and together they were paid a combined salary of forty dollars a month. "Since that barely covered the cost of our car," Nicholson recalled, "my conscience about a 'hireling' ministry did not bother me!"[11]

Over the next year, Nicholson got acquainted with Southern California peace activists and Japanese Christian church leaders. After he recovered from his illness, Reverend Fujimori had resumed his duties as the Japanese-speaking minister, but the Nicholsons stayed on to minister to the English speakers.

◆   ◆   ◆

In the wake of Pearl Harbor, so many church members were arrested that Nicholson made almost daily visits to the Immigration Service detention center at Terminal Island. Since he was fluent in Japanese, he was one of the few who could interpret for the detainees and help them prepare for their hearings.

He also ran errands for them, helped them take care of business affairs and consoled their worried families. There was a lot to worry about. The U.S. Treasury Department froze the bank accounts of many Japanese Americans, allowing only small monthly withdrawals (thanks to a plea by Eleanor Roosevelt) for living expenses. Outstanding loans were called in. Issei businesses and property worth $27.5 million were taken over by the Alien Property Custodian. Many employers summarily fired Japanese Americans from their jobs, and companies refused to do business with them. Later in December, at the request of the War Department, the FBI began unannounced and warrantless searches of Japanese American households to seize guns, cameras, radios, and other "contraband" items, and to look for evidence of connections with Japan.

Nicholson lived by Isaiah 6:8: "Here am I, send me," and responded unhesitatingly to every call for help.[12] He was determined to rally popular support for Japanese Americans. He urged a committee of the Church

Federation to issue a statement of support, but Pearl Harbor had aroused strong feelings, even among the godly. Dr. Martin, the Methodist chair, roared at the Quaker, "Shut up! After what those skunks...did...we can't trust any Jap!"[13]

Many service organizations were more open than the churches, Nicholson recalled. "[T]hey would...say, 'Nicholson, we don't know anything about the Japanese point of view.... You just talk freely.'"[14] Nicholson pulled no punches. He explained that he did not support Japanese militarism, or the attack on Pearl Harbor, but "Roosevelt himself was pulling the strings...to get [the attack] to happen. He wanted America to be so terribly upset that they go into the war." Many scholars today support this view, but in the immediate aftermath of Pearl Harbor, it was a highly unpopular notion.

No one from the service clubs ever reported Nicholson's statements to the FBI, but many church groups did, Nicholson recalled:

> When I talked in the churches...I completely left politics out...I didn't want to get in an argument. All I wanted was to get people sympathetic...[but] nearly always...somebody would ask some fool question. I was foolish enough to answer it honestly, and they would report it to the FBI.... [A]bout once a month, an FBI man would come here to see me.... They said, "You'd better be careful or you'll land in jail." I said, "That's okay. I'm ready to go to jail. A lot better men than me have been there."[15]

Nicholson had a special concern for the Issei who had been arrested as "potentially dangerous aliens." At that point, no one knew exactly how many had been arrested or what would become of them. By February 1942, almost 3,000 had been detained, often on little or no evidence. Nicholson was indignant:

> [T]he stories that were told to the FBI. "This fellow has a shortwave radio. He's in touch with a ship out in the ocean."... Oh, [the FBI was] kept busy investigating stories that weren't anything at all. The bomb in the house [turned out to be] a tin pan. It was absolutely absurd, but more and more people were picked up all the time.[16]

To accommodate the overflow, an abandoned California Conservation Corps camp in Tujunga Canyon was opened up. The director, Mr. Scott, was privately sympathetic to the detainees, Nicholson recalled:

ISSEI ARRESTED BY THE FBI IN SANTA BARBARA AWAIT SHIPMENT TO ANOTHER DETENTION CENTER. COURTESY OF UNIVERSITY OF SOUTHERN CALIFORNIA, ON BEHALF OF THE USC SPECIALIZED LIBRARIES AND ARCHIVAL COLLECTIONS.

He just thought they were wonderful people…. [H]e told me, "I could open this camp at any time and say, 'Gentlemen, you may go home to your wives and your families. Come back tomorrow evening by five o'clock.' They'd go home and have a good time, and they'd all get back by five o'clock, and they wouldn't do any damage while they were out…. [T]hese [are] perfectly loyal Americans."[17]

When the American Friends Service Committee learned that Nicholson was visiting the families of the detainees, it hired him to collect the names of the arrested and assess their families' needs. He traveled in Southern California and Arizona with the Binfords. Then he headed north to join fellow Quakers Tom Bodine and Floyd Schmoe as they recorded arrests in Japanese communities from Bakersfield to Seattle.

In late January, 600 detainees were transferred to Missoula, Montana. Nicholson and Schmoe took the train to visit them. Mr. Collair, the camp's director, privately opposed the mass arrests, telling Nicholson that after examining the letters the prisoners were writing to their families, he was convinced that "these were the most loyal people we have in America."[18] Collair blamed the arrests on "public opinion" generated by California agricultural interests intent on eliminating economic competition from Japanese Americans.

Since Collair was short of interpreters, Nicholson volunteered to stay for four or five days and translate for the hearings of fifty-two Issei men. The case was a striking illustration of random injustice. All but two of the men were "uneducated, hard-drinking laborers" at a Nevada copper mine. Their Issei foreman had deducted fifty cents a month out of their paychecks to send to the Japanese Army widows' and orphans' fund. Most of the workers were not even aware that the money had been taken. After learning the men's story, the examiners decided the miners were hardly a threat to the nation. They asked the men whether they wanted to return to the mine, go to an internment camp or stay in Missoula. The men voted for Missoula. Most were elderly single men who'd had a rough life. They'd never had such good food or nice quarters, they told Nicholson. They didn't have to work, and there was no *sake* to get them into trouble.

The examiners decided to send half the miners to an internment camp and keep

DETAINEES ARRIVING AT A DEPARTMENT OF JUSTICE DETENTION CAMP AT FORT MISSOULA, MONTANA. COURTESY OF 84-296, FORT MISSOULA HISTORICAL MUSEUM—W.R. PIERCE COLLECTION, K. ROSS TOOLE ARCHIVES, THE UNIVERSITY OF MONTANA—MISSOULA.

half at Missoula. "If [the authorities] sent...all [the miners] out, the public would be alarmed. They had to keep some," Nicholson explained. "There was no rhyme or reason. The whole business was a farce." Later, Edward J. Ennis, director of the Alien Enemy Control Unit, told him privately that in 4500 hearings, not one suspect was found guilty of espionage or sabotage.[19] This fact was not publicized, however.

While at Missoula, Nicholson also acted as a character witness for fifteen or twenty of his friends from Los Angeles. One was Mr. Hiraiwa, a man in his eighties who had been arrested because he was a veteran of the 1896 Sino-Japanese war. Nicholson urged the authorities to "send the old man back to his wife in Pasadena." After the authorities agreed to release him, a grateful Mrs. Hiraiwa offered Nicholson fifty dollars for travel expenses, which he refused. The government, on the other hand, paid him nothing for his work as a translator. They kept him busy until 10 p.m. every night without compensation, not even for lodging or transportation. "All I got was [a] pencil...and a few free lunches," he declared disgustedly.[20]

Hiraiwa was released by the FBI six weeks after his hearing, but that did not mean he was free. By this time, all Japanese Americans on the West Coast were being interned. On the very day that Hiraiwa was transferred from the detention center to the Santa Anita Assembly Center, his wife was taken from her home and interned at the Turlock Assembly Center. To cheer the old man up, Nicholson took him a birthday cake. When the assembly center guard began to poke holes in the boxed, commercially baked cake with a "rusty knife," Nicholson cried, "You crazy fellow! What do you think you're doing?"[21] The guard continued to mutilate the cake, saying, "There might be a bomb in it."

Mr. Hiraiwa languished at Santa Anita for six weeks before Nicholson succeeded in arranging for him to join his wife in Turlock. Nicholson offered to drive the old man, but the authorities refused. Instead they bundled the elderly Issei, who spoke almost no English, onto a bus by himself. He arrived in Turlock in the middle of the night and sat unguarded in the bus station until someone arrived in the morning to take him to the assembly center. "It just didn't make

IN APRIL 1942, MORE THAN 2,000 MEN WERE INCARCERATED AT FORT MISSOULA—HALF JAPANESE AMERICANS AND HALF ITALIAN NATIONALS. BY THE END OF THE YEAR, MOST OF THE JAPANESE AMERICANS HAD BEEN TRANSFERRED TO OTHER CAMPS. COURTESY OF 84.298, FORT MISSOULA HISTORICAL MUSEUM— W.R. PIERCE COLLECTION, K. ROSS TOOLE ARCHIVES, THE UNIVERSITY OF MONTANA—MISSOULA.

sense," declared Nicholson. "It made me so exasperated."[22]

Sometime in February, the detention center at Missoula was closed and "the whole 600 were shipped to Louisiana." Nicholson traveled to visit them. "I kept going to detention camps, and nobody else did it. I was the only one that followed these people up," he claimed.[23]

By this time he had parted ways with the AFSC, which considered him a bit of a loose cannon. Decades later, at the Los Angeles hearings of the Commission on Wartime Relocation and Internment of Civilians, he testified:

> The AFSC asked me to join them...until I got too dangerous and they fired me. I was getting into too much trouble with the FBI. I was too active. I was seeing authorities and talking against the evacuation.[24]

Furthermore, many Friends were uncomfortable with Nicholson's fervently evangelistic style. Without AFSC support, Nicholson had to cover his own travel expenses. Characteristically, he fell back on a higher power. "I'd start out from home with thirty dollars on me. I'd buy a ticket part-way, and then I'd trust on some money coming in, or I'd hitchhike, or get there some way. But I always got there."[25]

When Nicholson arrived at the army-run detention camp near Alexandria, Louisiana, he found the commanding officer convinced that his prisoners were dangerous. Nicholson went to work on the colonel. "Now, just wait a minute," he said. "...[t]hey're all loyal Americans. They would be citizens if they were allowed to be.... [They are] the cream of the crop, the leaders of the Japanese community.... Have you noticed—haven't they organized already? Don't they have a mayor [and] a city council?"[26] Nicholson's sunshine worked its magic. By the end of his visit, the colonel was shaking his hand and thanking him for a new understanding.

The tireless Quaker next visited the Issei ministers' wives and Japanese-language-school teachers incarcerated at a women's detention camp at Seagoville, Texas. To save on hotel bills, he slept on the train. After visiting the women at Seagoville, he headed for New Mexico. In transit, he reached into his pocket and found an envelope containing forty-three dollar bills. The Seagoville women had taken up a collection and quietly slipped it into his jacket.

To get to the isolated detention camp at Lordsburg, New Mexico, Nicholson had to walk four miles from the railroad station. The camp was run by an alcoholic martinet and an "obnoxious" lieutenant, who confiscated Nicholson's papers and banned unsupervised meetings with the prisoners.[27]

Nicholson had completed his detention camp tour and returned to Pasadena by February 19, 1942, when FDR signed E.O. 9066. Barely a week later, on February 26, Nicholson was at a Quaker meeting in Whittier, California, when he felt a strong impulse to drop in on Virginia Swanson, a Baptist missionary working with the Japanese fishing community on Terminal Island. She was surprised and pleased to see him. She had just received word that the residents were to be evicted from the island within forty-eight hours. Together, she and Nicholson got on the phone to notify the AFSC and other groups, which scrambled to find accommodations for the evicted families. *(See chapter: Virginia Swanson Yamamoto.)*

Soon mass evictions were in full swing throughout Southern California. Nicholson spent much of his time at the Santa Anita Assembly Center, doing errands and helping the internees tie up loose ends. He even obtained permission to take a young couple out for the day to be married in his Pasadena living room.[28] Noticing Nicholson's ease with the internees, Richard Neustadt, the regional director of the Federal Security Agency, offered him a job as "reassurer of the Japanese people," at whatever salary he wanted to name.[29] Nicholson refused, believing that he would lose people's trust if he took a government job.

In June, as the internees began to be transferred from assembly centers to permanent internment camps, Nicholson rented a truck to take "about a ton of cast-off books" from the Los Angeles Public Library, along with pianos, pulpits, benches and prayer books, to Manzanar. There, he was again offered a job, this time by project director Roy Nash. Again he refused, but Nash wrote a pass giving the Nicholson family free access to the camp.

As Nicholson hopped into the rental truck to return to Los Angeles, Mr. Yamamoto, a grocer from Terminal Island, handed him the keys and the registration to his stake-bed truck and asked the minister to bring some furniture up from Whittier. Dr. William C. Bruff, a member of the Whittier Friends Church, had lent the Terminal Islanders a warehouse to store their household effects. Not long after Nicholson retrieved the first load of goods, an arsonist set fire to the warehouse. The grocer's possessions went up in flames, but he gave Nicholson use of the truck so that he could continue to run errands for the other internees. Togo Tanaka, prewar English editor of *The Rafu Shimpo*, recalled:

Nicholson brought to the camp truckloads of things, but mostly he brought good cheer—and

Woman awaiting internment, Hayward, California. Courtesy of The Bancroft Library, University of California, Berkeley, WRA Photographs.

WILLIAM AND MIRIAM BRUFF

Members of the Whittier Friends Church, Dr. William Courtland Bruff and his wife, Miriam, supported Japanese Americans in many ways. When the Japanese-language school in Norwalk was converted into a hostel for Terminal Islanders, the Bruffs visited almost daily to check on the welfare of the evictees and to offer loans and other assistance. They also looked in on the Imamoto sisters, whose parents had taught at the Japanese school before being arrested by the FBI. On the evening before the Imamoto girls were interned, the Bruffs took them out for a farewell dinner. The couple also visited the Imamotos and other internees at Santa Anita, bringing discarded library books from the Los Angeles Public Library, symphony records for a music appreciation class, and sheet music for the chorus. Later, Mrs. Bruff accompanied Quaker missionary Esther Rhoads on trips to Tule Lake and Manzanar.

Grace Imamoto Noda remembers Dr. Bruff as a quiet man of low-key but genuine warmth, with graying hair and beautiful blue eyes. When the West Coast was reopened, Dr. Bruff sent Grace train fare so that she could return to Whittier and work as his medical receptionist. From the many Japanese Americans who visited the Bruffs' office and home, she learned the full extent of their commitment to the former internees.   *Nominated by Grace Imamoto Noda.*

ESTHER RHOADS

A lifelong missionary who went to Japan as an 18-year-old, Miss Rhoads taught at the Friends Girls School in Tokyo prior to World War II. She happened to be in the United States during the war, so she worked with Japanese Americans for the AFSC. After the war she returned to Japan to serve as principal of the Girls School, and as regional director of the Licensed Agency for the Relief of Asia (LARA). To allow her to control the military warehouses where LARA supplies were stored, the U.S. Army gave her a temporary commission as a lieutenant colonel. When Grace Imamoto went to Japan after the war, she lived with Miss Rhoads, whom she remembers as a very human person, not at all pompous, with a wonderful sense of humor.

Nominated by Grace Imamoto Noda and Stephen McNeil.

hope. When help was needed he was there. He [was] very earthy and pragmatic, the kind of person who pitches in and does things. I never met anyone who, having met him, didn't remember him with a smile. The evacuees liked and respected many people, but they loved Herbert.[30]

Nicholson's son Samuel often accompanied his father on the 500-mile round trips to Manzanar until he was required to report to a work camp as a conscientious objector. Nicholson also made 2,000-mile round trips to Arizona to visit the Poston and Gila River internment camps. He often took passengers such as Quaker workers Kirby Page and Esther Rhoads, or missionaries E. Stanley Jones and Roy Smith. Nicholson also visited the camps at Topaz, Utah; Heart Mountain, Wyoming; and Amache, Colorado, and participated in Dr. E. Stanley Jones's weeklong revival meeting at Minidoka. *(See box: Dr. E. Stanley Jones.)*

On every trip, internees gave Nicholson lists of things they needed. He collected the items and stockpiled them at the Japanese church until he had a truckload. Although internees could ask the WRA to ship belongings to camp, they preferred to ask Nicholson because it took weeks for the WRA to process a request. Furthermore, employees of the commercial trucking company contracted by the WRA often deliberately damaged the internees' possessions.[31] When Nicholson ran out of room in Yamamoto's truck and was forced to let the commercial trucking firm haul certain items, he insisted on loading the goods into the truck himself. Otherwise, internees' goods were apt to be damaged "accidentally on purpose," while being loaded.[32]

At Christmas, the minister drove truckloads of Christmas presents to Manzanar, Poston and Gila River. Every year, the First Methodist Church of

Los Angeles collected 5,000 gifts "at a dollar apiece" for the youngsters at Gila River.[33]

The tireless minister believed that nothing happened without purpose. He was once asked to drive a car to a family that had resettled in Denver, Colorado. After delivering it, he borrowed another car and drove out to visit his friends the Sonodas, who had resettled in Henderson County. When he stopped at a country store to ask for directions, a boy volunteered to guide him. Nicholson was appalled to find the Sonodas living in a shack. It was quite a comedown from their lovely prewar home in Brawley, in California's Imperial Valley. Promising the Sonodas that he'd return in the morning, Nicholson returned to town with his boy guide. At 1 a.m., he was asleep in his motel room when he was roused by a man holding a gun to his head. The man flashed a sheriff's badge and hauled him off to jail. The boy, getting back at Nicholson for not letting him drive the car, had falsely accused him of stealing money from the motel till.

Nicholson spent the rest of the night in the cooler, listening to the troubles of an alcoholic fellow prisoner. In the morning, when the sheriff asked him why he had been arrested, he replied, "God sent me here to help that poor alcoholic and to have a talk with you."[34]

"Baloney," scoffed the sheriff. He interrogated the Quaker for an hour and then locked him up again. Later that afternoon, the sheriff reappeared. Nicholson recalled:

> Although he did not apologize...he shook my hand and said he was very happy to have this opportunity to talk.... This man, like so many others, was emotionally upset and hated all Japanese. He had been extremely hard on those who had come to Henderson County. I told him that if he wanted to meet a loyal American, he should get acquainted with Tom Sonoda. He was grateful for things I told him and said he would surely get to know Tom.

Once again, Nicholson's friendly persuasion had opened a closed mind.

♦　♦　♦

Officials like Collair of Missoula, Scott of Tujunga Canyon and Edward Ennis of the Alien Enemy Control Unit were privately appalled by the internment and tried their best to be humane administrators. Others did not, and the consequences could be serious. On a second trip to Lordsburg, Nicholson found the alcoholic major still in charge. Nicholson asked the camp lieutenant about an invalid detainee who had died. He was told that the man had been shot to death for falling behind on a four-mile walk from the railroad tracks to the camp. "Don't tell the man's wife what happened," begged the lieutenant. "Just tell her he died of TB."[35] Thinking the lieutenant wanted to spare the widow's feelings, Nicholson kept his mouth shut. It was not until decades later that he learned that not one, but two detainees, Hirota Isomura and Toshio Obata, had been shot and killed while being transferred from another detention camp. Both were invalids who had been too weak to keep up on the forced march.[36]

◆　◆　◆

Nicholson found a happier scene on his first visit to Camp Shelby, Mississippi, in the summer of 1943. A volunteer Nisei combat team was training there, and a group of homesick volunteers from Hawaii had just arrived. Although the chaplain knew that Nicholson was a pacifist, he allowed him to speak to the men at church services.

By February 1944, Nisei volunteers in the 442nd had performed so valiantly in Europe that the War Department decided to draft Nisei right out of the camps. To discuss the new policy, the AFSC and the Friends of the American Way met with Dillon Myer, head of the WRA, at the Orange Grove Friends meetinghouse in Pasadena. Nicholson declared that it was not right to draft people from behind barbed wire. Myer agreed. But, he said, "one branch of government did not have the right to tell another branch what to do."[37] He urged Nicholson to take his complaint directly to Assistant Secretary of War John J. McCloy in Washington, D.C.

"All right," Nicholson replied. "I'm on my way." En route, he stopped in Poston. He found a group of angry Terminal Islanders planning a demonstration to protest the draft. "They were just going to tear things up because they didn't approve of being drafted into the American army when they were locked up in this place," Nicholson recalled.

"That's not the way to do it," he cautioned. He explained that he was on his way to speak to McCloy about opening the camps and suggested that they send a telegram to Eleanor Roosevelt. She had made a "great impression" on the internees when she had visited the camp some time earlier. Nicholson led a delegation of protesters to see camp director Wade Head. "I'm so glad you came!" Head told Nicholson. "We knew there was going to be a demonstration. We could do nothing to stop it." Head asked a project lawyer to help the protesters draft telegrams to Mrs. Roosevelt, McCloy and Myer in exchange for a promise not to demonstrate again until they

OUTDOOR CHURCH
SERVICE AT CAMP
SHELBY, JULY 1943.
COURTESY OF THE BANCROFT LIBRARY,
UNIVERSITY OF CALIFORNIA, BERKELEY,
WRA PHOTOGRAPHS.

learned the outcome of Nicholson's meeting with McCloy.

After stops at Gila River and Camp Shelby, Nicholson arrived in the nation's capital. While waiting to see McCloy, he paid a visit to the Army captain charged with implementing the new draft policy. The officer complained that the Nisei were a "lot of roughnecks," and pointed out a stack of letters from angry internees. Nicholson recalled:

> [H]e handed me a letter. It was a terrible thing! Swear words and poor language, not very well-written, but very dramatically.... "We don't want to get in your blank old Army."... It was terrific.[38]

Once again, Nicholson applied the logic of simple humanity. "Captain, you're Irish, aren't you?... If they put us Irish behind barbed wire with towers...and men there day and night with guns to shoot us if we tried to get out...and then they tried to draft us in their old army, do you think we Irish would go?"

The captain replied, "Of course we wouldn't."

Nicholson pulled a letter off the stack and handed it to him. "Now put yourself in their shoes and you read this letter." The man read the letter with a revised perspective. He smiled. "These fellows have guts, don't they? Say, Nicholson, I'm so glad you came in here and talked with me...I'm glad to see their point of view.... I hope you get those camps opened."

John McCloy agreed that the internees should be allowed to return home. "But," he told Nicholson, "I can't do anything about it because of public opinion." He pointed to a basket on his desk. "We get these letters every day saying 'Don't let those Japs back again.'"

The letters were running ninety percent against lifting the exclusion order, McCloy said. Many of them were illiterate tirades or mimeographed form letters generated by the Sons of the Golden West or by agricultural groups that had profited from the intern-

FRIENDS OF THE AMERICAN WAY

WILLIAM CARR, a Pasadena real estate broker, founded Friends of the American Way because he felt the Committee on American Principles and Fair Play (CAPFP) had not gone far enough in opposing the internment. According to Audrie Girdner, Carr's group was "perhaps the most effective" offshoot of the CAPFP. By June 1944, Friends of the American Way had received 150 offers of jobs and housing for returnees, including one from a factory owner who said he could employ twenty to twenty-five returnees. The group's campaign to reopen the West Coast generated so many letters that John McCloy selected Pasadena to host the first returning Nisei, a student named Esther Takei, who enrolled in Pasadena Junior College in September 1944. *Nominated by Harry Honda.*

HUGH ANDERSON was a Pasadena accountant and member of Friends of the American Way who devoted tremendous energy to helping Japanese Americans. While working as a state auditor after Pearl Harbor, he assessed Japanese American businesses for tax collection purposes. Thus, he witnessed firsthand the hardships caused by bank closures and property impoundment. He made a profound and continuing commitment to helping the internees. First, he stored furniture and property for evictees before going to Poston to work as a business administrator. After a little less than a year, he contracted polio and was forced to resign. He then tried to attract Caucasian investment in a guayule rubber plantation intended to help resettlers reestablish themselves outside the exclusion zone. When Esther Takei was chosen as the first Nisei student to return to the West Coast, he invited her to live in his home, despite hate mail and threats. After the war, he devoted a year to helping returnees recover their property. Among those he tried to help was the Hagiwara family, who made an unsuccessful attempt to regain their concession at the famed Japanese Tea Garden in San Francisco's Golden Gate Park, which they had created and cared for before the war.

ment. He pointed to a second basket and said he would be able to open the camps if the basket was filled with letters from the West Coast saying, "We want our friends back."

That was all Nicholson needed to hear. He immediately sent telegrams to Poston, to the AFSC in Philadelphia, and to the Friends of the American Way in Pasadena asking them to launch a letter-writing campaign. As he made his way back to California, he met with camp councils at Amache, Gila River, Poston and Manzanar. He advised the internees to ask their Caucasian friends to write letters to FDR, McCloy and Myer. Pragmatically, he suggested that they enclose stamped, pre-addressed envelopes to make the task as easy as possible.

Nicholson's meeting with McCloy occurred on March 20, 1944. By July, McCloy had received 150,000 letters asking him to lift the exclusion order. Since the largest number of letters had come from Pasadena, McCloy wrote a letter to the Friends of the American Way in Pasadena, asking for their help in arranging for the first internee to return as a test in September.

◆　　◆　　◆

On January 2, 1945, the entire West Coast was reopened to Japanese Americans, but after years behind barbed wire, many internees were nervous about leaving camp. Nicholson enticed twelve Manzanar Issei into testing the waters in Los Angeles. He took them to visit the local police chief and a bank manager, who assured them that it was safe to return to their homes. At lunchtime, one of the internees suggested they eat at a local hangout. The place was crowded with aircraft workers, and a sign in the window warned, "No Japs." But when the owner spotted an old friend among the internees, he rushed out of the kitchen to kiss him on both cheeks and offer the entire group a free lunch.

As the internees trickled back to Los Angeles, Nicholson used Yamamoto's truck to haul their furniture until Yamamoto opened a business and needed his vehicle back. Nicholson then focused on the 156 Japanese American invalids who had spent the internment confined at the Hillcrest tuberculosis sanitarium not far from Pasadena. Throughout the internment, Madeline Nicholson had faithfully visited these patients twice a week. A firm believer in the power of prayer, she had rushed to their bedsides to hold vigils whenever they were in crisis. As the patients began to be released, the Nicholsons invited them to stay in their guestroom. Eventually, they rented a larger house and established "Friendship Home" as a halfway house for those leaving the sanitarium.

After the returnees were settled, Nicholson looked for new challenges. He volunteered for the Heifer Project, a charitable organization conceived by Church of the Brethren relief worker Dan West to bring livestock to hungry nations. Remembering his prewar goat farm in Japan, Nicholson raised funds to take goats to war-torn Asia. He delivered his first shipment of 200 goats to Okinawa in October 1947. As he crisscrossed the country, he was saddened by the widespread destruction—a quarter of the civilian population was dead or missing, the harbors filled with sunken ships, and homes and fields devastated. "Everywhere, I asked the people, who had suffered so much, to forgive us," Nicholson wrote. "At most meetings, when I asked to be forgiven, someone would stand up and say that they too needed to be forgiven.... It was a wonderful opportunity to tell of the love of God...."[39]

Nicholson was a born storyteller whose loquacious charm reached out to everyone. One evening his son commented, "Daddy, you talked for six and a half hours today to over 6,000 people."

Six months later, Nicholson brought goats to Japan. He told a Japanese journalist about a Japanese American girl whose family had raised four goats for the project. The story was expanded and embroidered until it appeared in a fifth-grade reader as the touching story of an American boy who sacrificed to send a goat to Japan even though his father had been killed in the Pacific War. The fable struck a healing chord in the Japanese psyche, and Nicholson became known in Japan as "Uncle Goat." For three years he shuttled back and forth across the Pacific, preaching forgiveness and reconciliation and raising enough funds to ship more than 5,000 goats to Okinawa, as well as Japan and Korea.

In 1950, when the Nicholsons moved back to Japan to help the Worldwide Evangelization Crusade, the Japanese American Chamber of Commerce of Los Angeles sponsored a farewell banquet, which raised $4,000. The pair worked as missionaries in Japan until Nicholson turned seventy in 1961. They returned to the United States, where they continued to speak at churches, visit hospitals and renew ties with former internees who never forgot the couple's tireless efforts on their behalf. The Nicholsons saw their lifetime of service as "a very simple testimony of God's dealing with us." They were merely "earthen vessels...feebly overflowing with the treasure of DIVINE LOVE."[40]

Dr. E. Stanley Jones

"A wrong has been done. The report that the Japanese are content and that they are satisfied that evacuation was necessary does not square with the facts, so far as I could ascertain them," Dr. E. Stanley Jones proclaimed to thousands of internees in 1943.[41] Jones was an internationally famed evangelist and missionary who was stranded in the United States by the war. Learning of the internment from Gordon Chapman and other missionaries who had served in Japan, he launched a "barbed-wire preaching mission," bringing his renowned weeklong revival meetings to seven of the internment camps.

Jones went to India as a missionary in 1907, and soon developed a following. In 1925, he wrote the breakthrough *The Christ of the Indian Road,* which sold over a million copies and is still in print. His prolific writings taught generations of missionaries to cultivate mutual respect and understanding among different cultures and religions. Rather than uncritically accepting Western ways, he said, missionaries should encourage native peoples to mesh their own cultural values with Christ's teachings. Jones organized "round table conferences" for people of different religions, and borrowed from Hindu tradition to create Christian Ashrams, retreats for spiritual self-reflection. Honing his style at huge mass meetings in India, Jones became a compelling speaker at revival meetings around the world. When he carried these meetings to the internment camps, he brought with him an interdenominational array of prominent church people, and the meetings were attended by 1,000 to 3,000 internees, both Christian and non-Christian. During his October 1943 visit to Topaz, he delivered a sermon titled "Barbed-Wire Christians" that typified his blunt honesty:

> [T]o lump together everyone, loyal and disloyal, citizen and non-citizen, was a tragic blunder for which we are already paying dear. Besides laying out $80,000,000 a year to maintain the camps, we have struck a shattering blow at the loyalty of Japanese Americans.... Our blunder was made when we...allowed an army officer to decide, on the basis of the prejudice, hysteria and vested interests of a vocal minority of Californians, what the nation should have decided on the basis of the principles of democracy.... "These camps are a monument to American stupidity," I said to a high-up Caucasian official.... I waited for the officer to disagree with my statement. But he replied, "I entirely agree with you."...

> A returned missionary, back on the [hostage-exchange ship] *Gripsholm*...told me that when he arrived back in this, his "home" country, he was grilled from February 4 to March 28, eight hours a day and sometimes fourteen, to break him down and get him to confess to being a spy. He held up only through prayer, he said...and his spirit triumphed unsoured. These Japanese-American Christians are doing the same. Their spirits are unbroken.... Their faith in democracy is intact. Their faith in God holds too, in spite of everything.

After the war, Jones resumed his international ministry, spending half the year in the United States and half in India. He traveled to the world's trouble spots to promote international understanding. He became a good friend of Mahatma Gandhi and wrote a biography that Dr. Martin Luther King later said inspired him to apply the principles of nonviolence to the American civil rights movement. Jones helped subsidize schools, churches and clinics in India and continued to speak and write until his death in 1973. *Nominated by Rev. Paul Nagano.*

ELIZABETH & CATHERINE HUMBARGAR:
A SENSE OF THE POSSIBLE

In May 1942, after the San Joaquin County Fairgrounds in Stockton, California, became the Stockton "Assembly Center," the guards quickly grew accustomed to admitting a pair of high school teachers who visited their former students nearly every day. If the gatekeepers were surprised that two pregnant-looking ladies should have the energy for a daily trek to the dusty fairgrounds, they would have been more astonished to know that the women were neither married nor pregnant. If they had patted down Elizabeth Humbargar and her sister Catherine, they would have found waists thickened by salami and other contraband foods.

The two teachers smuggled in treats the young people craved, paying for them out of their own pockets because the internees' bank accounts had been frozen. Surrounded as they were by barbed wire, guard towers and soldiers with machine guns, many students were numb with shock during the first days of their incarceration. They were American citizens, born on U.S. soil, with constitutional rights they had learned about in civics class. "Most of the kids couldn't believe they were there," Elizabeth Humbargar recalled.[1]

But the unbelievable had happened. Just a month before the end of the school year, the students and their families found themselves behind barbed wire at the fairgrounds, redubbed the Stockton "Assembly Center" by the the Wartime Civil Control Agency (WCCA). Since the government had made no provisions for the students to continue their education, the young people were in danger of losing an entire semester's worth of academic credit.

Because the students had been taken out of school, the Humbargars decided to take school to the students. They worked full time at Stockton High, so they could not teach the classes themselves. Instead, they recruited a cadre of young internees—mostly college students—to organize makeshift classes at the fairgrounds. They persuaded school authorities to grant credit for the classes and to look the other way while they raided district warehouses for textbooks. Every day after school, the two sisters visited the assembly center to train and counsel the internee teachers and funnel them daily assignments from the teachers at Stockton High. In their spare time, the Humbargars collected 1,000 books to create a library.

◆　　◆　　◆

When asked why she went out of her way to help Japanese Americans when few were willing to do so, Elizabeth Humbargar deflected praise. "If it hadn't been me, it would have been somebody else. But the Japanese did it themselves through their honesty, their integrity, their diligence, their perseverance," she told the *Stockton Record*.[2] "All I ever did was what anyone would have done that knew the people."[3]

The Humbargars understood what it was to be on the receiving end of prejudice. They had been raised in the tiny farm community of Salina, Kansas, and ended up teaching in California because in the 1920s it was hard for Catholics to find jobs in Kansas. Elizabeth taught English at Stockton High School and sister Catherine taught math. The two sisters were well-liked and respected by students of all backgrounds, but perhaps because they had been marginalized themselves, they took a special interest in the school's minority students.

"I found the Oriental kids so delightful," recalled Elizabeth, "so good, so humorous. This was a new world for me!"[4] Soon she was the faculty advisor of the

NEWLY ARRIVING INTERNEES PASS THROUGH THE GATES OF THE STOCKTON ASSEMBLY CENTER.
COURTESY OF THE BANCROFT LIBRARY, UNIVERSITY OF CALIFORNIA, BERKELEY, WRA PHOTOGRAPHS.

school's 400-member Japanese American student club, and Catherine was an active, though unofficial, partner. Each year Elizabeth also took a "schoolboy" or "schoolgirl" into her home—a student who lived so far out of town that it was difficult to commute to school. These students stayed with her during the school week and returned to their families on weekends. (After the war, she would provide similar assistance to students coming from Japan to study in the United States.) Her dedication to Japanese American students drew the attention of the Japanese government, and in 1936 she was selected to be one of fifteen West Coast teachers to tour Japan, Korea and Manchuria.[5]

In the late 1930s, Stockton High's student body was divided into three tracks, X, Y and Z. The Xs excelled academically, the Zs were steered toward vocational training, and the Ys fell somewhere in the middle. The Humbargar sisters taught the middle category, where most of the Nisei students were clustered. The Nisei were good students, hardworking and well behaved, but the majority lagged a bit in language proficiency. Though they were American-born, most spoke Japanese at home. Working with these students sparked Elizabeth's lifelong interest in teaching English as a second language.

One former student, Grayce Kaneda of the class of 1938 (later known as JACL activist Grayce Uyehara), recalled:

> The Humbargar sisters loved to work with us. Those of us who were raised by the Issei were taught certain things—that education was of prime importance and we never brought *haji*, shame, to the family. The teachers had no problems disciplining us. We were always the best behaved kids in the school. We always did our homework, and we were good students.[6]

STOCKTON HIGH SCHOOL AS PICTURED IN THE 1939 YEARBOOK. COURTESY OF THE HAGGIN MUSEUM.

As devoted as they were to their own students, the Humbargars were always on the lookout for promising Nisei in the larger student body. One such student was Jim Doi. Now a respected educator in his own right, in 1940 he was a small, skinny farmer's kid, working hard toward college and a better life, but not quite sure what such a life might look like.[7] He grew up just outside of Stockton in the little hamlet of Racetrack, where his horizons hadn't stretched much further than he could see across the flat, fertile fields of the Sacramento–San Joaquin Delta. After graduating from a sleepy little grammar school with only three teachers and eighty students, Jimmie struggled to adapt to bustling Stockton High School, which drew 3500 students from the city of Stockton and sur-

JAPANESE AMERICAN
STOOP-LABORERS WEED
A CELERY FIELD ON
ONE OF THE DELTA
ISLANDS NEAR
STOCKTON. COURTESY OF
THE BANCROFT LIBRARY, UNIVERSITY OF
CALIFORNIA, BERKELEY, WRA
PHOTOGRAPHS.

rounding communities like Racetrack, French Camp and Bacon Island.

Just before the end of his junior year at Stockton High, he was rushing down the hall when he was collared by a teacher he knew only slightly. "Stop by my classroom after school, Jimmie," Elizabeth Humbargar told him. "I'd like to talk to you." Her deep-set eyes and hawk-like nose lent her an imposing dignity, but the smile she flashed him was friendly and unpretentious.

What could she want? Jimmie wondered. He knew that she was the advisor of the Japanese Student Club, to which he belonged. But why would she single him out from 400 other Japanese American students?

After school, Elizabeth Humbargar was waiting for him, along with her sister Catherine. Elizabeth got right to the point. "Jimmie, you've been nominated for the presidency of the Nikkei Club, the Japanese American student club."

Guessing what was coming, he took a step backward. "Look, Miss Humbargar, I don't know very many of the other students at all—I'm a real country boy!"

The teacher fixed him with a look at once encouraging and penetrating. "I want you to accept the nomination and take over as the president in your senior year," she said. "You owe it to your people."

That was all she had to say. Like many young Nisei, Jimmie struggled to reconcile the Japanese values of duty, obligation and cooperation with the American drive for individualism, initiative and achievement. In a single sentence, Miss Humbargar had coupled the expectations from both of Jimmie's worlds.

"I was never in any of her classes," Jim Doi recalled, "but somehow she made up her mind that she was going to try to point out to me some new possibilities of what I might try to be."[8] Over the next year, Jimmie was to learn that the Humbargars had high expectations of all the Japanese American students.

You might say the Humbargar sisters were our faculty representatives. They took up our causes and carried any problems immediately to the faculty council and the principal. And they were always on the lookout for anyone with a

Japanese face who they thought had the capacity to lead.

Not all aspects of the club presidency were glamorous, Doi recalled.

During senior year, I got picked to do a lot of different things. I worked for the Humbargar sisters, both of them. Whenever there was a problem regarding any Nikkei kids, I was delegated to take care of it. For example, many of the Nikkei students drove to school. It was the only high school for miles around, and served the whole area. Sometimes students would park their cars carelessly and block the residents' driveways. Or sometimes they would eat their lunches and leave some litter lying around. I was the one who had to go around, often among total strangers, and tell them that there had been a complaint and that the principal had asked me to ask them not to do certain things.

Today Doi laughs at the memory.

I got "dumped on" in that way. If you want to know how you become a leader, part of the job is learning to raise difficult issues in a diplomatic manner. I didn't particularly want to be a leader, but in those days, if some teacher picked you up and said, "You're gonna do this," you did it. That was the way it was. I didn't seek to be the president of the Nikkei Club.

STOCKTON HIGH'S JAPANESE STUDENT CLUB, 1941. CLUB PRESIDENT JIMMIE DOI IS SEATED AT CENTER.
COURTESY OF THE HAGGIN MUSEUM.

Going into his senior year, Jimmie was a top scholar. Although he didn't know it at the time, he was under consideration to be valedictorian of his graduating class. Like many Nisei, however, he was soft-spoken and shy, and spoke with a slight Japanese accent.

Elizabeth Humbargar suggested that I take public speaking and try out for the debate team. To help me with technique, Miss Ovena Larson, who was the head of the English department, would take me out to the football field, and have me speak, at first 5 yards, then 10 yards, 15 yards, 20 yards, 30 yards —until she could hear every syllable at any distance. And she had me practice my enunciation: "Kick-ING." "Fit-TING." By the time she got through to me, after one term, I had lost my Nikkei accent. That's how hard the high school teachers worked with us.

Another task that broadened his horizons was arranging for an annual speaker for the Nikkei Club. Someone suggested that Jimmie invite Amos Alonzo Stagg, who was then coaching the College of the Pacific football team.

Alonzo Stagg was one of the legendary figures in collegiate sports because of his philosophy. He didn't care just to win games; he wanted to build character. It probably would not have occurred to me to seek him out on my own. I went to see him because of our club. I went to his home...and he was very nice and quickly agreed to come speak. That got me over my fear of talking to very important people.

When Jimmie graduated from Stockton High in June 1941, he gave his valedictory speech loud and clear, without an accent. Although he had never been to the San Francisco Bay Area, the Humbargars encouraged him to apply to the University of California at Berkeley. He was accepted for admission in the fall, but he decided to defer enrollment until the spring semester so he could work for a few months and save some money. In December, Pearl Harbor was attacked. Before the new semester began, the university wrote to Jimmie and told him not to come. Throughout the anxious spring, while controversy about Japanese Americans swirled around him, Jimmie worked in a celery-packing plant. In mid-May, he and the other Japanese Americans of San Joaquin County were interned at the fairgrounds. It was an ironic turn of events for Jimmie, who said:

> I grew up just south of the fairgrounds. As elementary school kids, none of us could afford to pay the 25¢ to get into the fairgrounds on county fair days. We used to look for holes in the fence that we could climb through. It was odd to find ourselves inside the fairgrounds—locked up.[9]

◆ ◆ ◆

When their students were interned, the Humbargars leapt into action. They raided the high school storeroom.[10] When the principal spotted the two women carrying out stacks of disused textbooks, he looked the other way. It was not something he wanted to know about officially. A maintenance man cocked his eyebrow. "You got something to haul them with?" he wanted to know. He helped them load books and supplies onto his horse trailer and drove them to the assembly center. There the Humbargars commandeered the grandstand and an empty barn, which they outfitted with tables made of sawhorses and planks.[11]

Elizabeth Humbargar soon sought out Jimmie Doi. "I need your help," she said, and recruited him to teach two junior-year English classes. She managed to secure a few textbooks, but since there weren't enough to go around, she suggested that he focus on composition. Doi recalled:

> That was my first exposure to teaching. I would take the papers my students had written and correct the spelling and grammar. Then I would meet with the Humbargars, and say, "This is the way I see these." They would make comments and

suggestions, and I could go back and talk to the students. In college I would have been called a graduate assistant.

The Humbargars worked hard—they really did. They taught their regular courses at Stockton High during the day and came into camp every day after school, and sometimes on Sundays. They met with me at least three times a week, and I don't know how many other "teachers" they had. Imagine working a full day and then coming to the assembly center after school to advise all of us green trainees.

◆　　◆　　◆

Another Stockton High graduate who was recruited to teach was Barry Saiki. He already had a job as the editor of the Stockton Assembly Center newspaper *El Joaquin,* but Elizabeth Humbargar talked him into teaching classes in his spare time. He taught drop-in classes in California history and current events using outdated history books and current events newspapers she supplied.

Barry, who had been just about to graduate from UC Berkeley when he was interned, had not taken classes from either of the Humbargar sisters. But Elizabeth Humbargar had sought him out in 1937, early in his senior year at Stockton High. He recalled:

A MOTHER AND HER YOUNG CHILDREN OUTSIDE THEIR ROOM AT THE STOCKTON ASSEMBLY CENTER.
COURTESY OF THE BANCROFT LIBRARY, UNIVERSITY OF CALIFORNIA, BERKELEY, WRA PHOTOGRAPHS.

> I was selected from the public-speaking class to speak at the Armistice Day program. I was one of the finalists in a statewide contest on "What American citizenship means to me." My material was good, but my technique as a speaker was not very impressive in those days. Miss Humbargar approached me and said, "Catherine and I would be willing to stay after school and listen to your speech. We could give you comments and hints on how to improve it."
>
> The other faculty members were not particularly interested in us, but the Humbargars were outgoing. They showed the friendliness typical of Midwestern farm people. They approached people in order to find out what was up and determine what they could do to help. Their main motivation was to help.[12]

Most young Nisei were reserved, even shy, outside of their own group. They loved Elizabeth Humbargar for her ability to reach out and make them feel cared about. She encouraged everyone to go to college, even though in those days, because of discrimination, a college degree was no guarantee of a job. "She made me do something with my life," a former student recalled after her death.[13]

It was not just country folk like Jimmie who had limited horizons. The color line was a literal fact of life in Stockton. Most youths from the close-knit world of Japantown rarely ventured north of Weber Street. The gracious bungalows and well-trimmed lawns on the north side of town were a world away from the crowded workingmen's hotels and pool halls squeezed between downtown and the waterfront. The Eurocentricism, racism and classism of the dominant culture combined with the self-effacement of traditional Japanese values to keep most prewar Nisei "in their place."

Grayce Kaneda was an exception. Her role model was college-educated Mrs. Sudow, the only English-speaking Issei woman in the area, who taught at the Japanese-language school at the Japanese Presbyterian church.

> I was not a typical Nikkei. I was the kind that tried out for plays even if there were never any roles for me; I played in the marching band. These were things that the average Nikkei in Stockton didn't do.... I was fortunate that I didn't have a mother who thought that Japanese women are supposed to stay quiet and stay in the background.... I just believed fundamentally in equal opportunity and the democratic process.[14]

But even Grayce benefited from the Humbargars' advice and support. "Both of the Humbargar sisters took interest in me," she recalled, "and they always encouraged me. They felt that I had potential to be a very good speaker." Grayce had attended Stockton High just four years earlier than Jimmie Doi, but in her day, the school's debate team was closed to Japanese Americans. "It was an exclusive white club when I was there," she said. She developed her speaking skills by competing in the JACL's biennial oratorical contests. When she won her first Northern California JACL competition, she asked Elizabeth Humbargar to help her prepare for the national competition. Grayce placed second on the national level twice in a row.

When she was interned in the spring of 1942, Grayce was an honors music student at the College of the Pacific (COP) in Stockton. She had been practicing to perform at the senior piano recital with full orchestra, but she was interned before the performance date. Fortunately, her teachers vouched for her abilities, and COP granted her a degree in absentia. With typical energy, she began organizing choral music classes at the assembly center. Although she got plenty of encouragement from the Humbargars, Grayce used her own resources as well. "My father made his living cleaning homes on the north side of town," she recalled. "His clients happened to be the

GRAYCE KANEDA PLACED SECOND AT THE 1936 JACL NATIONAL ORATORICAL CONTEST IN LOS ANGELES. COURTESY OF GRAYCE KANEDA UYEHARA.

superintendent of schools and other people who made decisions for the school district. And I knew all the heads of the departments at Stockton High School and at COP because I had been so active. We had good connections with the people who ran the Board of Education, and they loaned us books to use at the assembly center."

Through the efforts of internee "teachers" like Grayce, Barry and Jimmie, ninety-two percent of the interned students received academic credit for the semester.[15] Elizabeth Humbargar was modest about her own role and graciously acknowledged the "great co-operation of Stockton High School teachers."[16] But in the memories of the Nisei, the Humbargar sisters stood out. Both were called "Jap lovers" and received crank calls and hate mail from the many Stocktonites who were glad to see their neighbors behind barbed wire.

"What offended me greatly was that so many Italians had signs on their cars saying 'Japs Go Home,'" Elizabeth Humbargar recalled.[17] But she chose to focus on the positive. "I'll tell you who were wonderful during the war," she said. "The Chinese. The night before they had to report to the fair-grounds, almost all the Japanese ate in Chinese restaurants. [In spite of the curfew for Japanese Americans,] the Chinese told them, 'You can stay as long as you want. They can't tell Chinese from Japanese anyway.'"

Throughout Stockton's long, sweltering summer, when temperatures routinely climbed above 100 degrees, the Humbargar sisters continued regular visits to the students at the fairgrounds. In September, the internees were transferred to a more permanent internment camp in Rohwer, Arkansas. The Humbargars continued their support, long distance. Soon the internees began to resettle in the Midwest and East, and they and their families needed letters of recommendation for jobs and school admissions, scholarships and financial aid. Elizabeth estimated that she and her sister wrote over 500 recommenda-tions—so many that government agents visited her home and placed her name on a list of "subversive" persons.

In early 1943, a secret POW camp for Japanese nationals was established at Byron Hot Springs, six-teen miles southwest of Stockton. Japanese American soldiers from the Military Intelligence Service

Grayce Kaneda graduated from Stockton High in 1938. Courtesy of Grayce Kaneda Uyehara.

(MIS) were assigned there as translators. Since the entire West Coast was now off-limits to Japanese Americans, the Nisei soldiers were confined to base. Elizabeth Humbargar made special arrangements for them to use her home as a surreptitious USO. Another former student and MIS member, Richard Hayashi, recalled that the Humbargars helped him make a secret visit from Pennsylvania to Stockton to check on a family business.[18]

In January 1945, the West Coast was reopened to Japanese Americans, and the Humbargars opened their homes as temporary hostels for returning students and their families. Elizabeth also helped reestablish the Stockton JACL after the war, petitioned Congress to suspend the deportation of "disloyal" Japanese Americans, and supported the Issei in their quest to become U.S. citizens. She modestly dismissed her activities as "a small bit of help."[19]

She left Stockton High School after the war to teach at San Joaquin Delta College, and endeared herself to a new generation of students coming from Japan and other countries to study in the United States. She was a pioneer in teaching English as a second language, and wrote several manuals and handbooks on conversational English. She retired in 1969 after forty-four years of teaching, but continued as a consultant to the Stockton school district's adult education program.

She maintained a lively interest in Stockton's diverse Asian American population—Japanese, Chinese, Filipinos, and Vietnamese Americans, saying:

> My association has been long and it has been tremendously rewarding, in friendship. I've learned a lot about the Oriental people; they have a great wisdom that they didn't learn here.... You give them an inch and they give you back a mile.[20]

◆　◆　◆

Elizabeth Humbargar's students honored her many times for what she had given so freely to so many. In 1949, they took up a collection to buy her one of the first televisions in San Joaquin County.[21] In 1970, friends and former students organized a testimonial dinner, which raised $15,000 to endow a JACL scholarship in her name. Admirers from as far away as Chicago and Hawaii arrived to honor her. Later, a second scholarship was established to honor her work with foreign-language students at San Joaquin Delta College.

In 1978, she became the second American woman ever to be honored by the Emperor of Japan with the Order of the Sacred Treasure, 4th Class. The Stockton JACL arranged for its president, Richard Tanaka, to escort Elizabeth Humbargar and Catherine

Humbargar Rovetta to Tokyo to receive the award. While they were there, the sisters were feted at a banquet organized by Barry Saiki and attended by over forty former students from all over Japan.

Long after her death in 1989, the mere mention of Elizabeth Humbargar's name could still bring a smile to the lips of former students. Beyond the friendship embodied in her warm, friendly gaze and unpretentious manner, Elizabeth and her sister Catherine passed on something far greater. They expanded their students' sense of the possible and taught them to aim high. When Jim Doi was appointed dean of the University of Washington's School of Education in 1979, he was the first person of color to be named dean at a Pac 10 university. When Lt. Col. Barry Saiki was named Chief of Military Security, G2, for the Sixth U.S. Army, with responsibility for security in the eight Western states, it was just twenty-two years after he himself had been interned as a security risk because of "military necessity."

From 1985 to 1988, Grayce Kaneda Uyehara played a key role in the passage of the redress bill in which the U.S. government offered an apology and $20,000 restitution to surviving internees. Uyehara was tapped by Mike Masaoka and civil rights icon Min Yasui to replace Masaoka in Washington, D.C. For three crucial years she left her family in Pennsylvania and worked in the nation's capital. She declined a salary, asking only compensation for meals, lodging and travel. "Thus," she said, "there was no necessity for raising a large sum to run the Washington office. I wanted to take personal responsibility for correcting the injustice suffered by our people."[22]

She added, "Without the loving support, encouragement and training I

JACK MCFARLAND

Jack McFarland, former sports editor for the *Stockton Independent*, organized recreational programs for the internees at the Stockton "Assembly Center" from May to September 1942, according to Barry Saiki and Fred Oshima, who were respectively the editor and the sports editor for the assembly center newspaper *El Joaquin*.

The internees had been abruptly uprooted from their homes and routines and crammed into makeshift quarters behind barbed wire at the San Joaquin County Fairgrounds. The internees faced an unknown future, and tensions ran high. Jack McFarland's mission as a member of the administrative staff was, in Oshima's words, the "sensitive psychological job of keeping a mass of confined and innocent humans busy inside a crowded, concentrated, barbed-wire fenced [compound]. His prime objective was to...prevent the evacuees from drifting into [an]...inactive, stagnant environment" by providing the internees with healthy diversions to occupy their time and attention.

Working with a very limited operating budget, McFarland enlisted the help of the internees to develop a comprehensive recreational program with offerings for every age and interest—from sports to arts and crafts and cultural activities such as *ikebana* (flower arrangement), calligraphy and tea ceremony. He scrounged for donated equipment and materials, improvised facilities and recruited a volunteer staff from the internees.

George "Pop" Suzuki helped McFarland organize team sports. Before the war, "Pop" Suzuki had been the legendary coach of the Stockton Busy Bees, the best Nisei girls' basketball team in the country. With his help, McFarland was able to recruit baseball and basketball talent and organize games that were enjoyed by players and fans alike. *Nominated by Barry Saiki and Fred Oshima.*

received during my high school years from the Humbargar sisters, I would not have accomplished the task." She said that the intellectual capacity she needed to argue on public issues and garner redress votes from members of Congress was born of the patient after-school coaching she received while preparing for those long-ago JACL oratorical contests. She considers herself just one of the many Stockton High Nisei whom the Humbargars "enabled to become strong communicators and who were no longer shy nor diffident, as most white Americans expected of us. I do think we found the strength to actively change many of the practices which were not American." For her work, Uyehara too was honored with the Order of the Sacred Treasure (Gold Rays with Rosette) in April 1995.[23]

For the Humbargars, doing the right thing was what people did, pure and simple. Decade after decade, they modeled their beliefs. By expecting only the best from themselves and others, they often got it.

PREWAR RELATIONSHIPS:
BUILT ON A SOLID FOUNDATION

EARL AND MARJORIE MINTON/EUGENE CALVO: BRIDGES ACROSS CULTURE IN MOUNTAIN VIEW

Some Japanese Americans who formed solid and supportive relationships with non-Japanese Americans before the war had an easier time during the internment because of support from friends, landlords and others. In her memoirs, Nellie Nakamura, a 102-year-old Nisei from Los Altos, California, recalled a relationship that began in 1920.[1]

Earl Minton owned the Minton Lumber Company in Mountain View. Mr. Minton provided the lumber to build a Japanese church in San Jose and a Chinese mission in San Francisco's Chinatown. His wife, Marjorie, was "a genuine Lady Bountiful" who did many things for the Japanese American community. In 1920, Marjorie Minton started a Sunday school for Japanese American children in the home of Yonejiro Tsuruda, Mrs. Nakamura's stepfather. Mrs. Nakamura recalled:

> Our house had a large kitchen. Mr. and Minton came over and said, "Can we hold a Sunday school class here on Sundays?" Mrs. Minton and her sister were the teachers. They brought two little pump organs and some folding chairs. And they started a Sunday school. At first there were only a few students, then there were more children, and the kitchen wasn't big enough.

> My stepfather donated a corner of his property so they could build the Japanese Community Church. Mr. Minton donated the lumber and acted as chief architect. All the Japanese people of the neighborhood helped build it. The church

73

stood for a long time, and the Japanese Christians brought their kids there for Sunday school.

The Mintons tried to promote appreciation and respect for Japanese people and culture by inviting their Caucasian friends to their home to celebrate Girls' Day. On this Japanese holiday, Issei and Nisei women and girls dressed in their finest kimonos and performed Japanese dances on the Minton lawn.

Mrs. Minton also gave free piano and voice lessons to several Japanese American children. One of them was Nellie Nakamura's daughter, Emmy, who recalled, "Everything about her house was so elegant. It was so unlike the humble surroundings that most of us lived in, but she taught us to believe that we could aspired to the finer things in life." One of Mrs. Minton's students, Ruth Okamoto, passed on these aspirations to her son Kent Nagano, who is now a celebrated conductor of classical music.

During the internment, Mrs. Minton tried her best to look after belongings stored in the Japanese Community Church. Nellie Nakamura recalled:

GIRLS' DAY AT THE MINTONS' HOUSE IN THE 1930S. MRS. MINTON, FRONT LEFT, WEARS A COMET-STREWN KIMONO. NELLIE NAKAMURA, FRONT, FOURTH FROM RIGHT, WEARS BLACK WITH A SPRAY OF FLOWERS. COURTESY OF NELLIE NAKAMURA.

> The whole Japanese community used it to store valuables that they couldn't take to camp with them. The place was just crammed full of furniture from everybody in that area, not just the Christians. Once we got to Heart Mountain, Mrs. Minton was glad to do anything for us. We would write and ask her to send us things that we had stored in the church. She'd go in there and find the things and the government would pay for them to be shipped to us. She said that every time she would check on the church, she could see that people had broken in. Lots of stuff was scattered around from people's boxes.

The Nakamuras also received help from their landlord, Spanish immigrant Eugene Calvo, who watched over their property and rented out their house.

> When we came back, at least we had a house to go to.... The Calvos kept our old house...[and the tenants] cleaned it up nice because they knew we were coming back. We lucked out. We were better off than a lot of people who had no place to come back to. People who didn't have a place to go stayed at the Japanese language school in Mountain View. They

just got a mattress and slept there. They had a big hall where people could just stay for awhile. People like Mrs. Minton and the Duvenecks, and others who were sympathetic to the Japanese, tried to do whatever they could to find homes and jobs for us. *Nominated by Nellie Nakamura.*

PANSY HAM: A COLORFUL INSPIRATION

Phyllis Mizuhara won second place with this essay in the Art and Literature Competition sponsored by California Civil Liberties Public Education Program and the California State Library Foundation.[2]

In the 1930s, at first glance, one wouldn't have guessed that Pansy Ham was a church administrator or a Sunday school teacher. She had brick red hair and carefully plucked eyebrows that arched gracefully over azure blue eyes. Her eyelids were shaded with blue mascara, her prominent cheekbones were highlighted with circles of artistically applied rouge, and her sunken cheeks made her small, heart shaped lips pucker up as if she were ready for a kiss. She dressed flamboyantly in brightly colored, almost garish, outfits. At our church social programs, Mrs. Ham would sometimes don a grass skirt and do the hula. She was definitely not the sedate, formal sort of person that one expected a church leader to be. I guess that she had acquired this colorful flair because she was also a successful painter and a high school and college art teacher. However, every bit of chutzpah that Mrs. Ham displayed was balanced with sincerity, kindness and a true Christian spirit.

PANSY HAM, 1980.
COURTESY OF THE MIZUHARA FAMILY.

In 1938, when I was eight years of age, she was my Sunday school teacher. Her class was fun because she was so animated and energetic. She also taught dancing to the young adults and instructed the girls on proper table manners and formal table settings—skills most of us had not learned at home.

Her association with the Japanese Christian Church of San Bernardino began in 1932, when she was 37. She volunteered to become the unsalaried assistant director of our Sunday school. She was recruited by the established First Christian Church to help our smaller church with our Sunday school programs. Her position lasted until 1942, when Californians of Japanese ancestry were ordered to move to concentration camps.

Our church became defunct, but Mrs. Ham did not abandon the Japanese community that she had worked with so closely for 10 years. She helped us prepare to move: finding places to store possessions, advising us on how to rent our homes, and on evacuation day, May 23, 1942, arranging transportation to the area where we boarded the bus that was to deliver us to some unknown, God-forsaken place. (After the war my sisters discovered that Mrs. Ham had stored our boxed belongings in her bedroom during the three years that we were incarcerated.)

In February of 1942, prior to our evacuation to Poston, the FBI arrested my father and sent him to a detention camp in

New Mexico. In July, after my mother, my three sisters, my brother and I were "ensconced" in our one-room home in Poston, Mrs. Ham wrote a letter to U.S. Attorney General Biddle on our behalf, asking for the release of my father from his concentration camp in New Mexico, so he could join us in ours. She vouched for his character, conduct and reliability. Our family felt that she went "out on a limb" for us. Being sympathetic to the Japanese was not a popular stance to take at that time. She also wrote letters attesting to the character and loyalty of other fathers detained in New Mexico, as well as for her Nisei friends who wanted to leave Poston to attend college or seek employment back East.

On May 10, 1980, my sisters and I planned a banquet to honor Mrs. Ham for her friendship, loyalty and support of the San Bernardino Japanese community. Since very few internees returned to San Bernardino after camp, many who attended the dinner traveled from various parts of California and from as far away as Maryland. Everyone enjoyed renewing old friendships and having the opportunity to show our gratitude and give thanks to a truly compassionate, caring and courageous person. Mrs. Ham, in her eighties then, still had her henna red hair and a little pizzazz left in her demeanor. Upon accepting a plaque of appreciation and a small gift, she said tearfully, "I didn't realize that I was loved so much!"

In the following years, Mrs. Ham's health began to wane. My sister Masako visited her weekly to see how she was faring. On January 31, 1989, Mrs. Pansy Ham passed away at 94 years of age. I feel indebted to her and all the other "Mrs. Hams" who went the "extra mile" to support the Japanese community in times of adversity, and who in doing so, may have experienced adversity themselves.

CLYDE AND FLORENCE MOUNT: FRIENDS INDEED

When World War II began, Clyde and Florence Mount were simply Harry Fukuhara's employers, but, as he recounts below, their concern and compassion during the chaotic months preceding the internment became the young Kibei's emotional anchor.[3] Colonel Fukuhara went on to a distinguished twenty-nine-year career in the U.S. military. His many honors include the Kunsho Award, Order of the Rising Sun (Gold Ray with Neck-Ribbon) which he received from the Japanese government for contributing to U.S.-Japan understanding.

Almost two years before World War II began, I started working in Glendale, California, for a couple named Clyde and Florence Mount. They began as my employers, but during the internment period, they lived up to the old adage "a friend in need is a friend indeed." During the worst days of my life, when I was trying to cope with internment as a scared, confused young adult with loved ones on both sides of the Pacific, the Mounts showed sincere and genuine concern for me and took me into their family. Their kindness laid the foundation of a relationship that lasted for the next thirty years.

I was what is called a Kibei. I was born and raised in the U.S., but in 1933, when I was 13, my father died and my mother took me and my siblings back to Japan. I completed high school in the city of Hiroshima and returned alone to California in 1938 to go to college.

In January 1939, I enrolled at Glendale Junior College and looked for a nearby job as a "schoolboy." I was hired by a pair of elementary-school educators; Mr. Mount was a teacher and Mrs. Mount a principal. I did chores for them and lived in their home, which was just a short commute from my college. Glendale was a well-to-do, all-white community just north of Los Angeles. It was a congenial area where the neighbors accepted me as a resident in the Mounts' home and even hired me to do occasional odd jobs for them.

The day Japan attacked Pearl Harbor, my life changed almost immediately. December 7 was a Sunday, and I was doing some gardening for a nearby family. As soon as the lady of the house heard the news over the radio, she came out and told me to leave immediately. She fired me on the spot!

The outbreak of war was especially traumatic for me because my mother and brothers were still in Japan, along with many other relatives. I worried about what would happen to them, as well as myself. I didn't know if we would ever see each other again. Not long after December 7, I decided to quit school because commuting was becoming increasingly difficult as the atmosphere in Glendale and Los Angeles grew ever more hostile to anyone of Japanese ancestry. I survived by doing odd jobs—the only kind of work I could get. There were lots of defense jobs opening up, but they were closed to Japanese Americans.

I continued to stay with the Mounts. I'd lived in this pleasant community for almost three years by that time and the neighbors who were familiar with my background were at least polite to me because the Mounts were highly respected in the community. As time went on, however, I began to realize that my presence was becoming awkward for Mr. and Mrs. Mount.

As war hysteria worsened, neighbors became involved in the war effort as air-raid wardens and other volunteer positions. They began to develop suspicions about me. When restrictions were imposed on the movements of Japanese Americans, the neighbors began to watch my comings and goings and quiz the Mounts about my activities. They warned the couple that I was flouting the five-mile travel restriction and the 9 p.m. curfew. Mr. and Mrs. Mount were very protective of me. Over the next few months, they vouched for me several times in the face of accusations against me. I didn't want to continue causing problems for them, so I decided that I had to find a new home.

In late February 1942, my sister, who had separated from her husband, moved down from Seattle with her little daughter. I moved out of the Mounts' home, and my sister and I joined forces to face an uncertain future together. In just a couple of months my role had changed from relatively carefree college student to head of household with two people depending on me. The next two months were stressful and difficult. I was not prepared for the extra responsibility or the financial difficulties that we encountered. It was a constant struggle to find work. Fewer and fewer Caucasians would hire me and the Japanese Americans could not afford to hire because their bank accounts were frozen. No one wanted to rent a house or room to a Japanese American, especially one without a steady job. Even the neighborhood grocery store refused our business.

The period from December 7 to May 1, when we were interned, were the worst five months of my life. Yet shining through all that turmoil and darkness, the sincere affection and compassion that the Mounts extended to me and my sister remains a bright and inspirational memory. As I was confronted with one difficulty after another, the Mounts were always ready to listen to my fears and frustrations. Their kindly words of encouragement were tremendous morale-boosters during a period when I had no one else to turn to.

Mr. and Mrs. Mount had no children. They had both devoted their entire careers to education and had developed very close relationships with people of different ethnic backgrounds. Years before, they had legally adopted a Mexican girl and befriended a boy of French and English parentage. During the last couple of months that I lived with them, the Mounts became deeply engaged in trying to help me.

When the newspapers began writing about mass internment, Mr. and Mrs. Mount were horrified. They were very vocal in their opposition. They insisted that it was illegal for our government to lock people up without due process of law. It was the beginning of my education on the Constitution. Mr. and Mrs. Mount helped me understand that I had civil rights, and they stressed that it was important for us Japanese Americans to speak up on our own behalf.

The Mounts tried to think of ways to help me avoid internment. Thinking that shedding my Japanese surname would help, they offered to legally adopt me so that I could use their last name. We dropped that idea when we learned that anyone with even one-sixteenth of Japanese ancestry would be interned. When the Mounts heard that Japanese Americans could avoid internment by moving inland, they suggested that I go to live with their relatives in Columbus, Ohio, and continue my education there. I gladly accepted this offer, and it would have become a reality if my circumstances had not changed.

By January 1942, I was having a hard time finding any work at all. When I heard that the Terminal Islanders had been ordered to leave their homes within 48 hours, I went down there to look around. A man who was desperate to sell his furniture agreed to let me take it and send him the cash after I sold it. I hauled away the goods and set them up in an empty lot on a busy street in Los Angeles. I sold everything right away to the commuters driving by. I got a much better price for the man than he would have gotten on Terminal Island, so I split the proceeds with him. As Japanese Americans began to be interned from other neighborhoods, I did the same thing for them. That was kind of the thing I had to do during that period. I really had to scramble to keep food on the table for my extended family.

By the time our little family unit was interned on May 1, our financial situation was so bad it was almost a relief to go to camp and let the government take care of us for a while. We were sent to the assembly center at the Tulare County Fairgrounds along with other internees from the southern California coast and the Los Angeles area. Tulare is located in the Central Valley south of Fresno; it felt like a long way from home.

During the next six months, Mr. and Mrs. Mount tried to keep up my spirits by writing me regularly. I always looked forward to hearing from them. On one unforgettable occasion, they made the 340-mile round trip from Glendale to visit me. Very few people at Tulare got visitors because it was a long haul over the Tehachapi Mountains, and gas and tires were rationed. The Mounts saved up their coupons for several months in order to make the trip. I was deeply moved by this thoughtful demonstration of their concern.

The Mounts stayed in touch with me when I was transferred to the internment camp in Gila River, Arizona. In November 1942, I volunteered for the Army's Military Intelligence Language School at Camp Savage, Minnesota. The Mounts were very proud of me for volunteering for military duty from the confines of an internment camp. They informed all of their neighbors that I was going to fight against Japan, and displayed a flag with a star on their front door to signify that a member of their household was in the service. They often reminded me that their home was also my home and insisted I use their address as my home address.

For the next several years, as I went from Camp Savage to overseas assignments in the Pacific Islands, Mrs. Mount faithfully wrote to me every week. In early 1944, while I was attached to the 112th Cavalry Regiment in the southwest Pacific near New Guinea, John Wayne came to visit us on a USO tour. He was surprised to see Nisei soldiers fighting in the Pacific. Since he had Nisei friends, he was particularly interested in our work interrogating Japanese POWs and translating captured Japanese documents. When he returned to California, he telephoned the Mounts to tell them that the Nisei were doing a very important job. The Mounts were proud and happy to tell their neighbors and students that John Wayne had met me and had personally vouched for the Nisei soldiers fighting in the Pacific. At the time, the exploits of the 442 Regimental Combat Team and the 100th Battalion were not yet known, so the Mounts were proud to spread news that Japanese Americans soldiers were contributing to the war effort.

Clyde and Florence Mount proved themselves to be true friends in time of need. After the war, we were able to share the good times as well as bad, and we remained close until the end of their lives. I realize now, over sixty years after we first met, how lucky I was to have been blessed with such dear friends who were a positive and affirming influence in my life and that of my family.[3]

GOOD NEIGHBORS: ARROYO GRANDE, RICHMOND, REDWOOD CITY, SAN JOSE, WATSONVILLE

According to the 1940 census, nearly two-thirds of the Japanese American workforce had jobs related to agriculture. The value of farms operated by Japanese Americans in California, Oregon and Washington was $72 million. The vast majority of Japanese Americans lost everything during the internment. The Issei, who were barred from owning land by the Alien Land Laws, lost control of the land they rented or leased before the war. Many of those who had managed to purchase land in the name of their American-born children could not keep up with mortgage and tax payments while they were behind barbed wire. A fortunate few were able to keep their holdings with the assistance of neighbors or other supporters.

Whether they were able to return after the war and rebuild their lives often depended on the attitudes of their Caucasian neighbors. On the central coast of California, for instance, almost no Japanese Americans returned to farm at Pismo Beach, but a few miles south in Arroyo Grande, conditions were more favorable, thanks to a few people who saw Japanese Americans as neighbors rather than enemies.

ARROYO GRANDE

The most prominent supporters of Japanese Americans in Arroyo Grande were J. Vard Loomis and his brothers. They were the sons of Edward Clinton Loomis, one of the area's early ranchers, who founded a feed and grain store in 1905. By the 1930s, E. C. Loomis and Sons was the principal agricultural supplier in San Luis Obispo County, with feed mills in Arroyo Grande, San Luis Obispo, Paso Robles, Lompoc and Santa Maria. The area's agriculture was split into two distinct cultures: the largely Caucasian cattle ranchers and dairy farmers, who grew hay and alfalfa and ran their cattle on rolling inland pastures; and the largely Japanese American produce growers, who irrigated labor-intensive vegetables in the fertile coastal valleys. E. C. Loomis and Sons served them both, offering feed and grain to the ranchers and seed, fertilizer and insecticide to the farmers.

After Ed Loomis retired, his three sons, Ivan, Clinton (better known as Buster) and Joseph Vard (known as Vard) managed the business. Vard, the youngest, was elected class president at Stanford in 1931. He was also a star pitcher on the baseball team.[1] After graduation, Vard joined his brothers at the family firm, handling sales. Personable and outgoing, he was a familiar and welcome sight throughout the county as he visited the farmers to take their orders. Kazuo "Kaz" Ikeda, now a prominent Arroyo Grande farmer, remembered:

> Vard was really friendly, and not only to the Japanese. When he talked to the farmers, it was not just for five minutes—he sat and talked for a half-hour or an hour. He really cared about people.[2]

Most of the truck farms in the Los Osos Valley, San Luis Obispo, Pismo Beach, Guadalupe and Arroyo Grande were operated by Issei like Kaz's father. Juzo Ikeda had begun farming in 1929 and was soon leasing forty acres of rich alluvial soil in the Arroyo Grande Valley. By the late 1930s, there were about forty Issei farmers in the area. They formed a growers' co-op—the Pismo-Oceano Vegetable Exchange—to ship produce to the East Coast.

Every year, the Loomises threw an annual "Japanese picnic" for their Japanese American customers. Families from Santa Maria to Morro Bay attended the gathering, Ivan Loomis's son John recalled:

> Dad would convince his suppliers...from the seed, fertilizer and insecticide companies to donate their products. We...sold nicotine...which was used to kill aphids on peas. Everyone, including the Japanese, was raising peas in those days. [The sales rep] would bring...cases of cigarettes in tins...thou-

EVERY YEAR THE LOOMISES THREW A PICNIC FOR THEIR JAPANESE AMERICAN CUSTOMERS. COURTESY OF GORDON BENNETT.

ARROYO GRANDE'S NISEI BASEBALL TEAM. BACK ROW: KAZ IKEDA, JUZO IKEDA AND VARD LOOMIS; MIDDLE ROW: HARRY KUROKAWA, SEIRIN IKEDA, JAMES NAKAMURA, FRANK SAKAMOTO, HARRY SAKAMOTO, SAB IKEDA; FRONT ROW: BEN FUCHIWAKI, GEORGE NAKAMURA, JOHN SAKAMOTO, HILO FUCHIWAKI, AND TARO KOBARA. COURTESY OF SANDRA LOOMIS CABASSI.

sands of cigarettes—and he'd give them all away. Then we had the local soda pop works...come out with a truck filled with iced-down soda pop....

On the day of the picnic Mr. Hayashi would come to our house with...crates of his own-grown lettuce, mayonnaise and cases of canned shrimp and crab.... He'd mix it all up in large washtubs....

They served sirloin steak, bread, beans, crab salads, coffee, and soda pop, followed by strawberry, vanilla and chocolate ice cream cups for dessert. After eating, cigars and cigarettes were passed around...before the games started.... After the picnic we'd have a baseball game, run races, play all kinds of games, and everyone went away with a prize.... Those Japanese picnics were wonderful.[3]

◆　◆　◆

When Kaz Ikeda became a teenager, Juzo decided that his eldest son and the other young Nisei needed a constructive physical outlet. At the time, baseball was at the height of its popularity, and every town and city had a sandlot team. Juzo decided the Japanese Americans of Arroyo Grande should have one, too.

He learned that Vard Loomis had played baseball at Stanford and enlisted his help. In 1931, they organized the Arroyo Grande Young Men's Association baseball team, which Vard coached for ten years, until the internment. Kaz, the catcher, was "quite a ballplayer," according to his cousin Haruo Hayashi.

The team traveled to Santa Maria, Santa Barbara, Bakersfield, Fresno and San Jose to play other Nisei teams. Vard drove the team, and wife Gladys often went along.[4]

One day, a bus full of African American musicians spotted the Nisei team practicing in an Arroyo Grande park and challenged them to a game. Being the only "white guy" and odd man out, Vard was selected to be the umpire.

It was one of the happiest days of his life, he later told his daughter Sandy—filled with laughter and good-natured teasing as each team called him "four-eyes" and "blind" whenever he made an unfavorable call.[5]

Vard was an honorary member of the Japanese Fishing Club, which invited him along on their expeditions. He acted as their "designated driver," which permitted the other fishermen to drink their fill of *sake*.[6]

On New Year's Day, the principal Japanese holiday, the entire Loomis family was invited to the Hayashi farm to pound sticky rice into *mochi*, or traditional rice cakes. John Loomis recalled:

> About one-third of the kids in school were Japanese American, including my best friend, Haruo Hayashi. Haruo and I and my cousin Gordon [Bennett] were so inseparable we were known as the Three Musketeers.[7]

After Japan attacked Pearl Harbor, the Loomises stood by their Japanese American friends, even though others in the community called them Jap-lovers. Kaz Ikeda's family had particular reason to feel grateful for Vard Loomis's help—so much so that Kaz would later name one of his sons after him.

At the outbreak of war, Kaz was twenty-three. He had recently graduated from Cal Poly in San Luis Obispo, and was helping his dad farm the sixty acres that Juzo had purchased in Kaz's name when he turned twenty-one. About a month after Pearl Harbor, Kaz was abruptly thrust into the role of head of household. His father broke his neck in an accident involving a runaway team of horses. He was paralyzed and required around-the-clock nursing care at the hospital.

Haruo Hayashi and Vard Loomis Courtesy of Sandra Loomis Cabassi.

When the Wartime Civil Control Administration (WCCA) ordered Japanese Americans to move east of Highway 1, quite a few of the Arroyo Grande farmers had to relocate. Kaz's family moved across the highway to the Arroyo Grande Japanese-language school. Then they heard that the exclusion zone would be extended to the middle of the state. Kaz and some other Nisei drove east of Highway 99 looking for a place to rent, but, he recalled, "They didn't want us out there. We couldn't find anyplace to rent, so we decided to stay put."[8]

When they learned they were going to be evicted, the family appealed to the WCCA. Juzo needed long-term nursing that was not available at the makeshift "assembly center" at the Tulare County Fairgrounds. Kaz recalled:

KAZ IKEDA IN FRONT OF THE FUKUHARA HOUSE, 1942. COURTESY OF SANDRA LOOMIS CABASSI.

The WCCA told us my dad could remain at the local hospital until adequate facilities could be built at Tulare. And Mother could stay with him. But Mom hardly spoke English and didn't know how to drive, so I asked if I could take her place. That's when Vard stepped in and said I could stay at his place as long as I needed to. He didn't hesitate for a second, but I heard he got a lot of flak from his friends.[9]

Kaz's mother and brothers went ahead to Tulare, while Kaz stayed with Vard and his wife, Gladys, and visited his father at the hospital every day. In exchange for the Loomises' kindness, Kaz offered to babysit their daughter, Sandy. For the next two and a half months, he was the only Japanese American in the area. Gladys Loomis recalled that Kaz's presence caused the sheriff to search their home for shortwave radios, and the young Nisei was once stopped by the police for being alone in a car with a young white woman—he was driving her home at Gladys's request. According to John Loomis, the authorities enjoyed exercising their power:

Soon after Pearl Harbor, we started having blackouts in Arroyo Grande. Most of the air raid wardens were guys that were 4F. They were quite a rowdy bunch. They would threaten to kill people for not having their lights properly shielded. They were mean hombres.[10]

Finally, the Tulare Assembly Center's medical facilities were ready, so Kaz and his father rejoined the family. They were eventually transferred to Gila River, Arizona, where the family cared for Juzo in their barrack until he died in the summer of 1943.

Meantime, the Ikeda farm had been rented out to a couple of young Portuguese men. Vard Loomis stopped by regularly to collect the rent, out of which he paid the property taxes.

Haruo Hayashi recalled that Vard also looked after the Fukuhara house during the internment.[11] The Fukuharas farmed the old Routzahn place, 200 acres of choice farmland near Oceano. Their house on Halcyon Road was just about the biggest in town when it was completed in 1941. After Pearl Harbor, the brand-new place became a natural target for the resentful and envious. When the Fukuharas were interned, they asked Vard and Gladys, then living in a modest little house, to move into their home and keep an eye on their property. Vard and his brother Buster leased the Fukuhara acreage and farmed it during their absence.

The Loomis brothers also arranged for the evictees to store their personal belongings in a large dehydrator building near their offices. Unfortunately, the building was somewhat isolated and easy to break into, so most of the furniture was stolen or vandalized by war's end.

Gladys Loomis recalled a day when one longtime Caucasian customer stormed into the family store. Buster, who had never really recovered from an early bout of rheumatic fever, was managing the operation from a cot set up in the store. The customer loomed over Buster's sickbed and roared, "You Jap lovers...if you don't quit, I am going to burn your store down!"[12]

◆ ◆ ◆

Ken Kobara's family also farmed in Arroyo Grande before the war. He said:

> I've lived in the same house for seventy years. I was born in this house. My father was one of the early ones to buy here in the area, in the 1920s. We owned about 25 acres. Before the war, all farmers in Oceano were doing well because they were raising pole peas. Our cool, moist climate was perfect for them. Even during the Depression, the well-to-do people still ate their peas, and they were willing to pay for them.
>
> During the war our property was farmed by Joe Silviera, a Portuguese fellow. His family owned part of the land my father bought, and he lived only 200 yards away. Joe was a young man at the time; he had worked for my father as a teenager.
>
> When we had to leave, we put all the furniture in one room of the house and locked up the room. We left the farm with Joe. He rented out the house, farmed the land and paid the taxes. He did very well during the war. He had twenty to twenty-five acres of his own and he also grew peas up on the hillside above Shell Beach.
>
> Joe was a nice man, but he was so outspoken that he didn't have too many Caucasian friends. In January 1945, the WRA said it was OK for Japanese Americans to return to the West Coast. A month or two later, Joe notified us that the people who were renting our house were moving out. He warned my dad, "You better hurry up and get back before someone burns the place down." So in February or March, my father and sister came back. They were the first Japanese Americans to come back to Arroyo Grande.
>
> Two agents from the WRA named Thompson and Lighter stayed here at night for several weeks. They parked their car in our yard about fifty yards away from the house and kept watch all night. My sister and my father slept in the hallway where there weren't any windows. They were afraid that people would shoot into the house.
>
> Father decided to start farming. He went to the hardware store he used to patronize for years before the war. The clerk welcomed him back, and he bought hoes and shovels and other items. Later, the store called and asked him not to come back, because some people were giving them a bad time. The people who used to deliver our gasoline told him they couldn't do it during the day—only at night, when people couldn't see. Father decided he couldn't farm under those conditions, so he went to work for Joe Silviera for a few months. He didn't start to farm again until August or September.

The rest of the family stayed in Utah until the end of the school year. We came back in June. When school started in Arroyo Grande in September, there were only a handful of Nisei: the Fukuhara boys and a few others. The teachers and the principal were really helpful, but it was pretty tough for the first three or four months. We had a terrible time, fighting every other week. The Fukuharas had an old Plymouth coupe they used to drive to school, and people used to flatten the tires all the time.

There were quite a few people who were helpful, though. Peter Bachino had an insurance company. Father had left cars and trucks with him, and got them back in good shape. After the war, nobody would sell us car insurance except for Peter Bachino. He picked up Japanese American accounts all the way up to Morro Beach.

Paul Wilkinson was a butcher in Arroyo Grande. Before we were evicted, there was still meat rationing. We didn't have ration cards, so he would slip us meat under the counter. In those days, everyone ran a tab, kept an account that they would pay off when they had the money. Before we went to the assembly center, all the Japanese went to pay off their tab, and he wouldn't take any payment. "You hang on to it. You're gonna need the money, so don't pay me," he told them. After the war every single family paid him back when they could afford it. There was not one deadbeat.

The people who stood by us, I could count on one hand. J. J. Snyder was an orphan who was a blacksmith. He was awful good to the Japanese. I remember one time he came to fix my dad's pump on Christmas Day.

W. A. Baxter and Sons was another one. When the internees were coming back, two WRA men went around and talked to local businessmen to see if anybody would take our business. Walter A. Baxter had a service station and auto repair business in Pismo Beach. He had three sons in the navy fighting the Japanese, but he knew the Japanese Americans in Shell Beach before the war—they were the nicest people, he said. He was the only service station in the area that would do business with us.

The other farmers in the area didn't want us back. They had gotten hold of the land we farmed before the war, and they knew that we would get the land back, so there was a lot of backstabbing. Many people returning from camp didn't own property. They needed a place to stay until they could get established, so lots of them stayed in the migrant laborers' cabins we had behind our house. The Japanese-language school was also used as a hostel.[13]

◆　◆　◆

Haruo Hayashi recalled:

Before the war, we owned a few acres, I wasn't old enough for my dad to buy land in my name, but the land was held in the name of a cousin. Some neighbors, Cyril Phelan and John Enos, farmed our property while we were gone. They took care of all the tractors and equipment, and kept everything in good running condition. After we got back, there were other farmers who offered to lend us equipment when we needed it.

I got discharged from the army in the summer of 1945, just before the war ended. I came back to pick up the family car and stayed over at the Bennetts'. They took a little flak from some of the neighbors, but they told me, "You can stay as long as you want."

There were quite a few good people. We were all farmers and we all got along. They had no hatred for the Japanese, before, during or after the war. There were a few people who were anti-Japanese. Some had signs that said, "No Japs allowed," but after ten, fifteen years went by, some of those guys wanted us to be their friends.[14]

Kaz Ikeda and his mother returned to Arroyo Grande in December 1945, a half-year after the first group returned. By that time, the most intense hostility had abated, he said.

The people farming around us, Caucasians, were nice people. When we started to farm, Edwin Taylor and Gus Phelan loaned us any equipment we needed. Joe Silviera, our neighbor, kept some things for us—a shotgun, radio, piano. After the war, we got them all back.

Maybe there were one or two that shied away from us, but most people treated us all right.[15]

◆　◆　◆

Gladys Loomis remained livid about the injustice done to her neighbors. In 1991, she said:

Never once was any disloyalty found in our area. Nearly all of the young men who played on Vard's Nisei baseball team who were of draft age volunteered immediately. Not one was drafted. Almost all of them worked in military intelligence because they were bilingual. Some served in the 442nd Infantry Combat Unit [sic], the most decorated American unit of the war.[16]

According to Gladys, one of the most important Issei in the area before the war never returned. Mr. Kawaoka chose to be repatriated to Japan rather than accept the humiliation of internment. His son Yosh served in the U.S. Military Intelligence Service under General MacArthur. After the war, he moved to Japan to join his family, and by the 1990s he headed his own steel company.

Among the Japanese Americans who returned to San Luis Obispo County, Hayashi noted:

There are very few Japanese American farmers left today. Much less than half the families came back after the war. A lot of people never came back, and a lot of people went into different lines of work—they worked for the county, or went into engineering or other professions.

We had to get bigger to survive. As people died or retired, we bought their land, so the remaining families each control hundreds of acres. Today there are only five family farms left in the Pismo-Oceano Vegetable Exchange: Ikeda, Hayashi,

Kobara, Saruwatari and Dohi. Business has been growing. We've had to adopt new technology.[17]

The community has not forgotten the Loomises. In 1980, the California Nisei Baseball Association played their championship series in Arroyo Grande. They dedicated their program to Vard Loomis. Not long afterward, the Ikeda family built a housing development on a portion of their land. They named one of the streets Vard Loomis Way.[18]

Nominated by John Ortega, Kaz Ikeda, Haruo Hayashi and Ken Kobara.

RICHMOND

Around the turn of the century, Issei Jiro Ninomiya bought a strip of land in Richmond, California, across the road from Swiss immigrant Frederick Aebi. By the time World War II broke out, the Ninomiyas and the Aebis had been neighbors for almost forty years. Both immigrants grew roses to sell in San Francisco, and both had passed on their businesses to their sons.[19]

In 1942, Tamaki Ninomiya and Francis Aebi were too busy to do much socializing, but as rumors spread that the Japanese Americans would be sent to internment camps, Francis Aebi gathered his family together and walked across the road to his neighbor's house. He offered to look after his nursery if he were forced to leave. He told his neighbor that he did not doubt that Ninomiya would do the same for him. "Love they neighbor as thyself," he said.

After E.O. 9066 was signed, the Ninomiyas showed Aebi how to operate their greenhouse watering system. Not long afterward, the FBI arrested Tamaki Ninomiya, leaving his wife and his young children to prepare for eviction alone. Soon they were interned in an assembly center, then the Amache internment camp.

Aebi struggled to care for the Ninomiya property as well as his own. Since flowers were not eligible for the farmers' rations of extra fuel needed to keep the greenhouses warm and productive, the grower uprooted the precious plants and replaced them with cucumbers and tomatoes, keeping just a few roses for better times.

For three years, Aebi tended both properties, working so hard he grew thin and gaunt. But when the Ninomiyas returned, he met them at the train station and welcomed them home to a thriving nursery, a freshly cleaned house and a healthy bank balance. The Aebi and Ninomiya nurseries continued to prosper side-by-side for another generation. Aebi still lives on the same property, across the street from the Ninomiya sisters.

Nominated by Harry Fukuhara.

REDWOOD CITY

At the outbreak of war, J. Elmer Morrish was branch manager of the First National Bank in Redwood City, California, south of San Francisco.[20] Active in business and community organizations, Morrish was known as a soft-spoken man with "a heart of gold." Among his customers were Japanese American farmers and flower growers, for whom he helped arrange mortgages and loans before World War II. When his customers were interned, many entrusted him with power of attorney and asked him to look after their property.

A collection of 2,000 letters donated to the Redwood City Public Library in 1990 documents how Morrish leased out the internees' land, paid their taxes and bills, and watched for vandalism. After the war, he supported the returnees as they reestablished their lives. Morrish kept his half of the correspondence properly business-like, but his customers wrote to him as a trusted friend, confiding their hopes and fears and sharing victories and frustrations. After Morrish retired, a grateful community sent him on a trip to Japan. Morrish died in 1957, but he is still remembered and honored today.   *Nominated by Harry Fukuhara.*

SAN JOSE

Even before the war, San Jose, California was considered friendly to Japanese Americans, partly because of the support and leadership of James Benjamin Peckham, a self-styled "country lawyer" descended from one of San Jose's founding families.[21] J. B. Peckham, also known as Ben, was the prewar lawyer of choice for Chinese and Japanese immigrants. Representing them when few others would, Peckham helped them get around the Alien Land Laws by holding their properties in his name until their American-born were legally old enough to gain title. On paper, he became one of the largest landowners in the Santa Clara Valley.

In 1942, when the local Japanese Americans learned that they were about to be interned, they again turned to Peckham for help. For a modest legal fee, he agreed to watch over hundreds of properties, collecting rents, paying taxes and holding the balance in trust until the owners could return. While internees were away, he ensured the survival of San Jose's Japantown by paying daily visits to shuttered stores and the boarded-up Buddhist church to prevent vandalism. When the West Coast was reopened to the Japanese Americans, Peckham and the Council for Civic Unity ignored hate mail, and assisted former internees returning to the area. The relatively welcoming environment attracted former internees whose old neighborhoods were more hostile. As a result, San Jose's

Japanese American population grew from 3,700 prewar to 6,000. Today, San Jose boasts one of the last three surviving Japantowns in the continental United States, in large measure because of J. B. Peckham's longstanding support. In 1993, former San Jose mayor Norman Mineta introduced a bill in the U.S. House of Representatives to name the city's new federal courthouse and federal building after J. B.'s nephew Robert F. Peckham, who, following family tradition, had become a distinguished jurist with a strong commitment to civil rights and racial equality. *Nominated by Norman Mineta and Harry Fukuhara.*

WATSONVILLE

On April 27, 2002, after two years of research by Mas and Marcia Hashimoto, Jane Borg of the Pajaro Valley Historical Association and Historian Emeritus Sandy Lydon of Cabrillo College, the Watsonville-Santa Cruz chapter of the Japanese American Citizens League organized hundreds of community members to participate in the reenactment of the evacuation of sixty years ago with a program titled "Liberty Lost...Lessons in Loyalty." The event paid tribute to the Japanese Americans of Santa Cruz County who were unjustly interned; to those who volunteered for military service from behind barbed wire, and to those in the community who befriended and supported the Japanese Americans and welcomed them back.

As the Japanese Americans of Watsonville prepared to be evicted from their homes, a number of neighbors stepped up to assist in whatever ways they could, even if their actions drew suspicion to themselves. At the Pajaro Valley National Bank, Edward Hall, Louis Lopes and Al Miguel made arrangements to safeguard bank accounts and property.[22] Ford's Department Store allowed the evictees to charge purchases, and agreed to mail them to destinations as yet unknown. Gim Lew of Canton Market forgave the Hashimoto family's ninety-dollar tab. George Cowles, W. D. Loveless, Stacy Irwin Stout, the Tomasellos and the Skillicorns agreed to watch over their neighbors' land and equipment. Walter Dutro agreed to look after the ornately beautiful Buddhist church, Carl Mehl Sr. made special arrangements to care for the ashes of the deceased, and Henry Martin stored furniture in his grain elevator.

Watsonville High School principal T. S. MacQuiddy urged departing students not to give up on their education and wrote recommendations for college applicants. Teachers Mae Lord and Dorothy Stroud Roark sent letters and books. Rev. Henry Babcock Adams of the First Presbyterian Church helped find a church gym to store property, mailed needed items to internees, and preached many sermons on the difference between Japan and Japanese Americans. Dr. Oscar Marshall cared for his patients when they were interned at the Salinas Assembly Center and escorted six mothers to the county hospital to give birth.

Some Pajaronians, including Nick and Rose Kalich, Louis Bechis and Tony Tomasello, later made the long trek to Poston, Arizona, to visit their friends behind barbed wire.

In early 1943, as discussion arose about releasing some Japanese Americans for military duty and resettlement, the *Watsonville Register-Pajaronian* editorialized: "Some American-born Japanese are loyal to America, but among their ranks are many who are not.... Words spoken and oaths sworn by Japanese tongues will bear little weight...so long as Pearl Harbor reverberates in American memories."[23] The Watsonville Pajaro Valley Defense Council passed a resolution opposing the return of Japanese Americans to the West Coast. A number of townspeople, including the ministers of several local churches, wrote the *Register-Pajaronian* to protest the resolution. In response, the defense council passed an even harsher resolution urging a constitutional amendment to strip the Nisei of their citizenship and forcibly return all Japanese Americans to Japan. Council chairman J. E. Gardner insisted:

> We should put a stop to the problem before it gets out of hand. The state of California should be unanimous....They should not be allowed to return —they should be sent back to Japan, or else in time they will be, economically and politically, in the saddle.[24]

Three members of the eighteen-member council voted against the resolution: Episcopalian minister Allan Geddes, attorney Phil Boyle, and Deputy District Attorney John L. McCarthy. McCarthy wrote vehement letters to the local paper condemning racism: "It reminds me of the days shortly after the last world war when the Catholics, Jews and Negroes were by the Ku Klux Klan declared un-American...and fiery crosses were burned."[25] At about the same time, resolutions to keep Japanese Americans off the West Coast were passed in several counties, including Santa Cruz, King, Sacramento, San Benito and Monterey.

When the U.S. government reopened the West Coast in January 1945, only about a third of the internees returned to the area. A few found their farms, homes and possessions in good shape, thanks to the oversight of their friends. But many more came back to nothing. Jobs and housing were hard to come by. Homes and land that had been rented before the war were no longer available and carefully stored possessions were stolen or vandalized.

The Watsonville Buddhist Church was turned into a hostel, while other families doubled up. George Cowles, Joe Crosetti, Mr. Franich and Tony Tomasello hired returnees to work in the fields, but most local growers spurned them. Rose Cowles loaned several families money to rent land to grow strawberries. Other returnees worked in the canneries of Monterey, cleaned houses, or worked as gardeners.

In town, some neighbors were extremely hostile. When Rev. Henry Babcock Adams assisted an ailing returnee, rotten eggs and dirt were thrown at his house. Undeterred, he hired unemployed returnees to turn his yard into a landscaping showcase. Chinese American Gim Lew welcomed Japanese Americans back to Canton Market. Dr. Marshall and his wife, Opal, remained outspoken supporters of the Japanese Americans, although they lost their only son, Mahlon, in the Battle of Leyte. The Marshalls braved name-calling and broken windows to meet returnees at the train station. When Opal Marshall learned that local grocery stores were turning away the returnees, she bought and delivered groceries. Unlike the *Register-Pajaronian*'s previous editor, Frank Orr wrote supportive editorials, and Chief of Police Matt Graves and Deputy District Attorney John L. McCarthy announced that incidents such as the attempted arson of the Buddhist church would be "prosecuted to the fullest extent of the law."[26]

Eventually "No Japs" signs disappeared from barber shops, beauty salons, gas stations, restaurants, grocery stores and other establishments. In 2002, the boards of supervisors of Monterey, San Benito and Santa Cruz counties unanimously rescinded their wartime anti-Japanese resolutions, and the reenactment commemorated stories of "liberty lost," of heroism and of support.

感谢

HELEN ELY (BRILL):
"THEY'RE GOING UP TO A PLACE CALLED MANZANAR, AND I WANT TO GO WITH THEM."

HELEN ELY BRILL, 1944.
COURTESY OF LAUREL BRILL SWAN.

Not long after her Japanese American students were interned, Helen Ely was offered a permanent position at her Compton, California, high school. On the heels of the Great Depression, tenure was a prize. She was one of only three teachers in her district to be offered it. Nevertheless, she recalled:

> I had the great delight of going to the superintendent and telling him I was leaving.... [H]e said, "Helen, you're crazy! You're going to Japs?" And I said, "Yes, they're going up to a place called Manzanar, and I want to go with them,"[1]

Helen Ely was a young woman when she made that fateful decision, but she came from a family with a tradition of activism. Her grandmother's barn had been a stop on the Underground Railway.[2]

Helen Weare Ely was born into a prominent pioneer family in Cedar Rapids, Iowa, in 1914. "My parents...believed very strongly in education," she recalled. The Ely men went to Princeton, while the daughters went to Scripps, a recently endowed women's college in Claremont, California. Miss Ely graduated in 1936 with a BA in humanities. At the height of the Depression, jobs were scarce, so she returned to school to earn a master's degree in history and a teaching credential.

In 1939, she landed her first teaching job in Compton, a farm community south of Los Angeles. About a third of the student body was Japanese American, she recalled.

93

When I walked into that schoolroom the very first day...and I saw these children with round heads, black hair...I thought: "My goodness, I've never seen them!" They weren't in Iowa...nor were they in college in Claremont when I was there.... I had an awful time pronouncing their names.... [The] first day they just tittered.[3]

Miss Ely was amazed by the ambition and determination of the Japanese American students. "Their parents were restricted by the dreadful laws then on the books.... [T]hey could not own land, nor could they vote," she recalled.[4] The children grew up helping their parents with the backbreaking labor of raising vegetables for the produce market. The parents spoke barely enough English to transact basic business, and yet the children were all taking Latin because it was a college requirement.

Miss Ely was not nearly so impressed by the community of Compton. "It turned out to be a perfectly awful town. It was the headquarters of the Ku Klux Klan."[5] When a Caucasian child in Miss Ely's class refused to salute the flag for religious reasons, representatives of the American Legion demanded that the girl be expelled. Miss Ely suggested a compromise: place the child in the back of the class, where her nonparticipation would be less obvious. The principal agreed.

◆　◆　◆

She was learning to stand her ground gracefully through "friendly persuasion." She became involved with the Quakers during college. *(See box: The Religious Society of Friends [Quakers].)* For three consecutive summers, she volunteered at American Friends Service Committee work camps, traveling to South Philadelphia to work with Italian American immigrants, south of the border to work with Mexican laborers, and Northern California to work with migrant laborers. These were transformative experiences for the sheltered Midwesterner.

I had had a very secluded...background. I had never seen poverty; I had never seen slum housing. I remember being goggle-eyed when I was taken to a birth control clinic, the only one in South Philadelphia.[6]

Seeking a year-round spiritual connection, she investigated the Friends Church in Pasadena. She was disappointed to find:

It was exactly like the Presbyterian Church I'd left...a choir and everything, exactly the same. But I then learned [about] the Orange Grove Meeting [also in Pasadena]. It's one of the great meetings out on the West Coast, and I just loved it.[7]

NOT EVERY JAPANESE AMERICAN FARM FAMILY WAS PROSPEROUS. COURTESY OF THE BANCROFT LIBRARY, UNIVERSITY OF CALIFORNIA, BERKELEY, WRA PHOTOGRAPHS.

8. **HELEN ELY (BRILL):** "THEY'RE GOING UP TO A PLACE CALLED MANZANAR, AND I WANT TO GO WITH THEM."

95

The Orange Grove Meeting was part of an association of progressive meetings that were taking hold on the West Coast. Like similar groups in Berkeley, Palo Alto, San Francisco and San Jose, California, and in Seattle, Washington, Orange Grove was particularly interested in pacifism and in the Japanese question. Every Sunday, Miss Ely boarded the interurban streetcar for a two-hour trip to Pasadena to listen to "these interesting people all talking about the war that was coming."[8]

In Miss Ely's view, newspapers and radio at the time had a heavily Eurocentric focus. "The Orient" was viewed through the filters of racial and religious prejudice as a remote, exotic place. The Quakers, however, were acutely aware that war with Japan was imminent. Anticipating that serious problems could arise for the local Japanese American population, they suggested that Miss Ely get acquainted with Compton's Japanese-language-school teacher, a "sweet Buddhist teacher" whom no white teacher had ever bothered to visit before. Through him, Miss Ely began to meet some of the Issei parents. "[The] kids came from humble, humble houses. You could see right through the [cracks in the] walls."[9]

"Then bingo! came Pearl Harbor," she said. Since it happened on a Sunday, she heard the news at the Orange Grove Meeting. The next day at school, the principal called an assembly to discuss the news. Miss Ely was concerned about the Japanese American students.

> I'll never forget them. They came to school; they didn't stay home. But their heads were bowed, and they were terrified. Many of them had had their fathers picked up by the FBI the night before. And their mothers were terrified—but the other school kids put their arms around them and they were just wonderful.[10]

There was no talk of an "evacuation" at that point, said Miss Ely. "It took the hysteria a little while, a couple of months, to get organized." But her aviation license was canceled. Although not many women flew in those days, she had been taking flying lessons just for the fun of it at a "little hinky-dinky airport" on the outskirts of Compton.[11] The government took over the airport, and "canceled all the licenses on the West Coast.... It was no fun anymore," Miss Ely declared. "Everything was very serious...we were going to have a war!"

Life had certainly turned serious for the Japanese Americans. On February 19, 1942, President Roosevelt signed E.O. 9066, which would soon force all Japanese Americans from the West Coast. On February 26, the Japanese Americans of Terminal Island were told they had to leave their homes in forty-eight hours. Miss Ely recalled:

The Religious Society of Friends (Quakers)

The Religious Society of Friends was founded in England in the mid-1600s by George Fox, who received a direct call from God at age twenty-three. Inspired by a passage from John 1:9—"The true Light, that lighteth every man that cometh into the world"—Fox roamed England to promote the idea that every individual holds the inborn capacity to understand the word of God and interpret it for himself. To Fox, it logically followed that everyone had direct access to God, and that priests and churches were unnecessary. Every person, male or female, slave or free was of equal worth and could be guided toward spiritual perfection by an inner light. Worship should be a simple gathering of souls in silence where any individual could be moved to speech by the Holy Spirit. There was no need for "empty forms" such as sermons, ritual or dogma. Spiritual gatherings were called "meetings," and a system of monthly, quarterly and yearly meetings facilitated organization on local, regional and national levels.

The "Friends of Truth" avoided alcohol, sports, theater and excessive finery. They were concerned with society's castoffs, and worked to end slavery and the abuse of the impoverished, the imprisoned and the insane. They refused to pay tithes to the Church of England, swear oaths in court, doff their hats to the privileged or fight in wars. These acts of civil disobedience displeased both Oliver Cromwell's Puritan government and the Restoration monarchy of Charles II. Within the movement's first fifty years, Fox and over 3,000 of his followers were imprisoned for their beliefs. When Fox advised one judge to "tremble at the word of the Lord," the judge derisively dubbed him a "Quaker," a label that came to be widely used, even by the Friends themselves.

Quakers who emigrated to the American colonies were often imprisoned or hung as witches and heretics. They found safe havens in Rhode Island, West Jersey and Pennsylvania, colonies that supported religious tolerance. By the late 1600s, Quakers were widely regarded as hard workers of high moral character. Nevertheless, they tended to congregate in their own communities, where they could practice simple living. They tried to remain neutral during the Revolutionary War, but most incurred enmity because they refused to pay taxes or fight. After the American Revolution, Quaker groups organized to work for better conditions for slaves, prisoners, and American Indians. Many Quakers were active in the Underground Railroad, which sheltered runaway slaves.

A series of schisms developed in the 1800s, and by the early 1900s, the movement was divided into four groups: the liberal Hicksites, who were interested in social reform and "unprogrammed" meetings; the evangelical and Bible-centered Gurneyites who instituted structured church services with hired pastors; the rural Wilburites, who maintained traditional Quaker speech and dress; and the Christ-centered Orthodox group.

Prior to World War I, all Quakers were strictly pacifist, but many Quakers joined the "war to end all wars." The American Friends Service Committee was formed by all four Quaker groups to help conscientious objectors find ways to serve their country in peaceful ways. On the West Coast, most Quaker meetings were established under the auspices of the Evangelical group, but by 1941, the Pacific Coast Association of Friends encompassed a number of unprogrammed Independent Meetings, including groups in San Jose, Berkeley, Palo Alto, Orange Grove (Pasadena), Mount Hollywood (Los Angeles) and Riverside, California; Corvallis, Oregon; and Seattle, Washington. Today, there are about 125,000 Quakers in North America (300,000 worldwide). Evangelical groups form the majority; about 35,000 are affiliated with unprogrammed meetings.

8. **HELEN ELY (BRILL):** "THEY'RE GOING UP TO A PLACE CALLED MANZANAR, AND I WANT TO GO WITH THEM."

97

And that was when, at Orange Grove Meeting, they made their famous telephone call to Esther Rhoads, that great person.... She was in Philadelphia, had had lots of experience in relief work, and she knew Japanese fluently.... [T]hey telephoned her and she said, "I'll come right away."[12]

A Quaker missionary who had spent many years in Japan, Esther Rhoads was familiar with the people and fluent in the language. Working under the auspices of the American Friends Service Committee, she converted a vacant Presbyterian school building in the Boyle Heights area of Los Angeles into an emergency hostel for the Terminal Islander. She persuaded a mattress factory to donate and deliver mattresses. Miss Ely said:

> And there was Esther Rhoads, I will never forget it, at the entrance to that building when they brought these terrified women, the fishermen's wives. And she'd be bowing to them, speaking their language. The rest of us were making sandwiches and soup for them!

> It made a great impression on me, and I knew that that's where I wanted to be. I still had a job...teaching, but this was something I could do [in the service of the evacuees].[13]

Sometime in March, eviction notices went up in Compton. Miss Ely saw an eviction placard posted on a telephone pole in front of her school. She took it down and saved it.

> [I]n very militaristic language it told that every head of household should report on a certain day...at 5 a.m. to the railroad station in Compton.... You can only take with you what you can carry in your hands. And you will be taken to an assembly center.... [I]t didn't say where it was. Then you will be taken to a camp, to a relocation center. They had all these euphemisms for all these places.

> In the meantime they had to get the camps built. So...the government asked for volunteers, young [Japanese American] boys to go off and build these barracks [at Manzanar]. A lot of fellows did. There was a great feeling, [that] we must be good Americans...show our patriotism.... [D]readful signs were showing up all over the place: "No Japs here."[14]

In the days leading up to eviction day, Miss Ely recalled:

> The evacuees had to sell everything that they owned, at very distressed prices. I remember the faculty at the school would sit there and say, "You

THE ORANGE GROVE MEETING HOUSE IN PASADENA. PHOTO BY SHIZUE SEIGEL.

know, I got a refrigerator yesterday for ten dollars, and it was new!" It was just awful![15]

The night before the students were to report to the train station to be taken away, Miss Ely telephoned her fellow teachers and asked them to go with her down to the station to say good-bye. She vividly recalled the coach's response:

> After these Nisei kids had won all of his track and field events for so long, he said, "Helen, of course they're good and of course they're fine and there's nothing the matter with them. But you can't tell.... [W]e've got to do this." And I said, "Well, at least come and say good-bye to them." And he said, "That's awfully early in the morning." And none of the teachers came [except my roommate].[16]

Miss Ely racked her brains to think of some small and affordable comfort she could pass out to the students as a parting gift. "I bought up a lot of gum. They weren't supposed to chew gum in school. But it was all I could think of to give out. I stood there giving out gum to them."

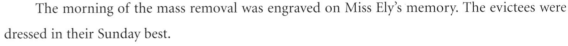

The morning of the mass removal was engraved on Miss Ely's memory. The evictees were dressed in their Sunday best.

> A lot of them had small children, babies, so you had to carry diapers and milk and everything. And the children were trained to carry as much as they possibly could. Rather than use suitcases, you got a blanket, and you put everything there and you picked up the blanket, all four corners.... [F]or the kids it was sort of a lark, they were all excited—"We're going someplace, we're going to an assembly center." Well, they didn't know it was Santa Anita, the racetrack in Pasadena.

> Their parents and their grandparents just didn't say a word. I can remember so well as each one got on a train car, there was a man with his gun there, a young fellow, even he knew, and everybody knew, that this was crazy. People were helping the older people get on the train. Oh, it was just heartbreaking, the whole performance.[17]

At the end of the school year, Miss Ely quit her job and sent the WRA an application to teach at Manzanar.

> The superintendent of schools absolutely couldn't understand.... It was still the Depression. You couldn't get jobs. And here I was throwing [a tenured position] over...to go teach "those Japs."... [H]e said, "Oh, I know they're good people! But you can't trust them! They've got to suffer just the way everybody else is suffering

TWO CAUCASIANS READING EVICTION ORDER. COURTESY OF THE BANCROFT LIBRARY, UNIVERSITY OF CALIFORNIA, BERKELEY, WRA PHOTOGRAPHS.

8. **HELEN ELY (BRILL):** "THEY'RE GOING UP TO A PLACE CALLED MANZANAR, AND I WANT TO GO WITH THEM."

99

because there are some bad apples in the barrel!"[18]

Miss Ely's family back in Iowa was inured to her independent ways. "They thought I was crazy to go off to that desert [Manzanar], but they went along with it."[19]

When school ended, Miss Ely had still not heard whether or not the WRA had accepted her application to teach at Manzanar, so she spent her summer vacation at a Quaker service camp near Palo Alto. At Hidden Villa Ranch, operated by Quaker activist Josephine Duveneck, she worked with other young activists at a migrant labor camp, and enjoyed spirited discussions about service. One Quaker tried to dissuade her from working for the WRA, saying, "Even though they need teachers, that's helping the government, and you ought to resist!"[20] He himself was refusing any involvement in the war, not even registering as a conscientious objector, and he was later sent to prison. Josephine Duveneck, however, encouraged Miss Ely. "If you don't go—if you wait for a perfect society, you'll never get it! They're going to need teachers…, You go ahead —get to Manzanar!"

Miss Ely was at Hidden Villa when she learned that her application to teach at Manzanar had been accepted. "I found out later, it wasn't very hard to get accepted," she said. Not many people applied for jobs at the "relocation centers."

JAPANESE AMERICANS AWAITING EVICTION.
COURTESY OF THE BANCROFT LIBRARY, UNIVERSITY OF CALIFORNIA, BERKELEY, WRA PHOTOGRAPHS.

Manzanar was the most accessible of the internment camps, situated "only" 225 miles northeast of Los Angeles. The High Sierra was a popular destination for hunting, fishing and camping, but the Manzanar site itself, in the rain shadow of spectacular snow-covered peaks, was desolate. There was nothing there, Miss Ely said, but sagebrush and jackrabbits until the guard towers, barbed wire and shoddily constructed barracks of the internment camp sprouted up on the barren plain.

Construction was still in progress when she arrived in August 1942. She was disappointed to learn that most of her Compton students had been sent to other camps. But she was ready to help any Japanese American; they had all been unjustly incarcerated.

The internment compound was about a mile square, and organized into "blocks" of twelve to fourteen military-style barracks arranged around common latrines, showers and a laundry room, plus a mess hall and a recreation hall. Each barrack was divided into one-room "apartments" ranging in size from 20 by 16 feet to 20 by 25 feet. The units lacked running water or kitchens, and were furnished only with cots, a single light bulb and a coal-burning stove. Whole families were crammed into single rooms, with only the largest families rating the larger rooms. Miss Ely was critical of the way that the administration kept to themselves in "nice little houses" with their own separate mess hall while the internees were crammed into flimsy barracks.[21]

The teachers were well paid, but conditions were hardly ideal. They were officially assigned civil service hours: eight to five, including Saturday mornings, but the school superintendent gave them Saturdays off, telling them, "Just don't make yourselves too visible in the camp." The staff saved up their two days off per month so they could "hitchhike down out of the valley if [they] were lucky and get to Los Angeles."[22]

In November 1942, Miss Ely gave a talk in Los Angeles to build support for the interned children:

> In September, when youngsters in other parts of California were trooping back to well-ordered school programs in buildings adequately equipped, we at the Manzanar Relocation Center were still looking around for empty barracks where we could conduct classes.

MANZANAR WAS SURROUNDED BY SAGE-BRUSH AND OVERSHADOWED BY THE HIGH SIERRA. COURTESY OF THE BANCROFT LIBRARY, UNIVERSITY OF CALIFORNIA, BERKELEY, WRA PHOTOGRAPHS.

> When you are really building your school from scratch, you can challenge every theory, every subject, and every textbook—in short, you have the opportunity to build the kind of school you want, though hardly with the necessary equipment....
>
> My school room is typical of most.... A linoleum covering on the floor and a Coleman stove constituted the only "furnishings" the first day my classes were held. For two weeks everyone sat on newspapers on the floor, but soon each room was given 20 folding chairs, and these plus a few orange crates now enable the majority of pupils to have seats, though of course, not desks. My 8th-grade Social Living class helped to make curtains and artificial flowers for the room, and later...an insulating material was installed over the walls.... [E]ven with our stoves the rooms are very cold...and pupils and teachers alike wear coats and mittens until the sun warms up the buildings about 11:00.[23]

Miss Ely was assigned to teach the U.S. Constitution to eleventh-grade students who were being deprived of their constitutional rights, an irony not lost on anyone. But she saw Manzanar itself as a living social science laboratory.

> Our textbook is really the community in which we live. Ten thousand people living in a mile square area provide a "workshop" unlike any other. The hospital, post office, fire and police departments, the cooperative stores…[t]he set up of [the] relocation center…like a pioneer community…grew from nothing and the children have themselves seen the community take shape. They know that it is their parents who have made it, not some remote city council. The churches, YMCA and YWCA, Boy Scouts, all recreation work—things so familiar in most towns—are still in the formative stages at Manzanar….

> A unit in the study of propaganda requires no more than the countless rumors and reports which are always current in a relocation center, where the ordinary channels of communication do not function as on the "outside." A favorite device of the pupils is to secure the latest magazine article or news report on Manzanar, and chuckle over the "facts" they read!

She made an appeal for compassion and support:

> Remember many of these boys and girls have been evacuated not once, but two or three times, they have seen their homes and possessions sold, often at great loss…. [E]verything that they loved—their homes and schools and play-mates—they know they will probably never see again. Coupled with all this is the fear of the future—economic and social—and their intense desire for security. So it is no wonder that they are confused and embittered. It is a real challenge to interpret democracy to these children, and I am sure that in the process we teachers have gained far more than we have given.

> One primary consideration motivates our classes: the resettlement of those children "outside." Every day they remain in the camps means that they are just that much more cut off from the swift current of events which is so changing the pattern of American life. It is impossible to appreciate the extent of our isolation at Manzanar, unless one lives there. What will happen to these boys and girls, the future leaders of their people, if they are kept in such seclusion…then suddenly expected to readjust in communities new to them, amid hostilities engendered by war?…

> The problem of the resettlement of these children and their families is our problem, and our privilege…. Write letters to those you knew! Mail from friendly people means so much in morale, and several times youngsters have brought us letters from their friends "back home," thrilled not only to have the news but perhaps more because they were remembered. Send books or magazines….

In the searing summer heat, Manzanar sixth-graders study out-doors, crouched in the shade of their bar-rack classroom.
Courtesy of The Bancroft Library, University of California, Berkeley, WRA Photographs.

She concluded with a quote from a small child: "[I]t summarizes better than I can the feeling of the boys and girls in a Relocation Center: 'Mother, when can we go back to America?'"

◆　◆　◆

Not long after Miss Ely wrote her report, a major incident occurred at the camp that underscored how far the internees were from the land of the free. On December 6, the day before the first anniversary of Pearl Harbor, one of Miss Ely's students—eleventh-grader James Ito—was shot and killed in what is sometimes called the "Manzanar riot."

The camp had gone through four directors in its first eight months of operation. The last of them, Ralph P. Merritt, had just been appointed in late November. Conditions in the camp had been tense for some time, and complex political undercurrents underlay Miss Ely's rosily naive depictions of the internees' civic life. A power struggle had developed between superpatriotic Nisei leaders of the JACL, who strongly advocated cooperating with the authorities, and the more militant Japanese-speaking Issei and Kibei (people who had been born in the United States and educated in Japan), who considered the JACL leaders to be overly accommodationist "informers." The administration had assigned many of the camp's leadership positions to the more Americanized Nisei.

AN INTERNEE IN HIS CRAMPED QUARTERS.
COURTESY OF THE BANCROFT LIBRARY, UNIVERSITY OF CALIFORNIA, BERKELEY, WRA PHOTOGRAPHS.

The Japanese-speaking group bitterly resented the fact that the best jobs were going to a group of inexperienced young men whose views did not represent the camp as a whole. On the night of December 5, 1942, Fred Tayama, a Nisei who had just returned from a WRA-sanctioned JACL convention in Salt Lake City, was severely beaten. He identified one of his six attackers as Harry Ueno, a Kibei who had organized the highly vocal Kitchen Workers Union.

Ueno was arrested for questioning and sent to the county jail in the nearby town of Independence. Back at Manzanar, a furious crowd of three or four thousand internees gathered to demand Ueno's release. They believed Ueno had been arrested to stifle his recent accusations that two camp administrators were stealing meat and sugar from the mess hall supplies to sell on the black market.

Merritt had Ueno brought back to the camp jail, but the crowd was not appeased.

8. **HELEN ELY (BRILL):** "THEY'RE GOING UP TO A PLACE CALLED MANZANAR, AND I WANT TO GO WITH THEM."

103

They demanded that the prisoner be released, while angry, knife-wielding groups split off to "get" Tayama and other informers. A crowd milled around the jail, taunting the authorities and throwing rocks. Tear gas failed to disperse the group, and when a driver-less car began heading toward the military policemen, the soldiers fired live ammunition into the crowd. Seventeen-year-old James Ito died instantly, and 21-year-old James Kanagawa later died of his wounds. Nine others were wounded badly enough to require treatment. Ito was shot through the heart at twenty-five feet, and the others were shot from the side or behind.

According to Miss Ely, many of the crowd were simply bystanders:

> [I]t was a Sunday and we all went out to see what was going on because it was the only amusement that there was....[24]
> The commander of the [military police] had gone off for the weekend, and these army rejects [the guards] were bitter men. It was the anniversary of Pearl Harbor. A lot of the young fellows [Nisei and Kibei]...came down...near the police station and they all started shouting "Banzai!"... The guard told them to quiet down and go home, and they wouldn't. They just jeered at them. They had no weapons or anything.... The guards were getting angrier and angrier and finally they threw tear gas to disperse the crowd.... When the tear gas came, I left.... And then, at that point, when everybody was dispersing.... Somebody fired, and people were killed.[25]

INTERNEES ARRIVING AT MANZANAR UNDER ARMED GUARD. *Courtesy of The Bancroft Library, University of California, Berkeley, WRA Photographs.*

Martial law was imposed. Through the night, the MPs, supplemented by the National Guard, patrolled the camp and broke up crowds that gathered in the streets and mess halls. Gangs of men hunted for Nisei whose names were on a "death list" of suspected informers that was read out at a mass meeting. Sixty-five Nisei, including Tayama, sought protection from the WRA. After sheltering in the military police compound for a few days, they were sent to a disused Civilian Conservation Corps camp in Death Valley until they could be resettled outside the exclusion zone. Ueno and fifteen of his supporters were sent to detention camps.

The shootings polarized the camp. Internees refused to report for work, bringing the camp to a virtual standstill. In an unpublished essay, Miss Ely wrote, "The whole camp was closed down. There was no school, no mail, nothing."[26] Martial law was imposed, and all work suspended until after Christmas. Nonessential civilian staff was evacuated. Miss Ely recalled:

> But I wanted to stay, told them I would run the telephone switchboard....

[The switchboard office] was just a little closet, and in there [with me] was one of the guards, with his gun. He had to guard me because this was the only contact between that camp of 10,000 people and the outside world. That poor guard.... It was getting close to Christmas and he was very homesick....

There was no mail service, so the post office soon was bulging just before Christmas. And then the miracle happened. Here came Herbert Nicholson, a Quaker, a really great spirit.... They let him into the camp. He had all these toys that people had donated. He drove out onto the middle of a firebreak. He stood there, throwing these things out of his truck, and people just caught them! And it changed the whole spirit of that camp.[27]

Although relative peace was restored, the Manzanar incident exacerbated tensions that had been simmering for months and hardened positions on all sides. To head off more trouble, the WRA accelerated its plans to separate the "loyal" from the "disloyal."

In the early spring, the War Department began recruiting for the all-Nisei 442nd Regimental Combat Team. Miss Ely recalled, "They had a lot of casualties, but they were fighting two enemies—they were fighting Japan and Hitler, of course, but they also were fighting for their interned parents and families in the camps." It was particularly heartbreaking, said Miss Ely, when furloughed sol-

HELEN ELY AT MANZANAR, 1943.
COURTESY OF LAUREL BRILL SWAN.

diers would visit. "[They] would come, in their uniforms, to that camp.... And here would be an armed guard to admit them. And then they'd find their parents.... Oh, gee, it was terrible. They never stayed their full time, they just left."[28]

Miss Ely had tried to learn Japanese when she first arrived at Manzanar, but "quickly gave it up," so she was not able to communicate much with the Issei. "But they were so grateful, those Issei, for anyone who would come and be a teacher in that camp. There wasn't anything they wouldn't do for you." Many of the Nisei did not speak much Japanese, either. When they tried to sign up for the Military Intelligence Service, they were rejected because they lacked the language skills. "It was a very disappointing thing for those kids. They were itching to get out of that camp and be in the armed forces."[29]

Other young people saw college as a way out of camp. Miss Ely wrote recommendations and helped students with their college application forms. College applicants had to navigate a complex maze of bureaucratic requirements. *(See chapter: Ralph and Mary*

Smeltzer.) School fees and living expenses were another problem. "Manzanar was probably one of the poorest of the camps," she said. When all was said and done, "very few actually went from Manzanar to colleges."[30]

Miss Ely was acutely aware of the hostility and resentment that many local people bore against the internees. The Owens Valley had been economically devastated when the Los Angeles water district drained the area of its water and turned farms and orchards into wasteland. The inhabitants who clung to the area led a relatively hard and bitter life, and the internees were an easy target for their accumulated resentments.

> After the riot, you couldn't go into the little town [of] Lone Pine, which was fifteen miles away. They wouldn't sell you anything if they knew you came from the camp. There was great anger in the valley because we had an X-ray [machine] in the camp and nowhere in that valley was there an X-ray.
>
> Of course it didn't do any good to try to talk to them. The X-ray was put in not out of sympathy for the internees, but because our government was deeply concerned that if the word got to Japan that we were not giving adequate medical care, [Japan]...would have a good excuse to treat the U.S. people interned in Japan badly.[31]

HELEN ELY AND BOB BRILL WERE ENGAGED TO BE MARRIED IN 1944. *Courtesy of Laurel Brill Swan.*

◆　◆　◆

Miss Ely was to stay at Manzanar for two years. In the spring of 1943, romance entered her life. Since outsiders were not permitted to visit the camp unless they were visiting a Caucasian staff member, Miss Ely had circulated her name to the Quaker and YMCA/YWCA networks, inviting people to come see the camp for themselves. "A lot of Civilian Public Service (CPS) men wanted to see Manzanar. It was the most accessible internment camp: all the others were a good long ways away."[32] One of the visitors was a conscientious objector named Bob Brill, Miss Ely recalled:

> I gave them "the tour" [which] always included "the children's village" for orphan babies. They were in cribs, in a long row on either side of a long barrack.... [T]here were 60 of these children.... I always loved to say, "Don't they look dangerous? These subversive little children! You have to lock 'em up behind barbed wire and machine guns, they're so dangerous!" It was so absurd.
>
> Then we'd go up to the hospital, to see the little newborns through a glass window. The glass window had been put in by this wonderful guy at Caltech, Bob Emerson, who would come up for the guayule experiment.

That was the next tour stop. Bob Emerson was trying to find a rubber substitute. They needed rubber because the Japanese had come down through Southeast Asia and taken over all of the rubber plantations in Malaysia and the Malay Peninsula, cutting off the supply. They didn't have nylon tires and such then. Well, you had to have rubber in the war, so there was a great effort made to develop a rubber substitute. The camp had a lot of good scientists, chemists, who worked on this.... Guayule is a plant that grows well in the desert. They got the rubber from the plant all right, but the project fell through because it was too expensive.[33]

Before her visitors left, she asked them for a favor. The end of the school year was approaching and students were planning the high school yearbook. They wanted to include photographs, but film was very difficult to obtain during wartime, particularly in the isolated Owens Valley. Miss Ely had appealed to every visitor, but no one had ever responded—until Bob Brill. Much later he recalled:

Helen had talked so enthusiastically about [the film] that it seemed to me a good thing to do. My parents were in New York City, where you can always get things, so I wrote and asked them to go to the Eastman Kodak store...and send some film to Miss Ely. So they sent it. I didn't think anything of it; this was a worthy thing.... Miss Ely seemed like a nice person.... I didn't think any further about it.[34]

About three weeks later, Miss Ely received four rolls of film in the mail. "I was so thrilled," she recalled. "And I ran across the

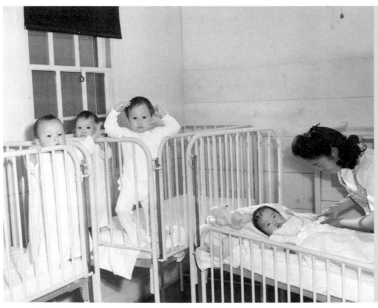

ORPHANS AT THE "CHILDREN'S VILLAGE" AT MANZANAR. COURTESY OF THE LIBRARY OF CONGRESS, PRINTS & PHOTOGRAPHS DIVISION, ANSEL ADAMS, PHOTOGRAPHER, LC-DIG-PPPRS-00426.

ANSEL ADAMS AT MANZANAR. Renowned photographer and environmentalist Ansel Adams became a good friend of Manzanar project director Ralph Merritt through their mutual involvement in the Sierra Club. Merritt invited Adams to photograph at Manzanar, and Dorothea Lange encouraged him to take advantage of the offer. Helen Ely wrote: "Ansel Adams...was a man of few words.... He just walked around and took these pictures....With each picture, we tried to give him a little bit of the story of the person. He never batted an eye. We didn't know whether he was in favor or opposed."[35]

Adams published *Born Free and Equal: The Story of Loyal Japanese Americans* in 1944. The trouble-plagued book and accompanying exhibition at the Museum of Modern Art were compromised by political and other considerations, and the results met with mixed success. Miss Ely surmised, "The time was not right to win over people. He thought that with his camera, he could change public opinion, but he didn't."

Adams donated the photos and negatives to the Library of Congress in 1965. In 1989, they were republished in the book *Manzanar,* with commentary by John Hersey. *Born Free and Equal* was reprinted in 1984 and in 2001. *(See box: The Truthful Eye.)*

firebreak to [photographer] Toyo Miyatake and I said, 'Look, here, we can have a yearbook now!'" She couldn't remember Bob Brill clearly, but she wrote him "the nicest thank you letter I could possibly write."[36]

When she went to Pasadena for Thanksgiving break, Bob Brill invited her to meet him at the Los Angeles Public Library. Within three days, he proposed and she accepted. Bob and Helen were of like minds. He was a fellow Quaker, a Yale graduate and a social activist doing his alternative service in a National Forest firefighting camp. After a long-distance courtship, they married in April 1944.[37]

In early 1945, Mrs. Brill left Manzanar to work for the AFSC in Los Angeles. The Evergreen Hostel in Boyle Heights was re-opened to assist internees returning to Southern California.

> We charged a dollar a day to keep somebody at Evergreen, and the Japanese did all the work.... [T]hey cooked and they cleaned up and they kept the place wonderfully, but we had sometimes 150 people there. I know it was against all health rules and everything, but those wonderful Japanese knew how to run things....[38]

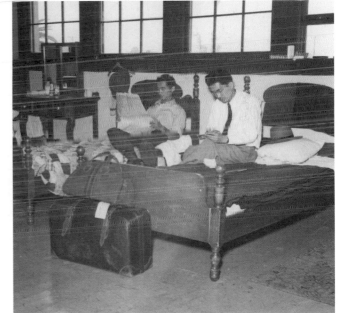

MEN'S DORMITORY AT THE EVERGREEN HOSTEL IN BOYLE HEIGHTS.
COURTESY OF THE BANCROFT LIBRARY, UNIVERSITY OF CALIFORNIA, BERKELEY, WRA PHOTOGRAPHS.

In spite of the low rates, the hostel turned a small profit, which was converted into fifty-pound bags of rice. Mrs. Brill and Esther Rhoads delivered them to the three Buddhist temples that were also serving as hostels. Mrs. Brill helped locate jobs and housing for the returnees, no easy task because anti-Japanese feeling still ran high. She worked at the hostel until the fall of 1945, when Bob Brill was released from alternative service.

The young couple moved to New York, where Bob Brill earned a master's degree in social work from Columbia University.[39] He then directed various social service programs in New York, Pennsylvania and Connecticut, while Mrs. Brill raised two daughters and taught high school. The Brills remained active in the Society of Friends, and held leadership positions on the local, regional and national levels. They remained fervently involved in social justice. They hosted State Department dignitaries, sheltered a succession of refugees, from the "displaced persons" of World War II through the Vietnamese "boat people." In 1982, they founded the Connecticut chapter of Parents and Friends of Lesbians and Gays (PFLAG).[40]

◆　　◆　　◆

Helen Ely Brill is remembered by many as a wonderful teacher and a hard-working organizer who radiated energy. She maintained lifelong contact with former students from Compton and Manzanar and often referred to her two years at Manzanar as the best years of her life. She was always ready to speak about the injustice of the internment to individuals and groups. It was a terrible thing, she often said, that should never happen again.

She passed away on April 14, 2003. Upon seeing her obituary in *The Rafu Shimpo,* Joe Nagano, a former internee and retired City of Los Angeles lab director, wrote a letter to the editor.

> Although I met Helen Ely Brill only briefly in Manzanar...I owe a lot to her for her caring concern and advice 62 years ago. I was 21 at the time and...she was deeply involved with Ralph and Mary Smeltzer in the Student Relocation Program, helping displaced college students to relocate to inland colleges and universities....
>
> On the day that I received my military pass to leave Manzanar, the president of Juniata [College] wired me to cancel my application because the community was opposed to my presence. I wondered, "What should I do?" I sought Helen Ely's advice and she said that since it was difficult to obtain military clearance to leave camp...[s]he suggested that I go to Chicago.
>
> With four hours of preparation, I followed her advice and...headed to parts unknown with $60 in my pocket. When I reached Chicago, I was assisted by the American Friends Service Committee and by Thomas Temple.... I was accepted at the Illinois Institute of Technology....
>
> Were it not for Helen's correspondence and encouragement, and the Disciples of Christ, who provided a scholarship, and others who helped, it would have been tough to survive the rigors of baptism under fire: working and studying in a strange city....
>
> I truly thank the Lord for the people like Helen Weare Ely Brill who touched the lives of so many of us Nisei. They gave the kick-off that we needed to...complete college and prepare ourselves...to launch successful careers after World War II. She was an inspiration to many students at Manzanar.[41]

HELEN ELY BRILL, 2000.
COURTESY OF THE PHOTOGRAPHER,
LAUREL BRILL SWAN,

THE TRUTHFUL EYE

Along with the euphemistic language of "evacuation" and "relocation," WRA used photography to gain public support for the internment. Staff photos of happy, smiling internees vastly out-numbered those that captured the confusion, heartbreak and anger experienced by those who lost their homes, their livelihoods and freedom.

Understanding the power of photography to illuminate injustice and promote social change, Ansel Adams and several other well-known photographers attempted to document the internment sympathetically and honestly.

DOROTHEA LANGE first established her reputation with her powerful Depression-era photographs of Dust Bowl migrants. In 1942, Miss Lange postponed a prestigious Guggenheim Fellowship to photograph the eviction of Japanese Americans from Northern California for the WRA. "It's too worthwhile to refuse," she wrote. Over the next four months, she took over 800 photographs. With deep psychological insight, impeccable composition, and a keen eye for irony, she created images that have become indelibly associated with the internment.

HANSEL MIETH AND OTTO HAGEL were self-taught photographers who emigrated from Germany in the late 1920s. Mieth and Hagel documented migrant laborers, Hoovervilles and waterfront strikes in stark, powerfully composed black and white. In 1936, Mieth was became the second woman to be hired as a staff photographer by *Life* magazine. She and Hagel married in 1941, and in 1943, *Life* sent them to Heart Mountain to shoot an in depth photo essay. The couple's empathy for the internees is evident in their poignant photos, which *Life* chose not to publish during the war. The collection was finally published in 1997 by former internee Mamoru Inouye, in the book *The Heart Mountain Story: Photographs by Hansel Mieth and Otto Hagel of the World War II Internment of Japanese Americans*. Although they were not Communists, Mieth and Hagel were blacklisted during the McCarthy era. As the couple's photographic assignments dwindled, they retreated their Sonoma County farm. Hagel died in 1973 and Mieth in 1998.

Nominated by Susanne Norton Coffey

MARGARET MATTHEW D'ILLE (GLEASON):
"A MORE POWERFUL BOMB THAN THE ATOM"

Margaret Matthew D'Ille Gleason has been deceased for almost fifty years, but every Christmas, a family in Lake County, California, celebrates her spirit. Mrs. Gleason's grandniece Susanne Norton Coffey reads aloud the story of her aunt's first Christmas at the Manzanar internment camp, when project director Ralph Merritt credited her with lifting the cloud that hung over the camp in the aftermath of the "Manzanar riot."

Mrs. Gleason, then known as Margaret D'Ille, was sixty-three when she agreed to serve as Manzanar's director of community welfare and head counselor. During her three and a half years at the isolated internment camp, she applied the wisdom acquired in a lifetime of social service, including ten years in Japan. She was a tall woman with strong features and an erect carriage, who leavened her innate dignity with a radiant smile and a wonderful sense of humor. She radiated "love, kindliness, sympathy, helpfulness and faith," said Los Angeles County Supervisor John Anson Ford, calling the combination "a more powerful bomb than the atom...transforming rather than destructive."

A dynamic leader of great warmth and charm, she was born Margaret Matthew in Springfield, Illinois, in 1879.[1] Her father, Winfield Scott Matthew, was a Methodist minister and a dean at the University of Southern California. Miss Matthew graduated from the University of California at Berkeley and taught school before joining the national staff of the Young Women's Christian

Association (YWCA) in 1903 to develop programs for adolescent girls.

In 1908, she went to Japan on behalf of the International YWCA. For ten years, her tact, humility, generosity and humor endeared her to everyone. "She was perfectly at ease," a colleague remembered, "with women of wealth and nobility [and] their complicated code of etiquette, as [well as with] the giggling young school girls, in whose company she joked and teased."[2]

In 1918, she went to Siberia to do relief work for the Red Cross. She was admired there for her executive ability and her talent for getting the best out of people. In 1920, Miss Matthew returned to the United States and rejoined the national YWCA staff.

In 1935, Miss Matthew married Arthur D'Ille, a diplomat whom she had met in Siberia. After only a year and a half of marriage, he passed away, and Mrs. D'Ille moved to San Francisco to do social work for the California Relief Administration.

In the summer of 1942, she became chief of community welfare at Manzanar. After a few months, an old friend, Ralph P. Merritt, was appointed as the new project director. Merritt had known Mrs. D'Ille and her brother for over forty years. When she had gone to Japan, Merritt's wife, Varina, had viewed her as a role model and an inspiration. The Merritts had lost touch with her over the years and were delighted to see her at Manzanar.

Ralph Palmer Merritt was an able administrator with deep ties to California and its land.[3] He was born in 1883 in the Central Valley and managed the sprawling Miller-Lux ranch before serving at the University of California as comptroller and on its board of trustees. During World War I, he served as federal food commissioner for California. He became the first president of the Rice Growers Association of California in 1920 and then headed the Sun Maid Raisin Growers. Raisins made him a wealthy man, but he lost everything in the Crash of '29. Shortly afterward he contracted polio and

MARGARET MATTHEW, *FIRST ROW, SECOND FROM RIGHT, WAS THE* ELDEST CHILD OF A METHODIST MINISTER. COURTESY OF SUSANNE NORTON COFFEY.

MISS MATTHEW, *STANDING SECOND FROM LEFT,* WORKED FOR THE YWCA IN JAPAN FOR TEN YEARS. COURTESY OF SUSANNE NORTON COFFEY.

RALPH P. MERRITT
BECAME THE FOURTH
MANZANAR PROJECT
DIRECTOR IN
NOVEMBER 1942.
PHOTO BY TOYO MIYATAKE. COURTESY
OF ARCHIE MIYATAKE STUDIO.

spent three years recuperating in the Owens Valley.

Merritt was familiar with the eastern Sierra because he was an avid outdoorsman who combined ranching and mining interests with strong ties to the Sierra Club and other environmentalists. In 1942, his old friend Herbert Hoover recommended him to head the internment camp at Manzanar, which had became increasingly troubled.

Merritt agreed to become the fifth director since its inception. On Thanksgiving Day of 1942, he walked into the mess hall to meet his staff of 200. He scanned the crowd for a friendly face.

> Suddenly I saw a hand beckoning and recognized the smiling face of Margaret. I knew I had at least one friend, and found that, as Mrs. D'Ille, she was the Director of Welfare for the War Relocation at Manzanar. With her background of long acquaintance with Japanese problems and people she was just the right person in the right place at the right moment.[4]

When he took the job, Merritt had been warned that trouble was brewing at Manzanar. The commanding officer at the Presidio of San Francisco advised him to exercise "firm control, by force if necessary." On December 6, one day short of the anniversary of the attack on Pearl Harbor, the camp exploded. *(See chapter: Helen Ely Brill.)* Merritt recalled:

> It was a tragic affair, no one person was to blame. There was no one cause, but many grievances of many kinds created uncontrollable mass emotions. Late that night the final tragedy was enacted with gunfire and men wounded and dead.[5]

Martial law was imposed and the violence quelled, but in the following days, the internees refused to report for work. Merritt recalled:

> No children came out to play. No lights burned at night. It was a dead city. Days went by and I could find no way to bring about the normal way of living....

> Two weeks after the riot I was sitting in my office listening to instructions coming over the long distance telephone, telling me to "get tough," when I looked up and saw Margaret standing near my desk. She had heard the conversation and she knew that I had no answer to the problem of restoring peace and harmony to the 10,000 people under my charge. She smiled at me and said: "What are you going to do now?" I told her that I did not know, but that I would not

admit that to anyone but her.

Then she said, "Ralph Merritt, have you forgotten your Christian upbringing, and have you forgotten that this is Christmas, and what Christmas means?" I was startled, and then she went on to say that there was a warehouse full of presents that had been shipped to Manzanar by the churches and friends who were interested in giving Christmas happiness to the more than 2,000 children who were behind our barbed wire fence.

Then she unfolded her plan, which was that I should send trucks and men to the mountains to cut trees and bring them back to the camp; that they should be set up in front of each of the barracks, decorated with lights, and that the presents should be distributed the day before Christmas, so that the people could prepare Christmas trees for Christmas morning, and each child might have his gift.

Then she reminded me that there was at Manzanar a "Children's Village" which was under her Department. Here there were...orphans all the way from little babies to boys and girls fourteen years of age. They had been picked up by the Army all the way from Alaska to San Diego as "security risks." On Christmas Eve in the Children's Village, she proposed that she and I arrange a great party for these children....

Margaret D'Ille, second from left, was the director of welfare at Manzanar from 1942 to 1945. Clipping from the *Manzanar Free Press.* Courtesy of Susanne Norton Coffey.

On Christmas Eve, Margaret and Varina and I walked through our dark, dead camp to the opposite corner of our mile-square barbed wire enclosure where our Children's Village alone was lighted and where happy voices welcomed us.

In the big hall we sat on the floor, Japanese fashion, surrounded by the excited and happy children while the Christmas scene of shepherds and wise men was enacted upon the little stage. Then there was a Santa Claus and presents and we began to sing Christmas carols. As we sang, I suddenly realized that, coming from somewhere, there was more singing than the voices of the little children gathered in that room. I got up and quietly walked out into the night.

The clear moon and stars were shining over the Sierras. From out there in the darkness there came a great volume of the Christmas carols that were also being sung by the children inside. I climbed up on a box and looked out on the upturned faces of boys and girls of Japanese ancestry, born in America and American citizens, the product of our own schools, who were standing there in the night, joining with the children of the Village in their Christmas carols. As they

WINTER STORM AT MANZANAR. COURTESY OF THE LIBRARY OF CONGRESS, PRINTS & PHOTOGRAPHS DIVISION, ANSEL ADAMS, PHOTOGRAPHER, LC-DIG-PPPRS-00332.

saw me they suddenly became quiet, wondering what this new Government Representative would say and do. I called out to them that we should sing for the children inside, and lead them in "Oh, Come All Ye Faithful."

Soon Margaret and Varina joined me, and followed by hundreds and hundreds of boys and girls and young people, we marched down through the camp, singing as we went....

Lights came on throughout the camp, voices in Christmas greetings called out to us, and Manzanar came alive. When we came to the spot where the riot had occurred and where men had been killed and wounded we stood together, not in the spirit of anger, but in the Christmas spirit which had re-created a new peace and good will for Manzanar. I called out to wish them all a Merry Christmas and they wished me and all of us a Merry Christmas. As their voices died out in the distance they were still singing the songs of Christmas.

When Margaret and Varina and I stood alone watching the Star that was over us, I turned to Margaret and said: "Peace has come again to Manzanar."[6]

◆　◆　◆

Another person who renewed his acquaintance with Margaret D'Ille was George Gleason, who had known her when he had worked as a YMCA secretary in Japan. He visited Manzanar frequently, often hitching a ride with Herbert Nicholson. Gleason and Mrs. D'Ille married in 1946 and lived in Los Angeles until her death in 1954. They were active participants in the Mount Hollywood Congregational Church, which was led by peace activist Dr. Allan A. Hunter, another supporter of Japanese Americans.

At Mrs. Gleason's memorial service, former internee Miya Sannomiya Kikuchi recalled her friend's influence at crucial periods in her life.

> I entered the University of California at Berkeley, a frightened and bewildered freshman. How well I remember seeing the name of Ralph P. Merritt (Comptroller) on many a receipt from the University. Little did I realize then what he and Mrs. Merritt would mean to me and my people in later years.[7]

A Nisei born in 1902, Miya Sannomiya was remarkable in her own right. After, she watched her parents struggle to make a living in the United States, she turned to education and Christianity as tools to counter racism. A Southern Methodist scholarship to an Alabama high school introduced her to the harshness of Southern prejudice. She returned to California just as the alien land laws were impacting the Issei. She was frequently called on to interpret for Issei in lawsuits, and a wealthy Canadian Issei offered to send her to law school. But she wearied of court battles and decided to become a doctor. She enrolled at UC Berkeley and joined the YWCA, where she met Margaret Matthew. She recalled:

> During my freshman year, and the following summer at the Asilomar YWCA Student Conference, Margaret came into my life. At the conference we girls had been sent out...to gather greens for chapel decorations. I...brought an armful of the poison oak to the chapel. It was a tall, slim, smiling person who gently relieved me of my burden, and took me to the infirmary where I was successfully treated and the poison prevented.
>
> I shall always remember the picture of Margaret's smiling face, as she sang by my side and helped me to learn the camp songs. What really broke the ice for me at this summer conference was stunt night. Margaret sat by me and handed me a peanut. When I started to eat it she stopped me with: "Wait and see what these are for when our turn comes." Down on the floor we dropped, and she, with her long body and tall nose, began to push her peanut across the rug. I, with my short body and snub nose, had a hard time following her. But, amid the laughter of the other girls, I did my stunt, and after that I was a regular member of the group. The push that night gave me a real start in student life.[8]

Her father's death interrupted her education. By the time she met Margaret again at Manzanar, Miya Sannomiya had operated her family farm, written a column for young Nisei for the Japanese American newspaper *Nichibei Shimbun*, and worked in the Japan and the United States for the semi-governmental Kokusai Bunka Shinokai (Society for International Cultural Relations). In 1938, she quit work to marry Yoriyuki Kikuchi, an Issei dentist living in Los Angeles. They were among the first to volunteer to go to Manzanar to help with construction. At the camp, she reencountered Margaret Matthew D'Ille.

> Once again Margaret met our needs when she came as Director of Social Work, and I worked with her as head of the Department of Family Relations. Later Mr. and Mrs. Merritt joined the staff. Speaking for other Japanese friends who may be too shy to talk to you today, I wish to say that Mr. and Mrs. Merritt and

SIXTY-FIVE ORPHANED CHILDREN LIVED IN MANZANAR'S CHILDREN'S VILLAGE. COURTESY OF THE BANCROFT LIBRARY, UNIVERSITY OF CALIFORNIA, BERKELEY, WRA PHOTOGRAPHS.

Margaret made the most wonderful, sympathetic and friendly advisers a group ever had.[9]

Dr. Kikuchi was appointed chief of the dental clinic. The Kikuchis were criticized for socializing with the Caucasian adminis-tration, and during the Manzanar riot, Dr. Kikuchi was one of the sixty-five who were targeted by militants. His family was among the first to leave camp to be resettled. In the 1950s, Mrs. Kikuchi met Margaret again, and she and her husband, George Gleason, became Dr. Kikuchi's dental patients. At Mrs. Gleason's funeral service, Mrs. Kikuchi recalled:

> Not long ago I fell ill. My doctor said that the only cure for me was to attain and keep a serene mind and a cheerful out-look. I wondered what I could do. Suddenly one day I saw the image of Margaret's smiling face at Berkeley, at Asilomar, at Manzanar. That picture meant that I should get closer to God and to my fellow man. If I should serve Him better by serving my fellow man more, as Margaret did, I should gain the serenity she always had.

> She has not left us, because the kindly, the gay, the wonderful things she did live on in us.[10]

Dr. Allan Hunter and the Mount Hollywood Congregational Church

Dr. Allan Armstrong Hunter, pastor of Mount Hollywood Church, was a prolific writer and an active and well-known proponent of a progressive and socially engaged Christian ministry that embraced pacifism, socialism, racial and gender equality, birth control, meditation and environmentalism.[11] He was a friend and admirer of Japanese Christian social reformer Toyohiko Kagawa. During the years leading up to World War II, he was West Coast chairman of the Fellowship of Reconciliation. In 1940, the church added to its constitution the determination "under no circumstances to lend this Church to war purposes,"[12] and during World War II the church sheltered over a dozen conscientious objectors.

Hunter opposed the internment and did what he could to help the Japanese Americans. Rev. Ray Kinney, the assistant minister, arranged for Mount Hollywood to take legal responsibility for the nearby Hollywood Independent Church when its Japanese American congregation was interned. Mount Hollywood's members served sandwiches and coffee to the evictees the day they left, and kept watch over the Independent Church and the internees' goods stored there. Hunter spent so much time at Manzanar ministering to restless and rebellious youth that pastor emeritus Dr. E. P. Ryland often had to substitute at Mount Hollywood on Sundays.

The congregation also supported the internees. They sent $100 to Heart Mountain to help establish a church, collected craft materials for a kindergarten teacher at Manzanar, and shipped Christmas and Easter presents to Manzanar children. When a Japanese American patient at Hillcrest Sanitarium urgently needed transfusions, eight conscientious objectors from Mount Hollywood supplied blood. And when a Buddhist family's baby fell seriously ill at Manzanar, a member of Hunter's congregation arranged for the infant to be brought to Los Angeles under guard for treatment.

In December 1943, Hunter testified before the Gannon committee hearings that he supported reopening the West Coast to Japanese Americans. As a result of the ensuing publicity, he received threatening letters, and the FBI tapped his phone. An FBI agent reported that he had a photo of Joseph Stalin on his wall (it was actually Albert Schweitzer). Some members left the church because of Hunter's uncompromising positions, and at one point he offered to resign. Instead, the congregation persuaded him to continue shepherding them through the confusion, pain and anger of wartime.

When former internees returned to Los Angeles, Mount Hollywood helped find them jobs and housing. In 1946, the Hollywood Independent Church gave Mount Hollywood $100 in appreciation for its help during the internment. To turn the gift into a lasting symbol of peace and Christian dedication, a cross was made from the charred remains of an atomic bomb-blasted tree. The tree had stood in the churchyard of the Hiroshima Methodist Church, where Rev. Kiyoshi Tanimoto, Independent Church's prewar pastor, was serving at the time of the nuclear attack. The simple wooden cross, inscribed "He is our peace," remains installed on Mount Hollywood's altar to represent the church's longstanding commitment to justice, and to commemorate its support for Japanese Americans during the internment period.

THE BELL FAMILY AT TOPAZ, 1945. *CLOCKWISE FROM TOP LEFT:* EARNEST, 14; ROSCOE; GLADYS; PAUL, 17; GORDON, 9; AND WINIFRED, 12. COURTESY OF THE BELL FAMILY.

THE BELL FAMILY:
MAKING THE BEST OF A BAD SITUATION

After Pearl Harbor, the Bell family in Berkeley, California, conscientiously prepared for the worst, installing blackout curtains, dimming flashlights with blue cellophane, storing food and water for emergencies, and strategically placing buckets of sand around the house to douse flames from firebombs. In a 1981 memoir Gladys Bell recalled:

> Our house…[became] the center of family practice and training for preservation, incendiary bombs, blackouts and attacks through the Golden Gate…. It was considered the right thing to call the enemy "the Japs" since they were the ones who bombed Pearl Harbor! We were not surprised at anything that we were told [by the authorities] to do, since we were in a warlike situation.[1]

At the time, Gladys's husband, Roscoe, was the state representative for California of the Federal Bureau of Agricultural Economics. Gladys kept busy raising their four children and doing volunteer work. As the country entered the war, Gladys walked the kids to and from school, scouting out places to run for cover in case of attack. At home, each child was assigned emergency duties—to fill the bathtub with water or turn off the natural gas valve. After the children had memorized the emergency drill, Mrs. Bell tested them.

> "One evening, as I was getting dinner I pretended there was [an alarm] and called out "blackout—everyone to his station." I turned off all of the lights and put a chair in front of the steps leading to the basement and called out that there

might be hazards. [The children] each did a magnificent job. We then quietly had our dinner.[2]

One evening while Roscoe and Gladys were out, they saw the lights go out in San Francisco, then Oakland, then Berkeley and up and down San Francisco Bay. They were concerned for the children, who were at home in the care of 14-year-old Paul. Three tense hours crept by. Finally, the all-clear sirens sounded, and Roscoe quickly called home. Paul was curt. "Hang up, Dad—don't you know you are not to use the phones during a blackout?" he said and clicked the receiver down. The parents groped their way home by the feeble light of their parking lights to find Paul calmly listening to the radio with the blue flashlight in his lap. The younger children had performed their emergency duties and were fast asleep in their improvised bunks in the basement shelter.

The next day, the school principal asked Gladys why their children appeared so calm when half his students were "scared, sick or absent." She described their preparedness exercises. "Well, it certainly paid!" remarked the principal.

◆　◆　◆

The Bells would soon be preparing the family for another big change. When Roscoe Bell registered for the draft at the age of thirty six, he had requested noncombat duty because he didn't feel he could "conscientiously engage in battle."[3] He was reclassified from 1A to 1AH because of his age and parental status, but he remained eager to serve his country in some way.

In the course of his work, Bell participated in California's Agricultural War Board, which oversaw the production and processing of the state's food crops during wartime. At the time the state produced over eighty percent of the country's canning tomatoes and a large proportion of poultry and eggs. Bell wrote in a 1982 memoir:

> Many other crops were critical to the war effort...and something like 80–90% were grown by people of Japanese ancestry.... There had long been, in California, animosity toward the Japanese, jealousy...prejudice.... These persons used the wartime hysteria as a means of fanning up the sentiment that the Japanese ought to be excluded, or interned, because they were "dangerous."[4]

The War Board was concerned that anti-Japanese hysteria would lead to violence against Japanese American farmers. It was also concerned that any mass removal of Japanese Americans would seriously impact the nation's supply of produce. Bell remembered his dis-

JAPANESE AMERICAN WORKERS HARVESTING CAULIFLOWER BEFORE THE EVICTION. COURTESY OF THE BANCROFT LIBRARY, UNIVERSITY OF CALIFORNIA, BERKELEY, WRA PHOTOGRAPHS.

belief on the March day when he learned that the government was planning to go ahead with the eviction. "We were shocked," he recalled, "because we could see what it meant not only to the people, but also to the meeting of wartime goals for food production."

In early July, Bell received instruction from Washington, D.C., to close the California office of the Bureau of Agricultural Economics. "This was a terrific shock to me," he recalled, "because [it] so obviously was essential war work."[5]

Finding himself abruptly jobless, Bell took his family camping in the Sierra to clear his mind and ponder the future. A colleague suggested that Bell apply for the post of chief of agriculture at the internment camp at Topaz, Utah. There were many reasons not to apply. The Utah desert did not sound appealing. Central Utah's highly alkaline soil and short growing season were not favorable for agriculture. Bell himself was a soils scientist with little hands-on farming experience. And the internment camp had few accommodations for families.

The family talked it over, and Roscoe prayed for guidance from God. Upon receiving an affirmative message from above, he decided to take the job. Mrs. Bell recalled:

> This would entail moving to a desert, renting our house furnished, taking along two trunks and all that we could get in the car, and a cat and tricycle! We would be working with the very same people (in looks that is) that we had prepared to save ourselves from—the Japs!
>
> Then we got to thinking—these were Americans, too! We had known a Japanese named Jobo Yasamura in college, and he was a wonderful person and friend....
>
> Certainly these new Japanese were in an awful, warlike situation and they would need people to help understand.... We decided as a family we would go and we would make the best of everything.[6]

Paul recalled, "My parents believed that the government was not serving its citizens well by the internment, so this was an opportunity for us to try to help the victims through their ordeal."[7]

Topaz was located about 160 miles south of Salt Lake City. After visiting the Tule Lake internment camp to observe operations there, the Bells drove to the camp with a

SINCE MUCH OF THE SOIL AROUND TOPAZ WAS HIGHLY ALKALINE, ONLY ABOUT THIRTY PERCENT OF THE PROJECT'S LAND WAS ARABLE. COURTESY OF THE BANCROFT LIBRARY, UNIVERSITY OF CALIFORNIA, BERKELEY, WRA PHOTOGRAPHS.

small trailer in tow, camping along the way. They arrived shortly before the first internees were brought in. Since staff accommodations were still under construction, the Bells had to stay in the town of Delta, about sixteen miles away. The town's lone hotel was so crowded that for several days the children had to sleep in a tent in 20-degree weather.

When quarters were available at Topaz, the Bells were assigned a suite of three rooms. Realizing that regular meals at the staff mess hall would be too expensive for a family of six, Mrs. Bell requested a stove. The procurement officer managed to dig up a rusty wood-fired range with a missing leg, a cracked top and an "ash-leaky oven." Propping up the stove with bricks, she eventually managed to get the apparatus to turn out angel food cakes and roast pheasant.

Because the country was at war, the Bells had to cope with rationing. Mrs. Bell noted:

> It became a habit for us to take turns buying groceries and running errands for two or more families, thus saving as much gas as possible. When we went on a vacation, we would wait until the end of a ration period and go as far as we could. Then we would wait until the new period had come in before we came back.... We learned to be very frugal in buying and cooking.[8]

Despite the dust and the cold, the Bells kept things in perspective. They had come to Topaz by choice. And although they were living in the same type of tar-paper barrack as the internees, they had three times the living space and plenty of furniture, including a piano.

The Bells were determined to engage fully in the life of the Japanese American community. Instead of associating exclusively with the Caucasian staff, they sent their children to school with the internees and attended internee church services. Mrs. Bell described their first morning at the camp church.

> [W]e arrived at the barracks just as Sunday School was letting out. There was a sea of faces—Japanese faces.... What should we do? I finally saw a lady, a little older than the others, so I went up to her and asked if it were all right to attend church there. She looked at me.... Then she asked, "Why, Mrs. Bell, don't you know that church is for everyone?" I was ashamed! She then asked us to sit with her, which we were very glad to do.

The Christian strength in these people...was and is a part of making Topaz and

ON THE TRAIN TO TULE LAKE, ROSCOE BELL TALKS TO AN INTERNEE. COURTESY OF THE BANCROFT LIBRARY, UNIVERSITY OF CALIFORNIA, BERKELEY, WRA PHOTOGRAPHS.

the people that it encompassed, the reason that these three years were the finest years of Roscoe's and my lives. We learned patience, depth of religion and tolerance in a way we had never known before or since. Our friendships [have] remained fast.[9]

Her husband agreed.

The church services in the center were very meaningful to us because of the enthusiasm and meaningful Christianity that was practiced by the church members with whom we were associated. Many were converts from Buddhism and had a more vital type of religion than many of [us] who have been raised in the religion of our parents.[10]

◆　◆　◆

Bell found that the Caucasian staff at Topaz differed widely in previous experience, competence and attitude. Most were sincerely interested in doing a good job, but some maintained that "a Jap's a Jap." And the townspeople of Delta were not particularly welcoming. They considered the Topaz staff "not quite American," because of their association with the internees.

As internees began to arrive at the raw new camp, all hands focused on receiving them and getting them situated. The first trainload of 200 arrived on September 12 from the San Francisco Bay Area. Many of the new arrivals were community leaders who were "able and willing to accept responsibility for helping others to adjust to the new life at Topaz," Bell wrote. It was fortunate that they felt this way, because—after the first meal prepared by the "appointed" (non-internee) staff—all services were performed by the internees themselves. One trainload, or 500 people, arrived each day, until the camp population reached about 8500. All who wanted to work were assigned jobs. Salaries were not necessary, the WRA reasoned, since housing, food, medical care and education were provided. Instead, workers were paid a "cash allowance" ranging from $12 per month for unskilled laborers to $19 for doctors and other highly skilled professionals. One reason for the low compensation was that a GI's base pay was $21, and it was believed that public opinion would not stand for the internees to by paid more than soldiers. Bell noted:

All of the actual operations of the Center were carried on by the evacuees, from police protection, fire protection, motor transport, motor repair, farming, irrigation, road construction, carpenter work, etc....under the overall leadership of the Civil

THE TOPAZ HOG FARM. COURTESY OF THE BANCROFT LIBRARY, UNIVERSITY OF CALIFORNIA, BERKELEY, WRA PHOTOGRAPHS.

Service staff, but the dedication of many evacuees far exceeded that of some of the appointed staff. Obviously good evacuee-administrative relationships were critical to smooth operations throughout the Center.

The Topaz residents included many unusually talented persons including a large number of well-trained and experienced professional people.... It was a bitter pill for a person who had graduated from medical...or dental school...to practice as professional for a "cash allowance" of $16 or $19 per month. Although the wage scale provided little incentive for work, the desire to serve in their chosen field was a great incentive for many and a great asset in all aspects of Center operation.[11]

There was also some benefit, Bell noted, for internees who had been barred in prewar California from teaching, social work and other professions. At Topaz, they had the opportunity to gain professional experience in their chosen fields.

◆　◆　◆

Once all the internees had been received into camp, Bell was able to concentrate on the agricultural program. The 17,000-acre project had adequate water for irrigation and two or three existing farmsteads with buildings. Bell's assignment was to plan and implement farming and livestock operations capable of feeding the entire camp population.

Aside from a handful of appointed staff, the labor and management of the farm program were supposed to come from the internees. More than half of the camp's population was from urban areas, but Bell was confident that agricultural talent existed among the internees—the challenge was to find it.

Gradually, unsolicited offers of help arrived. San Francisco landscaper Tom Takaki volunteered to recruit a crew to landscape the internment compound. A young woman named Sumi Ohye volunteered to work in the office, saying, "I worked in the state Department of Agriculture in Sacramento. I know agriculture; my father is a farmer."[12] When Bell protested that he didn't have a typewriter for her, she brought in her own.

In October, an elderly Issei arrived with interpreter in tow. Introducing himself as Mr. Matsuoka, he told Bell:

Rev. Nishimura tells me that you are Christian. I am Christian, too, and I want to

INTERNEES HAD TO CLEAR MOSQUITO-INFESTED BRUSH TO CREATE FARMLAND.
COURTESY OF THE BANCROFT LIBRARY, UNIVERSITY OF CALIFORNIA, BERKELEY, WRA PHOTOGRAPHS.

help you. Back in California, I was a dealer in farm supplies. Thus I was acquainted with farmers all over the state. I know the farmers and how they farm. I know those who have the greatest ability. I can help you select people who are competent to head the various parts of the agricultural operation.[13]

Bell recognized a good thing when he saw it, and appointed Matsuoka "Senior Counselor." Matsuoka helped Bell find well-qualified and dedicated people to head up various operations and to train the less experienced. Matsuoka had excellent rapport with the Issei, who felt free to ask him questions and voice concerns about all aspects of camp life. Through weekly consultations with Matsuoka, Bell was able to address points of concern and maintain a good relationship between the agricultural workers and the administration.

Rounding out the leadership were several college-trained Nisei agriculturists, and others who brought invaluable skills.

The land itself was a challenge, ranging from barren alkalis and mosquito-infested brushland to scattered pastures and fields of alfalfa and grain developed by previous landowners. Irrigation water was available, but ditches, flumes, and head gates needed to be repaired and extended.

Bell asked the Utah State Agricultural College to help conduct a detailed soils survey, which revealed that the project had no Class I farmland at all and seventy percent was Class IV or V (unfarmable). Arable parcels were widely scattered, and much time and fuel were needed to transport the internees to the work sites. Bell particularly resented the time lost getting the crews through the gates every day. Although some sentries simply waved the trucks through, others demanded that everyone get off the truck to have their ID cards carefully inspected every single time they passed in or out of the gates.

It was also difficult to procure building materials, tools and equipment for the "Jap camp." The supply officer cadged scrap wood from a military installation and begged a munitions factory for its reject ammunition boxes. To ease the tool shortage, he bought out a failing hardware store in Ely, Nevada, and scavenged for tools from disused Civilian Conservation Corps (CCC) camps and Works Progress Administration (WPA) projects.

Bell promoted the agricultural program as a training ground for internees interested in developing or improving their skills. He persuaded the Utah Agricultural Extension service to provide written information and daylong training workshops on raising poultry, swine and cattle, and growing truck and field crops.

The project's poultry enterprise was slowed by the remoteness of the poultry ranch and the lack of hen houses. In the absence of wood, an enterprising Nisei began making adobe bricks, but building progressed so slowly that egg production did not hit full stride—10,000 laying hens—until 1945. The program succeeded largely because of the experience and dedication of Mr. Yamane, the head poultryman, an Issei who was devoted to his chicks. He obtained permission to leave camp and live on the remote poultry farm so that he could tend the fragile chicks eighteen hours a day, seven days a week. He trained others to care for the chickens and expanded into turkey raising. That venture was discontinued after unfavorable publicity criticizing the "luxury" of turkeys for the evacuees.

The hog operation was also handicapped by the shortage of building materials, but by the second year, it provided the camp's entire pork supply. Relatively few Issei had any experience or interest in raising beef cattle, but Alden Adams, the high school agriculture teacher, trained his students to care for the animals. The students raised 1,100 head, enough to supply all of Topaz's needs and part of Minidoka's. The truck farm and field crops were also a success, as were bean-sprout and tofu-making concerns. In all, the agriculture program produced foodstuffs totaling $200,000 per year.

◆ ◆ ◆

In 1944, Bell was promoted to assistant project director for operations. In addition to agriculture, he supervised engineering, fire protection, motor transport and other departments. It was, he wrote, "an unexcelled opportunity to observe the differences in leadership abilities of the civil servants filling critical positions." Bell believed that without decent pay as an incentive, it was imperative for the Caucasians to cultivate "good understanding and good relationships" with the internee work force. When a Caucasian staffer treated the internees badly, there were consequences.

> [O]ne supervisor in the motor repair shop openly stated that he was the boss and that his job was to "herd Japs" to get the work done...even though members of his evacuee staff were as well (or even better) qualified as he.... It wasn't surprising that with this attitude the "deadline" of inoperable vehicles grew daily until about half of the equipment was awaiting repair. That supervisor resigned and was replaced by a person who established good staff relations and made use of the available talents of the evacuees.[14]

WOOD WAS IN SUCH SHORT SUPPLY THAT MANY FARM STRUCTURES HAD TO BE PAINSTAKINGLY PIECED TOGETHER FROM SCRAP LUMBER. COURTESY OF THE BANCROFT LIBRARY, UNIVERSITY OF CALIFORNIA, BERKELEY, WRA PHOTOGRAPHS.

Even with good supervisors, it was frustrating work trying to keep 200 "mostly worn-out" vehicles in operation, especially during the first year, when the repair shop lacked the proper equipment.

The engineering department was plagued with ongoing problems with the water supply. Believing that the camp would not be in use for very long, the army had installed the original water system with lightweight, used well-casings instead of cast-iron pipe. Alkali salts in the soil quickly corroded the pipe and the system was plagued with leaks. Bell wrote:

> One of the most miserable jobs in the Center was digging out the muck, patching up the pipe, and replacing sections of it.... Few people wanted to work on the water system, and you couldn't force people to work on it. Even paying a higher cash allowance wasn't enough to maintain satisfactory crews on the pipe line.

> It was a headache for almost three years. At one time as many as half the fire plugs in the city were dead.[15]

◆ ◆ ◆

Bell was an acute observer of camp psychology. He wrote:

> Living in a Relocation Center, a city that is surrounded by a barbed wire fence, guarded by armed military guards in guard towers and having to check through a military police guard as you leave...for any reason (even going out to work on the farm) is fraught with potential tensions.[16]

BELL CHAMPIONED LEARNING OPPORTUNITIES TO KEEP THE INTERNEES MOTIVATED, LIKE THIS VOCATIONAL TRAINING CLASS IN FARM CONSTRUCTION.
COURTESY OF THE BANCROFT LIBRARY, UNIVERSITY OF CALIFORNIA, BERKELEY, WRA PHOTOGRAPHS.

He noticed that changes or uncertainties in the administration's policies increased the number of hospitalizations from high blood pressure, and that war news could heighten tensions. He observed a huge generation gap between the Issei immigrants and the American-born Nisei. The two groups had vastly different preferences in language, recreation, and food, prompting one Americanized Nisei to exclaim, "I have never seen so many Japs in all my life." The older folks preferred to speak Japanese and longed for fish, rice, bean sprouts and tofu, while the Nisei were happy with American slang, hamburgers and hot dogs. On a budget of twenty-seven cents a day per person, plus rationing to contend with, the kitchen staff had its work cut out.

Tensions were so chronic among the appointed staff that an anonymous employee mailed copies of a cartoon satirizing political infighting in Washington to the fifteen principal members of the administrative staff. Scrawled on a drawing of Cabinet members taking potshots at each other was the notation, "x 8000 = Topaz." Some of the staff were outraged, and suspected the internees of trying to cause trouble, but Bell got a big chuckle out of the cartoon, and tacked it on the wall of his office.

> When I reached for the telephone to call the supply office(r) to chew him out because of delay...I would see this [cartoon] and think, "Well, Roscoe, maybe you had better simmer down before you call."[17]

Just before "disloyal" internees were to be transferred to the Tule Lake segregation camp, Bell wrote:

> It was a time of great tension because personal national loyalties were conflicting with family loyalties and [with] the authority of the Issei in the extended family. Many personal friendships, likewise, were involved and emotions ran high.[18]

One day the tensions erupted in the auto shop. Internee workers were talking about the impending segregation when they were ordered back to work by their Caucasian supervisor. When they didn't respond fast enough, he ordered them out of the shop, precipitating a walkout. Then the motor-pool drivers went on strike. The strikers warned the agricultural crews to stay away from work, and paid a visit to the poultry farm to warn Mr. Yamane that if he didn't quit work, he'd be beaten. Being a small man, Mr. Yamane did not resist. He went to Bell's office to beseech him to find someone to take care of his chickens. Bell pulled his children out of school to tend poultry until Mr. Yamane went to a meeting to plead for his precious birds: "[T]his is not the way to act toward chickens who can't take care of themselves," he told the strikers.

"You go feed your chickens," he was told, and he hurried back to the chicken ranch.

Bell found out later that the work stoppage ended after several residents spent the night going from block to block to persuade the internees to go back to work. "We can't do this to Mr. Bell," they reportedly said. The words resonated with the internees, Bell thought, because the entire Bell family had demonstrated their concern and sincerity by being deeply involved in the Japanese American community.

GLADYS BELL, 1945.
COURTESY OF THE BELL FAMILY.

◆　◆　◆

Since Mrs. Bell was not on staff, she was free to volunteer her energies wherever they were needed. She made many friends through the interdenominational Christian church. She recalled:

> Some of the pastors met with Mr. Raymond Sanford, who was in charge of the store, churches, school, etc., to see if they

could buy a dark red curtain or drape to put behind the pulpit for the Sunday service.... Mr. Sanford told them no—that if they really wanted to worship, they could worship in a horse barn!

These people had already been in horse barns at Tanforan [Race Track turned "assembly center"]; some had even had their babies there and remembered the smell of the horses as they suffered from morning sickness! So they didn't appreciate the suggestion.[19]

Father Tsukamoto, an Episcopal priest, told Mrs. Bell that when people had arrived at Tanforan, they had felt heartsick and afraid. The priest had told them, "We can either sit back and do nothing—and settle like Indians on a reservation—or we can treat it like a temporary situation that we can live with—and go on with our lives." Not all the internees agreed with this outlook, but the majority was determined to make the best of a bad situation.

With time on their hands for the first time in their lives, the internees developed an extensive program of activities, including sports and socials, as well as classes in English, writing, business, flower arrangement, doll-making, sewing and other subjects. Since Topaz was sited on an old lake bed, shells were plentiful. Art classes obtained permission to drive out under armed guard and collect shells, which they cleaned and assembled into jewelry, pictures, flowers and other objects.

INTERNEES WHO HAD BEEN FORCED TO LIVE IN HORSE STALLS AT TANFORAN ASSEMBLY CENTER DID NOT APPRECIATE A CAUCASIAN STAFFER'S REMARK ABOUT WORSHIPPING IN A HORSE BARN.
COURTESY OF THE BANCROFT LIBRARY, UNIVERSITY OF CALIFORNIA, BERKELEY, WRA PHOTOGRAPHS.

Roscoe Bell recalled:

Because photography wasn't permitted, many people made sketches, oil paintings and watercolors of Topaz life.... The art exhibits...were a source of great inspiration. Many persons who had artistic talents, but who had been too busy to express themselves, "blossomed in the desert." Wood carving, basketry, lapidary work and other art forms amazed all of us.... Especially notable to me were the beautiful creations from juniper knots and slabs recovered from the kindling pile.[20]

Mrs. Bell added:

Music was not neglected, even though there were not too many instruments. Dancing classes including tap, ballet, toe and Oriental were taught. All forms of music were to be heard...from jazz to classical, including Japanese. The Japanese instruments included the koto, the samisen and the flute. Japanese dancing was done by little girls up to the adults, with the proper kimonos and obis. They were beautiful.[21]

Being musical herself, Mrs. Bell was soon enlisted to play the piano at church services and amateur entertainments. One talented singer and entertainer named Goro Suzuki later built a postwar career under the name of Jack Soo. For the internees' second Christmas at Topaz, Mrs. Bell was asked to direct a 75-member chorus in Handel's "Hallelujah Chorus," an experience that thrilled everyone involved, she recalled.

Mrs. Bell attended dance and music recitals and served on committees that organized socials. She became so involved at the high school that the students began calling her "our own Mom Bell." She was also asked to be the Caucasian sponsor of the Topaz USO. Mothers, wives, sweethearts and sisters of servicemen met regularly in one of the barracks, she recalled:

> There would be a circle of ladies at one end who represented the European theatre and a circle at the other end representing the Pacific theatre. They would share letters, sadness, joy, sorrow, and at holiday time, they would keep food back from their meager mess hall meals and fix a box to send overseas. Sometimes they could add a few bought things from the co-op.... What a group of beautiful people!

> ...The 100th Battalion and the 442nd Infantry were renowned for their bravery and service to their country. We were proud of our boys, and it was hard to see them come home for a visit and have to sign in at the gate to see their parents behind barbed wire fences! One man had to have his father sign his pass, as he was an amputee! We didn't dwell on this, although we knew it was wrong, but we had to live with it at the time.

> One day we received a message that Mr. and Mrs. Kajiwara [she was president of the Topaz USO] had lost their son in action. It was my duty to go see all of the parents who had sad news, but this was the hardest. How does one comfort a mother who has lost her only son serving our country and she is a prisoner of war? I walked many blocks trying to think what to say. Finally I went to her and said, "I don't know how to tell you how sorry I am, and to think he was your only son!" She said, "Mrs. Bell, many thousands of American mothers are losing their sons.... [S]hould I be any different?" She made me feel a depth of spirit that I don't often find around people who have experienced tragedy."

◆ ◆ ◆

The soil within the mile-square internment compound was too alkaline to grow flowers or vegetables, as was done at some of the other camps. A few flowers for the hospital were raised at the camp farm. One patient, Mrs. Bell remembered, wept at the sight of fresh-cut flowers.

Flowers meant a great deal to the internees, who came from a culture that celebrated nature and the passing of the seasons. For weddings, funerals and other special occasions the women in the camp made flowers out of crepe

A NISEI SOLDIER STANDS IN FRONT OF A SERVICE FLAG SIGNIFYING INTERNEES FIGHTING IN THE WAR. COURTESY OF THE BANCROFT LIBRARY, UNIVERSITY OF CALIFORNIA, BERKELEY, WRA PHOTOGRAPHS.

paper, cutting, twisting, crimping and wrapping bits of paper to create beautiful and realistic roses, carnations, irises, chrysanthemums. Mrs. Bell wrote:

> There were wreaths, stars, triangles and blankets formed by using wire and moss, or any substance that would hold the flowers. People would stay up all night, if necessary, making flowers for a funeral, wedding or whatever. No flowers were used twice—the old ones were pulled out of the frame and new flowers of paper, cloth or silk were put into the old frames. Many tears of joy and thankfulness were shed because someone cared enough to make flowers for their loved ones.[23]

When two Topaz teachers decided to get married in camp, Mrs. Bell was moved by the universal character of the wedding party.

> [T]he bride, Patricia Bond, was Quaker, [the groom, Robert Maggiora,] was Catholic, the best man was Jewish and the bridesmaid was Quaker. The soloist was Mormon and the pianist Methodist.... [O]ne of the preachers was Congregational and the other was Presbyterian. The ushers were Buddhist and Presbyterian! It was impressive.

> The Issei Mothers Chorus helped me with the reception by making open-faced sandwiches.... I furnished the materials and told them how to make pinwheels, calla lilies and different shapes.... They used their own ideas and you never saw such attractive open-faced sandwiches.[24]

◆   ◆   ◆

FLOWER MAKING WAS A POPULAR CRAFT ACTIVITY IN CAMP.
COURTESY OF THE BANCROFT LIBRARY, UNIVERSITY OF CALIFORNIA, BERKELEY, WRA PHOTOGRAPHS.

The Bells had four children: Paul, who was 14 when they went to Topaz; Earnest, age 11; Winifred, 9; and 6-year-old Gordon. All four children attended school with the internees. Personable and friendly, Paul threw himself into sports and extracurricular activities, helping with school dances, the student newspaper and the yearbook. He recalled:

> The dances were one of the focal points. We spent all that time developing those fantastic crepe-paper decorations with romantic lighting, collecting the records, being there at the dance, and then cleaning up...so that the Protestant church could have service in the hall the next morning. I struggled to reconcile the investment of time and money in decorations only to have them all torn down so quickly, but we really did need the visual escape from camp drabness....

> Mom told me that it was a gentlemanly thing to take girls to the dances, but I shouldn't get serious with any of the Nisei girls because on the outside, attitudes toward mixed-race couples and their offspring was a tough road. I don't know how

she did it, but she had sort of an understanding with the girls' parents that I would be no part of serious dating.... [N]othing was expected other than to take another girl for an evening at the dance. I felt it was my job to book my date up with [dances with] as many cool guys as possible.... Oh sure, there were some gals that I really liked, but I doubt that they knew it,....[25]

Life at Topaz High was stimulating, but I always felt like an outsider. I couldn't have a...Navy pea coat [military surplus items were issued to internees as part of their clothing allowance]. My mom didn't knit, so I had no argyle socks. My pants were always too short.... My hair was light and wavy, not black and straight like all the cool guys. I didn't tan; I burned. I couldn't jitterbug. My attempts to learn Japanese were a disaster.[26]

Eventually staff housing was constructed, and the Bells moved from a tar paper barrack to a neatly painted, four-unit apartment building separated from the internee housing by a wide strip of bare dirt. The two-bedroom unit was too small to accommodate the whole family, so Paul and Earnest were assigned their own apartment in the dormitory for male staff. Paul wrote:

That move was sad for me, because already we staff had so many advantages. We now lived in special accommodations in a separate section of the camp. After I got reprimanded for letting one of my internee friends use the pool table in our recreation room, it was clear that the staff housing area was part of an intentional segregation policy. My parents even took some flak about inviting [some Nisei friends] and Nikkei farm workers over to our apartment for sit-down dinners with a tablecloth.[27]

After he graduated with the Topaz High class of 1945, Paul enlisted in the army. He and his family maintained lifelong relationships with friends from camp. He wrote:

An individual can make a whale of a difference.... [T]he residents of Topaz, many of whom thought of themselves as merely ordinary folks, demonstrated the human spirit of taking whatever life dealt them and making something good happen out of that experience. What a rich legacy my Topaz friends have given me.[28]

Roscoe Bell was transferred to another government job in the fall of 1945, a few months before the Supreme Court decision that ended the internment. About his three years at Topaz he wrote:

All in all, it was a tremendous experience...working with people who had every cause to be embittered, but were not; people who were optimistic and cooperative; and people we enjoyed.... [W]e felt that our years in Topaz [were] one of our greatest professional experiences because of the demanding administrative responsibilities coupled with deep personal experiences and the satisfaction of sharing with people at a very difficult time in their lives. It was for us, both individually and as a family, a faith-strengthening experience, from the beginning, with our guidance from God for us to go to Topaz.[29]

JOSEPH GOODMAN RESIGNED HIS POSITION AS ASSISTANT SUPERINTENDENT OF THE STEINHART AQUARIUM AND TAUGHT AT AN INTERNMENT CAMP. COURTESY OF LYSBETH GOODMAN.

DR. JOSEPH GOODMAN:
INVESTING IN DEMOCRACY

The new faculty advisor called the seniors of Topaz High School together. "Today, we will elect class officers and write a class constitution," announced science teacher Joseph R. Goodman. "And we will do it democratically."

The young Nisei internees hooted derisively. "Democracy!" they scoffed. "That's not how we got to Topaz!"

The 215 seniors had good reason to feel disillusioned. Where were their constitutional rights when they were uprooted from their homes in the San Francisco Bay Area and sent to a remote Utah internment camp? Living in tar-paper barracks under armed guard, it was difficult to feel anything but discouraged and angry.

Seeing the disillusioned faces of his students, Dr. Goodman felt sure that he was in the right place at the right time. "I decided to teach in a relocation camp," he wrote later, "because this group of students included some who could become scientists, doctors or leaders in society if they were encouraged to continue their education even under adverse conditions."[1] He told his students:

I believe the evacuation is unconstitutional. You are American citizens...incarcerated against your will without due process of law. I'm not going to whitewash the circumstances that put you here, but you can choose to be bitter or you can choose to look for the positive. You have a unique opportunity that students at an established school do not. You can choose your school colors, your mascot, and create songs, cheers and other school traditions.[2]

These were minor matters, but for students who had seen their lives spin completely out of their control, such decisions were the first small steps toward regaining a sense of self-determination. With one choice at a time, Goodman was determined to restore his students' faith in their right and responsibility to master their own destiny.

By the time the principal abruptly announced the abolishment of homerooms, the students had gained confidence. The student government was based on representatives elected from each homeroom, so some of the student body officers went to Goodman for advice.

"Do we have a right to petition the principal not to change the system, Dr. Joe?"

Knowing that the principal had made the decision unilaterally, without consulting with or informing the faculty, Goodman replied, "I don't think it would change his mind, but if your question is, 'Do you have the right to petition?' the answer is 'Yes, you do.'"

The next morning Goodman was called out of his first-period chemistry class by the school secretary. He entered the principal's office to find the student body officers already lined up and the principal in a red-faced fury. Brandishing the student petition, he began to read: "Two heads are better than one...." He tossed the paper aside and glared at Goodman. "What are you doing fomenting rebellion among the students?"

"The students came to me with the question, 'Do we have the right to petition?' I told them, 'Yes, you do have that right.'"

"You are relieved of all your duties as of this moment, Goodman. Dismissed!"

As they walked out, the student body president whispered to Goodman with barely suppressed glee, "The principal was practically hysterical."

The school was so short of staff that Goodman was quickly reinstated as a teacher. Eventually his advisory positions were restored as well. By the end of the school year, it was the principal who was gone.

The events were a practical demonstration of Goodman's fundamental belief that right triumphs over wrong, eventually. For adolescents caught up in the emotional tur-

IN AN ATTEMPT TO GIVE THE STUDENTS SOME SENSE OF CONTROL, SOME SCHOOLS ASKED THE STUDENTS TO CHOOSE THE SCHOOL NAME AND COLORS.
COURTESY OF THE BANCROFT LIBRARY, UNIVERSITY OF CALIFORNIA, BERKELEY, WRA PHOTOGRAPHS.

moil of the times, it was a powerful lesson. Former student Glenn Kumekawa, who was fourteen when he was interned, wrote:

> [Dr. Goodman] represented the very best of the America [that we] felt had abandoned us during those stressful days of internment. His presence with us was enormously significant for all of us.... He came...not as a benefactor, but as a participant.... His participation was strong, creative, supportive, and his outlook, expansive and unlimited in possibilities.[3]

◆ ◆ ◆

For Goodman, the run-in with the principal was just one marker in a remarkable journey of conscience that had begun in the summer of 1940, shortly after he earned a doctorate in chemistry at the University of Washington. He was a strong-minded, take-charge sort of person, who did not hesitate to translate his beliefs into action. He converted to Quakerism, and as he watched the clouds of war build up, he considered his future. "I believed it would take a dramatic and emotional incident to galvanize the people of the United States into action," he recalled later. "When this occurred it would be difficult to make objective decisions."

Goodman made his decision in advance. He became the first person to register as a conscientious objector with the Seattle draft board. He wrote:

JOSEPH GOODMAN, 1942. COURTESY OF LYSBETH GOODMAN.

> In sociological actions, there is no absolute good or absolute evil [but]...various shades of gray.... I decided to seek acts that were primarily constructive or good and [to] flatly refuse, even when ordered to do so, those that were primarily destructive or evil.... This thinking, plus the determination never to deliberately kill any person, led me to register as a conscientious objector in the draft.[4]

Not long afterward, Goodman was hired as assistant superintendent at the prestigious Steinhart Aquarium in San Francisco's Golden Gate Park. On December 7, 1941, the "dramatic and emotional incident" he had anticipated occurred at Pearl Harbor. Goodman briefly considered civil defense work and the Army Medical Corps before deciding that he wanted to work with the Japanese Americans. He had had no previous association with them, but it was already becoming clear that they might be targeted with discrimination on a massive scale.

In mid-December, about a week after President Roosevelt declared war against Japan, the young scientist stepped into the FBI office in San Francisco and asked to speak to an agent. "I am registered as a conscientious objector," Goodman told him. "I plan to move to the Japanese section of town. I plan to go there as a private citizen, with no affiliation with any group, political or religious, to help in communication between the people of Japanese ancestry and others in the community."[5]

The FBI agent wrote up a one-page summary of Goodman's statement and wished him well. "Thank you for coming in," he said. "It would have taken us three months to investigate you."

Goodman then visited Lincoln Kanai, the director of the Japanese YMCA, whom he had met a few months earlier. Through Kanai, Goodman rented a room from an Issei widower whose life had been turned upside down simply because he was an "enemy alien." He had been fired from his janitor job the day after Pearl Harbor. With his bank account frozen by the U.S. government, the old man needed cash. Ironically, his American-born son was in the U.S. Army.

Goodman continued to work at the Steinhart Aquarium during the day, but he spent evenings and weekends at the YMCA, helping organize youth activities. He also helped put together a mimeographed community information sheet to explain new developments affecting Japanese Americans. Churches, labor organizations and social groups were invited to join a community council to work on Japanese American concerns. Goodman remembered:

> Thirty-three people came to the first meeting. They asked me to be chairman, but I refused. After the meeting I asked some of them why they trusted me. How did they know I was not an FBI agent? They all laughed and said it was very simple. The FBI always came in two's, I was alone.[6]

The council met only a few times before the eviction orders were posted. In early April, the Japanese Americans of San Francisco were interned at the Tanforan Racetrack. Goodman ferried needed items to the makeshift assembly center south of the city, including athletic equipment and a piano from the YMCA.

With his landlord interned, Goodman moved to a room on the top floor of the Friends Center on Baker Street. Established just a few months before Pearl Harbor, the center served as AFSC offices, as well as a hostel for refugees from Nazi Germany. Space was so tight that the bed Goodman slept in at night was used during the day by another Quaker with a night job.

The secretary of the Baker Street hostel was Elizabeth "Betty" Baker, whose quiet

TOP: ANTI-JAPANESE POSTER AT SAN FRANCISCO'S SUTRO BATHS. *BOTTOM:* JAPANESE AMERICANS BOARD A BUS TO TANFORAN ASSEMBLY CENTER. COURTESY OF THE BANCROFT LIBRARY, UNIVERSITY OF CALIFORNIA, BERKELEY, WRA PHOTOGRAPHS.

TOP: BETTY BAKER WAS BORN IN PIEDMONT, CALIFORNIA TO A SOCIALLY PROMINENT FAMILY. *BOTTOM:* BETTY MARRIED JOE GOODMAN IN 1942.
COURTESY OF LYSBETH GOODMAN.

intelligence immediately attracted Goodman's attention.[7] She was the daughter of a wealthy and status-conscious Piedmont socialite, who had hoped to marry her off to Stephen Bechtel, a family friend who built his father's construction firm into one of the largest in the world. Miss Baker had rebelled against the values of her strong-minded mother, whose concern for appearances had included forcing Betty to wear high heels despite a physical problem that caused excruciating pain. Instead of marrying, Betty had earned a master's degree from the University of California and worked as an editor for a Berkeley publishing house. She joined a new social circle that included environmentalists Anne and David Brower, physicist Russell Varian and Quakers Betty and Francis Duveneck. She became a Quaker herself, and went to work at the youth hostel that Francis's parents, Josephine and Frank Duveneck, sponsored at Hidden Villa Ranch in the Los Altos Hills. When the Baker Street hostel opened, she transferred there.

Joe Goodman and Betty Baker married in July 1942. Betty's mother, appalled that Betty had married a man of no standing, disinherited her. Undeterred, the Goodmans stopped on the way back from their honeymoon at the internment camp being constructed near Twin Falls, Idaho. They were immediately hired as a teacher and a secretary.

Goodman resigned from his position at the aquarium, but the WRA canceled its employment offer because he was a conscientious objector. For the next several months, the young couple worked for the student relocation program that had been organized by the AFSC. In December, they were hired once again by the WRA and assigned to Topaz—Joe as a teacher and Betty as head of the social services department. Knowing that their salaries were not large, Robert Baker, Betty's brother, arranged to have the navy remit a portion of his lieutenant commander's salary to Topaz every month.

The Goodmans arrived in Topaz in January 1943. The isolated camp was built near the little town of Delta, Utah, on the alkaline flats of an ancient dry lake bed. In the far distance were mountains, including the camp's namesake Topaz Mountain, strewn with small crystals of the semiprecious gem. Construction had destroyed what little vegetation there was. Goodman recalled:

> Dust permeated everything, your hair, eyes, clothes, books, the rooms at school and...the homes in the barracks. When the wind blew strongly, it was difficult to see farther than two or three housing blocks. In the summer the temperature could reach well over 100°F. In winters it dropped to below 0°F and on occasion it snowed. These extreme conditions imposed restrictions on various activities and frequently made for very uncomfortable living.[8]

After Betty became pregnant, she was concerned that the living conditions at Topaz would affect the health of her unborn child. She reconciled with her mother and went to live with her in Piedmont.

Goodman remained at Topaz and became intensely committed to his students. Without enough textbooks to go around, and without a laboratory, equipment or supplies, Goodman taught six classes a day in five different subjects: chemistry, physics, advanced algebra, solid geometry and—after another teacher left—an eighth-grade history class. He also acted as senior class advisor and, with English teacher Elizabeth Boardman, as co-advisor for the school paper and the high school yearbook.

He established an honor system for tests, staying in the room just long enough to answer questions and then leaving until the end of the test. He put the students on their honor not to cheat. Other teachers protested, one in tears, saying that he was making them look bad. But Goodman stuck to his guns. He wanted to send a message to the students and to everyone else that he considered them absolutely trustworthy, even if the U.S. government did not.

Goodman later said, "Most of the time I felt a warm and giving relationship between the students and myself." His students knew him and understood why he was there, but when he walked anonymously around the camp, he triggered other reactions.

HIGH SCHOOL STUDENTS AT HEART MOUNTAIN.
COURTESY OF THE BANCROFT LIBRARY, UNIVERSITY OF CALIFORNIA, BERKELEY, WRA PHOTOGRAPHS.

> I soon learned...what it is like to be an obvious member of a minority in the society in which I was living. There were times when I walked through a resident block in daylight or after dark and could almost physically feel the pressure of stares, or of being looked at but not being seen. I did not feel in physical danger at any time, but on these occasions I felt I did not belong, was not wanted and in some cases perhaps even hated, because I was of the ruling white society that put them unjustly behind barbed wire.[9]

To help the students produce the yearbook, Goodman navigated a myriad of logistical barriers. He traveled to Springville, Utah, to find a publisher. He obtained permission from the assistant project director to take photographs if he could get hold of a camera. He learned that an internee optometrist, Dr. Henry M. Takahashi, owned a 35mm Leica that had been confiscated from him before he had been interned. WRA regulations did not allow Dr. Takahashi to possess the camera, but he could write a letter requesting that it be released to Goodman. Then

COVER ART FOR
RAMBLINGS, THE
TOPAZ YEARBOOK.
COURTESY OF GLENN KUMEKAWA.

PROJECT DIRECTOR
CHARLES ERNST.
COURTESY OF THE BANCROFT
LIBRARY, UNIVERSITY OF
CALIFORNIA, BERKELEY, WRA
PHOTOGRAPHS.

Goodman bought 100-foot rolls of film for the students to roll onto empty cartridges. He enlisted Emil Sekerak, director of the co-op stores, to help develop negatives and make prints.

Strict rules governed the nature of the photographs. No exterior views of the camp were permitted, except for a handful of group pictures taken with special permission against a blank wall. All other pictures had to be shot indoors, except for a track meet and picnics held outside the camp. Students such as Paul Tani, who served as technical editor for the annual, remembered Goodman as "deeply and actively involved in teaching others."[10] A particular highlight for Tani was when Goodman obtained permission for him and Editor Ken Shimomura to travel to Springville. "The publisher was extremely patient with us and treated us royally as we proofread the pages of the '43 *Ramblings.* It was wonderful to be free."

When it was completed, almost everyone was delighted with the annual. Even the Utah state librarian requested a copy for the state archives. Project Director Charles Ernst, however, was not pleased. He already regarded Goodman with distaste because of his conscientious objector status. He called Goodman into his office to air his grievances. First, he wanted to know how they had gotten the photographs. Goodman explained that he had gone through the proper channels to obtain permission while Ernst had been away in Washington. Second, Ernst wanted to know why the book did not acknowledge the WRA, the U.S. government or the project director himself. Goodman explained that the book had been published by the Associated Student Body of Topaz High School. The association alone had the right to decide its contents, since not a single penny of government money had been spent. The student body had raised the money through bake sales, advance sales and a handful of ads from Delta businesses.

Ernst was not satisfied. *Ramblings* was un-American, he declared. There should have been an American flag at the bottom of every page, instead of the "Topaz tree." Goodman defended the Topaz tree as "a symbol...developed by an internee statistician in the administration. If you draw a vertical line from the peak to the center of the base and rotate the figure 90°...the irregular line [charts] the age distribution of the Topaz population."[11]

◆ ◆ ◆

While Ernst preoccupied himself with bureaucratic minutiae, Goodman and certain other teachers worked hard to help the students emerge from apathy and resentment and realize that what they did could make a difference. They encouraged the seniors to plan a weeklong program of activities to mark their graduation. Goodman recalled, "Rather than have a few do most of the planning and work, we deliberately tried to involve as many of the students as possible. They were the ones who really made it go."[12]

The first few events went smoothly—a field trip to the mountains capped by a picnic; sack races and a muddy tug of war with the teachers, which the students gleefully won; a senior prom featuring a stairway painted on the wall, leading to a star-spangled ceiling. Then, Director Ernst tried to quash the senior banquet by forbidding food to be transferred from the regular mess halls to the school. The resourceful students ate dinner in their regular mess halls before gathering in the school dining hall, where they sat at

Special events like this dance helped make camp life more bearable for young internees. Courtesy of The Bancroft Library, University of California, Berkeley, WRA Photographic.

tables covered with white butcher paper with full place settings sketched in with crayons. Sympathetic camp cooks secretly sent over batches of cookies, and the students made hand-cranked ice cream with fresh cream they purchased from a local farmer.

Director Ernst and his wife made an appearance partway through the program but left after a few minutes, saying that they had not had dinner and needed to eat. "He apparently forgot that he had refused to transfer food from the block kitchens," Goodman chuckled. "[M]inutes later we got to our dessert of ice cream and cookies."

◆ ◆ ◆

After a short summer vacation, the fall term began with a large turnover in the Caucasian faculty, including a new principal. When the new boys' physical education director canceled at the last minute, Goodman volunteered to develop athletic programs for 450 boys.

Goodman organized a football team with two former members of the UC Berkeley football program, Keichi Kawamoto and Iwao Hashiguchi, as coaches. An hour before their first scheduled game at the high school in the nearby town of Delta, the county sheriff almost called it off. There might be trouble, he'd heard, from some of the young Caucasians who had recently returned from military service in the Pacific war. The game went on as scheduled, but not before Doc Joe gave his Nisei players a pregame talk. The Delta team might taunt them or play rough, he warned, but instead of starting a fight, they should channel their anger into the game and throw the ball farther and tackle harder.

The Delta team towered over the Topaz boys but lacked their quickness and agility. The young Nisei won 18–7. After the game, some of the Delta boys invaded the locker room to congratulate the internees, saying it was the cleanest game they'd ever played.

On the way out of town, the victors stopped at a restaurant for hamburgers, Goodman recalled.

> As we were leaving, a man sitting at the counter, who was apparently drunk, stopped me and said he wanted to talk to one of the players. This sounded like it might be trouble. I asked one of our quarterbacks, who was a quick thinker, to go with me to see what the man wanted. I motioned the rest of the players to go out and get in the...truck. The man said his son was the player who got a cleat cut on his cheek, the only injury in the game, and he also had lost a buck betting on the game. However, he thought it was a good game and he wanted to let us know that he was not resentful."[13]

The Topaz team finished the season second in the state for a school of its size.

Goodman and some of the other staff members did their best to provide the students with positive experiences, but they were powerless to ease many of the pressures that faced the young internees. Topaz teens were at a vulnerable age to begin with, and as they underwent the profound emotional and physical changes of adolescence, they had no privacy. Whole families were crammed into single rooms. Entire blocks shared latrines and showers and ate at a common mess hall. And there was no escape outdoors. More than 8,000 residents were squeezed into a mile-square compound they could leave only by special permission. The camp itself was surrounded by barbed wire and a vast expanse of flat desert.

In this isolated pressure cooker, tensions erupted between the generations, as

THE HOME TEAM SCORES A TOUCH-DOWN IN A GAME PLAYED AT TOPAZ AGAINST A LOCAL HIGH SCHOOL. COURTESY OF THE BANCROFT LIBRARY, UNIVERSITY OF CALIFORNIA, BERKELEY, WRA PHOTOGRAPHS.

parents and grandparents vainly tried to impose traditional values on their Americanized offspring. Family cohesion splintered as the young people ate and socialized with their friends rather than spending time with their families.

Circumstances often pushed the young people into leadership roles for which they were not prepared. Since many Issei spoke little English, Goodman's young students were often forced to translate and to explain new government regulations to their immigrant parents.

Several events caused confusion and dissension within the camp in early 1943, beginning with the government's attempt to recruit young men into an all-Nisei military combat unit. Most of Goodman's students were too young to enlist, but many had older brothers, and the recruitment drive sparked intense discussions pro and con. Some Nisei welcomed the opportunity to demonstrate their loyalty by volunteering to fight for their country, but others bitterly opposed risking their lives for a nation they felt had rejected them. Out of 23,606 draft-age Nisei men on the U.S. mainland, only 1,256 volunteered.

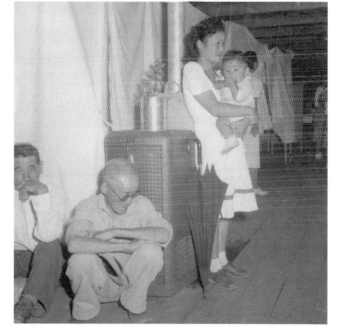

EXTENDED FAMILIES WERE CROWDED TOGETHER IN ONE ROOM, AND STUDENTS HAD LITTLE PRIVACY.
COURTESY OF THE BANCROFT LIBRARY, UNIVERSITY OF CALIFORNIA, BERKELEY, WRA PHOTOGRAPHS.

Whether or not they enlisted, all draft-age Nisei men were required to fill out an army questionnaire asking if they would be willing to serve in the U.S. military and to forswear loyalty to the emperor of Japan. *(See chapter: The Hannan Family.)* A short time later, the WRA began promoting a program to "resettle" the internees outside the camps. As a preliminary step, the agency required all adult internees, including women and Issei, to fill out an "Application for Leave Clearance" that contained similar loyalty questions. The intent was to separate the "loyal," who would be eligible to leave the camps, from the "disloyal." Glenn Kumekawa recalled, "With the results of the incredibly inept and fundamentally flawed 'loyalty questionnaire,' the 'disloyals' were to be segregated and sent to Tule Lake." Goodman called the questionnaire "fundamentally diminishing of our community, a tearing asunder of our fragile sense of solidarity as evacuees." In October 1943, when the camp's "disloyals" were sent to Tule Lake, students petitioned for time off from class to say good-bye to departing friends. The project director refused. "In our chemistry class on that day," Kumekawa recalled, "Doc Joe...engaged us to try to understand that ultimately friendship...justice...and peace [would] prevail."

A few months earlier, in April 1943, tensions in the camp spiked when James Wakasa, an elderly Issei bachelor, was shot and killed by a sentry while walking near the inner perimeter fence. Although the guard claimed that Wakasa had been trying to escape, physical evidence indicated that when he was shot, Wakasa had been walking parallel to the fence, not toward it, and was facing toward the guard, not away. The internees protested the killing with work stoppages, and the guards were moved from the inner to the outer fence line.

As students neared graduation, they were encouraged to apply for college outside of camp. They worried about how to pay for their education and about how they would be treated by people outside. Goodman and Assistant Principal Eleanor Gerard (Sekerak) gave many college applicants the encouragement they needed to navigate the bureaucratic maze and regain their freedom.

◆　　◆　　◆

STUDENTS IN AN AMACHE CLASSROOM. NOTE THE LACK OF DESKS. COURTESY OF THE BANCROFT LIBRARY, UNIVERSITY OF CALIFORNIA, BERKELEY, WRA PHOTOGRAPHS.

Goodman's draft board assigned him to a Civilian Public Service camp in January 1944. With two young children in tow, Betty Goodman moved to Southern California to be near her husband. She shared quarters with Betty Duveneck, whose husband, Francis, was serving at the same CPS camp. Mrs. Goodman recalled that local merchants refused to honor their ration coupons because their husbands were conscientious objectors. They had to supplement their diet with homegrown vegetables.

Goodman was sorry to leave his students behind. He wrote:

> I left feeling depressed and sad because the goal of helping these students seemed to have just begun and so much more needed to be done. Many friendships were being disrupted.
>
> Teachers can and do influence their students. Whether my impact on Topaz students...may have helped lead them into their careers is difficult or impossible to measure. There has been input by many others and the force of events also has influenced their lives. Only they can judge the success of my intent.[14]

Six months after his departure, a dedication appeared in the 1944 issue of the *Ramblings* annual:

> Doc Joe...served as faithful teacher and friend.... Our problems were his problems. He thrust himself beyond his responsibilities; he worked with the community as advisor to youth groups and with the church. Yes, "Doc" leaves a record of great activity and an intense interest in students and student affairs.

To those of us fortunate enough to have fallen within his friendly circle, he left inspiration and faith in man.[15]

Goodman maintained contact with his students over the years and attended numerous reunions. Of the 536 students who graduated from Topaz High in its three years of operation, the vast majority went on to productive lives, some to outstanding careers in politics, science, education, medicine and law.

After the war, Goodman went on to a long and prestigious career as a pediatrics professor at the University of California, San Francisco. As a medical researcher, he published significant papers on AIDS and on Alzheimer's disease. He ran marathons into his seventies and bottled his own Chardonnays and Cabernets in the garage of his suburban home. He died in April 2004, at the age of ninety-two.[16]

By acting on his principles, Dr. Joseph Goodman provided his impressionable young students with a powerfully positive role model. He provided "succor, support and validation" to the students, according to Glenn Kumekawa, at a time when "we needed that assurance for our own emotional survival."[17] In a memorial tribute, Kumekawa added:

DR. JOSEPH GOODMAN, 1993.
COURTESY OF LYSBETH GOODMAN.

> The legacy that Dr. Goodman leaves for us, is that there is under any circumstances, the possibility of good. That there is under whatever constraint, the possibility of hope. That there is extraordinary potential in everyone of us. That there is in service to others, unbelievable compounding returns.[18]

Like many former internees, Kumekawa went on to a distinguished career of his own, culminating as director and professor emeritus of the Intergovernmental Policy Analysis Program at the University of Rhode Island. In appreciation of Dr. Goodman's positive influence at Topaz, Kumekawa endowed a Nisei Student Relocation Commemorative Fund scholarship in his mentor's name.

OTHER TOPAZ STAFF

ELEANOR GERARD (SEKERAK) AND EMIL SEKERAK

Eleanor Gerard was a graduate student at UC Berkeley when the internment became a reality for her. It was on March 29, 1942, the last day that Japanese Americans were able to voluntarily leave the exclusion zone. Miss Gerard was one of a hastily assembled group of volunteers who worked until four o'clock in the morning to process travel passes for long lines of Japanese Americans anxious to avoid internment.[19]

Upon earning her teaching credential in June, she lined up a job to teach at a prestigious high school in the fall. During the summer, she learned that the promised job had been given to a man. Shortly afterward, a Topaz administrator encouraged her to apply to teach at Topaz.

One of the first people to spot her when she arrived at the Utah internment camp was Bill Oshima, who remembered her well when she was a student teacher at Oakland Technical High School because she had chided him almost every day for running in the halls. Miss Gerard instantly acquired clout among Topaz parents as the only teacher in camp with California credentials. The internees were deeply concerned that the quality of their children's education would suffer because most of the teachers had been credentialed under Utah's lower standards.

Indeed, the school was plagued with short supplies, high staff turnover, and an "idealistic" Stanford curriculum, which Miss Gerard thought was better suited for vocational studies than for college preparation. Some of the older students were soon spending half their time in work experience. Miss Gerard made a personal determination to hold her students to high standards of academics and deportment. Former student Paul Tani recalled:

> Eleanor encouraged us to extend our capabilities so that we could survive in the years beyond Topaz High School. She prodded us to read more, to write correctly, to participate in discussions, and to get along with others.... [W]e each had to pick a possible place to relocate...and...learn more about that place.[20]

When she heard her incarcerated students recite the daily Pledge of Allegiance, she felt a lump in her throat when they spoke the bitterly ironic words, "with liberty and justice for all." She was determined to keep her students' sights set beyond the barbed wire.

After an inspiring visit by Tom Bodine, field director of the student relocation program, Miss Gerard had an avenue for helping her students get out of camp. She became a "student relocation advisor" who helped students negotiate the labyrinth of academic, financial and bureaucratic obstacles to enrolling in a college outside the exclusion zone.

Miss Gerard's apartment became a center for student meetings and parties. Some of her students grew so devoted to her, she found out later, that they stood guard outside her room for several nights after threats were made against the staff.

She was one of the few appointed staff members to attend the internees' Protestant church. It was there that she met her future husband, Emil Sekerak.

Before he came to Topaz, Sekerak had never seen a Japanese American. He had been born and raised in Cleveland, Ohio, the son of a Russian immigrant.[21] He enrolled at Antioch College because he was attracted by the school's progressive ideals. He soon became fiercely committed to peace, and registered as a conscientious objector.

He was introduced to the co-op movement through Antioch's work-study program, and after graduation he was hired by the Ohio Farm Bureau to continue work in the field. Cooperative businesses originated during the Depression with growers' co-ops through which farmers could sell and distribute their crops without being exploited by middlemen. The cooperative concept then expanded into health care and consumer goods. By paying a small membership fee, co-op members gained access to high-quality goods and services and to consumer education. Costs were kept low through bulk purchases and the elimination of private profit.

When Sekerak learned that the WRA planned to operate all businesses within the internment camps on a cooperative basis, he applied for a position as a full-time co-op consultant at Topaz. Before he could leave for Utah, he was called up for alternative service. After one day at a Civilian Public Service camp, Sekerak succeeded in getting his Topaz job converted from a civil service position to a CPS position. As a result, Emil Sekerak was the lowest-paid person at Topaz. His monthly CPS stipend of five dollars per month was less than half the cash allowance of the lowest-paid internee.

Sekerak assisted WRA employee Walter Honderich, who supervised all of the camp's co-op businesses. The movie house, beauty parlor, barbershop and retail stores were operated under cooperative guidelines, but the day-to-day operations were managed by the internees. Many of the workers were seasoned businesspeople from the San Francisco Bay Area, with whom Sekerak genuinely enjoyed working.

Both Sekerak and Miss Gerard remained at Topaz until the camp closed. Miss Gerard then went to Washington, D.C., to help settle administrative details associated with the camps, and Sekerak went to Yakima, Washington, to help returning internees. In

1946, Sekerak and Miss Gerard married and settled in the San Francisco Bay Area, where Emil joined the Associated Cooperatives in Richmond, and Eleanor taught at Hayward High School.

Emil Sekerak has passed away, but every year on her birthday, Eleanor Sekerak is still joined by a group of students who gather from all over the country to thank her one more time. At the 2000 reunion of the Topaz High classes of 1943 and 1944, Paul Tani sent a tribute:

> Miss Eleanor Gerard was there [at Topaz] because God commissioned her to be our guardian angel.... In spite of unpleasant and hazardous conditions, she shepherded us with knowledge, with skill, and enthusiasm, with love and most of all by her example of being there with us....

> What a guardian angel! What a teacher! What a friend![22]

Mrs. Sekerak died on July 4, 2005.   *Nominated by Paul Tani.*

VICTOR GOERTZEL AND MILDRED GEORGE GOERTZEL

Because of his quiet, serious demeanor, Victor Goertzel didn't leave a particular impression on most students at Topaz High. Many would be amazed to learn the full story of Goertzel and his wife, Mildred. Goertzel's father, Sam, was a Jewish immigrant from Lithuania and a lifelong Communist who passed on to his son a strong belief in taking direct action against injustice. At age ten, Victor joined the Young Pioneers, a Communist youth group. Later he recalled:

> I was an idealist, and the Soviet Union represented the "motherland of the working class" to me. Every May Day I stayed home from school.... [T]he Pioneers was the in group whose respect I valued. It didn't matter what other children thought.[23]

He was in New York City on the night that Sacco and Vanzetti were executed in 1937, and he witnessed mounted police beating demonstrators. After his family moved to Los Angeles, Goertzel became an associate editor of his school paper. Shortly before he was to graduate, he wrote a rebuttal to an article attacking the Soviet Union. When the principal would not allow his piece to be published, Goertzel's Young Pioneer cell printed it as a leaflet and distributed it at the school entrance. Goertzel was suspended for ten days for insubordination. He returned to school with a lawyer from the Los Angeles chapter of the ACLU, but when he refused to recant what he had written, he was expelled.

Thinking his future lay in union organizing, Goertzel went to work in a marmalade factory. "One day's work convinced me that factory work was not for me," he recalled. He went back to school to earn his high school diploma and prepare to enter UC Berkeley. During that period he became disillusioned with Stalinism, especially after being called on to break up Socialist meetings in Los Angeles. He later wrote: "I was willing to break up fascist meetings but not Socialists, whom I saw as well-meaning but naive."[24]

He became an "unaffiliated leftist and peacenik" and earned a degree in psychology at Berkeley in 1938 before moving to Chicago for graduate work. There he met Mildred George, a brilliant and determined Indiana farm girl who had put herself through school by writing for local newspapers and producing a radio show.[25] Miss George had followed her mother's advice: "Don't waste your education by getting married," but she was captivated by the much-younger Goertzel when they clashed at Socialist Party meetings. In 1939, Goertzel and Miss George quit their jobs and went to Mexico to meet Diego Rivera, Frida Kahlo and other leftists. At the time, Goertzel was a Trotskyite, but he had always been troubled by the Communists' acceptance of violence to gain their ends. While in Mexico, he was introduced to Quakerism by Babette Newton, wife of the national peace secretary of the AFSC. He was "surprised and pleased" by the group's dual commitment to social justice and nonviolence. At first, Miss George was less impressed by the Friends because the Iowa Quakers she had known as a girl had seemed little different from mainstream Protestants. When the couple moved to Berkeley for graduate work, they discovered the unprogrammed Berkeley Friends Meeting and became lifelong Quakers. They married quietly at a Unitarian church.

Since they were actively opposed to World War II and the internment, the Goertzels volunteered to go to Topaz, where Victor was appointed guidance director of the junior and senior high school. He supported the students emotionally and acted as a liaison with the student relocation program. Former internee Tomoye Takahashi recalled that the Goertzels were "the nicest people you could imagine. We went everywhere and did everything together as two couples in camp...a steady foursome.... Mildred was like a sister to me."[26]

The Goertzels had been at Topaz for eighteen months when, Goertzel said, project director Charles Ernst "wanted to get rid of me because I was too close to the internees. He could find no fault with my work...so he had the Civil Service people investigate my past."[27] He was found to have falsified his employ-

VICTOR GOERTZEL, *CENTER REAR*, AT THE PHILADELPHIA HOSTEL. NISEI RESETTLERS GATHERED FOR WEEKLY SOCIALS TO VISIT FRIENDS AND CATCH UP ON CAMP NEWS.
COURTESY OF THE BANCROFT LIBRARY, UNIVERSITY OF CALIFORNIA, BERKELEY, WRA PHOTOGRAPHS.

ment application by omitting to mention arrests for sunbathing in the nude and for distributing peace literature. When threatened with firing, Goertzel appealed to national ACLU director Roger Baldwin, who interceded with WRA director Dillon Myer. As a result, Goertzel was permitted to resign instead of being fired.

The Goertzels moved to Philadelphia to direct a hostel for resettlers sponsored by the Philadelphia Council of Churches, the Citizens Cooperating Committee, and a chapter of the Women's International League for Peace and Freedom. Their stay at the hostel was brief, recalled Goertzel:

> We didn't like most of the wealthy Quakers we met, who were seeking cheap domestic help, wanted the Nisei girls to be "exotic," and were content to see a "little Tokyo" grow in Philadelphia. We strongly favor[ed] integration.[28]

After the war, Goertzel earned a doctorate and pursued a career as a clinical and research psychologist. In the late 1950s, he helped pioneer halfway houses for former mental patients. Mildred raised three sons and directed a school for emotionally disturbed children. In 1962, she wrote *Cradles of Eminence,* which remains a classic study on the childhood influences of famous people. Although her husband was listed as the lead author, she was the driving force behind the project. A sequel, *300 Eminent Personalitie*s, coauthored with Victor and son Ted, was published in 1978. Both Victor and Mildred remained active with the Quakers and with antiwar and civil rights organizations. In 1993, Victor was honored with the ACLU Civil Libertarian Award. He died in Seattle in 1999. Mildred died in 2000. *Nominated by Tomoye Takahashi and Harry Fukuhara.*

MURIEL MATZKIN (SHAPP)

Glenn Kumekawa recalled his time at Topaz High as a "time of bewilderment, bitterness and confusion." In a 1976 letter to Muriel Matzkin Shapp, he wrote:

> Those of us who went through that experience...remember with clarity as if [it] happened yesterday. Rightly or wrongly, those of us who were "evacuees," segregated and incarcerated as we were, could only perceive of the "outside" world by the representative[s] of that world within our camps. Many represented the administration, distant and impersonal. There were those, however, who represented the best in society.... Muriel, you were one of those special people.[29]

According to Miss Matzkin, the camp staff was "split right down the middle," with one group believing that incarcerating the Japanese Americans was the right thing to do, and the other believing that it was a terrible injustice.[30] Although there were no open rifts, the two groups kept to themselves. There was no doubt where Miss Matzkin stood. She was not much older than her students, and her unpretentious ease endeared her to many.

Prior to the war, she had earned a teaching credential in New York. She was job hunting when a former classmate told her that she was thinking of applying for a job in the "relocation centers." Miss Matzkin did not know what they were. At that time, many people back East knew nothing about the internment, since the few thousand Japanese Americans living on the East Coast were not affected. Intrigued by the camps, Miss Matzkin sent in an application to the WRA and was assigned to teach at Topaz.

She arrived just before school was to begin. She expected to be teaching biology, the field in which she was trained, so she was surprised to learn that she was also named head of the physical education department. She made a vivid impression on some Topaz High School students because, as part of the physical education curriculum, she explained the facts of life to them.[31]

Miss Matzkin was much better trained at biology than sports. She is fondly remembered as the phys ed teacher who couldn't serve the volleyball over the net. But she could rely on the internee staff to provide what she could not. "I had lots of wonderful help," she recalled, "because the residents, as we called them, were all very skilled people…. I had a woman who was a top shot at archery, and a man by the name of Yosuke Osono who was a great basketball coach and another guy who was a good football coach…. [W]e had people who really knew what they were doing who were backstopping me." Miss Matzkin was paid $50 a week, while the internee teachers were paid $19 a month. "It wasn't very fair," she said, "but then, of course, the whole relocation wasn't very fair."[32]

Topaz High's basketball team was her "pride and joy." The Japanese American players were small but nimble. When they ventured out to play the "hot-shot" six-footers on the local teams, "we beat them every time," she recalled with a grin. For students cooped up behind barbed wire, it was a great adventure to pile into the back of an Army truck and travel thirty or forty miles for a game. When the internees won, Miss Matzkin sensed that the locals were none too happy, but "we never had a sense that people were…going to throw bottles at us," she said.

Miss Matzkin later married Milton J. Shapp, a cable TV pioneer whose Jerrold Electronics made him a millionaire.[33] His company was a leader in equal opportunity in the workplace, hiring and promoting blacks, Puerto Ricans and women. Shapp was an early supporter of John F. Kennedy, and served as an advisor to the Peace Corps before running for governor of Pennsylvania in 1971. After defeating the Democratic machine in the primaries, he went on to become a popular two-term Democratic governor who instituted fiscal and welfare reforms, consumer advocate policies, and innovative programs for the elderly and handicapped.

As a young man, Shapp had changed his family name from Shapiro because he was concerned that anti-Semitism would stifle his career. It must have been a proud and satisfying moment when he was elected the nation's first Jewish governor.

Before she became Pennsylvania's first lady, Mrs. Shapp was a certified marriage counselor and taught at local hospitals. Within the governor's mansion, she created an educational facility for brain-damaged children and a senior citizens program.

Glenn Kumekawa had the pleasure of meeting Mrs. Shapp in the course of his work as executive assistant to the governor of Rhode Island. Both teacher and student were pleased and proud to see how far they had each progressed since leaving Topaz.

Nominated by Glenn Kumekawa.

ROBERT MAGGIORA AND PATRICIA BOND (MAGGIORA)

According to Eleanor Gerard Sekerak, Bob Maggiora was "a very popular teacher, very interested in his work."[34] He was born in San Francisco in 1918 to Italian immigrants.[35] His father worked as a maitre d' at the Fairmont and other prestigious hotels, and his mother worked in a French laundry. When Bob was in third grade, his father bought a ranch in the East Bay in what is now Fremont, and moved his family there. His father continued to work in San Francisco on weekdays and tended ten acres of apricots, prunes and grapes on weekends. Maggiora attended school in Fremont, where many of his classmates were Japanese Americans. Like himself, they were the American-born children of hard-working and family-oriented immigrants with deep connections to the soil.

Encouraged by his favorite high school teacher, English instructor Jack Reese, Maggiora became the first member of his family to go to college. When the war began, he was earning a teaching credential from San Jose State College and student teaching at his alma mater, Washington Union High School in Fremont. After graduation, employment prospects were dim because no school district wanted to hire a teacher who could be drafted mid-year. When Maggiora asked Reese for advice, his mentor suggested the internment camps, and sent him to Stanford to apply. Given a choice of camps, Maggiora chose Topaz because "that's where my Washington Union friends were sent. I needed to be where they were."[36] When his former classmates were interned, he felt that it was wrong and unconstitutional. He was also the child of immigrants from an Axis nation. Was he not as much the "enemy" as the Nisei? Just because he could not be picked out in a crowd and his parents had been permitted to apply for citizenship did not make them more "American" than their Japanese counterparts. And he had firsthand knowledge of the arbitrary nature of the detentions. His perfectly harmless uncle Eugenio had been arrested by the FBI and detained for about three months because he had once served in the Italian military.

When Maggiora got off the train in Delta, Utah, the first person he saw—the driver assigned to meet him at the station—was a man with whom he'd attended elementary and high school. Maggiora took it as confirmation that Topaz was the right place to be. He arrived at camp while it was still under construction. As the only certified business teacher, he was charged with developing the curriculum. For the first few months, he had no equipment, and was forced to teach typing by having his students finger keyboards hand-drawn on paper. But Maggiora encouraged his students to strive for the best. Former students remember him as a low-key but kind teacher who taught them the skills they would need in the outside world.[36] Maggiora deeply appreciated the Issei parents, who made it clear to their children that education was a number one priority, so class discipline was never a problem. Partway through his tenure, Maggiora was reclassified 4F at a pre-induction physical because of a leaky heart valve and poor eyesight. He could have returned to the Bay Area, where plenty of jobs awaited men who could not be drafted, but he decided to stay at Topaz for the duration.

PATRICIA BOND MET AND MARRIED BOB MAGGIORA AT TOPAZ, WHERE THEY BOTH TAUGHT HIGH SCHOOL. COURTESY OF HANNAH MAGGIORA WALLSTRUM.

In August 1944, Maggiora married a fellow teacher, Patricia Rose Bond. Miss Bond was born in 1921 to "birthright" Quakers.[37] She attended Earlham College, a Quaker university in Richmond, Indiana. Since she was the daughter of a Quaker minister who supported Earlham, it was a natural choice. She graduated in 1943, the year that Earlham's "first war yearbook" stated, "We at Earlham this year have been touched by something greater than ourselves: as a group, we have stood up for an idea; because conscience counted more than material, we have endangered our life as an institution and refused to train men in uniform."

Although Miss Bond knew no one on the West Coast, she knew that social injustices were taking place in Japanese American internment camps. The Quaker tradition of nonviolent protest led her to the Tule Lake "Relocation Center," where she taught English and Social Studies. When Tule Lake was segregated and tensions escalated, Miss Bond's health began to deteriorate. Though, as a Quaker, she saw the light of God in every person, she needed to leave, and was transferred to Topaz.

"I met my first love on the Project," Bob says about Patricia. They were married in Topaz on August 16, 1945, at the internees' nondenominational Christian church. The Maggioras stayed at Topaz until the camp closed, and continued to teach after the internment ended. They did whatever they could to support former internees, and took their children to every Topaz reunion, where, daughter Hannah recalled, the children learned how important it was to be looked upon for what you have to offer as a person rather than what you look like.

Nominated by Eleanor Gerard Sekerak.

FAR LEFT: 1946 SKI TRIP LED BY REV. EMERY ANDREWS.
BETTY JEAN AND BROOKS ANDREWS ARE THIRD AND
FIFTH FROM LEFT. NEAR LEFT:
REV. EMERY E. ANDREWS.
COURTESY OF BROOKS ANDREWS.

REV. EMERY ANDREWS AND FAMILY
THE PRIVATE COST OF PUBLIC SERVICE

In 1943, Nisei teenager Yukio Mochizuki was granted permission to leave the Minidoka internment camp in Idaho and resettle in Utah. En route, he had to catch a bus in Twin Falls, a town of 30,000 located about fifteen miles south of the internment camp. When he learned that the bus to Salt Lake City would not leave for some time, the young man decided to walk around town. Suddenly he was confronted by a mob, which threatened to take him into an alley and cut his throat. The young man was terrified.

"Are you a Jap?" the hostile men demanded.[1]

"I'm an American," Yukio asserted with all the confidence he could muster.

"'Then why aren't you in the army?" they jeered.

"I'm only sixteen."

"Aww, he's just a kid. Let him go," said one of the men.

As Yukio scurried away, he was relieved to see a familiar face—Florence Rumsey, a Baptist missionary he had known in Seattle. She escorted him to the home of Rev. Emery E. Andrews, where he spent the night. The next morning Miss Rumsey returned to feed

152

him breakfast and see him safely onto the bus out of town.

The hostel in Twin Falls was a vital haven for Japanese Americans. Because of the war with Japan, the atmosphere in Twin Falls was hostile to people who looked like the enemy, and lodging for them was nonexistent. Andrews and his family opened their home to countless internees in transit to or from Minidoka.

Prior to the internment, Andrews had been the active and well-liked English-language minister of the Japanese Baptist Church of Seattle (JBC). He and Miss Rumsey were among the JBC's four church workers who moved to Twin Falls when their congregation was interned at Minidoka. *(See box: The Ladies of the Church.)*

◆　◆　◆

Emery Andrews was born in Nebraska in 1894 and grew up on a farm near Modesto, California. He was ten years old when he first got the call to the ministry. He delivered his first sermon while still in high school.

ON A 1940 CAMP-ING TRIP, BROOKS ANDREWS, AGE THREE, STANDS IN FRONT OF THE "BLUE BOX" WITH HIS SISTERS BETTY-JEAN AND ARLEEN AND UNIDENTIFIED FRIENDS. COURTESY OF BROOKS ANDREWS.

He met and married Mary Brooks in 1916 after graduating from divinity school. After his ordination he acquired a taste for mission work by ministering to Italian and Mexican American communities while attending junior college in Southern California. In the 1920s he moved to Seattle to earn a sociology degree and a teaching credential from the University of Washington. In 1929, he became the English-language minister at Seattle's Japanese Baptist Church.

The first-generation Japanese immigrants were putting down roots and raising families. As the community flourished, Andrews was in his element. Fondly known by the community as "Andy," Andrews was outgoing and gregarious, with a sense of humor and a taste for practical jokes—ideally suited to minister to the young Nisei. He was an avid outdoorsman and an active Scout leader who loved to take his charges to the nearby mountains to hike and camp in summer and ski in winter. Rev. Paul Nagano wrote:

> His friendly smile and his willingness to lend a helping hand caught the eyes of the young and old alike, and he was soon loved and trusted by the whole Japanese community without regard for their religious affiliations.[2]

"Andy" and his battered vehicle, the "Blue Box," were a familiar sight as they transported "anyone in need throughout the Seattle area."[3] Andrews's son, Rev. Brooks Andrews, recalled, "[My father] was very active in the community...going out and visiting the families, encouraging them in their faith, finding out what their needs were, whether...physical or spiritual.[4]

The entire Andrews family was deeply immersed in the Japanese American community, in work, play and school. Brooks, the youngest of the four Andrews children, was the only Caucasian in his nursery school class. To the little 4-year-old, race meant nothing. "[W]e were living in an international community and so we had the African Americans, we had the Jews, and we had the Chinese and the Japanese, so it never occurred to me that life should be any other way."[5]

There was a shadow side to the Andrewses' public life, however. Emery and Mary Andrews had realized early in their marriage that they were not compatible. According to their daughter Arleen, "Mother was a shy and quiet person, and I'm sure she found being a minister's wife was difficult."[6] Bound by their respective religious values and by the mores of their time, the Andrewses tried to make the best of their relationship for the sake of the family.

According to Arleen and Brooks, their father did not develop one-on-one relationships with his children, but interacted with them as members of the scouting and youth groups he directed. Brooks said:

> He had a lot of energy when it came to his public interaction. He was out of the house often in the community. Because his own marriage was a failure there was not much energy put forth on the home front. The energy...was put into the community; that was where he received his sense of worth and value. At home he was distant emotionally, often coming home late and going right to his bedroom in the basement.[7]

THE LADIES OF THE CHURCH

Under the wing of the First Baptist Church of Seattle, the Japanese Baptist Church was established in 1899 by Rev. Fukumatsu Okazaki to serve Japanese-speaking immigrants. By 1929, the American-born offspring of the Issei were so numerous that an English-speaking minister was needed, and Rev. Emery Andrews was appointed.

Prior to the war, three Caucasian women worked alongside Andrews as missionaries at the JBC: Florence Rumsey, May Herd, and Esther McCullough. All four churchworkers followed the congregation to Idaho when it was interned, and all four resumed their ministry in Seattle after the war. Reverend Andrews and Misses Rumsey and Herd devoted their entire lives to the Japanese American community of Seattle. Sadly, little record remains today of the women who devotedly served the church. They were modest and self-effacing women in a male-oriented society.

FLORENCE RUMSEY

MAY HERD KATAYAMA

ESTHER McCULLOUGH

FLORENCE RUMSEY was a Japanese-speaking social worker who ministered to Issei women. She oversaw a home for abused women, and logged many miles visiting farm wives on isolated truck farms in outlying areas. After the war she continued to work for the church as long as she was physically able. Rev. Paul Nagano, who served the JBC in the 1970s and 1980s, recalled that during his tenure:

> Florence Rumsey was helping at the Fujin Home, a project of the church, but she became ill and I was honored to minister to her needs. I arranged for her to be placed in a nursing home...where she died. I vividly remember carrying her to my car, as she was only eighty pounds and weak. She was a saint and gave her whole life for the Japanese American community of Seattle.[8]

MAY HERD (KATAYAMA) assisted with the Fujin Home, the Sunday school and the nursery. She later married Mr. Katayama, a church member. The program for a 1977 birthday celebration at the church read:

> [O]ur beloved Mrs. May Herd Katayama...has served for over 49 years and continues to serve.... JBC is the result of the dedicated labors of the missionaries who gave their lives for [us].... Sensitive to encourage indigenous leadership, Mrs. K. has been gracious to take a back seat, praying, supporting and encouraging.... [S]he has not lost her keen sense of humor, her quick wit and deep faith.... More modest than most Japanese, she has the Meiji Era [quality] of humility.[9]

ESTHER McCULLOUGH supervised the Sunday school program before, during, and after the war until she left to get married.

THE JAPANESE BAPTIST CHURCH OF SEATTLE. SERVICES ARE NOW HELD IN A NEW SANCTUARY (PEAKED ROOFS TO FAR RIGHT). COURTESY OF THE JAPANESE BAPTIST CHURCH OF SEATTLE.

SPECTATORS WATCH
FROM THE BRIDGE AS
EVICTEES BOARD THE
TRAIN FOR MANZANAR.
COURTESY OF THE *SEATTLE POST-
INTELLIGENCER COLLECTION,* MUSEUM OF
HISTORY & INDUSTRY, PI-28058.

It fell to Mary Andrews to raise the children and run the household. Although she never spoke of her feelings, it was clear to her children that the situation pained her.

◆　◆　◆

On December 7, 1941, a different kind of pain entered their lives. After the bombing of Pearl Harbor, Brooks vividly remembers, the JBC's Issei pastor Rev. S. Hashimoto came to the Andrewses' house in tears to apologize. A couple of days later, 12-year-old Arleen answered a knock on the door to find two FBI men outside. According to Brooks, "We were immediately under suspicion as being sympathetic to the Japanese...and subversive in some way."[10] Some of JBC's Issei parishioners were arrested by the FBI, and Andrews worked hard to get them released. *(See box: FBI Arrests on Flimsy Pretexts.)*

Andrews was an outspoken opponent of the internment, which he considered one of the darkest episodes in American history. In a 1977 interview, he told Archie Satterfield of the *Seattle Post-Intelligencer*:

> [The] evacuation shouldn't have happened because the government, the FBI, had already picked up the potentially dangerous people and scattered them all over the country in various camps. The evacuation happened because there had always been a minority group in California who wanted to get the Japanese off the coast for economic reasons.... [And] Gen. John L. DeWitt had a personal prejudice against the Japanese.... I've always said that if there had been any other Army commander on the West Coast, the evacuation wouldn't have happened.11

As pressure increased to intern all Japanese Americans, the mainstream Baptist leadership "did very little" to oppose it, according to Reverend Nagano,[12] although Dr. Harold V. Jensen, pastor of the First Baptist Church, did testify against the internment at the local Tolan Committee hearing.[13]

Andrews and his coworkers resolved to stand by their flock. As the congregation prepared for eviction, storage facilities promised by the government failed to materialize. Andrews marked off the floor of the church gymnasium into ten-foot squares where each family could stack its belongings.

FBI ARRESTS ON FLIMSY PRETEXTS

In the aftermath of an attack on our nation, civil liberties can easily be swept aside. After Pearl Harbor, nearly 8,000 Japanese Americans were arrested as "potentially dangerous" enemy aliens with no concrete evidence of wrongdoing. Some were detained for as long as six years, yet not a single one was found guilty of espionage or sabotage. After 9/11, in an unsettling repetition of history, approximately 4,000 Arab and Muslim Americans were detained. Only a tiny fraction has been charged with crimes relating to terrorism.

According to a *Los Angeles Times* article by Teresa Watanabe, one of the Japanese Americans arrested in March 1942 was her grandfather, Yoshitaka Watanabe, an Issei produce vendor at Seattle's Pike Place Market.[14] Watanabe's daughter Toshiko still remembers the terror she felt as three FBI agents ransacked their home. They seized membership cards to the Japanese Chamber of Commerce and a couple of Japanese magazines. Then they arrested her father and took him away.

Rev. Emery Andrews wrote a letter to the U.S. Attorney in Seattle stating that Watanabe was a long-standing church member of good and loyal character; he was badly needed at home to care for his invalid wife and five young children. Nevertheless, the alien-enemy hearing board declared him a member of a subversive organization, and he was sent to detention camps in Montana and Louisiana for almost two years. After Andrews and other missionaries helped launch a letter-writing campaign and petition drive on behalf of the detainees, Watanabe was granted another hearing in November 1943. Noting that two of his sons had volunteered for the U.S. Army, officials paroled him to Minidoka, where he and his family remained interned until after the war ended.

Not until 2003 did Watanabe's family finally learn the reason for his detention. A Department of Justice file obtained through the Freedom of Information Act stated that Watanabe had been arrested because he was a member of Sokoku Kai (Motherland League), which was listed as a subversive organization. Ironically, Sokoku Kai had been equally critical of Japanese militarism, Western colonialism and American racism, and had opposed war with the United States. Watanabe's imprisonment arose out of compassion, not politics. He had never formally joined Sokoku Kai. He automatically became a member when he bought a subscription to the organization's magazine to help out a friend. In the FBI's view, subscription equaled membership equaled disloyalty.

The day of the eviction was seared into Brooks Andrews's memory. He stood with his family on the bridge that straddled the railroad tracks and watched his friends board the train. "I don't recall any conversation," he said. "We just stood there [with]...this blank, empty feeling of unbelief that this [was] happening."[15] Decades later he said:

> These American citizens were herded like animals to a holding site named, ironically, Camp Harmony, otherwise known as the Western Washington Fair Grounds [sic] in Puyallup, Washington.... No time was given to sell farms, equipment, homes...in an equitable fashion. Property was abandoned, sold for bargain basement prices, or simply given away. There were a few sympathetic Caucasians who tried to oversee property until the Nisei returned, if they ever would. My friends were only able to take with them those articles they could steal away in a suitcase or two.... No chairs, no lamps, no furniture of any kind; only a few boxes or containers that could be carried by hand....
>
> I watched from the bridge as I saw my friends, my people board the train, unknown to me that I was witness to a pale shadow of other trains, half a world away [in Nazi Germany].[16]

The first Sunday after the eviction was Mother's Day. Andrews walked into his church as usual. Sunday school classrooms that were usually filled with laughter and energy were cold and silent. The minister climbed the pulpit and stared out at the empty sanctuary, his eyes lingering on each pew as he envisioned the men, women and children of his vanished congregation.

◆　　◆　　◆

Evictees from Seattle and surrounding areas were taken to the Puyallup "Assembly Center," a converted fairgrounds thirty-five miles south of the city. At first, visitors were not permitted to enter, Brooks remembered.

> [W]e would just stand outside the barbed wire and...reach through...and shake hands or try to give hugs. And if we brought gifts they were immediately taken from us by the guards...looking for weapons.... One of my sisters...started crying and she said, "Oh, my friends, my friends, they're all gone."...[I]t was a heart-wrenching...time of separation.[17]

Euphemistically dubbed "Camp Harmony" by the Wartime Civil Control Administration (WCCA), the federal agency which had been created to operate the

RAIN TRANSFORMED THE PUYALLUP ASSEMBLY CENTER INTO A SEA OF MUD. COURTESY OF THE *SEATTLE POST-INTELLIGENCER* COLLECTION, MUSEUM OF HISTORY & INDUSTRY, 86.5.6680.1.

"assembly centers," the Puyallup fairgrounds had been transformed from what the Andrews children had previously thought of as a place of "joy and fun and entertainment" into a temporary holding pen for 8,000 human beings housed in horse stalls and hastily thrown-together barracks.

The Washington Council of Churches had largely sat out efforts to prevent the internment, but once the internees were behind barbed wire, it roused itself to lend support. As the council's assistant chair, Andrews visited Puyallup almost every day for the next four months to coordinate activities.[18]

Many area churches gave at least token support to the internees. Over fifty non-Japanese clergymen from the Seattle-Tacoma area participated in at least one church service at Puyallup. The Council of Churches and the Baptist Publishing House supplied Sunday school materials, choir robes and sheet music. Prior to the eviction, twenty non-Japanese church workers had served the area's seven Japanese Protestant churches, and most continued to devote much of their time to the internees. About half were former missionaries to Japan who spoke some Japanese. Eight Caucasian teachers helped Nisei internees organize Sunday schools and youth forums.

As the Council of Churches representative, Andrews also attended weekly meetings of the Evacuees Service Council, along with representatives from the American Friends Service Committee, the YWCA, the Fellowship of Reconciliation, the public school system, the Social Workers' Association and other groups. The Evacuees Service Council assessed the needs of the internees and cobbled together efforts to fulfill them. The WCCA insisted that school was unnecessary, but the council pushed for positive activities to occupy the internees. It organized a part-time school program and stocked it with old textbooks donated by the public school system. Lumberyards donated mill ends to use as kindergarten blocks, and the public library helped organize a camp library with 3,000 donated books and a ton of magazines. One local church spent $200 to buy out a Japanese bookstore and

MINIDOKA IN WINTER.
COURTESY OF BROOKS ANDREWS.

create a library for the Issei, only to have the WCCA ban all Japanese-language books except for Bibles and hymnbooks.

◆　◆　◆

After four months at Puyallup, the internees were transferred to the newly constructed Minidoka "Relocation Center" in south-central Idaho. Andrews and the Misses Rumsey, Herd and McCullough decided to accompany them. The WRA did not fund religious work. Caucasian missionaries were neither paid nor permitted to reside in camp, unless they were hired as teachers or social workers. They were required to find lodgings nearby and commute to the camp to serve their flock. Nor did the internee ministers—mostly Issei and a tiny handful of Nisei—receive government stipends for church work. Religious activities in the camps had to be supported entirely by the internees' own initiative, with help from outside groups like the mission boards of various denominations.

In spite of the tensions in her marriage, Mary Andrews did not hesitate to pack up her family and follow her husband to Twin Falls. According to Brooks:

> There was no question but that we would NOT stay behind. Our lives were wedded to the fate of the Japanese.... Mother was very involved but was not as high profile as Dad was in the community. She was close to the women...often being a counselor and mentor to them. I'm sure she was very sad to see the families incarcerated. Mother continued her relationships in the Minidoka camp. She was one that would give up her own desires for the good of another.[19]

As difficult as conditions had been at Puyallup, at least the assembly center had been near Seattle, with ready access to sympathetic friends and church groups. Now the Andrews family was moving 740 miles away from Seattle into a new community with strong anti-Japanese sentiments.

Emery Andrews traveled to Idaho in advance of his family. He recalled:

> [W]hen I got to camp, about 10 days after the first trainload of evacuees got there, I had to stay in a hotel while I looked for a house to rent. One evening, I went into a restaurant that had a "No Japs!" sign in the window. I must have said something.... I really don't remember. Anyway, [the proprietor] knew I worked with [the internees] and said he wasn't going to serve me....

THE ANDREWSES IN TWIN FALLS, *FROM LEFT:* BROOKS, BETTY-JEAN, ARLEEN, MARY AND EMERY. THE THREE UNIDENTIFIED JAPANESE AMERICANS ROOMED WITH THE ANDREWSES. COURTESY OF BROOKS ANDREWS.

So I went out the door, and as I went through, he gave me a shove and I landed on the curb....[20]

The restaurant owner's animosity was relentless. He reported Andrews to the FBI, and two agents came from Portland to interrogate Andrews for three hours. After Mary Andrews and the children arrived, the man stood on the sidewalk outside their rented home and harassed Andrews. Finally, he bought the house and forced the family to move.

The Andrews quickly rented another, nicer house across the street. Since it had more space than the family needed, the extra rooms were used as a hostel for Japanese Americans.

The Andrewses' guestbook recorded an average of 167 guests per month. Several young Nisei who found work in town roomed at the hostel during the week and spent weekends at Minidoka with their families. Other internees came into town for baptismal services, weddings or other business. Resettlers like Mochizuki stayed overnight while in transit. Caucasian staff members sometimes stayed at the hostel when they came into town for the weekend, and Caucasian visitors stopped there on the way to the camp. Perhaps the most poignant visitors were the young Nisei soldiers returning to visit their families behind barbed wire before going to Europe to fight for the country that had incarcerated them.

ANDREWS WITH TWO MEMBERS OF THE 442ND, JULY 1945. ANDREWS WAS ANXIOUS TO SERVE AS A 442ND CHAPLAIN, BUT WAS INSTRUCTED BY HIS SUPERIORS TO STAY AT MINIDOKA COURTESY OF BROOKS ANDREWS.

Since Emery Andrews was frequently absent on church work, Mary Andrews shouldered most of the burden of running the hostel, raising the children and managing her own household. Arleen wrote:

> I give my mother much praise for raising our family with God's help. My father was seldom at home.... I still feel that I never knew my father.[21]

Brooks recalled:

> My mother was very involved in the hostel.... She was always the gracious hostess and was anxious that everyone was comfortable and not left out. On occasion she would play the piano, if needed, for a Sunday School class or some other small gathering. When I think of my mother's role I recall the words of John Milton...."They also serve who stand and wait." Mother was kind and gracious in a strong way but never central in Dad's life.[22]

Arleen added:

> I don't remember that my mother ever complained about extra adults to feed and care for.[23]

◆ ◆ ◆

By offering shelter to internees, the Andrewses opened themselves up to hostility from their neighbors.[24] Signs posted in shops and restaurants warned, "No Japs allowed." Brooks said, "Life was not tranquil. We received innumerable threats and humiliation from local residents."[25] It was an ordeal for the entire family. "We were called vile names: 'traitor,' 'turncoat,' and worst of all: 'Jap lover!' We were accused of consorting with the enemy."

Andrews commuted almost every day from Twin Falls to the camp. During the week, the rest of the family had school and other obligations in Twin Falls, but Brooks recalled:

> [W]e always went to the camp on the weekends with Dad. I remember heat and dust in the summer, and mud and snow in the winter. On one occasion we arrived at camp in the midst of a windy snow storm. My father carried me on his shoulders because I could not walk.

> We always had to stop at the guard gate. Even though the guards knew who we were, they always inspected whatever we carried with us and asked questions regarding our business at Minidoka. The camp was surrounded by a high barbed-wire fence; guard towers were manned by soldiers with machine guns. We were told it was necessary for the internees protection. Why, then, were the guns pointed in toward the camp and not out?

AN UNIDENTIFIED WEDDING PARTY AT THE ANDREWS HOME IN TWIN FALLS, AUGUST 20, 1944. THE GROOM IS A MEMBER OF THE 442ND. MARY AND ARLEEN ANDREWS ARE IN THE SECOND ROW, FAR RIGHT. COURTESY OF BROOKS ANDREWS.

> Dad would go about his pastoral duties in the camp while my sisters and I went with my mother and visited our friends and playmates. I remember the unfit barracks in which our friends lived. One pot-belly stove stood in the corner, inadequate for heating the uninsulated room. Blankets were hung to partition the room for some semblance of privacy. In the summer we would go to the irrigation canal "swimming hole" for fun and picnics.[26]

◆ ◆ ◆

Back in Seattle, Andrews may have been late for supper because of church meetings or Boy Scout outings, but now his congregation was behind barbed wire, along with thousands of equally needy internees—Protestant, Catholic, Buddhist. In the face of a widened constituency with overwhelming needs, Andrews felt he had no choice but to respond. What might have been a mild case of pastoral workaholism before the war was transformed by the internment into a full-blown obsession.

In addition to his daily thirty-mile commute between Twin Falls and Minidoka, Andrews found himself making frequent trips to Seattle in his battered blue bus to fetch supplies and furniture for the internees, and to check on property and businesses they had left behind. He once recalled ruefully:

> Every time I came back to get something out of [the church] gym, it was always sitting on the bottom of the pile, and the piles were very high. When they left things with friends who said they would take good care of them, I'd almost always find them used or broken or sold or given away. It was terrible.[27]

During his three years in Idaho, Andrews made fifty-six trips to Seattle, averaging a trip every three weeks. Each round trip was at least 1500 miles. In one twelve-month period he logged 42,356 miles—on slow, pre-interstate roads that crossed searing deserts and wound through rugged mountains. In 1944, he also drove cross-country to visit church members who had resettled in the Rocky Mountain states, the Midwest, and as far east as New Jersey. Andrews said:

> [B]ecause I was gone so much making trips for the congregation, the church criticized me. They thought I should be teaching and preaching. It bothered me. Then the director of missions came out to the camp.... He told me that what I was doing had to be done, and that I was probably preaching better sermons that way than if I was in camp. I felt a little better after that, but he later lost his job for spending so much time with the Japanese.[28]

Andrews struggled to find enough ration stamps to keep the Blue Box in gasoline and tires, and he also contended with racism. On one trip with two Issei passengers, Andrews stopped at a southern Idaho gas station:

> I noticed the service-station attendant was awful slow coming. I got out of the truck to meet him. He said, "Are those Japs?" I told him, "They are Japanese fathers whose boys right now are over in Europe in the United States uniform fighting for you and me." It didn't make any difference. He wouldn't sell me any gas.[29]

On another trip with a Nisei girl, Andrews recalled:

> [W]e stopped for lunch in a little Idaho town. We went into a restaurant and waited and waited.... Finally the owner of the restaurant came over and asked if the girl was Japanese.

"NO JAPS" SIGNS LIKE THE ONE ON THE DOOR OF THE XXX CAFE WERE COMMON ON THE ROAD BETWEEN IDAHO AND WASHINGTON.
COURTESY OF BROOKS ANDREWS.

I explained that she was Japanese American and her brother was fighting in Europe. It didn't make any difference. She wouldn't serve us.

So we went down the street...[and] went into another restaurant.... The young Chinese manager was so gracious, so kind and so different from across the street. I felt at the time that he went out of his way to correct the situation.[30]

◆　◆　◆

One sweltering day in August 1945, Brooks was sitting on the front steps of the family house when all of the town's sirens went off at once. "What's going on?" he asked his mother.

"Well, the war is over," she replied.[31]

Minidoka closed its doors on October 28, 1945, and the Andrews family returned to Seattle in January 1946. Brooks recalled:

It was...like taking a deep breath and saying, "Oh, things are back to normal again. Like the poet said, "God's in his heaven and all is right with the world."

...Lincoln Elementary School in Twin Falls was...all Caucasian.... I had playmates at school but it wasn't like having my friends that I had [in Seattle]. And so coming back to Bailey Gatzert [Elementary School in Seattle]—it felt safe, it felt good.[32]

For the adults, the homecoming was not so simple. Andrews told Satterfield:

[W]hat did the people find when...they returned to Seattle? "No Japs!" signs in some restaurants, especially in the farming towns where they had lived before. They came back to cemeteries that had been vandalized with the tombstones knocked over, and they came back to their houses with the "No Japs!" signs painted on them and their farms grown over.

One particular family came back and the grass was waist-high. Several of us helped them get started again, and at the end of a couple of months, the crops were in and things growing. After the vegetables were harvested, we loaded his truck and took them down to Produce Row in Seattle. [The buyers] would not accept [the produce], even though I was driving the truck....

Finally, a Filipino neighbor told us to bring [the produce] over and he'd sell it like his own.... I could have broken a crate of lettuce over Dave

IN 1945, THE ANDREWSES AND FRIENDS STAND AT THE MINIDOKA GATE BESIDE THE "PROJECT CLOSED" SIGN. COURTESY OF BROOKS ANDREWS.

Beck's head.... He was head of the Teamsters then and they were keeping the Japanese farmers and businessmen out of Produce Row.[33]

Andrews also wrestled with church politics. At the time, mainstream Christianity was turning away from mission churches. Eager to disavow segregation and failing to understand the importance of cultural identity, several denominational organizations opposed the reopening of Japanese American churches. Instead, they favored integrating the returnees into established Caucasian churches. As a consequence, many Japanese American Christian churches on the West Coast never reestablished themselves after the internment.

In Seattle and other communities with large Japanese American populations, former internees campaigned hard for their ethnic churches, but it was not until 1947 that the Seattle Council of Churches and the Washington State Baptist Convention acceded to their wishes. The Japanese Baptist Church was the first of Seattle's Japanese Protestant churches to reopen. It served Japanese Americans from other denominations until their own churches were reestablished.

As the community found its footing, Andrews was constantly busy—finding jobs for returnees, reviving the prewar ski trips, ferrying church members to conferences. He was a member of the local JACL chapter and an honorary member of the Nisei Veterans Committee. He started English classes for postwar brides from Japan, and counseled new immigrants as they struggled to adapt to a strange new country. He even went to Hiroshima twice to help rebuild bomb-devastated housing.

In 1955, at the age of sixty-one, Andrews retired as the English-speaking pastor of the JBC. But he could not resign his sense of mission. He continued working as minister of visitation and then as pastor emeritus.

Andrews's tireless ministry eroded his ties with his family. In 1955, with Brooks almost ready to graduate from high school, Mary filed for divorce. Arleen explained:

> Mother kept our family together until we were old enough to care for ourselves. Her life back in Seattle was very stressful due to the friction with Reverend Andrews, and his activities away from home.[34]

Brooks reflected:

> [M]y mother and my father were separate in the same house for as far back as I can remember.[35]

The day of the final breakup, he recalled, he had retreated to the basement and his model railroad, as he often did when his parents argued.

Dad came in and obviously he'd been crying and he came over to me and told me that he and my mother were getting divorced and he hugged me.... [H]e said, "I'm so sorry." And it was an awkward moment for me because this [was] the first time my father ever hugged me to begin with, but [with] the circumstances that surrounded it, that hug was the totally opposite of what one would hope to have.... I don't recall any words I said to him. It was a very awkward moment, and then he left....

[My mother] was very quiet about [her feelings].... I'm sure she must have harbored a lot of anger and resentment. But being a minister's wife...you [didn't] divorce, at least in those days.... I think she held on as long as she could and [then she] got to the point where all of us were on our own and it was time to make that break.[36]

◆　◆　◆

Andrews continued to serve his community in large ways and small. Well into his seventies, he could be found helping a couple of elderly widows by cleaning up their old hotel in the International District or chiding the Baptist hierarchy for not welcoming Nisei ministers:

Over the years at least four young men grew up in our Baptist (Japanese) Church and our community of Seattle and went into the ministry. Although educated and graduated from our American Baptist seminaries, they could not get pastorates in our Baptist denomination. They had to go to other denominations. This attitude toward our Japanese Americans I could never understand.[37]

The community remained deeply appreciative of Andrews. In 1958, the Seattle Boy Scout Council awarded him its highest honor. In 1970, he received the Order of the Sacred Treasure, Fifth Class, from the Emperor of Japan for his lifelong work among the Japanese in America. Three months before his death, the Seattle community held a standing-room-only banquet where Andrews was lauded by countless organizations, including five Protestant denominations and two Buddhist sects.

In May 1976, at the age of eighty-one, Reverend "Andy" suffered a heart attack. In a final effort to connect, Brooks visited his dying father at the hospital every evening. Rummaging through the past for common memories, Brooks described aloud the many moments they'd shared: camping trips and picnics, hikes on Mount Rainier. "Do you remember this? Do you remember that?" he would ask

After the first Blue Box was demolished in a collision, Blue Box #2 carried on, c. 1949. Courtesy of Brooks Andrews.

his semiconscious father, and sometimes there was a glimmer of recognition. On the fifth or sixth evening, as Andrews breathed his last, Brooks's first thought was not of his own loss, but of the loss to the Japanese American community.

Over 1,000 mourners attended Reverend Andy's memorial service. By the time Mary died four years later, she had made a sort of peace with her ex-husband's memory and was buried in the same grave.

In a sense, his religious calling "stole" Andrews from his family. But Brooks is philosophical:

> [T]hat's a story that is not unusual for anyone who has been a high profile person in any endeavor.... I think my father had a huge amount of love and commitment to give, but it wasn't to his family. [I]t was to the community.[38]

> I think he loved me but didn't know how to express it. I am very proud of him; his example informed me as to what I do [as a minister] today.[39] I have very warm and fond memories being raised in the Japanese community. The community, as a whole, was an example to me of character-building, integrity and fortitude. I have never regretted for one moment living in the community.[40]

ROBERT COOMBS, 1991. Courtesy of the Florin Japanese American Citizens League and the Florin JACL Oral History Project, Department of Special Collections and University Archives, The Library, California State University, Sacramento.

ROBERT COOMBS:
A STEADY COMPASS IN AN UNCERTAIN WORLD

On the last day of July 2003, Robert Coombs's doctor told him that he had bladder cancer. "I'd like to operate tomorrow," he told his 86-year-old patient.

"Oh, no," said Coombs, "I'll be on a plane to Seattle."

"You can't go," the physician insisted.

"I've got to," replied Coombs calmly. "I'm going to go see my students." Coombs's "students" were pushing eighty themselves. Their association stretched back sixty years to the Minidoka internment camp in southern Idaho.

The doctor cautioned Coombs that if he didn't go under the knife the next day, he'd have to wait two weeks for the next opening in the doctor's schedule. Coombs refused to be stampeded. "I've waited all this time before you found it. Let's just assume that everything will be okay, and let's not worry,"[1]

Coombs went off to the three-day reunion, where his former students embraced him warmly, and he hugged them right back. When the veteran teacher and counselor returned to Sacramento, he sailed through the surgery without mishap, just as he had predicted. Placing the love of others before his own self-interest was a lifelong habit, one he had learned at his mother's knee.

Robert William Coombs was born in Visalia, California, on May 26, 1918, and grew up in Sacramento. When he was nine, his

168

father was killed in a boating accident, leaving his widowed mother to raise four children. Tragedy was nothing new to Mrs. Coombs. The eldest child of German immigrants in Cleveland, Ohio, she had begun caring for her younger siblings when she was still a girl. By the time she was thirteen, five of her six siblings had died. Her parents were too poor to afford the medical care and nourishing food they needed. Devastated, the young girl left her remaining family behind and hired herself out as a companion to an elderly blind woman who was moving to Whittier, California. The early responsibilities and sorrows helped her tap into a deep well of spirituality, which was nurtured by the Quakers of Whittier. In adulthood, Mrs. Coombs became, according to her son, "a very loving mother." He continued:

> We adored her. She had the capacity to explain to us what it meant to be human and love, no matter what people looked like...what their nationality was, what their racial characteristics were, the human being inside was the most important thing.... [T]hat's the way my twin and I were raised.... And we loved all people.[2]

On paper, Coombs's words may appear sentimental and trite, but the rich vibrancy of his voice carries all the wisdom and intelligence needed to keep on loving in difficult times.

IN SOME COMMUNI-
TIES, THE INTERNMENT
TORE APART GOOD
FRIENDS. COURTESY OF THE
BANCROFT LIBRARY, UNIVERSITY OF
CALIFORNIA, BERKELEY, WRA
PHOTOGRAPHS.

◆   ◆   ◆

The seeds for Coombs's future career were planted early. After his father died, his elementary school principal, Mr. Burkhart, took a fatherly interest in the orphaned boy and his twin sister. "[School] was wonderful," Coombs recalled. "Your teachers were your friends. They became part of your life."[3] Japanese Americans were also part of his life in east Sacramento, as classmates and neighbors. One Issei farmer, Mr. Miyao, made an indelible impression on him. During the Depression, many of the students were coming to school hungry. To supplement their meager diets, the PTA prepared hot, nourishing soups for lunch. Mr. Miyao faithfully contributed vegetables from his truck farm for the hot-lunch program. Coombs said:

> It was one of my first experiences with someone of a different race and [I] was aware that...he was doing...an outstanding kind of thing. Ever since then, I have always thought of the way he helped in the community."[4]

Like the Japanese American parents, Mrs. Coombs encouraged her children to go to college.

Coombs earned a teaching credential at Stanford University, where he was trained in a progressive new theory of education called the "core curriculum." For Coombs, the idea of teaching English and social studies as an interrelated whole rather than as separate disciplines was "like opening a door."[5]

After earning his credential, Coombs returned to Sacramento. Jobs were scarce. After one semester of substitute teaching, he landed a contract for the duration of the war to teach English and social studies at Sacramento High School.

With contract in hand, Coombs thought his future was assured. Unfortunately, he started his new job in February 1942, the same month that President Franklin Delano Roosevelt authorized the mass removal of Japanese Americans from the West Coast. All too soon, Coombs was saying good-bye to his students as they and their families were removed to temporary assembly centers. On the students' last day at school, he recalled, "The tears just flowed...the hugs and the kisses goodbye...[b]ecause these...kids had started kindergarten together. Some of them...were arm-over-each-other's-shoulder pals." The next day was also painful.

> When I walked into my room and the first class came in, to see all those vacant chairs. And the rest of the day, all five periods, vacant chairs.... [I]t was hard.... [W]e were not an isolated area where there might have been three or four [Japanese American] families that could be exposed to anger and bitterness.... There was a goodly population in Sacramento. And when you start kindergarten with youngsters and you grow up with them, you don't see differences.... [Y]ou're pals, you're buddies.[6]

With more than 300 of the school's students gone, Coombs and ten other teachers lost their jobs at the end of the school year. As he scoured the Central Valley for another teaching job, he was dismayed to learn that with the Japanese Americans interned, teachers throughout Sacramento, Solano and Placer counties had been thrown out of work.

Finally, he sought help from a former professor at Stanford, who told him that Stanford had been selected to set up K–12 programs at three of the ten internment camps, based on the "core" method that Coombs had been taught at Stanford. The professor handed Coombs a partially completed application to teach at the high school at Minidoka. He even provided him with an envelope pre-addressed to the WRA in Washington, D.C., and rattled off a list of items to pack, including all the textbooks he would need to teach a core class. Nine days later, Coombs received instructions to report in Idaho. "I was going...into the unknown.... I thought, 'This is going to be an amazing experience.'"[7]

In a way, Coombs said, going to Minidoka "was a miracle" that was made possible because a period of ill health had rendered him undraftable. While Coombs was at Stanford, his weight and stamina had suddenly plummeted. Doctors could not figure out what was ailing him. Although he was able to complete his education and hold a teaching job, he was not considered fit for the rigors of military service. A few years after the war, a thyroid condition was diagnosed and his health was restored by medication and diet. Throughout the internment period, however, his 4F designation shielded him from the draft.

Soon after he received his acceptance notice from the WRA, Coombs paid a courtesy visit to the Sacramento school superintendent to tell him about his new position. He was shocked when the man roared, "Don't you ever come back and ask for a job here in Sacramento!"[8] Several neighbors criticized him for "helping the Japs" when his brothers were in military service. The opposition only strengthened Coombs's determination to work at Minidoka. "I could not live with myself...if I had decided not to go," he said.[9]

By the end of August, Coombs was en route to the Idaho wilderness. The idealistic young teacher chose to live in the camp, not in the nearby town of Twin Falls. He wanted to participate as fully as he could in the life of the internee community and to be available to his students in the evenings. As he approached the camp for the first time, "the desolate area gave me a jolt," he remembered.[10] At the camp itself, the wind whipped freshly bulldozed earth into clouds of dust. Barbed wire and sentry towers ringed the raw new compound, and a guard inspected everyone at the gate.

The first day's exploration revealed that Hunt Junior and Senior High School was composed of a block of twelve military-style barracks, just like the ones that housed the 9,000 internees. Each flimsy barrack was divided into three barren classrooms furnished with a coal-burning stove and nothing else. The accommodations were hardly better in the men's staff dormitory. But room-and-

JAPANESE AMERICAN NEIGHBORHOOD IN SACRAMENTO TWO DAYS BEFORE EVICTION. COURTESY OF THE BANCROFT LIBRARY, UNIVERSITY OF CALIFORNIA, BERKELEY, WRA PHOTOGRAPH 15.

board was only $42 a month, and at $2,000 per year, Coombs was earning twice what he had made in Sacramento. The spartan accommodations and desolate landscape didn't deter the eager young teacher.

> This was going to be a challenge and I was ready for it. The nice thing about it was that the Junior/Senior High School principal [Dr. Jerome Light] with his wife and four young sons were going to live there. I thought if they are going to do it, I could do it without any problem. They kind of cheered me on because they were glad I was that kind of person, ready to take on whatever came my way.[11]

Jerry Light, who had also been trained at Stanford, was charged with overseeing the development and implementation of the curriculum. On their first day in camp, as Light's four lively sons explored their new surroundings, they soon encountered the barbed wire encircling the internment camp. The boys were shocked, literally, to find it was electrified. Their outraged father persuaded the chief of military police to turn off the power.

The fence incident was a sobering reminder that they were living in an American concentration camp. As he tried to get to sleep on that first night at Minidoka, Coombs thought about his parting conversation with his mother.

DR. JEROME LIGHT, PRINCIPAL OF HUNT JUNIOR AND SENIOR HIGH SCHOOL.
COURTESY OF YOSHI ASABA MAMIYA.

When her neighbors had criticized Coombs's decision to teach Japanese Americans, his mother had stood up for him. As a German American she had experienced the sting of prejudice during World War I. She reminded Coombs, "You are helping young Americans.... There are no hyphenated Americans. We are all Americans." As the raw Minidoka wind blasted lava dust against the flimsy tar-paper walls of his barracks, Coombs knew he had come to the right place.

The majority of the Hunt High School staff, especially at the beginning, was there because they wanted to be there. The teachers included Helen Amerman (later Helen Manning), a fellow Stanford graduate, and Margaret Hester, Ecco Hunt and Elma Tharp, missionaries in their sixties who had taught for many years in Asia. Some of them had been stranded in Japan by the sudden outbreak of war and had arrived in New York City that same month on the *Gripsholm,* the last shipload of Americans permitted to leave Japan during wartime. Coombs considered the missionaries to be "magnificent ladies" whose excellent Japanese-language skills were "a very valuable help" in communicating with Issei parents.[12]

In late August, many of the faculty had not yet arrived, and the school was not yet open. All hands present put in the government-mandated 8-to-5, plus a half day on Saturdays, preparing the curriculum. None of them had ever had the opportunity to design a school from its outset, and many considered it an exciting and challenging opportunity. Committees and subcommittees were organized to develop plans for various subject areas and grade levels. "It was a very active community of teachers who had come from states all over the country...with many interesting ideas and methods [they were] willing to share. We were all willing to try new ideas," according to Coombs.[13] One colleague was Marguerite Askew, a French and Spanish teacher who had taught at the university and high school levels in North Dakota. She and Coombs would develop a particularly close relationship.

TEACHERS AT MINIDOKA'S HUNT HIGH SCHOOL. COURTESY OF THE JAPANESE AMERICAN ARCHIVAL COLLECTION, DEPARTMENT OF SPECIAL COLLECTIONS AND UNIVERSITY ARCHIVES, THE LIBRARY, CALIFORNIA STATE UNIVERSITY, SACRAMENTO.

Only Light, Coombs and Miss Amerman had training in the Stanford core curriculum. Some of the more traditional teachers were irked by the new system. They felt perfectly capable of teaching the way they had always taught, without having to adopt the new-fangled Stanford ways.

Coombs, on the other hand, thought the progressive curriculum embodied a "new vision of teaching and a new vision of school, [of] what public education could become."[14] The new approach taught young people how to adapt to and even anticipate the unavoidable technological, social and personal changes of a rapidly and continually evolving world. Within their lifetimes, Coombs's students would see radio evolve into television and eventually the Internet, and transportation develop from cars to planes to spaceships.

The ability to deal with change was of particular value to the students at Minidoka, who had been ripped away from everything safe and familiar. As they faced an uncertain future, their ability to respond positively to new circumstances would be crucial.

Their first adaptation had to be made even before school began. The school schedule was pushed back because the students were sent out to Idaho farms to harvest sugar beets and potatoes. When classes finally began in November, conditions were

RAIN COULD TURN THE UNPAVED GROUND INTO A SEA OF MUD.
COURTESY OF THE BANCROFT LIBRARY, UNIVERSITY OF CALIFORNIA, BERKELEY, WRA PHOTOGRAPHS.

makeshift. Furniture consisted of picnic tables and benches made in the project carpenter's shop. Blackboards were nonexistent, and the textbooks that had been ordered had not yet arrived. Teachers were reduced to copying text out of sample textbooks onto rolls of butcher paper pinned to the walls.[15]

The weather was often a problem. During the freezing winters, the coal-fired stoves needed to be stoked constantly. Students sitting near the stoves roasted while those in far corners of the room froze. To equalize the suffering, Coombs would have the students rotate seats. When they stood up, the unstable picnic tables threatened to tip over.

The omnipresent dust sifted in through cracks in the walls. "Once the lava soil…was hit by a wind, everything and everybody became gray with lava dust," Coombs recalled. "At times, the wind would bring rain and in a minute, one was covered with mud. The thaw would bring a new problem…as the mud became inches deep and shoes, galoshes or rubbers were lost in the mud."[16] In the spring, sagebrush pollen gave Coombs hay fever. In the summer, temperatures skyrocketed.

Because of a teacher shortage, Coombs taught enormous core classes of fifty to fifty-five students. He and the other teachers were assisted by Nisei "teacher's aides." In Coombs's eyes, these internees were invaluable. "A number of these young adults held advanced degrees in the sciences, math, English and history, and brought a new dimension to the educational program at Hunt…. We have never forgotten the outstanding job they did for the students and the faculty."[17]

Most of the students were "very cooperative" and eager to learn. Since being evicted from their homes in the spring, they had lost weeks of schooling while sitting in makeshift assembly centers. In the fall, they had missed almost two more months because of the sugar-beet and potato harvest. Most were now eager, Coombs said, "to make up for lost time and have an opportunity to once again look toward graduation…. A large majority of the student body had been excellent students in their former schools."[18]

Coombs cut a memorable figure on campus. Calvin Ninomiya did not have him as a teacher, but recalled him as "a lanky, slim (almost skinny), blond-haired young man, well over six feet tall, bounding across the dusty walks at Hunt High School. Obviously, he stood out physically among a student body of uniformly shorter, black-haired youngsters."[19]

Coombs taught public speaking and tenth- and eleventh-grade English/social studies core classes. The core classes were taught in double periods, where the two disciplines were interwoven in a flexible and organic fashion. Students read literature and wrote essays related to the history and geography they were studying. "We did a lot of...reading aloud and discussing...[a]nd our writing always reverted back to the history program," Coombs said.[20]

The core curriculum approach invited a responsive and flexible teaching style, said Coombs.

> I never said, "Well, we can't get into that, we're doing such and such today." To me, it was necessary to handle somebody's question, or maybe they were disturbed by something, and it was important for all of us to get involved and talk about it.... It gave us many an opportunity to talk about a lot of things, and I encouraged them, the girls particularly, because they were apt to be quiet and not say anything.[21]

Only a few years older than his students, Coombs seemed approachable and friendly to the young internees. Former student Eugene Uyeki said:

> Bob Coombs was a good friend as well as [a] thoughtful and sincere teacher. "He was young enough...that...we could relate to him.... I remember chatting with him between classes, joking around as well as continuing with topics from class.... He always took the time to listen to us with good cheer, and humored us along when we were frustrated with one thing or another—such as the lack of school supplies, or the dusty storms...or our sense of being singled out unfairly...by the U.S. government.[22]

"The kids knew that I liked them," said Coombs.[23] His loving warmth and calm manner made him an excellent counselor. Whenever he was faced with an enraged adolescent, Coombs said he would "just sit and look at them very quietly and say, 'Now what happened?' And the kids would say, 'Mr. Coombs...why don't you yell at me like my mother does? Like my father does?' And I would say, 'Because I don't like to yell.'" Coombs laughed at the memory. "That's part and parcel of how I was raised, you see."

COOMBS PLANTED A GARDEN OUTSIDE HIS CLASSROOM. COURTESY OF THE JAPANESE AMERICAN ARCHIVAL COLLECTION, DEPARTMENT OF SPECIAL COLLECTIONS AND UNIVERSITY ARCHIVES, THE LIBRARY, CALIFORNIA STATE UNIVERSITY, SACRAMENTO.

Coombs provided the students with opportunities to talk and write about their lost homes and about their present situation, but many did not want to express their feelings so publicly. A few students vented their pain and rage by trying to provoke him in class, but Coombs refused to rise to the bait. One student was so angry that "it was dangerous to him physically and mentally," Coombs reported.[24] Counselors arranged to get him away from the camp environment and placed in a home in the Midwest, where he could feel more free. Three counselors worked closely together to help this boy and other students. They were Catholic priest Father Leopold Tibesar, Methodist minister Reverend Machida, and Episcopalian priest Joseph Kitagawa.

◆ ◆ ◆

Conditions at the camp slowly improved. The textbooks finally arrived. So did donated books, magazines and encyclopedias from service clubs all over the country.

Coombs planted a flower garden outside his classroom. The students initially scoffed at his plants, but soon they were coming around to help weed and water, and their parents admired his garden and invited him to visit theirs. "I dearly loved to go visit their dads and moms," he recalled.[25] "I was always amazed at what was done by mothers and fathers to make their living and sleeping quarters at least livable. They used every means available to bring some comfort to their small one-room apartment."[26]

Coombs's dealings with the parents were limited by the language barrier. He and some of the other teachers had begun taking Japanese lessons from the missionaries when they first arrived, but once school activities got under way, no one had the free time to continue. Two of the missionaries who taught seventh and eighth graders visited students and parents at home quite frequently and built strong relationships, but Coombs's sophomores and juniors were less chummy with their teachers, perhaps, Coombs theorized, because they were older and more self-sufficient.

Coombs and the rest of the staff lived "up the hill" in the staff residential complex. Three Issei ladies were assigned to keep the staff barracks clean, but Coombs continued to make his own bed until the ladies asked him to stop. "They were beautiful elderly ladies," Coombs recalled, who would dust and sweep in the morning and do it again in the afternoons after a dust storm deposited another layer of fine grit over everything.

When the ladies learned that Coombs went into Twin Falls every few weeks, they asked him to make some purchases for them. When he agreed, they handed him a long shopping list: knitting needles and yarns, embroidery thread, sewing patterns. The first time Coombs took the list into a Twin Falls shop, the saleswoman looked skeptically from the list to the young bachelor and asked him where he was from. "[W]hat difference does it make who's buying these things...?" Coombs asked her. "After all, it's money in your pocket, isn't it?" Thanks to Coombs's persuasion, the woman overcame her reluctance to traffic with "Japs." Soon she admitted that her prejudices had been foolish and automatically held out her hand for a list whenever Coombs entered her store.[27]

The shopkeeper was not the only Idahoan to benefit economically from the internees. After the students helped save the harvest in the fall of 1942, many farmers came to rely on the internees for seasonal labor. "[T]heir crops were very valuable and they were being saved, every spring, every fall," Coombs said. "And they realized it."[28] Eugene Uyeki viewed the farm work as a mutually beneficial exchange:

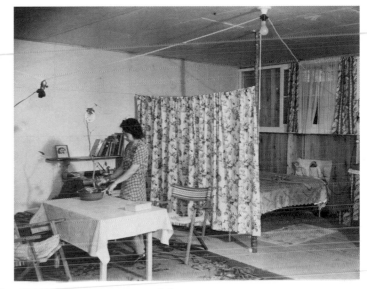

> The farmers treated us fairly. I'm sure that they were very happy to get any kind of help when there was a severe labor shortage. We were all happy to get out of camp for a short time and earn a bit of spending money and...experience life outside of the confined quarters in the Center.[29]

BEGINNING WITH A BARE ROOM FURNISHED ONLY WITH COTS AND A POTBELLY STOVE, INTERNEES MANAGED TO CREATE A CRAMPED ILLUSION OF HOME

◆ ◆ ◆

Coombs was very close to his mother, and wrote her four or five times a week in a running chronicle of camp life. His first Christmas in camp was brightened by Mrs. Coombs's decision to spend her one-week vacation at the camp. Coombs obtained permission from camp authorities for his mother to stay in a guest room in the women's dorm. Every day Mrs. Coombs sat in on her son's classes, much to the delight of the students, who flocked to talk with her during class breaks.

Mrs. Coombs "loved every minute" of her visit, according to Coombs, and went back to Sacramento with many tales to tell the ladies of her Presbyterian church. "That church was very mission-minded," explained Coombs. "[T]here was no mission involved [in the Christmas visit], but there was love involved...the kids just loved visiting with my mother."[30]

◆ ◆ ◆

The majority of the school's administrators and faculty were dedicated to helping the students, according to Uyeki:

Most...were quite conscientious and supportive.... I don't recall any who were tyrannical or hostile.... [S]ome of the teachers were better prepared or [were] better teachers, but that's not different from [any school].... I think all of us students were gratified that the teachers were willing to come to the relocation centers to teach us. I'm sure that it was not a popular calling at the time.[31]

Wishing to ensure that universities around the country would honor the graduates' diplomas, the superintendent and the principal worked hard to get the school recognized by the North Central Accreditation Group before the end of the 1942–43 school year. Hunt High School became the first high school in the entire state to earn accreditation. "Once that news reached Idaho educators, they came to Hunt to see what we were doing," Coombs said.[32]

With some pride, Coombs called the school "the very best possible. We were very proud of the end result of our plans and our work. Our students upon graduation were accepted in many of the finest universities and colleges in the Midwest and the East Coast." The curriculum included "electives of all kinds" to fulfill graduation and college entrance requirements, said Coombs.

When the students began to apply for college, Uyeki recalled, Coombs and Helen Amerman counseled them about the specialties and entrance requirements of various colleges. Most of the teachers were helpful in writing recommendations for their students. However, enrollment was complicated by WRA regulations involving military security. Students were not permitted to attend schools located near railroads, war-related factories, or military training programs. They also needed a sponsor to accept responsibility for overseeing them, and they needed to demonstrate that they had funds for tuition, supplies and living expenses. Fathers Tibesar and Kitagawa and Reverend Machida coordinated their efforts with the Japanese American Student Relocation Program to help connect students with colleges, sponsors, scholarships, housing, employment and other needs.

◆　◆　◆

The teachers also helped organize and supervise extracurricular activities because "there was not much to do in this desert town surrounded by sagebrush

REGULAR SATURDAY NIGHT DANCES WERE A POPULAR FEATURE AT CAMP HIGH SCHOOLS. COURTESY OF THE BANCROFT LIBRARY, UNIVERSITY OF CALIFORNIA, BERKELEY, WRA PHOTOGRAPHS.

and barbed wire, " as Coombs put it.[33] Calvin Ninomiya added, "A continuing effort was made by the school authorities, and perhaps, more by the student government...to simulate the types of activities that they had enjoyed in their former school.... There were all sorts of student clubs [including homemaking, photography, drama, speech and science clubs], dances, sporting events. There were very successful student fairs and carnivals."[34]

According to Coombs, the teachers who lived at the camp were always happy to help after school and on the weekends.

> We did not like the idea that the youngsters whose living quarters were very small, whose study places were limited, of a weekend would just drift. So we had activities Saturday afternoons, and Saturday evenings we had dances. Friday evenings we would have parties for one reason or another. We would make up reasons for parties. Some of us would go into town to buy favors, crepe paper, napkins, and so on.[35]

In the 1943–44 school year, Coombs served as the teacher-advisor for both the student newspaper and the yearbook. Calvin Ninomiya was one of the students involved.

> The preparation and production of the student paper and the annual were largely extracurricular activities, and involved a considerable amount of evening work.... [O]n many occasions Bob went to his quarters after school ended, had dinner, and then walked [a half-mile] back to [school to] work with us on the paper or the annual.

HONOR ROLL OF MINIDOKA INTERNEES SERVING IN THE ARMED FORCES. COURTESY OF THE BANCROFT LIBRARY, UNIVERSITY OF CALIFORNIA, BERKELEY, WRA PHOTOGRAPHS.

> We encountered a "cost over-run" in producing the 1944 annual. Since I was the student editor, I had to confess to Bob late in the spring that we were over-budget. He has long claimed that I was the one who often counseled him: "no *shin-pai*," don't worry. At this critical instance, however, he was the one who made it possible for me to have "no *shin-pai*." He assured me that he would contact the local vendors who had done the engraving, layout and printing, and simply tell them that we had no more funds. He must have been persuasive, as we were never dunned for further payment.[36]

◆ ◆ ◆

In 1943, the WRA escalated its efforts to get the internees out of the camps and resettled outside of the West Coast. Efforts were made to recruit students into the army. None of Coombs's students enlisted, but many young Nisei did enlist or were drafted. A large billboard listing the names of those in the service was erected at the entrance to the camp, with

CAMP-MADE PICNIC
TABLES SERVED AS DESKS
FOR THE STUDENTS.
COURTESY OF THE BANCROFT LIBRARY,
UNIVERSITY OF CALIFORNIA, BERKELEY,
WRA PHOTOGRAPHS.

a gold star marking those killed in action. Those stars weighed heavily on Coombs's mind, and on the minds of the camp sentries as well.

> A number of the [guards] wondered just why they were there. Their cry was almost, "These are the mothers and fathers and brothers and sisters of boys that had been killed. We are guarding them!" This bothered them; it bothered them a lot.[37]

Coombs advised his tenth and eleventh graders that their first priority was to finish high school.

> Graduation from high school is the most important thing that you should have on your mind, and then the rest will take care of itself [b]ecause by the time you're a senior, you're going to have ideas of where you want to go and what you want to do.[38]

In his public-speaking class, he tried to get his students to plan for the future. "Now what?" he would ask them. "What's going to happen? What are we going to do? Where are we going?" His questions encouraged students to explore and act on their own thinking rather than simply trying to please their teachers or parents. And Coombs would not let his students sink into the inertia of hopelessness or resentment. "[T]ell me about something that's perfect," he challenged his class.[39] "...[T]here's no such thing as perfection. You do the best you can with what you have...." As their counselor and teacher, Coombs felt he had to speak bluntly yet lovingly. "[The] only way that they could get some kind of peace," he explained, "[was] to realize that this is an imperfect world, this is an imperfect time."

Coombs told his students they had their whole future ahead of them but "they had to work at it, work it out." The silver lining of the internment, he believed, was that by being uprooted from their segregated communities, students were exposed to opportunities and options they may not have previously conceived of. In the succeeding decades, he was proud that many former students were able to say, "I am somebody that I never thought I was ever going to be." Eugene Uyeki, for instance, became a sociology professor and provost of social and behavioral sciences at Case Western Reserve University, and Calvin Ninomiya a high-ranking official in the U.S. Treasury Department.

◆　◆　◆

The WRA was also encouraging entire families to leave camp and resettle outside the exclusion zone. The exodus created mixed emotions for the teachers because the brightest students with the most initiative worked the hardest at getting out of camp. "Just when we were getting going well with a group of youngsters, a family would leave to relocate. We lost many leaders that way," Coombs noted.[40]

Of course, the teachers were overjoyed to see their students regain their freedom. "[T]he WRA had one major aim and that was to relocate as many families as possible, as soon as possible. It was very necessary to prepare the families to move on east to make new homes and start a new life."[41] The teachers encouraged former students to stay in touch, and write to their former classmates about their experiences in the outside world. When discussed in class, these letters helped prepare more students to leave.

Sometime in the middle of the 1943–44 school year, school principal Jerome Light was transferred to an internment camp in Arizona. Always an outspoken advocate of the school and the students, he had clashed repeatedly with a camp administration that Coombs described as "manipulative"[42] and "aggressive."[43] He had also attracted jealousy from Idaho educators who resented the fact that the "Jap" camp's high school had won accreditation and was placing its students in some of the best Eastern schools. When Light was forced out, Eugene Uyeki remembered,

> [S]ome of the students thought of organizing a march to the administration to support him. We wondered if this would be effective or if the administration might feel threatened...so there was no student action. We had no specific information about the causes of the departure...but we had gotten to know him as sympathetic to our concerns. So we must have thought that the administration was removing him because he was supportive of the students.[44]

Coombs was also ignorant of the specifics of Light's departure. He admired Light greatly, however, and speculated that the principal was forced out partially by his own success. As the school's achievements received statewide attention, Idahoans came to view the camp's administrative positions as a source of fat salaries and personal advancement.

> Several of the Idaho teachers realized they would be better off out of the school and in the political end of it, and they pulled all the political strings necessary to get appointments up the "hill," as we called [the administration complex], to go on up the political [ladder] in the State of Idaho.... They had another agenda, and they thought we were a bunch of do-gooders, because we stuck our nose into the business of making sure everything was right for the young people.[45]

◆　◆　◆

After three years of internment, former internees return to Sacramento. Courtesy of The Bancroft Library, University of California, Berkeley, WRA Photographs.

Coombs himself left the camp in November 1944. After twenty-eight months at Minidoka, the pollen, lava dust and frigid winters had taken a toll on his health. Some teachers were being released because of declining enrollment, so he decided it was time to return to a healthier climate.

Marguerite Askew also left camp in 1944 to teach in Montana. "[A] warm and supportive person with a wonderful sense of humor," according to Uyeki, she and Coombs had developed a romance. But employment prospects were uncertain, and so was Coombs's health, so the couple decided to postpone tying the knot.

Back home in Sacramento, "it was not always a bed of roses," Coombs recalled, when he told people what he'd been doing for the past two years. "I took [the criticisms and hostility] on the chin," he said.[46] In his mind, he'd made his own unique contribution to the war effort, and "nobody could take it away from me."

When he heard of injustices, he did not hesitate to speak his mind. "One of the things I was unhappy about in this valley was the way some of the Japanese growers...were treated. Some of the Caucasian growers promised they would take care of the orchards, see that they were pruned.... In too many instances, folks came back and found their trees were shattered because of not being cared for."[47]

Coombs stayed with his mother and found work in the payroll office at McClellan Air Force Base. One day, he was startled to receive a phone call from Calvin Ninomiya. The young Nisei had been undergoing military training in Texas, when he was called home on a family emergency. He'd gotten as far as McClellan on a military transport, and needed a place to stay while he waited for a flight to Seattle. Coombs was delighted to invite him to stay with him and his mother. "I appreciated a sympathetic friend," Ninomiya recalled, "because...my father [had just been] killed in a hit-and-run death accident on the very day that he and my mother had returned home to Seattle after three years of confinement at Minidoka."[48]

Since Coombs and his mother had both lost family members early in life, they were able to offer the young man profound and wordless solace.

◆ ◆ ◆

In 1945, Coombs was able to return to teaching after his old mentor Mr. Burkhart became associate superintendent of the Sacramento school district. The prewar superintendent who had threatened to ban Coombs from teaching had departed.

Once his employment was secure, Coombs was free to marry his sweetheart, Marguerite Askew. Ninomiya said about her, "I always felt that Miss Askew was wonderfully professional and provided credibility for the level of instruction at Hunt High. She and Bob made a great couple, and were the parents of three children." Coombs worked as a teacher, and then as a junior high school counselor, until his retirement in 1978.

Hunt High School's first graduating class held its first reunion in 1983, forty years after they graduated. Alumni from all over the country gathered in Seattle to meet with classmates and eight of the teachers, including the Coombses and Helen Amerman Manning. It was the first time that most students and teachers had seen each other since they left camp. They were pleased to find that most of their classmates had settled into comfortable lives and interesting careers.

At the reunion, Coombs told his former students with characteristic modesty:

> Your future life was very important to us [teachers] and it is my hope that we were able to assist you so that your lives have been successful and happy. No matter how cold it was or how warm, windy or dusty, we all grew up in many ways with each other. My life was fulfilled because of my service to you.[49]

About his Minidoka mentor, Calvin Ninomiya wrote:

> If there is one quality that Bob has displayed consistently through his adult life, it is his unalterable sense of fairness. Although he says he took on teaching at Minidoka because his Sacramento students had been evacuated and he needed a job, the real truth is that it was his contribution to the nation's war effort to see loyal American youngsters... survive the most extraordinary trauma of their young lives. His legacy, and that of others like him who voluntarily shared the Japanese American war relocation experience can scarcely be assessed. Bob's life has been crowned in goodness. The humanity and compassion that he has extended to us over the years by both deed and thought have been truly superlative.[50]

MARY BLOCHER AND
RALPH SMELTZER JUST
AFTER THEIR MARRIAGE
IN 1940. COURTESY OF
MARY BLOCHER SMELTZER.

REV. RALPH AND MARY SMELTZER:
"WE WERE ALWAYS INTERESTED IN MAKING SOCIETY BETTER"

On the night of December 7, 1942, Ralph Smeltzer answered a frantic knock on the door. Smeltzer and his wife, Mary, were schoolteachers at Manzanar. Disdaining staff housing, they were living at the far corner of the camp as houseparents for a group of young internees. Earlier that day, there had been a demonstration, which had turned violent. *(See chapter: Helen Ely Brill.)* Now gangs of angry men were roaming the camp looking for people who had been denounced at a public meeting as government informers.

One of the hunted was Togo Tanaka, a neighbor and friend. It was Tanaka's wife who was at their door. She begged Smeltzer to drive her husband to safety. Before the war, Tanaka had been the English editor of *The Rafu Shimpo*, a Japanese American bilingual newspaper in Los Angeles. At Manzanar he worked as a "documentary historian" for the WRA's Japanese American Evacuation and Resettlement Study (JERS), headed by sociologist Dorothy Swaine Thomas. Some viewed the daily reports of camp activities that Tanaka wrote for her as spying for the government.

The internment had polarized feelings. Those who, before the war, had fought shoulder to shoulder for equal rights now found themselves on opposite sides. Tanaka's former friend Joe Kurihara became one of his most vociferous opponents, warning that the JERS reports could be used by the government "in ways that would be detrimental to us." While Tanaka and other JACLers urged

184

Manzanar Nisei to enlist in the U.S. Army to demonstrate their patriotism, Kurihara strongly disagreed, saying:

> I served my country, the United States of America, in World War I. I fought and bled on the battlefields of France, and I know what it means to...be willing to give my life for this country. But since this government...has seen fit to regard me as a "Jap," by God, I'm going to be a good Jap, 100%! I will never do anything to fight for the United States.[1]

Smeltzer was a conscientious objector himself, but he did not hesitate to act in the face of danger. He drove his car to the place where his frightened friend was hiding, clutching a knife for self-defense. Gently but firmly, he talked Tanaka into leaving the knife behind and spirited him into the car. As Tanaka crouched down on the floor of the car, Smeltzer sped without lights along the camp perimeter. It felt like the longest mile he had ever driven. As he approached the front gate, he gunned the engine and aimed the car at an angle across an open field. They reached the guardhouse safely, but the guards told Smeltzer that if they had been more alert, they would have shot at the vehicle as it raced toward them. Tanaka and over sixty others on the hit list were transferred for their own safety to a disused Civilian Conservation Corps camp in Death Valley before being resettled outside the exclusion zone.

MARY BLOCHER'S PARENTS, *UPPER LEFT,* ON THEIR WEDDING DAY IN 1901. MARY'S GRANDFATHER WAS A PREACHER IN THE CHURCH OF THE BRETHREN. COURTESY OF MARY SMELTZER.

◆　◆　◆

Smeltzer was an ordained minister in the Church of the Brethren, one of the three historic peace churches in the United States. The Brethren share similarities with the Mennonites and the Religious Society of Friends (Quakers) but have their own distinct origin and history. The denomination arose in Germany in 1708.[2] Although the Brethren held to no formal creed, their core beliefs emphasized a personal redemptive experience and reliance on the Holy Spirit and on the New Testament for guidance. They believed in emulating Christ by practicing peace, service and simple living. They founded their first American colony in Pennsylvania in 1723, and in the 1940s had about 180,000 members—mostly farmers and country folk, a mixture of liberals and conservatives, living primarily in the Tidewater states, in the Midwest and on the West Coast.

Ralph Smeltzer and his wife, Mary, were both born and raised in the church, and they maintained a lifelong commitment to social justice. Ralph Emerson Smeltzer was born in Chicago in May

26, 1916, and grew up in Southern California. Mary Evelyn Blocher was born in Texas on October 17, 1915. Her grandfather had been a Church of the Brethren preacher, and in 1921 her parents moved to La Verne, California, so that their children could attend Brethren schools. Mary and Ralph met in the late 1930s while attending La Verne College, a Brethren institution. Ralph was outgoing and energetic—a cheerleader, a member of the debate team and editor of the campus newspaper. "We had a lot in common," Mrs. Smeltzer remembered. "We were both interested in the same things. We were both outgoing people and we were always interested in making society better."[3] After Mary finished graduate school and began teaching in Northern California, Ralph proposed.

The couple was married on June 29, 1940. They taught for a year in the Imperial Valley before moving to Boyle Heights. In the spring of 1941, Smeltzer was ordained in the ministry. When required to register for the draft, he declared himself a conscientious objector to all military service, combatant or noncombatant.

Not long after Pearl Harbor, he paid a price for his pacifism. The Los Angeles school district directed its teachers to sell defense stamps to the students, and Smeltzer refused, offering to grow a victory garden instead.[4] The school district retaliated by taking away his job as a long-term substitute teacher, forcing him to take short-term assignments for the rest of the semester.

In March 1942, the Smeltzers attached the following statement to their income tax returns:

> We protest the use of this for war purposes. We feel it a privilege to contribute to the support of our democracy, the U.S.A. We do not believe in the method of War in solving its problems. Consequently—we strongly disapprove and protest the use of any of this money for war purposes.[5]

The FBI dispatched agents to investigate the young couple and considered placing them under "custodial detention." Neighbors, former employers and landlords confirmed that the Smeltzers were unquestionably loyal to the United States. They were "radical in respect to war" only because of their deeply held religious beliefs.

The Smeltzers were radical even for Brethren. Of their fellow parishioners at Calvary Church, Mrs. Smeltzer recalled:

> I think they felt like we did [that the internment was wrong], but they just weren't activists. They just let it go, just like a lot of church people now. Like, for instance, the war in Iraq. A lot of people didn't want it, but they just kind of let it go and don't do anything.... Of course peace people are stronger against it, but we can't do that much. I've often said about our church that society and the culture affect us much more than we affect them. That's just how it is. We're a small group.[6]

According to Mrs. Smeltzer, most Brethren are service oriented, but in a middle-class context. "They don't do very well relating to the poor. They do relief work, like helping after a natural disaster."[7] But the Smeltzers wanted to do more. "We weren't interested in the relief stuff. We were more interested in things that could change society."[8]

The Smeltzers found like-minded people at the monthly meetings of the American Friends Service Committee, which was attended by activists such as pacifist Congregational minister Allan Hunter and Quaker Herbert Nicholson.

Between March and May 1942, the Smeltzers logged almost 700 miles visiting Japanese American communities and attending meetings. "All spring," Mrs. Smeltzer wrote, "Ralph wrote long reports about the happenings and we would ride in the middle of the night downtown to the main L.A. post office to mail them to [church headquarters] in Elgin, Illinois."[9] When M. R. Zigler, director of the Brethren Service Committee (BSC), visited Southern California, the Smeltzers persuaded him to commit some of the BSC's limited resources to helping the Japanese Americans.

On February 26, the residents of Terminal Island were given forty-eight hours to leave their homes. In a letter to the Brethren Service Committee, Smeltzer wrote:

CHILDREN WAITING TO BE INTERNED. COURTESY OF THE BANCROFT LIBRARY, UNIVERSITY OF CALIFORNIA, BERKELEY, WRA PHOTOGRAPHS.

Although the Friends Service Committee had been making elaborate evacuation plans for several weeks they were caught off guard. Not altogether, however, for they had already been completing arrangements for temporary housing. Their evacuation personnel was not prepared and did not function except for a few persons who [happened to be] on the scene when the evacuation orders came. Our daily paper did not even carry the news and the first I knew of it was Dr. Bruff calling me...and asking if I would like to help about forty Japanese get settled temporarily in a Japanese language school near Whittier. It happened that I was not called to teach that day, Friday, February 27, so I went to [assist in any way I could]....

The atmosphere [at Terminal Island] was one of tension, nervousness, speed and confusion on the part of the evacuees and suspicion on the part of the army men who were riding up and down the street with their machine guns and fixed bayonets. The Baptist Mission and Miss Swanson...were assisting as the nerve center for the proceedings.... Mr. and Mrs. Nicholson and Bill Mahlin were the only Friends upon the scene. Two members of the Federal Security Agency were also lending a helping hand. You can imagine the exhaustion of these people who had worked all day Thursday, Thursday night and all day Friday. And you can also imagine the nervousness they felt...seeing a good number of...looters...stealing right and left...and finally realizing that the midnight deadline was fast approaching. I did what I could and then returned to Los Angeles with the Nicholsons.[10]

The Smeltzers assisted at the Evergreen Hostel, which was located near their Boyle Heights home, but, Smeltzer continued, "Until the Army makes its next announcements...we don't know how to plan or...what part we can or should play. Right now the entire service picture is quite hazy."

Within weeks, the evictions were in full swing. In one community after another, Japanese Americans received notices to report at designated sites to be transported to makeshift "assembly centers" at fairgrounds and racetracks. The American Friends Service Committee (AFSC) decided to serve breakfast to the departing internees, and the Smeltzers joined the effort, arising at 5 a.m. to offer a cup of coffee and a sandwich to the evictees as they prepared to be herded onto buses and trains. Since the pickups were scheduled for early morning hours, the Smeltzers could spend a couple of hours with the internees before work.

During summer vacation, the Smeltzers helped direct a Brethren work camp in Farmersville, near Visalia in Tulare County. They supervised young adults and college students who built a community house out of tamped earth and cement blocks, and operated a day camp for children of Dust Bowl migrants. They also sent a petition, signed by twenty individuals, to President Roosevelt and other government officials protesting the eviction.

> [T]hese Japanese-Americans are as good or better citizens than most of us, and to say that they are potentially more dangerous than some other group is fascist in the extreme unless well-backed up by facts....
>
> Reports of high anti-Japanese feeling have always been traceable to just one or two individuals to whom it would almost invariably be advantageous, in a business way, to have Japanese removed.... [T]he rest of the people around here...feel friendly toward them and sympathetic with their problems.[11]

The Japanese Americans had not yet been evicted from eastern California. The army had cleared the coastal areas first, declaring that those living in the eastern half of the state would not be interned. As a result, a number of Japanese Americans had relocated east of Highway 99. During the summer, the authorities decided to evict them as well.

DESPITE OPPOSITION FROM GROUPS LIKE THE AMERICAN LEGION, SOME CAUCASIANS WENT TO THE ASSEMBLY SITES TO SAY GOOD-BYE TO THEIR FRIENDS AND NEIGHBORS. COURTESY OF THE BANCROFT LIBRARY, UNIVERSITY OF CALIFORNIA, BERKELEY, WRA PHOTOGRAPHS.

The Smeltzers organized the churches in the nearby town of Lindsay to provide transportation for evictees who needed help getting to the assembly site. They also made plans to hand out lunches and refreshments as the departees boarded the train.

The military was grateful for the help, because no provisions had been made for feeding people in transit. But when the local American Legion post learned of the plans, veterans and police officers harassed the church groups. Mrs. Smeltzer recalled:

> The situation was so serious that all helpers were called together early on evacuation day to reconsider our plans and have a prayer meeting. We decided that Christianity was on trial in Lindsay that day, and we must go ahead. Our tormentors surrounded us at the train station, shook their fists, and hurled derogatory remarks, but did not harm us.[12]

◆ ◆ ◆

Looking ahead to the fall, the Smeltzers applied for work at Manzanar. Although Ralph originally hoped to do religious work, the couple was hired to teach high school math and biology. They moved to the camp in September. The camp itself was desolate, but Mary never tired of the Sierra Nevada. The peaks that rose in a steep wall just west of camp offered an endlessly fascinating visual feast as light shifted throughout the day, and snow levels and vegetation changed with the seasons.

The camp had Protestant, Catholic and Buddhist churches for the internees. The Smeltzers attended the Protestant church and, in the absence of a Nisei minister, soon found themselves helping provide leadership for the Nisei youth.

Mary vividly remembered when classes began in October.

> We started teaching in empty rooms. Students brought newspapers to sit on the floor as they leaned against the walls. We had one set of books for all our classes. In spite of all the handicaps, this proved to be one of the easiest teaching situations we ever had. Students were well-motivated and self-disciplined....
>
> Life at Manzanar was very oppressive to most "detainees" as well as to the Caucasian administrators and teachers. Caucasian personnel were housed in two separate blocks at the corner of the center and were not encouraged to fraternize with evacuees.... We became very uncomfortable living in separated and better conditions than the Japanese Americans.[13]

The Smeltzers applied for permission to live among the internees. Eventually, Margaret D'Ille, the director of social services, offered them positions as houseparents to a group of young Kibei men. Kibei had been born in the United States but educated in Japan. Many had become so immersed in Japanese language and culture that they had a very difficult time readjusting to American life. Incarceration in American concentration camps did nothing to increase their sense of belonging.

Being less Americanized than the Nisei, they preferred their own company, and a group of single Kibei men age eighteen to twenty were assigned to a dorm sponsored by the Young Men's Christian Association (YMCA). In Manzanar the organization was re-dubbed the YMA, Young Men's Association, to be inclusive of the many non-Christians.

AFTER REQUESTING CLOSER CONTACT WITH THE INTERNEES, THE SMELTZERS WERE ASSIGNED TO BE HOUSEPARENTS TO A GROUP OF YOUNG KIBEI MEN. *Courtesy of Mary Blocher Smeltzer.*

"We were in Block 36, Barrack 14, Apt. 1," Mary wrote, "the farthest possible block from the other *hakujin*, as the Caucasians were called."[14] The Smeltzers lived in a large room at one end of the barrack. As in a typical block, everyone used the bathroom and laundry facilities in the center of the block. The Smeltzers dined with their charges in the block mess hall every Saturday evening, but the rest of the week they were required to eat at the staff dining hall at the other end of camp. They drove back and forth to work and meals in their "trusty Model A Ford."

"We had good times and good relationships with the young men, enjoying their music and art," Mary wrote. A young man named George Yano gave the Smeltzers a set of twelve "priceless" watercolor paintings. The exquisitely rendered Manzanar scenes are still treasured by the Smeltzer family.[15] In spite of the weekly meals together and occasional parties in the Smeltzers' room, the Kibei remained reserved and diffident. "I don't feel like we really knew them," Mary admitted. "They were very Japanese-y. I imagine [George Yano, the young painter,] went back to Japan long ago."[16]

Their neighbor Togo Tanaka helped them understand the gap between the Kibei and the Nisei. Later Tanaka recalled:

There was this terrible division within the camp between those who spoke and thought in the English language and those who spoke and thought in the Japanese. In the midst of war, it was an impossible situation.[17]

The Kibei might have eventually warmed up to the Smeltzers, but the couple stayed in Manzanar for just six months. "From the time we arrived at Manzanar until we left," Mrs. Smeltzer wrote, "we worked to get the Japanese Americans out of the concentration camps."

As Ralph Smeltzer tried to help the internees find ways to get out, his correspondence with the BSC barely hid his frustrations with the gap between the internees' needs and what the BSC was prepared to offer. In November, Leland S. Brubaker, the BSC's director of relief and rehabilitation, wrote that the BSC had notified the Students Relocation Council that four small Brethren colleges and a seminary were willing to accept students of "Christian character," but no applicants had yet been heard from. Could the Smeltzers recruit applicants at Manzanar?[18]

SMELTZER WITH A
TODDLER AT THE
BROOKLYN HOSTEL.
COURTESY OF THE BANCROFT LIBRARY,
UNIVERSITY OF CALIFORNIA, BERKELEY,
WRA PHOTOGRAPHS.

Smeltzer replied:

> We are glad to know that Brethren Colleges want Japanese students.... Incidentally the third one applying at Manchester happened...to be a fellow here—a grand boy, leader of the Manzanar Christian young people and a strong pacifist. Unfortunately Manchester decided it could not afford three Japanese students and turned down his application. Drake University is to benefit now by his presence....
>
> If we had known other Brethren Colleges would accept students we would have been urging applications there.... The reason you have not heard further from the student relocation council is that there have been no students interested in our colleges.... Brethren Colleges are unknown among Japanese.... [H]aving attended large universities in the west, they are reluctant to even consider small schools in the east....
>
> You indicated that the BSC stands ready to help them financially if it is necessary. We are glad to hear this as those students who have been able to pay their own way have already been relocated for the most part. In relocating additional students, the student relocation council has all but exhausted its funds.... We are contacting various students who we feel would fit into our colleges.[19]

The Smeltzers persuaded Joe Nagano to apply to Juniata, but his acceptance was withdrawn at the last minute. (*See chapter: Helen Ely Brill.*) Juniata's president complained that Nagano's financial need was greater than the college was prepared to meet, and that "some of my friends have suggested that [Nagano's enrollment] might be opening a sore spot in the community."[20]

The Smeltzers replied:

> Since living here with these people we have grown to know them, love them and have such confidence in many of them that we do not realize how people feel who do not know them personally....

> You can no doubt sense the feeling that came over us when the telegram arrived asking Joe to change his plans.... Your community situation must of course be considered and you no doubt know much more about handling it than we do. It seems to us, however, that the only way that Japanese Americans can ever be accepted...is to just go there and live as normal a life as possible.[22]

The Smeltzers also had to contend with Anetta Mow, the director of the BSC's clothing department, who wrote:

> [D]uring the past year, it has been impossible to send shipments to Shanghai, China, and the clothing has been accumulating in our three storerooms.... If you could use the clothing [at Manzanar], it would certainly be a splendid way to put it to use.

> Of course it is true that relief clothing...is not of uniform type. We have constantly urged that all clothing be clean, repaired and in good wearable condition. Nevertheless, some people seem to fail to read the instructions as thoroughly as they should.[23]

Smeltzer replied that the new WRA clothing allowance would help alleviate the need for used clothing and added, "In many cases Japanese are too proud to accept used clothing or any other form of charity."[24] There were exceptions, he continued, and several groups had asked him for used clothing to make rag rugs and other sewing projects.

Smeltzer said nothing about Mow's offer to send Sunday school craft projects as Christmas presents or about her enthusiastic endorsement of the bundles of "little Eagle Booklets" she was putting in the mail:

> All age groups from the Juniors through to adults find these booklets intensely interesting because the stories are well written and they are quite thrilling. I hope those who receive them will realize that they are fine stories of outstanding Christian men and women.[25]

The Smeltzers received this letter about a week after the "Manzanar riot." Two internees were dead, including a 17-year-old high school student, and nine others were wounded. With schools and churches closed and the camp under martial law, Smeltzer could only reply, "We are glad for the concerned attitude you have shown toward our work. We too believe [helping the internees] is in accord with our 'creed' and that our church should be doing more about it."[26]

◆ ◆ ◆

By this time the Smeltzers had decided on a way to be of substantial assistance to internees wishing to leave Manzanar. As early as July 1942, even as they were still filling the camps, the WRA was developing policies to encourage internees to apply for "indeterminate leave" and "permanent resettlement" away from the West Coast. The WRA's plans to move large numbers of people out of the camps were met with resistance on several fronts. Many Issei were reluctant to leave camp for an uncertain future in an unknown state. Many communities were hostile to the idea of accepting Japanese American residents. And although many Nisei were eager for a taste of freedom, their parents were anxious about sending them into a potentially hostile environment. Applications for leave clearance also met with many delays within a convoluted bureaucracy.

"At first," Mary Smeltzer remembered, "the only way a person could get out of camp was to secure a job before leaving. For most this was practically impossible to do."[27] Thomas Temple, Manzanar's chief of community services, made an exploratory trip through the East and Midwest. He and two Nisei who had made a similar trip reported that many employers outside the exclusion zone were receptive to hiring Japanese Americans. The Smeltzers decided to develop a resettlement hostel in Chicago where internees could stay until they found jobs and permanent housing.

Through the BSC, they learned that enrollment had dropped because of the draft at Bethany Theological Seminary, a Brethren institution in Chicago, Illinois. The school was willing to host up to fifteen internees in its dormitories. On January 10, 1943, Thomas Temple took a group of thirteen Nisei to Bethany on a trial run. The young men quickly found jobs at the Curtiss Candy Company, the Cuneo Press and other companies. Just as rapidly, Temple became disenchanted with:

> ...the grand scramble to get on the band wagon and take credit for the hostel idea.... Tom Holland and a young Japanese...buzzed around telling me how pleased they were with "their idea."... After three or four days of watching both the Friends and the WRA...I came to the conclusion that I would withdraw and let them go about their business in their own way."[28]

"A friendly handshake, a helping hand and a warm greeting from the hostel directors make relocation seem worth all of its courage and effort to this young lady and her elderly mother," according to the slide-show script. *Courtesy of the Church of the Brethren Historical Library and Archives.*

The hostel on Sheridan Road was in a sprawling old mansion on the Chicago lakefront. The slide-show script read, "[I]t provided a colorful contrast to the old drab dusty relocation camp barracks. What a welcome sight after a long, hard, dirty train ride!" Courtesy of the Church of the Brethren Historical Library and Archives.

Smeltzer wrote back:

> Our experience with the WRA here and...with the AFSC somewhat bears out your criticism. It is unfortunate that there can't be more cooperation. Jealousy and narrow-mindedness does our cause no good.[29]

Temple and a group of internees rented a couple of apartments in Chicago's South Side where they could live cooperatively. He wrote Smeltzer to suggest that they collaborate to open their own employment hostel, independent of the WRA and the AFSC.

> So many of the placements which have been made through other churches seem to be unsuccessful and unsatisfactory. It seems to be a policy to find a hole and then force someone into it—regardless of suitability or acceptability. There are plenty of jobs open of all kinds.... [A] few days' effort will generally result in finding the right sort of opportunity.[30]

Meanwhile, Brubaker offered the Smeltzers positions as directors of the Bethany hostel at a salary of $100 per month, which was twenty-five dollars less than the going rate for live-in domestic help. As for Temple, Brubaker wrote, "We have stated that Temple is not at all connected officially with the BSC.... We intend to work very closely with the WRA, the Friends, the Methodists...and any other who might be interested in this work."[31] A week later, Brubaker wrote that Temple was developing plans for long-term co-op living arrangements, but that "it is not the purpose of the BSC to develop permanent living quarters for Japanese.... [W]e do hope

these people can be kept moving."[32] Temple went his own way and eventually bought a house on the South Side to use for long-term resettlement.

In March 1943, Ralph Smeltzer drove the Model A to Chicago, stopping in Arizona at Poston and Gila River to publicize the new hostel and set up a referral network. Meanwhile, Mary accompanied five Nisei by bus and train.

Bethany Seminary was located on the near Westside. The hostelers used the institution's existing services, sleeping in the student dormitories and eating at the seminary "boarding club."[33] With the booming war economy, jobs were plentiful in Chicago, so the average hostel stay was less than two weeks. The Smeltzers contacted administrators at several camps to arrange for a regular influx of internees.

The FBI continued to keep an eye on the Smeltzers, checking for evidence of subversive activity and monitoring their activities at the hostel. Not until

September 1943 did they finally conclude that the couple was "extremely religious and friendly to the Japanese," but that there was no indication they were undermining the war effort.[34] By this time, Ralph was also serving as director of the Ministry to Resettlers for the Church Federation of Greater Chicago.

Meanwhile, various church and community groups opened hostels in cities such as Minneapolis, Cleveland, Des Moines, Cincinnati and St. Louis. The WRA opened relocation offices to help resettlers find work. Internees could apply to the hostel of their choice directly from the internment camps. At Bethany Hostel, hostel secretary Virginia Asaka (later Morimitsu) handled applications from the camps, and the Smeltzers offered counseling on jobs and housing. Mrs. Smeltzer observed:

> It took quite a brave person to come to a strange city after having been locked up for six to eighteen months. Many families in the centers felt it risky to let their children...go out alone into a hostile unknown world. The hostel served as a bridge, a safe and secure place to begin a new life.[35]

But the reception was not always positive. Mrs. Smeltzer will never forget taking Mr. Minowa to the county hospital when he fell ill. He was an older man whose blue eyes betrayed his half-German and half-Japanese heritage. The hospital staff "just looked daggers" at him, Mrs. Smeltzer recalled.[36] More than sixty years later she said, "I can [still] almost feel the look on their faces when I brought that man there." Fortunately, Mr. Minowa received adequate treatment and recovered from his illness.

The slide show's description of the Sheridan Road hostel's fifteen-bed men's dormitory read, "Notice the many comforters made by Brethren women. One hundred of these beautiful comforters were made available to the hostel by the BSC." Courtesy of the Church of the Brethren Historical Library and Archives.

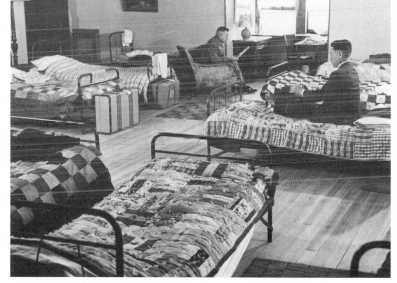

In the fall, the Smeltzers moved the hostel to 6118 North Sheridan Road, an old mansion on the lakefront near Evanston. Formerly used as a rest home, the three-story house could accommodate thirty-five hostelers per day. The average age was twenty-two, and the average length of stay was less than twelve days. Hostelers were expected to pay a dollar a day for room and board, which rose to $1.50 once they found a job. Bertha and Charles Kimmel, who had been employed in the Civilian Public Service, volunteered to help run the hostel.[37] According to an informational brochure, the Smeltzers had a busy schedule:

> The directors stand ready to welcome resettlers and to give a helping hand where it is needed: finding jobs and homes, giving advice about Chicago,

The Greater New York Resettlement Hostel in Brooklyn. The Smeltzers are in the second row from the top. Courtesy of the Church of the Brethren Historical Library and Archives.

introducing strangers, referring hostelers to places of entertainment or worship, storing baggage, counseling on various personal problems, providing recreational and social activities and visiting former hostelers. In addition to being host and hostess, they keep records, pay the bills, repair the premises and keep the hostel operating smoothly. As mother and father of the large hostel family, theirs is a twenty-four hour job, without including calls to interpret the hostel program to civic and church groups. The hostel directors endeavor to make relocation as easy and attractive as possible for those persons still in relocation centers.[38]

By March 1944, more than 1,000 former internees had passed through the Bethany and Sheridan hostels. At the time, resettlement policy favored dispersing Japanese Americans within the general population, on theory that "Little Tokyo" enclaves would discourage "assimilation" and attract resentment. After discussions with an interdenominational resettlement committee and with the WRA, the Smeltzers decided to close the hostel on Sheridan Road, even though they had recently renewed the lease.

The WRA suggested opening a hostel in New York City, and after a survey of various boroughs, J. Henry Carpenter of the Brooklyn Council of Churches helped the Smeltzers locate a former fraternity house in Brooklyn. It was a typical row house on Clinton Street in a neighborhood with many doctors' and dentists' offices. Shortly before the lease was signed, a local newspaper published news about the planned hostel.

Resettlement efforts in Chicago had met with little local resistance, but New York mayor Fiorello La Guardia and New Jersey governor Walter Edge made public statements opposing the resettlement of Japanese Americans to their area. In Brooklyn, 136 neighbors signed a petition opposing the hostel. The controversy raged for a month and made national news. Most local newspapers and religious and service organizations supported the hostel, but the American Legion and the Veterans of Foreign Wars adamantly opposed it. The fraternity postponed signing the lease several times. When threats were made to the Smeltzers' lives and property, the local WRA administrator offered to let them back out of the project. The Smeltzers refused.

On May 2, 1944, officials of Alpha Chi Rho met to decide whether to approve the lease. Four national board members, including a congressman and a naval officer, participated in the decision to lease the house and support the hostel.

About a week later, the first resettlers arrived. The press was camped on the doorstep and a policeman was posted in front. A small crowd gathered to demonstrate their opposition, but no trouble developed. For some weeks, the policeman visited regularly to record the names and the comings and goings of the resettlers. But the hostel soon became an unremarkable part of the neighborhood. In the first year of operation, it served over 700 former internees.

In August 1944, after the Brooklyn hostel had been operating for several months, the Smeltzers turned over its operation to Cecile Burke and moved to Elgin, Illinois, where Ralph had been offered a position as administrative assistant at the Brethren Service headquarters.

The Smeltzers were not yet thirty at the time, but they were to devote the rest of their lives to public service. Ralph oversaw Japanese American resettlement work from Elgin, and then directed Brethren Service relief work with displaced persons in war-torn Austria from 1946 to 1949. In 1953, after attending graduate school at the University of Chicago Divinity School, he became director of peace and social education for the Brethren Service Commission.

During the 1960s, he became involved in the civil rights movement, earning the title of the "peacemaker of Selma." He became a social justice consultant for the World Ministries Commission in 1968. In 1971, he moved to Washington, D.C., to direct the Church of the Brethren's Washington office and represent the church's peace position during the Vietnam era.

Ralph died of a heart attack in 1976, just short of his sixtieth birthday. After his death, Mary joined the Peace Corps and taught in Botswana for two years. In 1982, she worked for a year at the World Friendship Center in Hiroshima, Japan. She now lives in a Church of the Brethren retirement community in La Verne. Now almost ninety, she is not as active as she used to be, but she still volunteers with troubled youth. Sturdy and unpretentious, she remains gracious and friendly to all, ready to speak about the injustice of the internment to anyone who asks. In 1975, she wrote:

> As I reflect on our work with the Japanese Americans, I have a stronger feeling than ever that the entire evacuation was a very evil and unjustified affair. No matter what we...or the Church of the Brethren did, this deep scar will remain on our history—an event that says much about us as a nation.[39]

IN 1948, RALPH WAS JOINED IN AUSTRIA BY MARY AND THEIR TWO DAUGHTERS. COURTESY OF MARY BLOCHER SMELTZER.

JACK IKEMOTO AND FAMILY WITH ELIZABETH "LIBBY" WILBUR AT THE FRIENDS HOSTEL IN DES MOINES, IOWA. COURTESY OF THE BANCROFT LIBRARY, UNIVERSITY OF CALIFORNIA, BERKELEY, WRA PHOTOGRAPHS.

ROSS AND LIBBY WILBUR:
ROOMS, MEALS AND FELLOWSHIP IN DES MOINES

Seventy percent of those who left camp in 1943 and 1944 were between the ages of fifteen and thirty-five. Marvin Uratsu had not even graduated from high school when he decided to venture forth from camp:

When the notorious segregation program was implemented, our family was sent from Tule Lake [internment camp in California] to Amache, Colorado. I had just finished my junior year at...Tri State High School in [Tule Lake].... "A]fter arriving at Amache, I sought permission...to leave camp and finish my senior year at an "outside" school, thinking it would enhance my chances to enter college. Of all the places available to me, I chose Des Moines, Iowa, not even knowing exactly where it was. I was so happy to get out of camp, it did not matter where I went, so long as it was "outside."

I left camp...by train and on the next morning early, I arrived at the depot in Des Moines. As soon as we arrived, even before I wondered what to do next, a gentleman came up to me, picked up my small suitcase containing all my worldly goods and introduced himself as Ross Wilbur, director of the Friends hostel in Des Moines. It was a great relief for me to be met like that. It simply was a great feeling.

He took me to the hostel located at 2150 Grand Avenue in his station wagon. Shortly thereafter, [after giving me a chance to freshen up], Mr. Wilbur said, "Let's sit down and talk about what you would like to do." I told him I would like to earn my room and board by doing odd jobs around the house where I was to stay and go to school. Right away, he said he knew a family interested in having a "schoolboy."

On the same afternoon, Mr. Wilbur arranged an interview for me with a Mrs. Margaret Allen...and within another couple of hours I had a place to stay...[while I finished] my senior year at the Theodore Roosevelt High School in Des Moines.

Through all these years, I have not forgotten what the Friends did for me. Now when I look back...my time with the Friends and Mr. Wilbur was very short...for me but it was a giant step forward.[1]

Uratsu was one of over 700 guests who stayed at the American Friends Hostel in Des Moines during its two-year existence.[2] The ten-room boarding house was leased by the American Friends Service Committee in September 1943. It was a rambling old house near the train tracks that had seen better days, but it was a definite improvement over camp. After the hostel's first director, a conscientious objector, was drafted and assigned to a medical unit, the establishment was operated by Ross and Libby Wilbur, an energetic young Quaker couple with a baby daughter. Ross, a social worker, was paid $100 a month.

Journalist Bill Hosokawa, who later authored *Nisei: The Quiet Americans,* stayed at the Des Moines Hostel for ten days in October 1943. Hosokawa had worked as a reporter in Singapore and Shanghai before the war. He and his young family had returned to the United States just weeks before Pearl Harbor. They were interned at Heart Mountain, where Hosokawa edited the weekly *Heart Mountain Sentinel.* WRA director Dillon S. Myer met him on an inspection tour of the Wyoming internment camp, and persuaded his friend, newspaper owner Gardner Cowles, to hire Hosokawa as a copy editor for *The Des Moines Register.*

Like many resettlers, Hosokawa left his family behind in camp while he established a foothold in his new city. He went to work at 5 p.m. and returned to the hostel at 2 or 3 a.m. He spent his days looking for a place to live. After he found suitable housing, Hosokawa sent for his wife and son.

The Des Moines Relocation Committee and a local coalition of churches, schools and individuals contributed to the hostel's upkeep, but the Wilburs stretched the hostel budget by being resourceful. They supplemented the menu with chickens and rabbits raised in the backyard, and fresh and home-canned

ROSS WILBUR, *RIGHT,* AND AN INTERNEE MOVE FURNITURE. COURTESY OF THE BANCROFT LIBRARY, UNIVERSITY OF CALIFORNIA, BERKELEY, WRA PHOTOGRAPHS.

vegetables from their vegetable garden. To pay for a Christmas Eve turkey, the Wilburs had to take up a special collection from residents and visitors. The holiday meal occasioned mixed feelings, since almost everyone still had family behind barbed wire.

By September 1944, some 500 former internees had settled in the Des Moines area, including sixty families. During the previous ten months, an average of eighteen people a day had stayed at the hostel for periods ranging from a few days to several weeks. The Wilburs organized a furniture pool, from which resettlers could borrow basic household furnishings until they could afford to purchase their own.

In March 1945, WRA photographer Hikaru Iwasaki shot a series of photos of the hostel and of former internees who had resettled in the area. The glossy photos and chattily informative captions were intended to encourage internees back at the camps to take a leap into the unknown. The caption to one photo of hostel guests reads:

> Mr. Sakamoto, an accountant, is employed by the Iowa Power and Light Company, and Mrs. Sakamoto acts as dietitian at the Hostel. Mr. Oji has been picking tomatoes for a cannery; Mr. Yoshida is steward at the Hawkeye Post of Jewish War Veterans; Miss Kanatani, who is employed in the Kansas City, Missouri Relocation Office, is visiting at the Hostel; and James Chikahisa is a print shop worker at *The Advertising Press*.[3]

Iwasaki photographed Issei Asajiro Nishimoto, formerly of Los Angeles and the internment camp at Jerome, Arkansas, managing the produce department at Love's Modern Meat and Food Market. Nishimoto said, "The people are very nice here. I hope to stay." Sally Kusayanagi, a stenographer at National Screen Corporation reported, "The people I am staying with are a minister and his wife, who are more than hospitable to me. As for the place I am working, it is just grand. The people here have accepted us as one of them, and they treat us swell." Sachi Furuto, a coworker, added, "Our employer himself has more than willingly taken us in. The other employees have followed him, and accepted us as one of them."[4]

Other Japanese Americans were photographed as they attended Drake University, and worked in factories, locker rooms, gas stations and restaurants. A handful were working as professionals—pharmacist, physician, school principal, osteopath—but the majority were working in menial positions: factory hands, locker-room attendants, clerks, building custodians, waitresses, cooks, gas station attendants.

There were isolated instances of discrimination, but not at the virulent levels expressed in California. Neighbors objected when Henry Miyahara bought a home in Des Moines, but Bill Hosokawa purchased a home in August 1944 and stayed in Des Moines until June 1946, when he began a long and distinguished association with *The Denver Post.*

The International Association of Machinists, Des Moines local, refused to issue union cards to Japanese American machinists. But Jeri Tanaka completed courses at West Technical High School and landed a job as a welder at the Modern Lighting and Manufacturing Company. Like many others, she left camp alone and sent for her mother and sister after she got settled.[5]

By the fall of 1945, as the stream of resettlers slowed, AFSC headquarters decided to close the Des Moines hostel. The 727th and last guest was registered on October 26. The furniture was sold and arrangements were made for other groups to carry on the hostel's role as a Japanese American community center. Ross Wilbur landed a new job as a state child-welfare consultant.

A couple of weeks before the hostel closed, Ross and Libby Wilbur held a "sayonara tea." Present and former guests gathered to share memories and say good-bye. They took up a collection and presented the Wilburs with a farewell gift of $150.[6]

Ross Wilbur sent the money to the AFSC office in Philadelphia as payment for a farewell gift of their own to the Japanese American community: the keys to the rusty '35 station wagon that had met Marvin Uratsu and so many others at the train station.

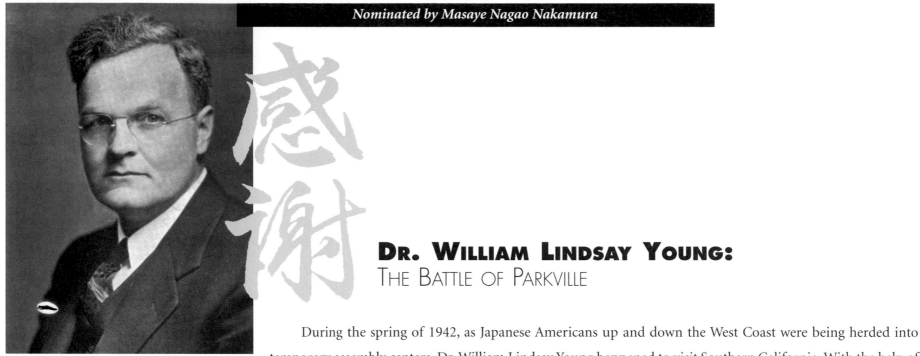

DR. WILLIAM LINDSAY YOUNG:
THE BATTLE OF PARKVILLE

WILLIAM LINDSAY
YOUNG,
C. 1941. COURTESY
OF FISHBURN ARCHIVES,
PARK UNIVERSITY.

During the spring of 1942, as Japanese Americans up and down the West Coast were being herded into temporary assembly centers, Dr. William Lindsay Young happened to visit Southern California. With the help of Raymond Booth of the AFSC's Pasadena office, Young was able to visit some Japanese Americans in their homes and neighborhoods, as well as at the Santa Anita Assembly Center. As the president of Park College, a small liberal arts college near Kansas City, Missouri, Young was particularly concerned about the Nisei college students whose educations were being abruptly cut short by the internment. He returned to Missouri determined to do what he could to help them.

With a determined jaw and steely eyes framed by metal-rimmed spectacles, Young cut an imposing figure. He had made a dramatic rise from dire poverty to the highest rungs of leadership in the Presbyterian Church. Young, who was born in Illinois in 1893, had to change schools twenty-two times before the fifth grade as his father, a Scottish coal miner, moved the family from one coal field to another. Young himself went to work in the mines at age thirteen, and later worked as a steelworker, steam fitter and plumber.[1]

Marrying Theresa Kruger in 1916 represented a turning point. The young couple worked hard to put themselves through school, and in less than ten years, Young was university pastor at the University of Montana, where he also founded and directed a school of religion. He then worked for the National Board of Christian Education of the Presbyterian Church before becoming president of Park College in 1937. A biographical sketch from the period reads,

> Dr. Young's intimate acquaintance with poverty and toil in his youth, his rapid intellectual achievements and his swift rise to leadership in the church all fit him perfectly for the Presidency of Park College. At Park every resident student has a part-time job.... By earning part of their expenses many worthy and capable young people have received an education who couldn't hope to get it otherwise. More important is the practical training young people get, before graduation, in the duties they will face later in the work-a-day world. "The need of the day is for men and women who aren't afraid of work, who know how to use their hands, who are conscious of the dignity of labor, who know how to work creatively and co-operatively in an increasingly complex and maladjusted society," says Dr. Young.[2]

Young believed that Park's primary objective was "to aid students in Christian character growth," but his view of a Christian education was not limited to academics.

> The professor of Bible is no more responsible for advancing the Kingdom of God than any other professor or member of the administrative staff. Caretakers, workers in the green house, the farm, the heat plant, the carpenter shop, the print shop, the Commons [the kitchen and dining hall], should be individuals whose influence is of a positive Christian character.[3]

Furthermore, he was committed to the "growing edge" of social change:

> Every social advance involves disturbances that tax the patience and understanding on the part of all who would be creatively helpful in the process.... Theologically, politically and socially, [my predecessor Dr. Hawley] was to the right of center while I was to the left.... I came to Park with no preconceived blueprint for changing its social, religious or educational program. I preferred to exercise patience in first getting an understanding of the entire situation. Once I found the growing edge I began to formulate plans to aid and abet the growing process....[4]

The new president increased student and faculty input into Park's decision-making processes, and counted as one of his proudest achievements the beginning of a slow and gradual campaign to admit Negro students. When Young had arrived at Park, he recalled,

> No Negro could eat in the commons or worship in the chapel.... Such steps as the following were taken. The Kansas City YMCA was invited to bring its members, including Negroes, to an all-day conference on campus where both the commons and the chapel were used. Great Negro leaders...were invited to speak at school assemblies with the children from the Negro school invited to attend as guests. The local Negro minister...was invited to audit some Bible courses.... Finally, Negroes of the Parkville community were invited to attend the college motion picture shows for the first time. The end

result [in 1950] was the admittance of Negroes as regular students.[5]

Young's dynamic leadership and his skills as an articulate speaker and writer did not go unnoticed. In 1940 he became one of the youngest men ever to be elected to the highest office in the Presbyterian Church: moderator of the General Assembly.

When he finished out his year's term in May 1941, he and his wife, Theresa, were honored by Park's board of trustees. "These two," the commemorative program read, "whom we honor tonight represent the democratic way of life we treasure and defend in America. In our land of liberty and opportunity they have risen from the ranks to occupy positions of high trust and leadership."[6]

Young was less than fifty years old and at the apex of his career. It is not surprising that he believed he had the power and the duty to help the displaced Nisei that he had met in Southern California.

◆　◆　◆

Young was not the only educator who wanted to help the young Nisei. On March 21, barely a month after President Roosevelt signed E.O. 9066, educators, students and representatives from religious groups met in Berkeley, California, to coordinate efforts to help Nisei college students continue their studies outside the exclusion area.[7] The meeting was hosted by Henry Kingman of the UC Berkeley YMCA and attended by officials from thirty West Coast schools, including presidents Lee Paul Sieg of the University of Washington, Robert Gordon Sproul of UC Berkeley, and Remsen Bird of Occidental College. Participants agreed to establish the Student Relocation Committee, and Quaker Joseph Conard was named executive secretary. Funds would be solicited from the YMCA and YWCA to open a central clearinghouse in Berkeley to coordinate the work that had already begun in the Pacific Northwest and Northern and Southern California. Sproul stated that Nisei college students represented the best of future Japanese American leadership. An investment in their good treatment and education was "insurance" in future relationships with Japanese American community.

PARK COLLEGE IN 1938 WITH THE TOWN OF PARKVILLE IN THE FOREGROUND. COURTESY OF FISHBURN ARCHIVES, PARK UNIVERSITY.

At around the same time, W. C. Coffey, president of the University of Minnesota, circulated a letter to his Midwest colleagues to test the waters. A number of voluntary resettlers had arrived at his doorstep seeking admission to his university, and he was concerned that an over-concentration of Nisei at one school would draw negative public attention to both the students and the school. His colleagues expressed varying degrees of sympathy for the Nisei students, but were concerned about opposition from their boards or from the community. Coffey then turned for help to Milton Eisenhower, the first director of the WRA, reasoning that a national student relocation program would be able to deflect public criticism from the admitting institutions and scatter students in small numbers to a large number of schools.

In early May, Eisenhower asked Clarence Pickett, executive secretary of the American Friends Service Committee, to organize a national student relocation committee. The WRA would select and certify the students, Eisenhower wrote Pickett, but the government could not be seen as "coddling" the Japanese Americans. Therefore, it was necessary to establish an independent, privately funded agency to generate public acceptance of student relocation, to persuade educational institutions and their local communities to accept the students, and to raise funds for both student aid and for its own operation. Pickett convened an organizing conference in Chicago later that month, which was attended by prominent educators and representatives of religious organizations, as well as the YMCA, the YWCA, the JACL and the AFSC. The meeting established the Student Relocation Council (later renamed the National Japanese American Student Relocation Council) to carry on the work that had been started in Berkeley by the Student Relocation Committee. (*See box: Tom Bodine and Harvey Itano's Independence Day.*) At the time, it was estimated that 2300 college students had had their college educations interrupted by internment.

To defuse public opposition and preserve the myth that mass incarceration was a military necessity, an elaborate selection process was devised. Students could only attend schools that had been cleared by the military, which meant no institutions that conducted defense training or research or that were located within twenty-five miles of major power installations, defense industries, or railroad terminals. Thus, military restrictions ruled out many institutions in urban areas, including ones headed by some of the most ardent supporters of student relocation. Such conditions forced many students to look to small, obscure colleges like Park.

Student applicants were ranked according to academic and personal qualifications; they had to provide character references and show bankbooks. Before they left camp, they had to be accepted by a school and provide evidence that they had the financial

UNIVERSITY OF COLORADO, BOULDER.
Responding quickly to appeals from the West Coast, the university regents declared in March 1942 that they would accept Japanese American students.[8] By July, a plan was developed to accept up to sixty out-of-state Nisei, distributed among the various colleges to reduce the impact of their presence. Because of prescreening imposed by the U.S. Army, no more than twenty out-of-state Nisei were ever enrolled at any one time.[9] Total Nisei enrollment peaked at seventy-two, including Colorado residents.

UNIVERSITY OF NEBRASKA. About fifty Nisei students were admitted to the University of Nebraska in the fall of 1942 with help from Chancellor Chauncey S. Boucher, Registrar George Rosenlof, and members of the campus faculty and ministry. Below, from left: George John Furutani, Sukeo Oji and Joe Nishimura.[10]
COURTESY OF THE BANCROFT LIBRARY, UNIVERSITY OF CALIFORNIA, BERKELEY, WRA PHOTOGRAPHS.

backing to pay for tuition and expenses for a year. With their parents behind barbed wire, students needed a patchwork of scholarships, grants, part-time jobs and savings to meet the financial requirements. The applicants also needed sponsors in the receiving community, and statements from the mayor, police chief or other community officials that there was no reason for them not to come.

Joe Conard's uncle Henry Conard of Grinell College in Iowa was an early supporter of student relocation. Grinell offered two full scholarships, and by May, three Nisei students had arrived on campus to a cordial reception by the students. But most Nisei applicants would spend a long and frustrating summer behind barbed wire.

Margaret Cosgrave, registrar at Fresno State College, had been alerted to the problem of relocation in early spring when several Nisei students sought her help in transferring outside the exclusion zone. She traveled to Berkeley in March to attend the Student Relocation Council's organizational meeting, and returned later to devote her summer vacation to the effort. She described the student relocation office as busy and enthusiastic, if lacking in the necessary experience to evaluate students properly.[11] It was not until after school started in September that the first two students from Fresno State were able to leave the Fresno Assembly Center. *(See box: Margaret Cosgrave and Mary Baker.)*

◆   ◆   ◆

Meanwhile, back in Missouri, William Lindsay Young had stayed in touch with Raymond Booth of the AFSC, who connected him with Joe Conard when the Student Relocation Council was organized. By June 1942, Young had secured agreement from Park's faculty and its board of trustees to accept six Nisei for admission in the fall, provided they (1) could demonstrate the ability to do college-level work; (2) were native-born U.S. citizens; (3) were a members of a Christian church; and (4) had the necessary financial resources.[12] But Young was

Margaret Cosgrave and Mary Baker

Kazue Sekiya Iwatsubo recalled, "At the time of internment, I lived in Fresno and was a sophomore at Fresno State College. There were quite a few Japanese Americans at the school, maybe about 100. Before the war, there was no overt discrimination against us, but we were not asked to join the Caucasian groups. We Nisei tended to stick together.[13]

"After the war broke out, we were sure we would have to move. My parents wanted me to go away to school. My piano teacher, Miriam Withrow, suggested I go back East, but at that time, none of the state colleges were accepting us. We had to find a private institution to admit us. I didn't know where to go, so Miss Withrow talked to Mary Baker, the dean of women. Miss Baker was very interested in anything Japanese. [According to Gary Okihiro, Miss Baker had once been a missionary to Japan, was fluent in Japanese, and knew many local Japanese American families.][14]

"Miss Baker suggested Drake College in Des Moines, Iowa. From what I understand, Hubert Phillips, a sociology professor, whom I never met personally, had connections at Drake. He did a lot of letter-writing to pave the way for me and Masako Ono to be admitted. Margaret Cosgrave was the registrar. She helped us get our papers in order. We needed letters of recommendation from teachers and other people, and we had to show that we had a certain amount of money in the bank. I think she helped other students, too, and she spent her summer vacation working at the student relocation office.

"Masako and I were the first to leave the Fresno Assembly Center for school. We needed to be prepared for the Iowa winters, so two armed guards took us to downtown Fresno to shop for clothes. When we left for Des Moines, armed guards took us to the train station. We arrived at Drake sometime in September. School had already started. Most of the people there had never heard of the internment. Drake was an excellent school. We lived in a home-like dormitory where the other girls were very nice to us. We were Buddhists, and they respected that.

"The Quakers arranged for us to go around and speak to different church groups. The people were cordial and interested. They had so many questions. It was a pleasure to be able to educate people about what had happened to the Japanese Americans. I was not a public speaker, but I was not particularly shy. The reception was so good, and I was happy to try to pave the way for others to leave the camps. Masako and I were the first to arrive, but eventually there were about a dozen Nisei students at Drake. I think our classmates were encouraged by our experience, and quite a few of them left camp and went to Oberlin and other schools.

"The Quakers made sure that we had a place to stay during school breaks, with Quaker families. We heard rumors about a student in Denver who had been refused service at a coffee shop, so her Caucasian friends emptied the salt and pepper shakers all over the table and stalked out. Another time, we heard, she was spat on in the street. But nothing bad ever happened to us.

"For a short period, I was hired to play the organ at an African American church. The minister would pick me up every week in his car and bring me home. I think by the end, he was paying my salary out of his own pocket. It was $25 a week, which was a good sum in those days.

"I earned an Iowa teaching credential at Drake, but when I came back to Fresno after the war, no one would hire me to teach music. Arthur Berdahl, the head of Fresno State's music department, who had taken care of my grand piano during the internment, eventually helped me get a job as a secretary in the music department. I was not too disappointed. I wasn't sure that I wanted to teach anyway."

sure he could do more. With a student body of less than 600, Park College was not a large school, he wrote Conard in early July, but he believed it could easily absorb twelve to fifteen Nisei students. The Nisei would not require special treatment because the student population was already diverse, drawing from twelve foreign countries and many states. Furthermore, with one in twelve students planning to enter the ministry and many others planning careers in Christian work, Young did not doubt that the students would do the right thing.

But, Young reported, a small cloud had appeared on the horizon. He was having difficulty securing a statement of approval from officials of the town of Parkville, a community of 600 or 700 located across a creek from Park College. Mayor H. H. Dyer had told Young that it would be difficult to convene a meeting of the town council, and the mayor himself, as a relative newcomer, was unwilling to act without the council's full support. Young asked Conard if he could waive the required statement of approval from town officials. He asserted that the college was a self-contained community where students studied, slept, ate and worked. If trouble should arise in any part of the town, the problem could easily be resolved by restricting students from going to that area.

Conard wrote back to suggest that the local sheriff write the necessary document. Holt Coffey, sheriff of Platte County, readily agreed to write a letter, which aroused fury in town. The local chapters of the American Legion and the American War Mothers were outraged, and the mayor and the city council threatened to take legal action to keep the Nisei from coming to Park College.

Three Nisei students arrived on campus in late August. In accordance with the Student Relocation Council's strategy of sending out the brightest and the best as a kind of advance guard, the three included a ministerial student with a brother in the army, a former student body vice president, and a valedictorian who had also won an American Legion essay contest on American democracy. Their arrival spilled the controversy into the Kansas City newspapers. Mayor Dyer stated that he didn't know any Japanese Americans personally, but he agreed with a veteran who said, "If the FBI is so sure that these Japs are loyal citizens, why didn't it let them remain on the West Coast instead of sending them to a concentration camp?" The internees should be kept behind barbed wire, Dyer declared, rather than be dumped on Parkville. In

NISEI STUDENTS WITH SOME OF THEIR CLASSMATES AT PARK COLLEGE. COURTESY OF FISHBURN ARCHIVES, PARK UNIVERSITY.

response, Dr. Young mailed a two-page letter to 1,000 residents of Parkville and Platte County. The WRA had assured him, he wrote, that "you may be confident that any student relocated at your college...will have undergone a thorough investigation as to his loyalty to the United States." He continued:

> Does this minority group that sets itself up as the epitome of patriotism...know more than the Federal Bureau of Investigation and intelligence divisions of the army and navy, which investigate each and every one of these students?
>
> What about the thousands upon thousands of young men and women already in our colleges whose parents were born in Germany? Nothing has been said about this group. Is an American-born Japanese any worse than an American-born German according to our way of life? Or is war hysteria making us lose sight of our democratic ideals and the priceless guarantee that all Americans are free, equal and have the same opportunities?
>
> Let those with an intolerant viewpoint think about Sgt. Peter Gunji Kawahara who was graduated from Park College in 1940 and returned to his native Hawaii to live with his Japanese parents. Shortly afterwards, he enlisted in the United States army and today he has shrapnel wounds from Pearl Harbor.[15]

Young wrote a similar letter to Park alumni, headlined, "Your college wants your opinion immediately about a vital matter."[16] He needed their support for a September 4 meeting of the college board of trustees. By this time, the controversy had attracted national attention. The vast majority of letters and telegrams sent to the campus supported Young's position, but the two-and-a-half-hour board meeting was tense. Eventually the vote was twelve to three in favor of admitting the students, but Young's rapport with the board was never the same.

The Kansas City Star lauded Young for his stand. The campus paper headlined the semester's first editorial "Welcome, Nisei." In his opening address to the students, Young appealed for them to keep "cool heads in these hot times".

> We stand today unified in singleness of purpose under one flag. Whether our fathers were subjects of king or emperor in the East or in the West, we here today owe but one undivided allegiance, and that is to the Constitution of the United States of America.
>
> War breeds hysteria and...[f]eelings become intensified.... If we are not careful...we are apt to do damage to those very values which we are now anxious to preserve.... We will not tolerate un-Americanism on this campus. Any act of disrespect to a fellow American citizen, simply because his forebears came from an enemy country, will be construed as a violation of the Constitution...an affront to Park's Catholicity, and a betrayal of the Christian faith....[17]

Eleanor Roosevelt sent a letter congratulating Young on his "splendid stand."[18] A total of nine Nisei eventually enrolled at Park, and several went on to distinguished careers. Arthur Kamitsuka, one of Park's three Nisei pioneers, did indeed go into the ministry. His work experience milking cows at Park College served him well after the war when he became a Presbyterian missionary in Hokkaido, Japan. He and his wife, Lily, were assigned to serve at a newly established dairy college, where they developed a work-study program modeled on that of Park College.

Another alumnus, Dr. William Yamamoto, sent Park College a substantial sum when he received his redress check in 1991. While a student at Park, Yamamoto had never met Young personally or shaken his hand, but he was just the sort of person whose potential had had gripped Young's imagination during the early days of the eviction. Yamamoto wrote:

DR. WILLIAM LINDSAY YOUNG. COURTESY OF FISHBURN ARCHIVES, PARK UNIVERSITY.

> Our family of five was dirt-poor in Pasadena living in a small apartment between the Union Pacific and Santa Fe tracks. All non-whites lived in this band and issued forth as gardeners, charwomen, day laborers.... My father always exhorted us to study and excel at school...and so study I did. My first year at Pasadena Junior College I entered a competitive exam in chemistry and won a scholarship to the University of California, and so poor as we were, I had achieved one of my parents' and my goals. Then came Pearl Harbor.... It amazed me when one day walking back from school I read the yellow poster on the telephone pole stating all Japs were to be relocated....
>
> In profound dismay I spoke first to my teachers—and then to my school advisors. One of them, Miss Emma Munday suggested I write...and see if I might be admitted to Park.... I sent in papers for admission and [Dean Sanders] admitted me to Park on "condition" that I could present myself to Park in time for enrollment.
>
> I have always found my fellow men benign, kind and helpful...but never such outpouring of kindness, concern and generosity from people in the community—offers to help store our chattel, legal advice, and help from the churches. My teachers came in on Saturdays and stayed late so that I could finish the term...or take books to camp to complete my studies....
>
> With scholarship in one hand and admission to Park in the other, I went to Santa Anita Assembly Center....
>
> In August...I heard that Dr. Young had arrived at the camp office to get the release of two students, Peter Mori and Toki Kumai.... The story is that Dr. Young came to Mr. Hillyard (camp director), and asked for parole of two students to Park. Mr. Hillyard is reputed to have said, "And you have a third student?" Without missing a beat, Dr. Young is said to have said, "Of course, I'll take him, too!" So a jeep drove up that afternoon and took me, my seventy-five pounds of belongings and my father's only savings. Peter and Toki, whom I barely knew, and I got on a car under FBI arrest and were

placed on a "sealed" train.... We arrived many hours later in Kansas City. [19]

Though it was past midnight when they arrived, the students were met at the train station by two representatives from Park. Yamamoto was soon embraced by the "kindly and familial" atmosphere at Park. "For me Park has made all the difference," he wrote. "Dr. Young...was and to this day to me is an Olympian figure that reached down and blessed all my days by saying, 'Oh yes, I'll take him, too!'"

Masaye Nagao Nakamura, a retired teacher, has spoken frequently about her experiences at Park College:

I was the last to be accepted at Park from Santa Anita. Three other students had already left, so I had to go by myself. It was at the end of August. They came for me in a truck, three armed soldiers. I thought they would invite me to sit in the cab of the truck, but they made me sit in the back of the truck, on my suitcase, with two soldiers with rifles guarding me. On the ride to Union Station, people on the street could see me. Everyone was staring, and pointing at me. When we got to the station, a conductor directed me to the train, which had been held up, waiting for me, so the passengers were irritated and resentful. When I climbed aboard, there were no empty seats. As I walked up the aisle, carrying my suitcase, I could hear people muttering, "Dirty Jap, what's she doing here." Since there were no seats, they told me to sit in the little vestibule at the front of the car. When the conductor entered to collect the tickets, I handed him my ticket, and he spit in my face. I was so startled, I was dumbfounded. I heard everybody gasp, but no one said a word. I sat stock still as the spit rolled down my face. I sat there for the whole trip without moving. Even though passengers disembarked and seats were vacated, I didn't move, not even to go to the bathroom.

As the hours went by, sitting there feeling sorry for myself, I thought the conductor had to have a reason for treating me as he did. Maybe he had a son in the service. Maybe he knew someone who was killed at Pearl Harbor. But to this day, whenever I see a conductor, I get a funny feeling.

Towards the end of my journey, just a few stops before Kansas City, a young couple boarded the train. They looked at me quizzically, and proceeded into the car. Later I felt a hand on my shoulder. It was the young woman. She was smiling at me. "Why don't you join us?" she said. "There's a seat open across from us." They had so many questions. They wanted to know who I was, and why I was on the train. I told them the whole story. I was so relieved to find sympathetic ears for the story of the internment that I almost forgot to get off the train. They had to remind me when we got to Kansas City.

Dr. Young and another person from Park met me at the train station. He was a tall, heavyset man, and I felt a bit intimidated at first, but they gave me a very warm, warm welcome. "All students are eager to meet you," he said, "but there's just one thing: the townspeople are up in arms and they might harm you. You must promise me not to go into town unaccompanied. If you need to go, ask some of the students to go with you." After dinner, I got to the dorm and opened a package of food my mother had given me. All our neighbors at Santa Anita had given up their desserts so that I could have something to eat on my journey, but I had been too upset to eat on the train. I shared the treats with my dorm-mates and we had a little party.

The students were wonderful. They all greeted us with real warmth. But the townspeople were not happy. Threats were made against us and against Dr. Young. I learned later that when the first Nisei had arrived, the other students were so concerned for their safety that they stood guard all night outside their rooms.

During the first six weeks, I went to town two or three times, and the Caucasian students were always happy to accompany me. There was no trouble. One day, I ran out of stamps—I wrote to my mother every single day. There was no one around to ask, so I decided to slip down to the post office by myself. As I came down the hill, I noticed two guys sitting on the bridge, staring at me. I started to feel afraid, but my pride wouldn't let me turn around. My heart was pounding, my knees were shaking. I could see myself swinging from a tree—they had threatened to lynch us.

After I passed the two, they followed me and others joined them. There was a little crowd of people following me. I got more and more nervous. Fortunately, the post office wasn't very far, just on the corner. I walked in and they followed me in. The woman behind the counter asked me what I wanted. I don't know how I managed to find my voice. I asked for some postage stamps. "You speak English?" the woman asked. This was a question I was used to hearing, even in California, so I replied with my standard speech, "Why of course! I'm an American, just like you. We are a nation of immigrants. Most of us came from someplace else originally. I just happen to look like the people we're now at war with, but I pledge allegiance to the same flag as you."

She gave me the stamps, and I think she said, "Thank you. Come again." I turned around and the crowd of people was still there. They were absolutely silent. They parted and made a path to the door. I walked out with my head high and went back to school. When I got back to my dorm, I fell exhausted onto the bed.

Very soon came a knock on the door, and the housemother said, "Dr. Young would like to see you."

My heart sank! When I got to his office, he was grim-faced. It was clear that I was in trouble. I feared I might even be expelled from school. "You have done a very foolish and dangerous thing," he said. "You not only put yourself at risk, but those around you. We took a risk to invite you here, and we're responsible for your safety."

I must have looked crest-fallen because he lightened up. "If anything had happened to you, I would have never forgiven myself." After a stern lecture, he put his arms around me, and said, "I understand how you feel. I might have done the same thing. But you must realize you did a foolish thing and must pay a penalty."

I braced myself for the worst, but he said, "I'm going to ground you for a month. You can't socialize with friends, go to Kansas City. You must be in your room after dinner every evening." I was sorry to give up some activities, but I was relieved to be able to stay in school, and without distractions, I made good grades.

Within two or three months, the atmosphere in town settled down and we were able to go there without any trouble. Students even took odd jobs in town—babysitting or yard work.

Over Christmas break, I took a Greyhound bus to Heart Mountain to see my family. I arrived in the middle of a snow-storm. Father was waiting for me outside the gate. I felt so bad when I saw the conditions they were living in. I felt guilty going back to my pleasant life at Park, but Father said, "Study hard. You've got to graduate."[20]

But Young was to depart from the campus on the hill before the Nisei graduated. After a decent interval to let the dust settle, Young left Park in January 1944 to become regional director of the National Conference of Christians and Jews.[21]

When Young left Park College, many alumni and religious and educational leaders wrote the college to express their shock and dismay. In an essay written in 1956, Young was gracious and diplomatic:

It is...not necessarily an adverse reflection on the former administrations when new leaders seek to improve the services of the college.... The Board of Trustees, as a whole, were well advanced in age and had served the college long and faith-fully. It is to the members' credit that they endorsed many changes, even when it seemed painful for them to do so.[22]

Young served the National Conference of Christians and Jews until his retirement in 1958 and died a year later. He would have been pleased to know that his spirit was evoked at what is now Park University in the wake of 9/11. In the fall of 2002, the Nisei stu-dents were invited to attend a commemorative convocation on the sixtieth anniversary of the Battle of Parkville. President Dr. Beverley Byers-Pevitts greeted Park's students with Young's rallying cry from sixty years before:

Let us prove to the world that while emotions surge about us like a billowy sea, while tides of hatred tend to render rational processes almost impossible, we will strive with the help of God to demonstrate democracy at its best on this hillside.[23]

TOM BODINE AND HARVEY ITANO'S INDEPENDENCE DAY

After having set the highest academic record in UC Berkeley's class of 1942, Harvey Itano received his diploma behind barbed wire at the Sacramento "Assembly Center." At graduation exercises in Berkeley, university president Robert Gordon Sproul noted his absence, stating, "He cannot be with us today. His country has called him elsewhere. Mr. Itano hopes to enter the field of medicine and has taken his books with him."

Prior to his internment, Itano had been accepted by several medical schools including the University of California, San Francisco, but all withdrew their acceptances except for St. Louis University, a Jesuit school in Missouri. According to Itano, "I did not apply to the Student Relocation Council for help because I did not know about it. I do not recall just how my medical school acceptance was brought to the attention of the authorities." In a November 1992 article for the Friends Journal *(reprinted with permission of* Friends Journal*), Tom Bodine recounted his role in Itano's release. Bodine, a Quaker and a conscientious objector who served as field director of the National Japanese American Student Relocation Council, wrote:*

On the morning of the Fourth of July, 1942, I received a telephone call at our office in Berkeley, California. We were hard at work accumulating, sorting, and analyzing transcripts of the roughly 2,000 Nisei who had been enrolled or were about to be enrolled in colleges on the West Coast. The phone call came from the offices of the Western Defense Command in San Francisco and summoned me to come there at once.

I drove across the Bay Bridge and reported to an army officer whom I took to be Colonel Bendetsen. *(See appendix: Why the Mainland and Not Hawaii: Decisions Leading to Mass Incarceration.)* In his office with him was a civilian gentleman to whom I was not introduced.

Bendetsen had before him an article I had written for *Christian Century,* criticizing conditions in the Puyallup Assembly Center outside Tacoma, Washington, where I had visited as a staff member of the American Friends Service Committee. He scolded me for what he felt was an unfair criticism of the army and threatened to deprive me of further visitor's permits if I ever wrote anything of the sort again.

He then asked me if I knew what day it was. When I replied "the Fourth of July," he asked me if I knew what the Fourth of July commemorated. He replied to his own question by saying it stood for the Declaration of Independence, which promised "life, liberty, and the pursuit of happiness." He went on to assert that none of the evacuees had been deprived of any of these in the evacuation, first into assembly centers and later into the relocation camps. He asked me if any evacuee had been deprived of life, and paused for me to agree with him. I thought of some of the older evacuees living in army-style barracks with central latrines, but admitted that no one had been deprived of life.

He went on to declare that no evacuee had been deprived of liberty. When I started to demur, he said, "Young man, do you know the meaning of liberty? The word is derived," he said, "from a Greek word referring to liberty of the spirit. It has nothing to do with physical liberty." I was about to protest vehemently when the civilian present caught my eye and winked at me, so that I remained silent.

"And as for the pursuit of happiness," he went on, "these people have never been happier. They are fed and housed and don't have to work. They are creating gardens and taking classes and enjoying themselves." With that, he opened the bottom drawer of his desk and took out a sheet of paper and began to read to me the menu of the Fourth of July dinner that was being served in all the centers that day.

At this point, the civilian interrupted and identified himself as John J. McCloy, the assistant secretary of war, who had come out to the West Coast, among other assignments, to sign a release for Harvey Itano, the 1942 Gold Medalist at the University of California in Berkeley. Itano had been accepted at the St. Louis University School of [Medicine] in a class due to start July 6. A decision had been reached in Washington, D.C., that the Japanese American college students in the camps were to be released to study on college campuses in the East, away from the West Coast. John J. McCloy wished to symbolize this as the intention of the Roosevelt administration by signing a release order for Harvey Itano.

A soldier secretary was summoned, the release order was dictated, typed, and signed by McCloy, then handed to me! I was told to drive to Tule Lake immediately and to take Harvey Itano to Klamath Falls, Oregon, to catch a train to St. Louis. I was told to hurry, as St. Louis University required that students report for classes on time and Harvey Itano should not be late. (In war-time, civilians did not travel by air; Harvey Itano was to travel by train.)

I dashed to my car and drove to Tule Lake. On arrival, I reported to the camp commandant on duty, who, it being July 4th, was a young army lieutenant, younger even than myself. The lieutenant expressed amazement and didn't believe me, nor the release form signed by the assistant secretary of war. He was certainly not going to release one of those "Japs" under his control.

I reminded him how serious it was for a soldier to disobey orders, stressed the urgency of Harvey Itano's release, and suggested he phone the offices of the Western Defense Command to learn if the release order was for real. He telephoned, and I could hear the officer he spoke to in San Francisco blister him for disobeying an order.

Whereupon the young lieutenant cried to me to hurry, and we jumped in his jeep and drove wildly through the camp, scattering dogs and children and old people out of our way. We drove up to the Itanos' barracks, and the soldier pounded on the door, certainly frightening Harvey's parents. None of them had seen me before, but Harvey quickly packed, said his goodbyes, and off we went.

Gas rationing had not yet come to the West Coast, but the blackout had. For part of the ride to Klamath Falls, I drove with slits of light for head lamps. We arrived at the railroad station an hour or so late, but fortunately, it being war-time, the train was also late. We stood in the pitch-dark on the platform as the train pulled in, huge and black and frightening. I still remember how brave Harvey Itano seemed to me as he left the relative security of my company and climbed the steps of the train to go off into the unknown.

Harvey Itano graduated from medical school with honors and later became a surgeon in the U.S. Public Health Service and Professor of Pathology at the University of California in San Diego.... By the end of the war, the National Japanese American Student Relocation Council had helped a total of 3,500 U.S. citizens of Japanese ancestry find their way from camp to college.[24]

Student Relocation and Resettlement:
Esther Torii Suzuki/Fujiko Kitagawa

The Good Lives On

By Esther Torii Suzuki. Excerpted with permission from an article published in Friends Journal, *November 1992.*[1]

Three months after President Roosevelt signed Executive Order 9066, our family, in Portland, Oregon, was assigned the number 15327. We were allowed two suitcases each, or the equivalent, which amounted to cardboard boxes and duffel bags. With one week's notice, our household possessions were sold off for less than garage sale prices.

I was barely 16 years old, and although my depth of despair and feeling of futility may not have compared to those older who lost businesses or jobs, or who had families with toddlers, I was devastated. Not given permission to leave "camp" for my high school graduation exercises, I received my diploma through the mail. My Quaker teacher mailed me my only copy of the commencement exercises. My scholarship to a local college was not valid since I could not remain on the West Coast.

The detention camp at the Pacific International Exposition Grounds, where we were sent, was called the Portland Assembly Center.... The days dragged endlessly on, but I was lucky enough to get a job. I saved every cent for college.

Since we lived in an exposition center where rodeos were performed, manure from horses remained.... The stench was overpowering.... Our living cubicle...was partitioned off from the other cubicles by eight-foot-high walls. The mattresses were stuffed by us with straw. Our one doorway had a canvas hanging for privacy, and the security guard came by two times a day and flipped the canvas open to count our heads.

I was busy writing letters all over the country trying to get released. Like the pieces of a giant cosmic puzzle, after a time things started to fall into place. The first person to assist me was Margaret Rodman, a long-term substitute teacher at Lincoln High School, and a Quaker. She felt that Macalester College, a small, private Christian college in St. Paul, Minnesota, could possibly be the answer for me. The red tape was indescribable, but the college accepted me, the college was cleared by several agencies to be acceptable to enroll Japanese Americans, and letters were received from the St. Paul police chief and fire department and other representatives of the community acknowledging my acceptance. All these papers were handled by the National Japanese American Student Relocation Council, and the final approval for release came from the War Department.

Margaret Rodman's interest in me did not end. She found a teaching job in a small town in Oregon for one year. Since there wasn't a Quaker meeting there, she tithed from her $100-a-month salary and sent me $10 a month for nine months. I was so excited and grateful that I wrote her a letter of thanks immediately. She answered, asking me not to write my name on the return address; the inquisitive postmistress had questioned her about who she knew in St. Paul. The anti-Japanese feeling was so strong in her small town that she feared losing her job if they found she had a friend of Japanese ancestry.

Life on campus was safe at Macalester. The tenor of the mood was set by the faculty, and the students followed the lead of student leaders, most of whom were active in the Fellowship of Reconciliation. Fellow students invited me for holidays since I could not go home to where my family was incarcerated. The first Thanksgiving, I was invited to Eau Claire, Wisconsin, which meant I had to get permission from the U.S. Attorney's office.

One friend from the Church of the Brethren said her mother, who lived on a farm without electricity, felt that the evacuation was a national shame and she wanted to do something personally for me. She did my laundry in a gas-operated washing machine with homemade soap, so I smelled clean in all my classes. She ironed with a flatiron heated on a wood-burning stove. This dear person packed in large homemade oatmeal cookies, which smelled like homemade soap, but I ate them with relish.

One classmate's father was a chaplain in the navy, and her mother was director of Christian education in a Presbyterian church in St. Paul. When she heard I skipped breakfasts to save money, she gave $10 to the dean to give to me anonymously.

I missed Japanese food, and one classmate's father, who was on the faculty and came from Japan when he was 17, cooked sukiyaki for me.

One religion professor, Dr. Edwin Kagin, had been a missionary to Korea, and in the first week of school he gave me two

Mrs. Suzuki also described three other teachers who supported her during her years at Lincoln High School:

Mrs. Nell Armstrong, my math teacher, saved me the day after Pearl Harbor. A boy came up behind me while I was getting books out of my locker...knocked me to the ground...spit on me and called me, "Dirty Jap." Mrs. Armstrong witnessed this and took us both in front of the homeroom class and said, "Esther is not the enemy and anyone who lays a hand on her will have to answer to me." I was safe as long as she was in sight. She wrote me a letter of recommendation for college, and also got a brilliant Japanese American boy into her Iowa alma mater.

Ruth Arbuckle, my English teacher, had met with me every Friday after school during my sophomore to senior years, in a one-on-one book club of which I was the only member. She helped me prepare a speech for the JACL oratorical contest, wrote me a letter of recommendation for college, and gave me *Elements of Style* as a parting gift at the train station when I set out for Macalester College.

Mrs. Alice Albrecht, an art teacher, hired me for three years to do Saturday morning chores at her home. When I left for Macalester, I went first to Mrs. Albrecht's house, where I took my first bath in four months, a bubble one at that. I was used to taking showers in one large room where showers were spaced three feet apart with no partitions between. Mrs. Albrecht took me by cab to the train station and gave me a three-gardenia corsage which extended from my shoulder to my navel. How I wished she had given me something to eat instead, but coming from her background, this was the only appropriate gift for a trip.

persimmons. He said he understood prejudice because he was subjected to it in Korea, where everyone commented on his big nose. (I didn't think his nose was big at all.)

The other religion professor, Dr. Milton D. McLean, was advisor to the six Nisei students on campus. He opened up his home every Sunday night for popcorn and apples and we looked forward to going to this warm, loving home.

My parents [were sent to the Minidoka internment camp and] remained in camp for the duration so my sister and I could pursue our college education. While at Minidoka, my mother made Indian moccasin pins, one inch long, decorated with multicolored beads. She was paid five cents each for them. A man sold these at souvenir stands, state fairs, and in the old five-and-ten-cent stores for considerably more. Working late into the night by the one dim, naked light bulb suspended from the ceiling in their 12-by-12-foot room, mother earned my train fare from the college to Minidoka for a one-week visit in 1943—the best vacation I had in my whole life. The hours that went into the countless tiny moccasin stitches would be like counting the grains of sand in the desert.

It is fifty years later now, and I am serving on the Alumni Board of Directors of Macalester College. At an alumni weekend in June 1992, a couple of classmates came up to me and said they still remembered my unfinished speech, described in an article I wrote for the November 1991 *Macalester Today*. The article started with this paragraph:

I enrolled at Macalester in September 1942 when I was 16. For my first assignment in freshmen speech class, I began by declaring, "The happiest day of my life was the day I left for college." But suddenly I remembered my father, mother, and two sisters standing on the other side of the barbed wire fence in Oregon waving goodbye, smiling bravely through their tears. I broke down and couldn't continue.[6]

A WEB OF KINDNESS

Mrs. Fujiko Sugimoto Kitagawa, widow of the Rev. Daisuke Kitagawa, wrote in a February 2004 letter:

I have attempted a report of the various groups and individuals who helped during those dreadful days following December 7, 1941, at least those whose assistance my parents and I personally experienced. There were many other helpful church groups besides the Evangelical and Reformed Church (now part of the United Church of Christ) and the Episcopal Church, but I have confined this report to the two churches that directly affected me and my family. I was very happy to be able to make contributions to the various groups who had helped us during those dark days, using the redress check sent me by the government a few years ago.

We were members of the First Evangelical and Reformed Church (E & R Church) in San Francisco. The Rev. and Mrs. Carl Nugent, who had previously been missionaries in Japan, were serving the church's Nisei members as World War II began. When members of the church were interned at Topaz, Utah, the Nugents chose to move there, too, to continue their ministry to camp inmates.

A Caucasian woman whose name I am sorry to have forgotten, who had been taking flower arrangement with my mother in San Francisco, helped us arrange to store our possessions in a commercial storage facility. Unlike many other evictees, whose possessions were looted from government warehouses, we were able to recover all of our things when my parents eventually resettled in Chicago.

When I had to withdraw from the University of California, Berkeley, in mid-March 1941 in order to evacuate "voluntarily" from San Francisco to Zone B, Mary Blossom Davidson, the Dean of Women, called me into her office. She told me that I would be treated exactly the same as the men who were being drafted into the armed forces. Although it was the middle of the semester, I received full credit for all but one of my courses based on the grades I earned at mid-term exams. I very much appreciated this consideration.

I then began hoping for the possibility of going to an inland college. Our former pastor the Rev. Arthur Felkey and his wife, who had moved elsewhere well before the war began, were graduates of Heidelberg College in Tiffin, Ohio. They recommended me to the college, so after just two and a half months at Tule Lake, I became one of the first students to leave camp. If I remember correctly, the Home Department of the national E & R Church assisted me with train fare.

My parents were apprehensive about my leaving the comparative "safety" of Tule Lake and going out into a hostile country, but they realized that camp life was not a healthy one physically or psychologically. They wanted me to continue my education, so they encouraged me to go in spite of their fears, for which I am eternally grateful.

Heidelberg College, a small liberal arts college then associated with the Evangelical and Reformed Church, is today consistently ranked as "one of America's Best Colleges" by *U.S. News & World Report*. It was founded in 1850 by the Reformed Church, which later merged with the Evangelical Church—well before World War II. The college provided me with tuition scholarship and a job in the college office. I was one of five Nisei from the San Francisco E & R Church who were admitted to Heidelberg in the fall of 1942.

Heidelberg's president, Dr. Clarence Josephson, and the college were severely criticized for admitting us Nisei students. In fact, Dr. Josephson was formally charged by some board members with being a Communist, with the presence of us Nisei as one of the reasons. Fortunately, he was completely exonerated.

All the professors were kind and helpful. I was invited to dinner at several of their homes. The students were friendly, but some knew nothing about Japanese Americans and wondered how we had managed to cross the Pacific during wartime!

The townspeople were a somewhat different story. President Josephson assigned his secretary to take us shopping in nearby towns for some months in order to avoid the animosity of the townspeople. Years later, I learned that when I volunteered to help roll bandages for the Red Cross, they threw away the ones that I had touched, and asked our college group not to come back in order to avoid the possibility that I might be with them. When a huge railroad accident occurred just behind the campus, some townspeople muttered that it was probably sabotage by us Nisei students.

Dr. Josephson and his wife invited another Nisei and me to stay in their home during the first Christmas holidays when the dorms were closed. We were treated as guests, and not even allowed to help with the dishes. During the summer break, I stayed with Mrs. Meta Beck and her two daughters. She was criticized by some for taking in a "Jap," especially since her husband was an E & R missionary who was at risk in wartime China.

I stayed in contact with two of my professors, Dr. Allen O. Miller and Dr. John Kolehmainen, and their wives for many years afterwards. They and the Josephsons visited us in Minneapolis and/or Chicago and Geneva, Switzerland. The Josephsons kept in touch with us until their deaths.

After two years at Heidelberg, I married the Rev. Daisuke Kitagawa, an Episcopal priest whom I had met at Tule Lake. The Rev. Dr. George Wieland, head of the Domestic Missions Department of the National Council of the Episcopal Church, traveled from New York City to Chicago to officiate at our wedding. He was very helpful to Episcopalians of Japanese background during our ordeal.

My husband, who was born in Japan, had come to the United States in 1937 for advanced religious studies with the intention of eventually returning to Japan. But after two years at the General Theological Seminary in New York City, he was ordained a priest of the Episcopal Church. He served for two years before the war at two Japanese American parishes in the state of Washington. Although he was an Issei, he had much in common with the Nisei in age and outlook, and was affectionately called Father Dai. His bilingual skills and cross-cultural perspectives made him an effective bridge between the Issei and the Nisei.

Shortly after our wedding, we arrived in Minneapolis, Minnesota, where my husband served as civilian chaplain to the hundreds of Nisei soldiers studying the Japanese language at the Military Intelligence Service Language School (MISLS) at Fort Snelling. Although a Caucasian chaplain was already assigned to the post, MISLS Personnel Procurement Officer Lt. Col. Paul Rusch recognized that the Nisei soldiers had particular needs. Having known my husband as a student at St. Paul's University in Tokyo, Rusch recommended him to the camp commandant, Col. Kai Rasmussen. My husband was still technically an "enemy alien" at the time, and as a pacifist, he was opposed to serving in the military, so Rusch negotiated with the Rev. Dr. George Wieland to assign my husband to Fort Snelling. Thus, the National Council of the Episcopal Church provided support for my husband's civilian ministry to the Nisei soldiers. Many MISLS recruits felt deeply conflicted between their own sense of American patriotism and their Issei parents' distress at the possibility that their sons and their relatives in Japan might face each other in battle.

In addition to serving the MISLS students, my husband also ministered to the resettlers who were arriving in the Twin Cities of Minneapolis and St. Paul. He assisted them in finding jobs and housing, and mediated in trouble spots. He spent many hours speaking about Japanese Americans to local religious and civic groups. Among the groups that assisted him were the Episcopal Diocese of Minnesota and its bishop, the Rt. Rev. Stephen Keeler; the Minnesota Council of Churches; and the Minneapolis and St. Paul Councils of Churches. The Minneapolis Council of Churches and its head, the Rev. Howard G. Wiley, provided an office with phone service and a part-time secretary for five years. In the early days of the resettlement process, the Lutheran Church sponsored a hostel that provided temporary shelter for the incoming resettlers. Also welcoming and assisting newcomers were the Minneapolis Resettlement Committee, chaired by Mrs. Lawrence Steefel, and the St. Paul Resettlement Committee, chaired by Mrs. Ruth Gage Colby. Minneapolis mayor Hubert Humphrey appointed my husband to the Mayor's Council on Human Relations and generally supported the Japanese American community.

In 1949, a large mansion was purchased by the national Episcopal Church to serve as a community center for the rapidly growing number of Japanese Americans, with my husband as director. The Episcopal Church placed no restrictions on the use of the building, and the community assumed responsibility for its care and upkeep. We used the second floor as our living quarters and opened the downstairs for various uses, including Issei Christian services, Buddhist services, JACL meetings, and meetings of various interfaith and social groups. Chief among them was the Rainbow Club, which my husband started to promote interracial friendships involving both children and adults.

At about the same time the Japanese American Community Center was established, the US government began actively urging Native Americans to leave their reservations, very much in the same way that we Japanese Americans were encouraged to leave the internment camps. In 1950, Dillon S. Myer, who had directed the WRA from June 17, 1942 until its end on June 30, 1946, was named commissioner of the Bureau of Indian Affairs by President Truman. Myer began a policy of encouraging Native Americans to resettle outside their reservations, and many began coming to the Twin Cities. In many ways, they needed as much or more assistance than we Japanese Americans because many had had little or no experience of city life. We Japanese Americans had been helped in so many ways in our resettlement process that we in turn wanted to assist these new resettlers. My husband encouraged them to form their own groups, and they were invited to hold their meetings and powwows at our community center. My husband assisted them in various ways to adapt to life in the city, and they joined the work parties that maintained the Community Center.[3]

EARL FINCH, 1946.
COURTESY OF THE 442ND VETERANS CLUB
ARCHIVES.

Nominated by Ted Tsukiyama and Yuri Kochiyama

Based, with permission, on a series of articles by Mark Santoki originally published in the Hawaii Herald.

EARL FINCH: THE "ONE-MAN USO"

When a slender, soft-spoken Mississippian died in Honolulu in 1965, Hawaii's Sen. Daniel K. Inouye sent a telegram to be read at the funeral. The distinguished veteran of the 442nd Regimental Combat Team recalled a March day in 1943 when he was nineteen and his unit arrived at a Mississippi train station:

An Army band was piping away but the reception was cold....

Ringing in the men's ears were epithets they had heard along the way—dirty Jap. Many were still suffering from the barbs of discrimination and war hysteria.

In the back of the crowd at the station was a white man. Everyone saw him. He was standing up and waving his hat and shouting, "Welcome, welcome."

The man was Earl M. Finch. He soon became known to the Nisei soldiers as the "One Man USO."

We know he suffered from criticism from his neighbors. He was spat upon by some of them. But he continued in his pursuit of human brotherhood....

Here was a man who started his one-man civil rights movement 22 ¹/₂ years ago without fanfare, without demonstrations, without violence. And I think in many ways he was successful. We thank God that Earl Finch was there to greet us in Mississippi.[1]

Earl Finch never sought fame, and the Japanese American soldiers he once called his "boys" are fading away. But the remarkable tale of the slender man with the outsized heart deserves to be told and retold.

◆　◆　◆

Earl Melvin Finch was born in 1915 in tiny Ovett, Mississippi. Times were hard when Finch was a boy, and he went to school barefoot because his father could not afford to buy shoes. He had to quit school at age ten and go to work. By his twenties, he was a competent businessman and a clean-living bachelor who did not drink or smoke. He was also a devoted son, who lived with his aging parents and took them to church on Sundays.

By 1943, the family had moved to Hattiesburg, a southern Mississippi town of 25,000. World War II brought thousands of raw recruits to nearby Camp Shelby for basic training. In a stroke of good timing, Finch and a partner opened an army surplus store on Hattiesburg's Main Street. Business was booming as GIs snapped up work clothes, army and navy goods, and sports equipment. Finch also owned a bowling alley and a second-hand furniture store. At twenty-seven, he was financially comfortable, but not wealthy.

At the time, he was a shy, sensitive man with few friends. His father was a janitor and he himself was dismissed as uneducated and low-class. The young man was influenced by the populist ideas of Louisiana politician Huey Long. Although he had never traveled more than 100 miles from home, he rejected Southern ideas about class and race. Some of his childhood friends were Jewish, and he was friendly with African Americans. He respected both the people and their culture.

Finch had tried to enlist after Pearl Harbor but did not pass the army physical. After his younger brother Roy joined the military, Finch decided to contribute to the war effort by treating the troops to a little Southern hospitality. Acting on the theory that those farthest from home were the loneliest, he wined and dined Chinese airmen and French and British sailors.

During the summer of 1943 Finch met his first Japanese American soldier. On his way home from work one evening, he noticed some short, foreign-looking men in American uniforms. "They looked like the loneliest human beings in the world," he said later.[2]

He approached a burly little GI who was peering through a store window. "Welcome, soldier," he said. Although he did not know it at the time, those were life-changing words. A brief conversation led to a dinner invitation, and Richard Chinen and another Nisei followed Finch to his home. Finch's mother, Aloise, who was confined to a wheelchair, greeted them warmly and cooked up a hearty meal of fried chicken and black-eyed peas.[3]

The mild-mannered Finch was captivated by his new friends. Chinen, who had an infectious grin and abundant charisma, had been a notable amateur boxer in prewar Hawaii. Over dinner, he explained to the Finches how Japanese American GIs had ended up in Mississippi. Chinen had been a member of the Hawaii Territorial Guard until he and other Japanese Americans were booted out after Pearl Harbor. Determined to demonstrate their loyalty, the men had joined the newly formed Varsity Victory Volunteers and endured months of construction and maintenance duty while lobbying to be sent into action.

More than a year after Pearl Harbor, on February 1, 1943, President Roosevelt sanctioned the formation of a segregated unit of Nisei soldiers, the 442nd Regimental Combat Team. In Hawaii, nearly 10,000 Americans of Japanese ancestry (AJAs) immediately volunteered for the new outfit, and almost 2700 were accepted, including Chinen. The unit was filled out by 1200 recruits from the mainland, and in March they arrived at Camp Shelby for training. The 100th Infantry Battalion, about 1400 Hawaii Nisei who had enlisted before Pearl Harbor, had been there since January.

AFTER THE WAR, MEMBERS OF THE 100TH/442ND INVITED EARL FINCH TO HAWAII TO REPAY HIM FOR THE LAVISH PICNICS AND ENTERTAINMENTS HE HAD HOSTED IN HATTIESBURG. COURTESY OF THE 442ND VETERANS CLUB ARCHIVES.

Chinen confided that Mississippi congressman John Rankin had accused AJAs of sabotage at Pearl Harbor. "We don't want them," Rankin had declared to Congress. "Instead of sending these Jap troops into Mississippi as they are now doing, they should be put into labor battalions and be made to do manual labor."[4]

"Don't pay him no mind," advised Mrs. Finch.

After a pleasant evening, Finch never expected to see his guests again. He was surprised and pleased when he got home the following day to find the Nisei on his porch chatting with his mother. They had brought a dozen red roses to thank her for her hospitality. Finch was deeply impressed by the token of gratitude. Having grown up a stranger in his own land, Earl Finch finally connected with kindred spirits who genuinely valued kindness and reciprocation.

As he got to know the Japanese Americans, he realized that they did not take for granted the democratic values they were fighting for. They had faced discrimination and exploitation in Hawaii, and now, as they trained to free Europe from Hitler, they were met by Southern bigotry. Finch decided that if no one else would befriend these strangers, he would.

◆　◆　◆

The Finch home was tiny—much too small to hold more than a handful of soldiers—but the businessman owned a 350-acre ranch outside of Hattiesburg where he could entertain more expansively. There, Finch took Chinen and his friends horseback riding and "possum hunting." He also hosted hundreds of Japanese American soldiers at barbecues and watermelon picnics—even a rodeo for 600 guests. In a February 1944 letter, 442nd chaplain Hiro Higuchi wrote his wife about the Southern benefactor who spent thousands of dollars on parties for the Hawaii boys. One evening, he wrote, Finch hired a group of professional Hawaiian musicians to play for a hushed and appreciative crowd who were taken back, if only for an hour, to the Islands they loved.

Finch initially limited his generosity to the easygoing and expressive Nisei from Hawaii. He was unaware of the growing rift between the Islanders and the former internees from the mainland, who seemed to be reserved, even sullen, in comparison. The Hawaii "buddhaheads" thought mainland "kotonks" were as hardheaded as coconuts, and just about as difficult to knock sense into. And they wondered about the lack of patriotism. While 10,000 Nisei in Hawaii had clamored to enlist, only 1,200 out of 23,000 draft-age Nisei volunteered from the mainland.

At first, neither Finch nor the buddhaheads fully understood that most of the mainlanders had lost everything when they had been evicted from their homes on the West Coast and sent to internment camps. They had volunteered for the 442nd from behind barbed wire. They felt a pressing need to assert their loyalty and vindicate their families' honor, but while they were preparing to risk their lives for their country, their families remained unjustly confined.

As friction increased between the kotonks and the buddhaheads, Mike Masaoka, a powerful leader in both the JACL and the 442nd, appealed to Finch for help. While it might appear that the Hawaii boys needed the most help because they were the farthest from home, Masaoka explained, the mainlanders were in even greater need of validation and support. Once Finch understood the situation, he made sure he included the mainlanders. Relationships between the Island and main-

A MAINLAND SOLDIER HELPS HIS MOTHER PREPARE TO BE INTERNED. COURTESY OF THE BANCROFT LIBRARY, UNIVERSITY OF CALIFORNIA, BERKELEY, WRA PHOTOGRAPHS.

land Nisei also improved after Col. Charles W. Pence, the 442nd's commander, arranged to send some busloads of buddhaheads for a sobering look at the realities of life in America's concentration camps.

Over the next few months, Finch entertained several thousand Japanese Americans. Like any good host, he had an instinct for the detail that delivered the biggest bang for his budget—like sending watermelons on ice to Camp Shelby for the sweltering recruits to find at the end of a forced march. To appeal to homesick palates, the resourceful entrepreneur obtained soy sauce, bamboo shoots, tofu and Asian vegetables from Chinese restaurants in Chicago and New York. He delivered cases of mangoes from Bermuda and pineapples from Cuba to the mess hall. He had a cow slaughtered so that the AJAs could enjoy a sukiyaki dinner.[5] At Christmas he bought up all the cigars in Hattiesburg for his new friends.

Finch's extravagance attracted the attention of the press. In the spring of 1944, *The Saturday Evening Post* described a dinner he threw in Little Rock, Arkansas, for fifty Nisei. Finch ordered a thirty-pound tuna and shocked the chef by telling him to serve it raw. As the homesick grunts devoured their sashimi, the hotel staff looked on in wonderment.

Although Finch liked to ride and hunt, he was not particularly interested in sports until he learned that the 442nd included some of the best athletes in the country.

He sponsored the 442nd baseball and basketball teams. When the Nisei won the Camp Shelby baseball championship, he invited them to his ranch for a victory bash featuring a team trophy and individual medals that he commissioned.

When the Amateur Athletic Union (AAU) Swimming Championships were held in New Orleans, Finch arranged for ten Nisei swimmers to compete. He paid the team's train fare and put them up at the posh Roosevelt Hotel. Although they were out of shape, the Nisei won the team title and several individual events. Finch treated them to a victory dinner at the hotel.

◆　◆　◆

The Nisei appreciated Finch, not only for his hospitality, but also for his efforts to help them gain enough acceptance to walk around Hattiesburg without being harassed.

Nisei troops had been confined to Camp Shelby when they first arrived. When they were

As the time approached for them to head for Europe, soldiers kept abreast of the news. Courtesy of The Bancroft Library, University of California, Berkeley, WRA Photographs.

finally granted furloughs, they were told to use facilities designated for "white" folks, not "colored." Essentially, the Nisei had nowhere to go for recreation: they were barred from the Negro USO (United Service Organization) and unwelcome at the Caucasian one. Nor were they invited to the community dances and church socials held for Camp Shelby's other GIs.

Finch and other sympathetic Caucasians helped organize a separate club for the Japanese American soldiers. The "Aloha" USO was operated by Nisei wives who had relocated to Hattiesburg to be near their soldier husbands. Finch visited the club almost every day. There he received 200 letters per week from soldiers and their families and friends, who often enclosed small sums to help finance his hospitality.

Two of the ten internment camps for Japanese Americans, Jerome and Rohwer, were located in neighboring Arkansas, about 300 miles from Hattiesburg. The Aloha USO soon became a vital conduit between the Camp Shelby Nisei and the Arkansas internees. When the 442nd arranged a dance at the Aloha USO, Finch rented buses to bring Nisei girls from Rohwer and Jerome. He sent the 442nd basketball team to play the internee teams. At Easter, Finch persuaded Camp Shelby soldiers of all races to chip in more than $2300 for internee children.

THE "ALOHA" USO WAS A HAVEN FOR NISEI SOLDIERS. Courtesy of the Bancroft Library, University of California, Berkeley, WRA Photographs

Finch expected neither thanks nor special treatment, and the Nisei soon viewed their Southern benefactor as just one of the guys. On his frequent visits to Camp Shelby, the GIs would say, "Eh, howzit, Earl," and keep on shooting craps, in an unspoken expression of respect and acceptance.

◆   ◆   ◆

By September 1943, the 100th Infantry Battalion was in Italy. At Salerno and Monte Cassino, Anzio and Rome, the Nisei dogfaces were thrown into the thick of the action. After the 442nd shipped out to Europe in May 1944, an anonymous soldier wrote to Finch:

> In the last push, Mr. Finch, just before I was hit, several of my men died in my arms. Through gasping breath and blood, one of their last wishes, Mr. Finch, was "tell Mr. Finch *aloha* and good luck." We have never forgotten you, Mr. Finch. We will never forget you to the last...your sympathy, your kindness. So with the last message of your brave friends...till we meet again I bid *aloha* and goodbye.[6]

While training at Camp Shelby, the GIs had been instructed to make out wills and name an executor. Since the families of the Hawaii boys were living under martial law in the faraway Islands, and the mainlanders' families were in internment camps, some 1500 Nisei turned to Finch, who was both close at hand and trustworthy.[7] Thus as the names of the dead began to trickle in, it fell to Finch to handle their affairs. In a single year, the onetime homebody covered 75,000 miles, crisscrossing the nation to visit the bereaved and to comfort wounded Nisei convalescing in U.S. hospitals. Among the many injured soldiers that Finch visited was future senator Spark M. Matsunaga, then a 26-year-old first lieutenant recuperating at Fort Snelling, Minnesota.

To lift morale, Finch organized the Shelby Serenaders, a Hawaiian music group recruited from the new crop of trainees at Fort Shelby. With ukuleles, bass, and a male hula dancer in a grass skirt, the Serenaders entertained recovering dogfaces in New York City and Washington, D.C. They were so well received that Finch sponsored a tour that covered 35,000 miles to entertain some 25,000 wounded soldiers around the country.

About twice a month, Finch hosted special outings. On October 30, 1944, he flew to New York to take five wounded AJAs to a classy dinner show at the Cafe Zanzibar. Finch's flashy generosity attracted favorable attention to the Nisei troops and helped open American hearts to their special plight. In a United Press article, Sgt. Robert Oda and Pfc. Tamotsu Shimizu confided that the need to prove the loyalty of Japanese Americans was never far from their minds, even in the thick of battle.

EARL FINCH SPONSORED A MUSIC GROUP FROM THE 442ND THAT ENTERTAINED WOUNDED TROOPS AT WALTER REED HOSPITAL. COURTESY OF THE BANCROFT LIBRARY, UNIVERSITY OF CALIFORNIA, BERKELEY, WRA PHOTOGRAPHS.

The once-shy Southerner had become expert at building sympathy and respect for his boys, as in this letter to the editor of the *Honolulu Star-Bulletin:*

> In my visit to the army hospital I talked to many boys from Hawaii. All that I have talked to are cheerful and their morale is high. They are well liked by their fellow patients and I have many ward nurses tell me that they enjoy having the Japanese-American boys in the wards due to the cheerful, tonic effect they have on other patients who may be lonely or depressed. From day to day we can see the increasing evidence that their sacrifices have not been in vain. Every day more Americans are becoming aware of the great part these fellow Americans are taking in winning this war.[8]

In January, the *New York World-Telegram* dubbed Finch a "One Man USO" after he threw a huge Hawaiian party at the Hotel Astor for 150 returning soldiers. In June, Finch hosted a Chicago reunion for twenty-two wounded vets. By this time, the 100th Battalion had suffered so many casualties—900 out of an original troop strength of less than 1400—that they were folded into the 442nd. By war's end the Nisei soldiers had earned America's respect, but at a terrible price. The 442nd was the most-decorated unit in U.S. military history, for a group of its size and length of service. Japanese American soldiers had seen intense action in Italy and France, and had suffered a casualty rate three times its troop strength. In the bitterly contested rescue of the "Lost Battalion," 800 Nisei were killed or wounded to rescue 211 Texans from behind enemy lines.

◆　◆　◆

As World War II drew to a close and Japanese Americans returned to the West Coast, Finch helped some mainland GIs find jobs and loaned others money to start their own businesses. But it was the boys from Hawaii with whom he had the strongest bonds. In March 1946, Finch was invited to visit Hawaii for the first time, to pay tribute to the valiant Nisei who had died in action, to honor their families, and to reunite with old buddies from Camp Shelby.

On his trip to Hawaii, Finch honored the casualties of the 100th/442nd. Courtesy of the 442nd Veterans Club Archives

The visitor was greeted by the largest and warmest reception ever accorded a private citizen in territorial history. For twenty-five days, veterans and their families toasted their friend as he toured Oahu, Maui and the Big Island. He visited war memorials and attended luaus and picnics where thousands gathered to fete him. Modestly, Finch declared, "All I tried to do for [the soldiers] in my small way was to entertain them. I tried to show that I had faith in them."

Gold-star mothers lined up to hold his hand and shed wordless tears of gratitude for his generosity toward their fallen sons. But Finch was also thinking of the future. "The greatest service I have ever given in my life was given for these boys," he said. "Now that they are home, I know that they want only the opportunity afforded any other American citizen for building a successful future life in their communities, and I am going to do my part to see that they get it."

Finch's farewell reception was attended by some 2,000 people. He was presented with a check for $10,000 to continue his hospital visits. Finch encouraged the audience to do the same:

> Yesterday afternoon I visited Schofield Barracks hospital where I met a veteran who hadn't had a caller for three months. He cried when I came in to talk to him. You don't have to go with a big basket of gifts; just a big handshake, to tell him, "I hope you get out soon."[9]

The *Hawaii Hochi* editorialized that Finch had opened "new channels for the outflow of a spirit of love and respect" and a "new faith in the tenets of democracy." *Honolulu Advertiser* editor Ray Coll Jr. confessed that he had never appreciated the Nisei "until Earl Finch came to town." Once again Finch served as a lightning rod. In the climate of the times, it seemed to require the curious spectacle of a concerned Caucasian to draw public attention to the marginalized.

Finch's visit helped usher in an enduring postwar role for the 442nd. Their blood sacrifices were unassailable evidence of Nisei patriotism, repeatedly cited in efforts to repeal the Alien Land Laws, acquire citizenship rights for Asian immigrants, and gain redress for the internees. In Hawaii, 442nd vets played significant roles in the labor movement and in Democratic politics.

But Finch's bridge building was not restricted to the military. Two days after his departure, a tsunami devastated the Big Island, killing 159 people. Little more than a month later, he sent a check to help rebuild a school. Enclosed was a note explaining that the $150 had been donated by both white and black children in Hattiesburg's segregated school system.

> This is not a large sum. But I sincerely feel that it is an expression of the love that our children have for the children of Hawaii, a love that children the world over have for one another.[10]

In the ensuing months, Finch visited 3,000 hospitalized Nisei in Philadelphia, New York, and Chicago and then scurried to the nation's capital to watch with teary-eyed pride as Harry S. Truman awarded a Presidential Unit Citation to the 100th/442nd. "You fought not only the enemy," said the president, "but you fought prejudice—and you have won."

◆　◆　◆

The end of World War II did not end the need for Nisei troops. While the 442nd was distinguishing itself in Europe, Japanese Americans in the Military Intelligence Service (MIS) had played key roles in the Pacific War. Their work is less known because much of it was secret and not made public until decades later. Instead of being concentrated into segregated combat units, MIS translators were distributed to various units to decipher captured enemy maps and battle plans, interrogate prisoners of war and undermine enemy morale.

Before they went overseas, Nisei brushed up on their Japanese at the Military Intelligence Service Language School (MISLS) at Fort Snelling, Minnesota. MIS veteran Tom Kawamoto met

THOUSANDS FLOCKED TO LUAUS AND OTHER GATHERINGS TO HONOR FINCH ON HIS FIRST VISIT TO HAWAII. COURTESY OF THE 442ND VETERANS CLUB ARCHIVES.

Finch in 1946, when Finch asked him to drive his Cadillac into town, where it was loaded with 2500 cigars before Kawamoto headed back to Fort Snelling followed by a truck stuffed with 1800 pints of ice cream.[11]

When the MISLS relocated to the Presidio of Monterey, Finch traveled to California several times to arrange dances and social events. In August 1946 he chartered a boat to take forty-five men deep-sea fishing in Monterey Bay. Another time, he offered to pay the tab at a local Japanese restaurant for any uniformed Nisei. Caucasians from nearby Fort Ord liked to pick fights with the feisty Nisei, and brawlers sometimes landed in the hospital. When that happened, MIS officers phoned Finch, Kawamoto recalled.

> Sure enough, about a week later he's right there. He would go up on the mike and yell at the boys, "Eh you guys, don't fight! They are American and you are American.[12]

◆　◆　◆

In the summer of 1947, the 442nd Veterans Club decided to build a clubhouse, and held a five-day "Go For Broke" Carnival in Honolulu to raise $125,000. Two pages in the carnival program were devoted to Earl Finch:

> Myths and legends have grown up around Earl M. Finch. His boys will tell you of his fabulous wealth, of his ranch which is so wide that he needs a plane to cover every inch of the ground, and of his diamond store. Actually, he is a man of modest means, but he has given everything for the boys whom he loves. Jealous people have reported him to internal revenue collectors, but every investigating agency has found him over and above board. His record is clean, and he has been absolved of any "racket."... If one were to dedicate the carnival, it would be dedicated to the man from Mississippi and the friend of Hawaii's men, Earl M. Finch.[13]

Future senator Daniel Inouye and other prominent vets pitched in to help organize the event. Finch and Tatsuo "Tats" Matsuo went to Hollywood to book the entertainment. Mainland acts were reluctant to commit to going to Hawaii. Finally, Martha Raye, a popular comedienne, agreed to sign, but only if she was paid in advance. Longtime Hawaii promoter Ralph Yempuku explained:

> They weren't going to come to Hawaii and get stranded and not get paid. They didn't know Tats. They didn't know Earl. They didn't even know where Hawaii was.[14]

Finch took the necessary cash out of his pocket and laid it on the table, in $100 bills. With cash up front, Finch and Matsuo were able to fill the entire bill with comedians, musicians, dancers, an aerial artist, and even a stuntman. This early foray into Hollywood earned Finch credibility in the entertainment industry.

On his way home after the carnival, Finch entertained the Hawaii Swim Club, which was on its way to Texas to compete in the 1947 AAU national championships. Three of the nine defending champions were 442nd vets.

◆　◆　◆

Many questioned Finch's activities and the motivations behind them. When he first befriended Camp Shelby's Nisei, he was threatened and spat upon by Hattiesburg residents. Military intelligence initially suspected him of spying for Japan. The FBI screened his mail for evidence of sexual deviancy or nefarious business dealings. Hawaii's Emergency Services Committee sent Chinese American YMCA leader Hung Wai Ching to Hattiesburg to make sure that Finch was not taking advantage of GIs making out their wills. Finch was investigated countless times, but no group ever found evidence of wrongdoing. Finch once declared:

> The last thing I would think of is making money off my friends. It happens to be in my nature to be friendly, but it seems to be the nature of humans to look with suspicion on anyone who makes friendship an avocation. When these boys came to my home state they were in a strange land surrounded by an almost hostile people.[15]

In a sense, Finch was himself a stranger in his own homeland. His very being was in opposition to racism, classism and small-town meanness. Yet, though he was vilified in his hometown as a "Jap lover," Finch couldn't seem to find it in his heart to hate anyone. Of his Mississippi neighbors, he said:

FINCH IS GREETED WITH A HULA ON HIS FIRST VISIT TO HAWAII. COURTESY OF THE 442ND VETERANS CLUB ARCHIVES.

> They just didn't understand, that's all. They were good people. I felt sorry for them. Their way of life had long gone, but they didn't know it. They still clung to the long dead past. I was often asked why I did what I did. I was accused of being a homosexual, a draft dodger. Name it, and I was labeled. I guess I felt that those boys at Camp Shelby needed a friend. They were Americans, away from home. I had no ulterior motives. I just liked them, that's all.[16]

In the end, the Nisei's battlefield valor won them respect even in Hattiesburg. Vindicated for his faith in them, Finch could have remained in his hometown. He found himself home less and less, however, because his "boys" had returned to Hawaii and California to pick up their lives. With the war over, the hordes of Camp Shelby trainees slowed to a trickle, and business dried up at the army surplus store and the bowling alley.

With little to hold him in Hattiesburg, Finch could leave his parents in the care of his brother and take his money out of Hattiesburg. In 1949 he moved to Honolulu and joined veterans Harold Watanabe and Ken Okamoto in forming the Asiatic Trading Company, a modest enterprise that imported candy to Hawaii and exported aloha shirts to the United States.

At thirty-four, Finch reinvented his life once more. The personable newcomer made new friends as he delivered candy and serviced vending machines and penny scales in small neighborhood stores owned by local Japanese families. Hideo Sakamoto observed:

> No matter where he went, he would talk to the old Japanese men.... [P]eople liked him so they bought candy from him. He had a nice heart and people could tell, so they would say, *"Mottekinasai* (Bring some)."[17]

As his business took him around the Islands, Finch was able to stay in touch with his army buddies. Four or five times a year he would deliver candies to Kauai and take a few days off. Democratic Party organizer Turk Tokita recalled:

> We would make a big campfire and roast lobsters and fish. He used to eat with us. He never used to drink but would buy all the beer. He was a humble guy. Once, he came to our house and at that time we still lived in a plantation home with four, five bedrooms and a flat, tin roof.... He stayed with us a couple days and my mother was really thrilled.... Earl was such a benevolent man. He was almost like my father.[18]

FINCH, *LEFT*, AND SEIJI NAYA, *CENTER*, IN JAPAN, 1951. COURTESY OF MR. AND MRS. SEIJI NAYA.

In 1953, Finch was honored at the tenth reunion of the 442nd, along with Brigadier General Charles W. Pence, first commander of the 442nd, and Mary Kochiyama, a mainstay of the Aloha USO. The event marked another change in Finch's life. A decade after meeting his first Nisei, Earl Finch no longer felt needed. His "boys" had started families, gone to school on the GI Bill, and were now claiming their rightful place in the mainstream. As Finch himself had hoped, the vets were busy making inroads in academia, law, politics and business. They no longer had time to shoot the breeze with their friend from Mississippi.

◆　◆　◆

In 1950, Finch had traveled to Tokyo to explore business opportunities and visit his friends in the MIS, who were now serving key roles in Occupied Japan. At the time, the nation was still struggling to recover from the devastation of war. Almost all its major cities had been heavily bombed, and more than two-and-a-half million people had died. Finch did what he could to help, touring the nation's orphanages, passing out blankets, lollipops and comic books from Hawaii. He decided to establish a charitable organization to bring college students from Japan and Okinawa to study in Hawaii and the U.S. mainland.

The following summer, he spotted his first protégé in Seiji Naya, a collegiate boxer who visited Hawaii as a member of Japan's amateur boxing team. Finch was involved in boxing through his old friend Richard Chinen, who had returned to the sport after the war. Finch was deeply impressed by the 18-year-old Seiji, an orphan who had lost not only his parents but also his foster parents. The handsome, disciplined teenager was intellectually and physically gifted, working his way through college as he climbed the ranks of amateur boxing.

In March 1952, Finch visited Japan again, taking 10,000 letters from Hawaii schoolchildren, 100,000 pieces of bubble gum and 50,000 lollipops. He lobbied for his scholarship plan with Japanese leaders, and then he went to Osaka to offer Seiji Naya a four-year scholarship to the University of Hawaii, to be paid out of his own pocket.

FINCH WELCOMES HIS ADOPTED SON SEIJI NAYA TO HAWAII.
COURTESY OF MR. AND MRS. SEIJI NAYA.

Two months later, Finch eagerly welcomed his new son to Hawaii, telling the media, "I am not expecting anything in return. I only hope that Seiji will make good use of any aid, and become a good citizen."

The young man majored in business at the University of Hawaii and captured the national collegiate featherweight championship two years in a row, in 1954 and 1955. In 1957, as Seiji prepared to leave for the Midwest for graduate work, Finch adopted a second Japanese national, an 18-year-old waiter named Hideo Sakamoto. Unlike Seiji, Hideo had parents in Japan, who did not stand in the way of his opportunity to make a new life in Hawaii. Finch provided Seiji and Hideo with a house to live in while they attended school and worked part time at Finch's trading company.

Finch loved his adopted sons dearly. The proud papa could not bear to watch Seiji's boxing matches, but waited anxiously at home. When Seiji's age and Finch's marital status stood in the way of a legal adoption, Finch lobbied for an act of Congress. He encouraged his sons to shape their own dreams. He was equally proud of Seiji, who earned a PhD in economics and went on to a highly distinguished career, and Hideo, who contented himself with a low-key, family-centered life.

◆　◆　◆

In the late '50s and early '60s, Earl Finch's life took yet another turn. Building on his experience with Go

For Broke Carnival, he launched into show business with MIS veteran Ralph Yempuku. "Richard Chinen was very instrumental in convincing me that Earl was a real up-front guy," Yempuku recalled.[19] Grasping the incredible potential of rock 'n' roll, the enterprising pair decided to bring the new sounds to Hawaii. They recruited popular teen radio host Tom Moffat to help select the acts and emcee the shows. Over the next seven years, they produced a Show of Stars about every other month, featuring four or five top acts that played Honolulu before touring the neighbor islands. Finch and his partners booked everybody who was anybody, including Chuck Berry, Jerry Lee Lewis, Buddy Holly, the Everly Brothers, Ritchie Valens, Paul Anka, Frankie Avalon, Connie Francis, Bobby Darin, the Platters, Sam Cooke, the Drifters, Chubby Checker and the Beach Boys.

By the time the series ended in 1964, Yempuku and Finch had promoted thirty-four shows and sold 680,000 tickets. Yempuku reflected on his friend with affection and respect:

> I trusted that man. But as a businessman Earl wasn't that good or *akamai* (smart). He got involved in quite a few things but never to the extent where he...made it big.
>
> I think Earl was too good to be a good businessman. He didn't take advantage, that's why he never made it. He was too scrupulous, too kind, too gentle, too moral. He was always giving things away. A damn fool. But that's what he was. There weren't too many businessmen of that caliber during the days that he lived.[20]

◆　◆　◆

By 1965, Finch had lost contact with many of his Nisei friends. Son Seiji had married and left home, and Hideo was an adult. For the first time in two decades, Finch had no one to take care of. His younger son observed:

> He was lonely. One time I came home and he was drinking. He never drank, but when I came home and saw the scotch, half of the bottle was gone.[21]

At forty-nine, the "Old Man" seemed perfectly healthy. Not knowing about the heart condition that had kept Finch out of the army, Hideo was shocked when Finch said that he did not have long to live.

"Why? What are you talking about?" Hideo cried. "No, Daddy, no talk like that."

Several weeks later, while Hideo was still in denial, Finch sent him to visit his natural parents. Hideo was in Japan when he learned that his adoptive father had died of a heart attack.

THE ONCE-SHY MISSISSIPPIAN BECAME A POWERFUL ADVOCATE FOR THE NISEI SOLDIERS. COURTESY OF THE 442ND VETERANS CLUB ARCHIVES.

Finch's timing was impeccable. In Wisconsin, Seiji no longer needed his support. He had just landed a job as an assistant professor of economics. Before he could express his gratitude by sending his adoptive dad part of his paycheck, Finch was dead.

The 442nd Veterans Club handled all the funeral arrangements. On August 29, 1965, over 300 friends attended a memorial service conducted by three former 100th/442nd chaplains. Sen. Daniel Inouye sent an eloquent telegram from Washington, and the honorary pallbearers included some of Hawaii's most prominent leaders, among them Gov. Jack Burns, Mayor Neal S. Blaisdell, Brig. Gen. Kendall Fielder, Hung Wai Ching and Congressman Spark Matsunaga.

◆ ◆ ◆

Just after World War II, hundreds of new parents named their sons after Earl Finch, but few today have heard of him. He sought neither fame nor fortune, but in his unpretentious way he had a profound effect on many. One vet commented:

> The thing that I liked about this man was he was down to earth. You could talk to him as a friend, not as a haole [white person], as a friend. In those days, haoles were a level above us. But he made it so that we were the same level as them. After he got to be friends with me, I never thought the haoles were better than us. But before that I thought they were superior.[22]

Many questions remain unanswered about Finch, who rarely spoke about himself, even to his sons. Sadly, he did not live to see the extent of his elder son's success. Dr. Seiji Naya became an international expert on Asian development. He served as a Rockefeller Foundation Fellow in Thailand, as chief economist at the Asian Development Bank, and in the cabinet of the State of Hawaii. He is currently professor emeritus at the University of Hawaii and Distinguished Visiting Fellow at the East-West Center.

Finch's benevolent heart touched many a father's son, including Steve Sato, who was three years old when his father died in Italy as a member of the 100th Infantry Battalion. Sato still remembers Finch kneeling to talk to him with tears streaming down his cheeks and taking a 442nd ring off his own finger to give to the fatherless boy. It remains, Sato says, one of the nicest gestures he has ever experienced.

Many have tried to analyze the reasons for Earl Finch's generosity. Yet the truth may be stunningly simple: it feels good to give, and it feels even better when it's appreciated. From his boyhood, Finch had instinctively turned toward the light. Growing up in an atmosphere of poverty and bigotry, he maintained an open-minded and open-handed compassion. But Richard Chinen's simple gift of roses provided the other half of the equation. Love met with love creates more love; generosity and appreciation go hand in hand.

THE HANNAN FAMILY:
JOAN OF ARC AND HER LITTLE SISTER

Mother + Miss Crotts

Daddy March 1946

Mari 4/46

PHOTOS WITH MARI HANNAN'S HAND-WRITTEN CAPTIONS, FROM LEFT TO RIGHT: NELL HANNAN, ON LEFT, WITH MISS CROTTS, HER BOSS AT TULE LAKE; LAWRENCE HANNAN, 1946; MARI HANNAN IN FRONT OF THE HANNAN HOME AT THE TULE LAKE "SEGREGATION CENTER," 1946.
COURTESY OF OF THE BRENNAN FAMILY IN MEMORY OF MARI (HANNAN) BRENNAN.

On December 17, 1944, the Western Defense Command declared that internees were free to return to the West Coast. As the camps slowly began to empty, Lawrence J. Hannan signed on to work as a project lawyer at Amache. He brought his family to the Colorado internment camp in the summer of 1945. His elder daughter, Mari, quickly made friends with the Nisei children. Mari's sister, Helen, who was then twelve, recalled:

> Mari practically had a daycare center in our house. All these little ones would be down in our quarters all day playing board games and card games like "Fish," and making French-fried potatoes.... I don't think we endeared ourselves to the staff for associating with the internees. They kept their distance, but Mari was a real mother hen to the Japanese children. She was a 16-year-old girl, who should have been thinking about boys and makeup and clothes, but she was totally engrossed in the lives of the internees and what she could do for them.
>
> Mari used to gather up as many children as she could stuff in our father's convertible and take them into the nearby town of Granada for ice cream cones, and a trip to the town wading pool.... The other mothers did not want the children in the wading pool with theirs, as if something was going to rub off. Mari took a lot of abuse. People would glare and make remarks about people who didn't belong there and who ought to go back where they came from.... But Mari didn't care. I sort of felt like Joan of Arc's little sister. She forged on into battle, and I'd be standing there in amazement....

HELEN HANNAN PARRA TODAY. COURTESY OF HELEN HANNAN PARRA AND MARY JOHNSON.

It had never entered the head of anybody on the staff that they might take some of these little kids into town for a little frolic, until Mari came along. Everybody was dumbfounded.[1]

The summer that Lawrence Hannan took his wife, Helen ("Nell"), and their three children, Margaret Mary ("Mari"), Helen, and Larry Jr., to Amache, Helen was twelve years old. Lawrence, Nell and Mari are now deceased, but Helen proudly recalls her family's contribution. "The internment was so wrong!" she says. "The little bit that you could do felt like you were putting your thumb in the dike, but our family felt that you had to do what you could."[2]

Doing the right thing was a time-honored tradition in the Hannan family, stretching back to Helen Hannan's maternal great-great-grandfather, Thomas Duffy.[3] He and his brother had been schoolteachers in the 1830s, when the British occupied Ireland and made education a capital crime. The Duffy brothers were forced to become "hedge masters," who literally hid in hedgerows and ditches while teaching Irish children on the sly. With the British hot on their trail, the Duffys changed their name and went undercover in England. It would be three generations before the family felt safe enough to reclaim the Duffy name in the 1880s.

Lawrence Hannan had an equally strong sense of justice. A Chicago lawyer with a wife and three children, he was an army reservist who had been called into active duty in August 1941. He was transferred to six different postings around the country in less than four years to train troops for the European theater.

Hannan's military career stalled after he defended a young Jewish soldier he believed to be the victim of anti-Semitism. "My father got him declared innocent in the Court Martial," declared Helen, "but at the cost of all hope of his own advancement in the Army. The General made his life miserable and determined to be rid of him."[4]

On May 8, 1945, Nazi Germany surrendered unconditionally, and the war in Europe ended. The army released Hannan from active duty. His prewar position at Chicago Title and Trust was waiting for him, but Hannan had heard that the WRA was seeking lawyers to work in the internment camps. "He decided that he could do more good there even though it meant less money and much worse living conditions," said Helen. When Amache closed three and a half months later, Hannan requested a transfer to the Tule Lake Segregation Center, where the family remained until the camp closed in the spring of 1946. Helen recalled:

> As far as I know, my father didn't know any Japanese-Americans before he went to WRA. He was not a "crusader," but he held very strong moral convictions. As a lawyer he recognized that a great crime had been done by the government against its own citizens in violation of the "due process of law" guaranteed by the Constitution. They had been imprisoned without being accused of a crime, tried and convicted.[5]

Although she missed the comfortable home they had left behind in the Chicago suburbs, Nell Hannan completely supported her husband's decision. She was a devout Catholic who felt fortunate compared with her own mother, who had been sent to work at a rope factory in England at the age of four while caring for an invalid mother. The tales of her mother's Dickensian sufferings instilled a deep well of compassion in Nell. At the height of the Depression, when her husband's law office cut his hours and salary in half, she felt fortunate that he had a job at all. She kept a pot of soup on the stove to feed the hungry strangers who knocked on the back door. They were not "bums," she explained to her children, but hardworking men who had lost their jobs.

COL. LAWRENCE J. HANNAN. NOTE MARI'S HANDWRITTEN CAPTIONS IN THE MARGINS. COURTESY OF THE BRENNAN FAMILY.

During wartime, the family had grown accustomed to makeshift lodgings as they followed Hannan around the country to military assignments, but they found Amache to be strikingly desolate.

"The dust and sand never stopped blowing, and there was no vegetation to speak of," Helen remembered.[6] With no vacancies in the staff quarters, the Hannans were assigned to a military police barrack that had been partitioned into four apartments. In contrast to internee accommodations, where up to seven people were squeezed into a single 16-by-20-foot room, the five Hannans luxuriated in "three bedrooms," Nell wrote, and a "living room–dining room combination and a kitchen, very modern with cabinets of all types and sizes, a very fine electric stove and a refrigerator which would take care of the requirements of the average hotel."[7]

Helen recalled that "the staff had their own little world, literally with a white picket fence around it. They had little white cottages, with green grass around a sort of little village square...plunked down in the midst of this desolation. And they kept themselves that way, by and large."[8] The staff could almost imagine themselves on some imperialist outpost, isolated from the internees' area, which they euphemistically referred to as "the Japanese colony."

"The town of Granada," she wrote, "was very hostile to anyone from the camp.[9] They went out of their way to be unaccommodating." The bank refused to open an account for Hannan because he worked at Amache. The drugstore hid magazines under the counter and sold them only to the locals.

Within the camp, most of the staff were, in Helen's words, "of the bureaucratic mind-set: they were there to do a job and get paid to do it. They did not mingle with the people from the 'colony.'... Some of the staff had almost what would amount to a bad attitude."[10]

In contrast, the Hannan children quickly befriended the internees. Helen recalled:

We just sort of took to each other. The day we got to Amache, July 14, 1945, was Mari's birthday. The servers in the mess hall were girls from the colony, and somehow they got wind of it. They came over to wish her a happy birthday. She began talking to them, and they became life-long friends. Mollie and Edna Fujimoto...introduced her to other teenagers from the colony.... All her friends were colony kids.[11]

In a 2003 interview, Helen Hannan Parra, at age seventy, felt she could speak freely about the injustice of the internment. In contrast, her mother's chatty letters to friends and relatives focused at first on the mundane details of daily life. Disapproval of the "Guvamint," as Nell called it, was expressed obliquely. But the Hannans' sympathies came through in their actions. Only two weeks after their arrival in Amache, Nell wrote, "It has been decided by the powers that be that Amache is to be the first camp to close.... Larry might not have taken the job had he known, but we are...just the kind of people that are glad we didn't know because we wouldn't have missed it for the world."[12] The "Guvamint" was anxious to keep lawyers on the federal payroll and offered Hannan his pick of assignments. He asked to be transferred to another internment camp. Nell wrote:

> Larry's work is very fascinating, general practice—but there is a great deal of variety to it. There are the private affairs of the evacuees, mostly California property—leases, rentals, incomes, etc., and in addition there are the deals of those who are not returning to California but who are disposing of property and relocating.[13]

The family joined the internees for Mass at the camp's Catholic church. The resident priest was Father John Swift, a Maryknoll missionary who had lived in Korea. Soon Mari was taking Japanese-language lessons from Father Swift and helping him with choir practice. "Preparing a little child for first communion has given her an 'in' to the evacuees' homes," wrote Nell. "She crosses into their area three times a day and finds everyone anxious to assist her."

The entire family tried to learn Japanese, Nell reported. "At home we have a big blackboard on one side of our kitchen...and it's covered with Japanese. The rest of us try...we can't seem to keep up with Mari." By the end of August, Nell wrote:

> We stand by and watch the camp fold up around us. The internees are free to go, and the sooner the better the organization will like it. Most of them are very nice people and now that they are free to return to the West Coast, they are only staying because they can't get possession of their property or a place to live.[14]

The Catholic church closed when Father Swift left for the West Coast to help with resettlement. He made arrangements with priests in nearby towns to accept the internees at their Masses, and asked Mari to drive the internees to church. The Hannans were at Amache when the Pacific war ended in August. Helen recalled:

While there had been wild rejoicing in St. Augustine at VE Day, we didn't celebrate VJ Day in camp. We knew many people who had lost family members in the atomic bombings and it seemed indecent to rejoice under the circumstances. We were all just quietly grateful that it was over.[15]

Amache closed on October 15, and two weeks later, the Hannans arrived at the Tule Lake "Segregation Center" in California. As at Amache, Lawrence Hannan was to serve as a project attorney. However, the Hannans soon found that the atmosphere at Tule Lake was very different from Amache.

◆   ◆   ◆

POSTCARD OF KLAMATH FALLS, OREGON, THE NEAREST TOWN OF ANY SIZE TO THE TULE LAKE CAMP. IMAGE REPRODUCED BY PERMISSION OF EASTMAN'S ORIGINALS COLLECTION, D-51, DEPARTMENT OF SPECIAL COLLECTIONS, GENERAL LIBRARY, UNIVERSITY OF CALIFORNIA, DAVIS. POSTCARD COURTESY OF THE BRENNAN FAMILY.

Situated on Bureau of Reclamation land near the Oregon border, Tule Lake had originally been one of the ten WRA "relocation centers," but in July 1943, it was designated a "segregation center" for internees believed to be disloyal to the United States.

By late 1942, the WRA had become concerned that the internees would develop a "welfare" or "reservation" mentality if they languished behind barbed wire for too long. Planning began to allow "loyal" internees to resettle outside the exclusion zone or enlist in the military. To winnow the loyal from the disloyal at the ten internment camps, the army and the WRA each developed a questionnaire that included two controversial questions: (1) would the respondent be willing to serve in the U.S. military, and (2) did the respondent forswear allegiance to the Japanese emperor or to any foreign government?

The questions aroused confusion and controversy because they were poorly phrased and explained. Four percent of all internees refused to sign the WRA form. Another twelve percent answered "no" to at least one of the two "loyalty questions." Some Issei feared that if they answered "no" to the loyalty questions, they would be deported. Others argued that as aliens ineligible for U.S. citizenship, they would be stateless if they rejected their Japanese ties. Some Nisei refused on principle to forswear allegiance to a country with which they had never had ties. As for serving in the military, while 1200 Nisei did volunteer for the 442nd, countless others were opposed to fighting for a country that had taken away their freedom.

Controversy over the loyalty questions ran highest at Tule Lake. At other camps, an average of ten percent of the internees answered "no-no" to the two loyalty questions, or refused to fill out the form. At Tule Lake, it was forty-two percent.[16] The camp had already witnessed more strife than any other, so when tensions there erupted over the loyalty issue, the WRA designated Tule Lake as a segregation center where "troublemakers" from other camps would be sent.

Tule Lake's population swelled to more than 18,000 as internees were transferred from other camps. The segregants included "no-nos" and Issei who had asked to be repatriated to Japan, as well as parolees from Justice Department detention camps. Many Issei brought along their Nisei children, who did not really wish to go to Japan but felt obliged to stay with their parents. To complicate matters, about 6,000 of Tule Lake's "loyal" respondents elected to stay rather than be transferred out to a "loyal" camp. Allegiances within the overcrowded camp ran the gamut from militantly pro-Japan to resolutely pro-American. All the internees were denied leave clearance, as well as the self-governance that prevailed at other camps.

Tensions between the internees and the administration erupted in October 1943 after farmworkers went on strike and strike-breakers were brought in from other camps. Martial law was imposed in mid-November. More than 350 dissidents were arrested and held in the stockade without trial for up to nine months, and 1200 Issei were shipped off to Department of Justice Camps.[17] As a result, even moderates became embittered and turned against the administration.

On December 17, 1944, the Western Defense Command reopened the West Coast to Japanese Americans. The WRA announced that all the camps would be closed by the end of 1945. At Tule Lake, the Hoshidan, a small but determined pro-Japan group, employed rumors, intimidation and violence to convince many Issei that anti-Japanese feeling on the West Coast ran so high that it was safer to go to Japan. The militants urged the young Nisei to renounce their American citizenship and accompany their parents.[18]

Most Nisei felt trapped between the militant

Hoshidan Sunday Morning

HOSHIDAN MILITANTS EXERCISING AT TULE LAKE, FROM MARI'S ALBUM. THE PHOTO WAS PROBABLY SHOT BY ROBERT H. ROSS, THE WRA'S CAMP PHOTOGRAPHER. MARI MAY HAVE FOUND THESE TEST STRIPS IN THE DARKROOM TRASH, OR DEVELOPED THEM HERSELF FROM DISCARDED NEGATIVES USING PHOTOGRAPHIC SUPPLIES THAT HELEN PURCHASED FOR HER. COURTESY OF THE BRENNAN FAMILY.

attitudes of both the government and the Hoshidan. By July 1945, 5,589 Tule Lake Nisei—more than seventy percent of those age eighteen and up—had renounced their citizenship. Ninety-seven percent quickly regretted their decision and asked to have their citizenship reinstated. The WRA and other agencies were sympathetic to the renunciates, but the Department of Justice remained intransigently opposed for over twenty years. Its attorneys contested every legal action seeking the restoration of citizenship until 1968. Despite government opposition, ninety percent of renunciates eventually regained their citizenship, thanks largely to the tirelessly dedicated efforts of San Francisco attorney Wayne Collins.

◆　◆　◆

When the Hannans first arrived in Tule Lake, they had no idea of its bitter history. What had seemed a bit like an adventurous lark at Amache turned somber at Tule Lake, where the threat of imminent deportation hung over thousands of heads. Before the camp closed, that threat would become reality for 1,523 Issei, 1,116 Nisei renunciates and 1,718 minor children who had no choice but to accompany their parents to Japan.[19]

Since the WRA planned to resettle or deport all 16,000 of the camp's remaining inhabitants by February 1, there was much work to be done. "They are broadcasting for every able-bodied person to come in and help get things settled," Nell Hannan wrote.[20] Despite rusty secretarial skills, she began work at the camp hospital. As secretary to the medical social worker, she helped make arrangements for chronically ill patients to leave the camp. In letters home, she wrote:

MARI'S COPY OF A PHOTO BY ROBERT H. ROSS, WITH HER NOTES. COURTESY OF JOHN R. ROSS.

> The work is fascinating. We deal with the lives of people, some of which read like books.... I get an insight into the lives these people lived before evacuation. [21]

> We have situations here that would take Solomon himself to solve. When these people were first rounded up...and placed in various concentration camps, the idea was conveyed that all who were not citizens would have to return to Japan. Some were...older, and weary of being pushed around, were glad of the opportunity so they prevailed on their...children...to renounce their American citizenship. Now the old folks don't have to return to Japan, but the children do.[22]

Behind Barbed Wire

Side of Processing Bldg 3/20/46

In January she wrote,

> People are getting out fast and now even the hospital can be evacuated. We are finding beds in charitable institutions in Washington, Oregon and California for the ones who want to stay here, and there will soon be a hospitably-equipped ship (they hope) for the ones who wish to go to Japan.... The older ones change their minds from day to day about whether to repatriate to Japan and it makes a lot of paper work.[23]

Mrs. Hannan and her colleagues did not resent the extra work caused by indecision. "We go right on trying to negotiate a bed for them until they will actually be placed on the ship."

Helen recalled:

> My mother was sort of a mother hen to the ambulance drivers and orderlies and all these young kids who were waiting for their hearings. She was so concerned over them that the doctor had to put her on medicine for her nerves.... She was totally absorbed in each one of them individually, that they would get through their hearings all right.[24]

◆   ◆   ◆

Although Lawrence Hannan's official duties involved the internees' property issues, he too soon found himself helping the internees. Helen said:

> He would spend hours preparing young Nisei renunciates for their hearings.... These kids had never been to Japan in their lives. They had no place to go in Japan.... They were being given a chance for a hearing in which to explain why they should be allowed to reclaim their citizenship and so he was preparing them for this.[25]

He advised one renunciate, "Just tell them the loyalty questionnaire made you mad. It's as simple as that...you lost your cool, but you never meant to renounce your citizenship." When she thinks of the young internees, Helen still sputters with indignation. "These people had brothers who were fighting in the war while they were locked in camp...as my father used to say, 'You try locking up a couple of Irishmen like this, and you'd have non-stop riots....'"

Helen recalled:

> My parents greatly admired the way the internees were so dignified in this outrageous situation they were in.... They didn't just sit down and pout. They had like a small town existence there, with their clubs and their various things, and

Hoshidan

HOSHIDAN MILITANTS EXERCISING AT TULE LAKE, FROM MARI'S ALBUM. THE FULL-FRAME PHOTOS WERE TAKEN BY ROBERT H. ROSS. COURTESY OF THE BRENNAN FAMILY.

イケヂリ サン ト ノ ガワ ヨシナサン

they would make beauty out of anything. There was scrap lumber around from building the barracks. They would carve it into beautiful things.... And each one would have their little scrap of garden...somewhere so they could grow a few things.... They did their best to have a normal life.[26]

The Hannans also sought relief in the small joys of daily living. Nell Hannan confided in a letter that some of the patients' cases were so sad, they would "tear one up into bits and then tear up the bits but then in the midst of it will come something humorous or good and wholesome so there is almost always a balance."[27]

As at Amache, the Hannans turned to the church for uplift and community. They attended the internees' Mass and befriended the resident priest, Father Hunt, another Maryknoll missionary. He had returned from Japan on the exchange *Gripsholm*. Larry Jr. served as altar boy, and the Hannan daughters laundered the sacramental linens, which they lightheartedly called the "Sacred Wash." As Father Hunt prepared to return to Japan with the repatriates, Nell mended his clothes, which were "falling apart, he was so poor," Helen observed. In a letter, Nell wrote:

> To Father Hunt the physical well-being of his people is very important. He gets them feeling good...and then he goes after their souls. Very few of his congregation are baptized, and their backgrounds are all mixed, up with Buddhist temples, etc., but Father keeps a cozy place and any sort of treat he can find.

> Some of these people are going back to Japan very soon and since they are not allowed to leave the camp, they can do nothing to prepare themselves. Father Hunt buys lipsticks, slips, anything they ask. Yoyos by the hundreds!... Sometimes, he will be delayed by a half-hour starting his daily Mass, handing out bits of string for tops.[28]

"There are no shopping facilities except mail order," Nell reported. "They can't even buy a toothbrush in camp and neither can we." So the Hannans shopped for the internees on weekends, and Mari, who attended high school in the town of Tulelake, shopped every day after school. Helen admired her big sister's courage.

> I remember Mari going into the drugstore to buy Dixie Peach hair pomade. All the fellas, the young Japanese American internees, used it.... It's a good brand if you have really thick, heavy hair. The clerk just looked at Mari and said, "What do you want that for? The only people who use it are the Japs in the camp."

> I wanted to slink out of there, but Mari put on her most quelling "Queen Victoria" look and said, "Oh, really? Then I'd like six jars of it." She just stood there looking at them and defied them not to give it to her. And she got it.

MARTIN AND MARGARET GUNDERSON

Yuzuru Takeshita was a confused and angry young Kibei on his first day at Tule Lake's Tri-State High School. Born in the U.S. and taken to Japan at age eight, Yuzuru had been rejected as too American in Japan and too Japanese in the U.S. His family was initially interned at Topaz, but after Yuzuru's brother persuaded him to actively protest the loyalty questionnaire and join him as a no-no boy, the family was transferred to the segregation camp at Tule Lake. Yuzuru was asked to help teach Japanese to children planning to return with their parents to Japan, but he chose instead to continue his English language education at Tri-State High School. He recalled that he entered Margaret Gunderson's classroom filled with rage and cynicism, but her statements on the first day of school made a powerful and lasting impact. The internment should not have happened, she told the students. The failure lay, not in the Constitution, but in political leadership. The Constitution and the Bill of Rights were a blueprint for democracy, but each generation must work toward its realization. When she urged the students to stand firm against any encroachment of their freedom, Yuzuru felt affirmed in his right and responsibility to dissent with an unjust government.

Mrs. Gunderson's words carried particular weight because she and her husband lived their beliefs. Prior to the internment, Martin Gunderson had been school superintendent of Alameda County (in the San Francisco Bay Area), and Margaret had taught high school in San Leandro. After their Japanese American students were interned, the Gundersons quit their jobs to serve at Tule Lake, Martin as principal and Margaret as teacher. Margaret Gunderson mentored Yuzuru during the turbulence of the next two years. He renounced his citizenship, but later decided he wanted to remain in the U.S. In December 1945, he asked Mrs. Gunderson to give him an American name to celebrate his psychological "return to America." She suggested that he adopt "John" as his middle name, after her father.

After his release from Tule Lake, Yuruzu's brief stint in the U.S. Army was marred by his disqualification from the Military Intelligence Service (MIS) because he had renounced his citizenship. His rights were later reinstated when a federal court ruled that all renunciations made by internees under the age of 21 were "null and void." The Gundersons worked with the ACLU to support the court case. Yuzuru John Takeshita later became a sociology professor who made many trips to Asia as a family planning consultant. As he began to hear stories of the suffering inflicted by the Japanese military during wartime, he recalled that a childhood friend had died as a kamikaze pilot, and a soldier friend had come back from China hinting of Nanking-style atrocities. Grieved by the universal suffering caused by war, he was inspired by the long-ago example of the Gundersons to put his beliefs into action and actively work for peace and reconciliation among former wartime adversaries. *Nominated by Yuzuru J. Takeshita.*

> She took an awful lot of abuse because the shopkeepers caught on pretty quickly where she was coming from. She wanted men's clothing...and men's shoes in small sizes.... People would look at her...and say, "Well, maybe I'll give it to you and maybe I won't.".... But as my father said, "She had all the guts of an Army mule." Nothing could have put her off. She was going to bring back what was needed if she had to come back to the camp with the store and all their stock under one arm.[29]

◆   ◆   ◆

On the day before Christmas, the Hannans felt somewhat low-spirited because 1800 deportees were scheduled to be taken to Portland, Oregon, the following day and put aboard a ship to Japan. Powerless to stop what they believed to be a grievous injustice, the Hannans dedicated themselves to good works, rendering kindnesses large and small to anyone who asked.

> We decided to go to the town of Tulelake again for a few Christmas groceries.... What a town! Deep gooey mud everywhere. We should have stood in bed. Stores with the usual day-before Christmas people—"Marge, what shall I get the little woman?" but this year, there was so little for the clerks to offer.... We were trying to find gloves for a hospital clerk who was...leaving for Japan on Christmas Day. The usual futile search and final decision on something that would do. Then home, hungry and feeling akin to the mud.... No family was ever lower.... Just recovering from colds, no endurance, no food! Home and a bowl of steaming hot soup—spirits soared.[30]

Their spirits revived, Mari and her father decorated the old family crib to make a Christmas crèche and an old doll baby playing the part of the baby Jesus. They invited "children from the colony" to their home for a small good-bye party complete with presents, small items the deportees could pack into their luggage. Then the Hannans took their homemade crèche to the Midnight Mass at the staff church. "We had confessions...outside because there was no real confessional inside," Nell wrote.[31] The small portable organ was packed away in Father Hunt's luggage, so the priest asked for volunteers to sing a cappella.

TWO OVERLAPPING PHOTO STRIPS FROM MARI HANNAN'S PHOTO ALBUM. COURTESY OF THE BRENNAN FAMILY.

> Some visitors, mostly non-Catholic...sang throughout the Mass, with beautiful harmony.... It made for much peace and good cheer and everyone felt good in spite of the fact that they were gathered from the far corners of the country. A colored woman who does welfare work, and a Japanese and Italian, people from the state of Washington and from Washington, D.C., and from Maine and California.[32]

Having their Baggage Searched in Stockade

On Christmas Day, the Hannans piled into their car to

bid farewell to the deportees. When the car ran out of gas, they began walking, and were soon engulfed, Nell wrote:

> The exodus looked like something mentioned somewhere in the bible, maybe the last judgment day, as the deportees streamed from their barracks.... We had to walk around to try to find the hospital clerk. For all I know she was Buddhist, but nevertheless I asked St. Anthony to find her, and he did....
>
> Hours later deportees were still streaming slowly through the gates in the rain.... Babies were strapped on backs, and we could see the galoshes that Mari had been buying for the deportees for months.... The children—American citizens—who in many cases were being taken much against their will, but who are scarcely at an age to take care of themselves, were fingerprinted so they can come back when they are of age.[33]

Later that day, internee children came to the Hannan home to play, and Nell baked cookies for them to take home. Early the following morning, an internee child "appeared with a bag of potatoes to be French-fried so that they could be taken with the family on the 27th when another crowd left via train to embark for Japan at Portland." A total of 3551 deportees were shipped to Japan on December 29, followed on February 23, 1946, by 432 more.

Nell continued:

> Now we have an influx of Department of Justice men and women. Fifteen are conducting hearings and there's a flock of stenographers with them. Also the opposition—the Civil Liberties Union and their Lawyers stand by and occasionally listen in at the hearings.[34]

To another friend, she wrote: "Right now it's pretty tough, as the hearings have begun, and a lot of young people are looking pretty glum."[35]

The school for staff children was closed, so the Hannans sent Helen to the Sacred Heart Academy in Klamath Falls. She stayed at the boarding school during the week and returned to the camp on weekends. Helen's friend Alice Yoshikawa also went. Helen recalled:

> My father paid for Alice to come.... Her family couldn't have afforded it. I think they were making $19 a month.... Tuition at that time was $60 a month. It was a huge sum!... The sisters were wonderful.... We were just part of a mini-United Nations there.... My classmates all just loved Alice. They thought she was just the

PHOTO FROM MARI HANNAN'S PHOTO ALBUM. COURTESY OF THE BRENNAN FAMILY.

Inside Processing Building

sweetest thing in the world. It seemed that the children at the boarding school there were not poisoned like the rest of the town.[36]

Meanwhile, Mari stopped going to school. "The Tulelake school in town was a joke," Helen remembers. "My father let Mari quit high school in that semester and just hang around the camp. He said, 'What you're learning here is much more important.'"

Mari had become interested in photography. She filled a large album with photos of the camp. Mari believed that she was preserving an important record of camp history. Some of the photos were ordinary snapshots, but many were copies of images taken by the official camp photographers. The official government photos are now available to the public, but at the time, they were not. During the last months of the camp's operation, staff photographer Robert H. Ross cleaned out the files and threw out duplicates. He gave internee Jimi Yamaichi tacit permission to retrieve the discards by saying, "I can't give you any of these pictures, but if you see any of them lying around, I can't tell you what to do with them." Since Mari is deceased, we don't know whether Ross had a similar conversation with her. According to Helen:

PHOTO FROM MARI'S ALBUM, WITH HER HANDWRITTEN CAPTION, WAS PROBABLY TAKEN BY ROBERT H. ROSS. COURTESY OF THE BRENNAN FAMILY.

> She would use the camp darkroom. She'd slip in at night when no one was there. Obviously, she brought her own supplies. It wouldn't have been honest to be using theirs. All the photographic supplies that Mari needed…I would buy…during the week in Klamath Falls. Mari would write down carefully everything that she needed, and I was just her mule. I would get on the bus Friday night and come carrying all this stuff.[37]

Many of the photos in Mari's album are printed on narrow slivers of photographic paper. We do not know whether they were photographers' test strips that had been developed and discarded by Robert Ross, the official camp photographer, or whether Mari developed them herself, using discarded negatives and the supplies that Helen purchased for her in Klamath Falls. Helen felt sure that "if they had caught her at the time, they probably would have fried my father alive…. But he was totally supportive of her." The sense of secrecy lingered around the photographs for decades. Mari never discussed the photo album with her family, and her daughter

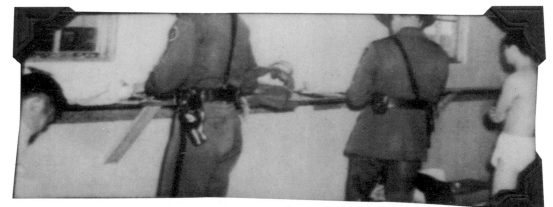

Boy's Searching Room - Stockade
3/20/46

Mary Johnson said, "I had the feeling...that the album was...secretive. We didn't really show it, or tell anybody we had it."

Several photos depicted the high school gymnasium burning down. Helen recalled the dramatic event:

> There was going to be a farewell dance because the camp was breaking up and everyone was going their separate ways. It wasn't easy, but they finally got permission. They decorated the gym, everything was set. The dance was to be held Saturday night. That afternoon, in broad daylight, the gym burned down.
>
> We were driving back from Klamath Falls and we saw the smoke in the distance, and with one accord we knew what it was. My mother always believed the fire was set. Somebody just being nasty, and denying the students one little pleasure that they wanted to have. No one ever knew who did it. I don't think the authorities wanted to know. It was simply "an unfortunate accident.[38]

The last of the internees was scheduled to leave Tule Lake on March 20, 1946. On the last day, some still did not know whether they would be freed or transferred for further detention to Crystal City, a Justice Department detention camp in Texas. The Hannans felt that "further detainment of the people in Crystal City was very wrong, adding insult to injury."[39]

Mari wrote a three-page account of the camp's final tense day. She babysat her friend's toddler while driving internees around the camp, picking up their mail, taking them magazines and candy bars, and helping them pack. She laughed and cried with them as they learned whether they were destined for Crystal City or for freedom.

The day began with a visit to Mari's good friend Helen Ikejiri. Helen and her daughter, Shigemi, were voluntarily joining Helen's husband in Crystal City. Two-year-old Shigemi had become Mari's little mascot, and Mari took her everywhere. "Helen gave me all of her personal papers to keep for her and a carton of things to send to her," Mari wrote.[40] Detainees had learned that the Justice Department was not giving receipts for the cash they were confiscating. Not having much faith in the government's plan to seal the money in envelopes marked with the owners' names, several people entrusted their cash to the Hannans and asked them to

Rushing to Fire

THE HIGH SCHOOL GYMNASIUM BURNING DOWN JUST BEFORE A DANCE WAS SCHEDULED TO BE HELD. COURTESY OF THE BRENNAN FAMILY

mail checks to relatives.

Mari learned that a friend, Tom Ariza, had been told that he was free to leave.

I wanted to cry and sing at the same time," Mari wrote. "My heart stopped beating for a second and I was so intensely happy I didn't know what to do. After all these weeks, since the detained list came in, such wonderful news at the last minute was almost too much of a shock to bear.

But not all the news was good:

Shigemi and I went to Jane Tsuji's house to give Jane her picture, which I took the other day. Her father is one of the six segregated parolees who was not freed. So the whole family is going to Crystal City. They have a baby just two months old.

Mari was torn between joy and heartbreak throughout the day. Her friend Helen's brother-in-law, Yosh Nogawa, learned that he was being sent to San Francisco to testify in a suit brought by civil rights attorney A. L. Wirin on behalf of the renunciates. Yosh's goods were packed together with Helen's in a big trunk bound for Crystal City. Suddenly he needed to retrieve his things. Mari rushed home to get her own suitcase, which she lent Yosh. As she and Yosh struggled to pack it, more free lists were announced, and they were surrounded by people yelling, "I'm free! I'm free!"

By the time the packing was finished, Helen and Shigemi had missed the breakfast serving at their mess hall. Mari took them home and fed them sandwiches and milk and then walked with them to the processing office. They rushed to be on time, then ended up waiting in the cold for over an hour. Mari wrote:

Everyone was thoroughly chilled standing outside. The wind penetrated. We wrapped Shigemi in a blanket and I held her, standing behind Yosh. He acted as a shield from the wind.

When Helen and Shigemi's names were called, Helen carried their bags and Mari carried Shigemi. Mari was told that she could ride in the truck with her friends as far as the stockade.

I couldn't go in. I might have bombs in my pockets, I suppose. But the truck didn't stop at the stockade entrance. It rolled right in, me with it. I was glad, because I had wanted to be with my friends in the stockade....

Here Mari's account stopped, but according to Helen, Mari had blended in with the other passengers with her dark hair and eyes, carrying a Japanese American baby. In her album is a photo of her sitting in the truck with the detainees, and she was able to stay with her friends a little longer.

The camp was emptied of internees on March 20, 1946, but the Hannans stayed on at Tule Lake while Lawrence wound up his work as project attorney. He was then hired by the Bureau of Reclamation to research land titles on the Central Valley Project, a huge power and water project that included Shasta Dam. The Hannans moved to Sacramento. There, Helen recalled,

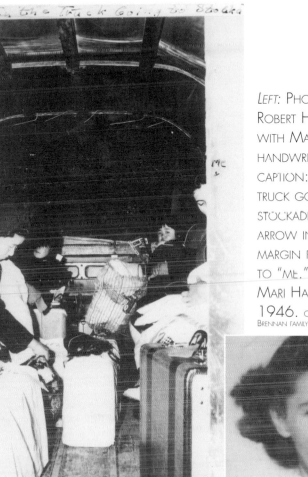

Mari kept up her friendships with a lot of the girls that she'd known in camp, who also relocated in Sacramento.... One day, she met a friend who had been a really great secretary in camp.... She was working as a maid because she was afraid to apply for a secretarial job.... She was afraid she'd be rejected. So Mari grabbed her...shoved her through the door of a big insurance company in downtown Sacramento and said, "Don't come out until you've applied for a job." Her friend applied for a job and got it. Then she went out and got her friends who were also working as maids, and they applied for jobs and got them. So even after camp, Mari was still giving them a little helping hand when she could.[41]

LEFT: PHOTO BY ROBERT H. ROSS WITH MARI'S HANDWRITTEN CAPTION: "IN THE TRUCK GOING TO STOCKADE." NOTE ARROW IN RIGHT MARGIN POINTING TO "ME." *BELOW:* MARI HANNAN, 1946. COURTESY OF THE BRENNAN FAMILY.

Mari did not forget her friends at Crystal City, either. She carried on a correspondence with U.S. Attorney General Tom Clark urging him to restore the renunciates' citizenship and cease attempts to deport them to Japan. She planned a career in the diplomatic service after college, but married Robert Brennan instead. After rearing ten children, she went back to school in the 1970s to become an obstetrical nurse.

Packing to leave Tule Lake April, 1946

MARI SURROUNDED BY PACKING CRATES IN THE HANNAN'S LIVING QUARTERS. COURTESY OF MARY JOHNSON.

Lawrence Hannan worked for the Bureau of Reclamation until his death in 1964 at age sixty-five. He never lost his sense of justice. Just before his death, he was assisting a Native American whose land had been falsely claimed by a Caucasian. "He was still going around with his antenna up for any injustices," Helen recalled.[42]

Former internees never forgot the Hannans, Helen said.

People were forever coming to our house for years, bringing fruit and flowers and vegetables, and one time, two live chickens. They were so grateful for the things that he had done for them in camp.... One young man who opened a florist's down in Los Angeles used to send us twenty pounds of fresh-cut flowers every Christmas. They never got over being grateful.[43]

Nell Hannan died in 1971 and Mari Hannan Brennan passed away in 1986, two years before President Ronald Reagan signed the redress bill, which offered the internees an apology and redress for the wrong that had been done them.

It was only after redress that the remaining Hannans began to talk about their years in an American concentration camp. Now seventy, Helen Hannan says, "Up until the redress, it was all pretty much swept under the rug. The government didn't want to talk about it, and the people who had been in the camps didn't want to talk about it. They felt somehow a stigma, although they had done nothing." She told a story that underscored the importance of having Caucasians bear witness to the injustice of the internment:

I met a man once who had a very good position at one of the big aircraft plants down in the L.A. area. When he heard that I had been at Tule Lake, too, he confided to me, "I always have this bad feeling inside of me, that I had been put in prison."

I told him, "You were put in prison because the government did something bad to you. You were seventeen years old, for heaven's sake. What wrong could you have done? You didn't do anything bad."

He said in a tone of amazement, "You know, no one has ever told me that—I feel much better now."[44]

DEVOTED TO THE DHARMA:
REVS. ERNEST SHINKAKU HUNT, JULIUS GOLDWATER AND SUNYA PRATT

REV. ERNEST SHINKAKU HUNT (1876–1967)

Rev. Ernest Shinkaku Hunt, who was born in England, was interested in religion from childhood. After graduating from college, he joined the British Merchant Marine to see the world.[1] Later, he entered the seminary and studied for the Anglican priesthood. Shortly before ordination, he remembered an exchange he had had years before with a Buddhist monk in Ceylon and decided against taking his final vows as a Christian minister. Instead, Hunt eventually made his way back to Asia to study Theravadan Buddhism. After receiving ordination in the Southeast Asian tradition, he went to Hawaii in 1915. He studied under Bishop Yemyo Imamura of the Honpa Hongwanji Mission of Hawaii and received a second ordination in the Jodo Shinshu tradition. He was given the name Shinkaku in 1927 and asked to develop a Buddhist curriculum for the Nisei generation. With his wife, Dorothy, he developed English-language lesson plans, guidelines, sermons and services for weddings, funerals and other special occasions. The Hunts also wrote words and music for many gathas, or Buddhist hymns. Their work was widely disseminated throughout the Hawaiian and mainland Jodo Shinshu churches, and much of it remains in use to this day. Their Sunday school literature has also served as a model for Tibetan and Zen Buddhist groups as immigrants seek to make traditional teachings accessible to their Westernized children.

Hunt's services took on a new urgency after the attack on Pearl Harbor. He was the only Buddhist minister remaining when all of the priests of Japanese ancestry were arrested and sent to detention camps on the mainland. At a time when all things Japanese and Buddhist were viewed with hostility and suspicion, Hunt made "courageous sacrifices at great personal risk."[2] He stopped the military police from smashing or confiscating butsudan, the household altars that devout Buddhists kept in their homes; supported the wives and children of the ministers who had been taken away; and continued to teach Buddhism and hold services in the Hawaiian Japanese community. He trekked to remote plantations with a butsudan strapped to his back and ministered to the forgotten patients of a tuberculosis sanitarium. His demonstrations of selfless service made a deep impression on a generation of young Nisei, many of whom later became religious and secular leaders in Hawaii's multicultural society.

Because of his unique status as a Caucasian Buddhist, Hunt suffered discrimination from both Christians and Buddhists. Rev. Newton Ishiura recalled an incident in 1929 when a Catholic bishop and an Anglican dean threatened to leave a meeting because of Hunt's presence, calling him an apostate, a defector from the Christian faith. On the other hand, many conservative Japanese Buddhists resented his broad, nonsectarian vision of Western Buddhism. Hunt's views were respected by Bishop Imamura, but after his mentor's death, Hunt was subjected to "prejudice and confrontation."[3] Eventually he left the Jodo Shinshu organization and joined the Hawaii Soto-Zen Mission, where he taught until his death.

REV. JULIUS GOLDWATER (1908–2001)

Born in Los Angeles to a German Jewish family, Julius A. Goldwater, cousin of Sen. Barry Goldwater, learned about Buddhism in Hawaii as a teenager. After studying with Rev. Ernest Shinkaku Hunt and Bishop Yemyo Imamura of the Honpa Hongwanji Mssion of Hawaii, Goldwater returned to Los Angeles and in 1928 founded a Buddhist study group that would evolve into the Buddhist Brotherhood.[4] In 1937, after taking instruction in Japan and China, he received ordinations from both Jodo Shinshu and a Chinese Buddhist sect.[5] That same year, he was asked to serve at the Los Angeles Hompa Hongwangi Betsuin Temple in Little Tokyo, working mainly with the Young Men's and Women's Buddhist Associations.[6] Goldwater made a particular impression on young Arthur Takemoto, who saw him as a man who truly lived his faith.[7] Takemoto remembers him as a jovial, friendly man who

20. **Devoted to the Dharma:** Revs. Ernest Shinkaku Hunt, Julius Goldwater and Sunya Pratt

257

livened up the young adult ministry by persuading the conservative Issei to allow the Nisei to hold dances, socials, theatricals and other events.

At the time, the Betsuin, or district temple, oversaw the Gardena and Senshin temples and eight sub-temples in Southern California. Immediately after Pearl Harbor, all of the Betsuin ministers, except for Goldwater, and most of the temple board were arrested by the FBI. Goldwater organized the ministers' wives and Nisei church members to carry on with services and other temple business. He then traveled to the San Francisco headquarters of the the Buddhist Mission of North America to urge it to take proactive measures to separate the temples in North America from the mother organization in Japan. This included changing the organization's name to the Buddhist Churches of America (BCA).[8]

Back in Los Angeles, Goldwater arranged to house evictees from Terminal Island at temples and language schools, and organized space in temple buildings to store members' belongings. Before the Betsuin's board of directors was interned, it gave Goldwater power of attorney to oversee the Betsuin's bank account and properties.

Beginning at the Santa Anita "Assembly Center," where he conducted weekly services, Goldwater worked very hard on behalf of the temple throughout the war years. He accepted responsibility for watching over the far-flung church properties, paying taxes and mortgages, and guarding the internees' stored property. He and the Buddhist Brotherhood visited patients interned at the Hillcrest Sanitarium in La Crescenta.[9] Goldwater also traveled to internment camps in California, Wyoming, Colorado and Arkansas at his own expense. He was not a member of the wealthy branch of the Goldwater family, but he had a trust fund that provided him with pin money.[10] Although he was called a "Jap lover," his house was defaced, and his conservative relatives thought of him as "some kind of clever traitor,"[11] Goldwater was not deterred. He had an honest and outspoken personality that some called prickly and irascible,[12] and others called feisty.[13]

In March 1945, as the internees began to trickle home, Goldwater established the first resettlement hostel in California at the Betsuin. He convinced Arthur Takemoto to return to Los Angeles to assist, secured bedding and kitchen utensils from the WRA, and solicited donations of furniture.[14] He prepared to welcome the congregation home, but was soon to have a rude shock.

When the temple leaders returned from camp, they found a changed world. Thousands had been attracted to Los Angeles to work in defense plants, and so many African Americans from the Deep South had moved into the deserted Little Tokyo area that it was known as Bronzeville. Accommodations were in such short supply that some tenants were sleeping five to a room. Temple buildings, which had been rented out to raise money for the mortgages and taxes, had become overcrowded and unsanitary, and the tenants had fallen behind on rent.[15] Furthermore, the temple bank account was depleted, and the State Banking Commission, which had picked up the temple mortgage from the Yokohama Species Bank following Pearl Harbor, was now calling in the loan.

Many argued that Goldwater had done the best he could under very difficult circumstances, but a few were quick to blame him for the state of the properties and the finances. They criticized Goldwater for spending temple funds without authorization, even though the money had gone toward such items as building maintenance, packing and shipping stored belongings to internees in camp, and printing 3,000 Buddhist service manuals for use by camp ministers. The disgruntled few persuaded the Betsuin's board to sue Goldwater for $10,000, charging mismanagement of temple finances.

Many felt the charges were baseless and politically motivated and that Goldwater had made good-faith decisions that demonstrated compassion and sensitivity to the needs of interned temple members. Goldwater himself was deeply hurt by the action, but he continued to serve the community. He resigned from the Los Angeles Betsuin and transferred the resettlement hostel to the Senshin Buddhist Temple, where he continued to manage it with the help of Takemoto and Rev. and Mrs. Kanmo Imamura. He also encouraged Takemoto to become a Buddhist minister. In the spring of 1946, the Betsuin's lawsuit went to trial. It was a long, drawn-out process, during which many bitter statements were made. Although the Betsuin won the judgment, the judge chided it for filing suit. Goldwater parted ways with the BCA and paid the restitution out of his family inheritance.

He continued to be deeply involved with Buddhism for the rest of his life. As new Asian immigrant groups began arriving in the mid-1960s, he helped Vietnamese, Cambodian, Thai, Sri Lankan and Korean Buddhists establish temples, often providing funds out of his own pocket.[16] He taught hundreds of Buddhists privately and cofounded the Buddhist Sangha Council in the 1980s. Many former internees continued to be grateful for his wartime efforts. In 1991, one woman sent him $500 out of her redress check. He wrote her that, though he accepted the check in the spirit in which it was given, he would never cash it. He continued to teach Buddhism until his death. *Nominated by Rev. Arthur Takemoto.*

Rev. Sunya Pratt (1898–1986)

For fifty years, Rev. Sunya Pratt nurtured generations of young Buddhists in the Pacific Northwest.[17] Her family emigrated from

England in 1919 and moved to Tacoma, Washington, in 1931. After she began the study of Buddhism, an article she wrote came to the attention of Bishop Kenju Masuyama of the Buddhist Mission of North America (now the Buddhist Churches of America). At a time when Christian denominations were successfully reaching out to a growing population of young Nisei through English-speaking Caucasian missionaries and ministers, the Buddhist church lagged behind. Services and Sunday schools were still conducted in Japanese by Issei ministers. Masuyama understood the vital necessity of developing an English-language program to reach out to both the Nisei and the American public. He instituted a program to train Nisei ministers, and when he met Miss Pratt, he immediately recognized her as a valuable resource for the church. He told her, "In America there is a need for a person who can understand the two minds—the Japanese and the English minds. The Japanese mind knows Buddhism but not the English mind. I want to put Buddhism into the English mind."

With the bishop's encouragement, Miss Pratt began to volunteer at the Tacoma Buddhist Church. She had no official status at first, beginning as an assistant at the Sunday school. She soon revealed a gift for expressing Buddhist teachings in clear and simple English and was given responsibility for teaching an English-language curriculum. The Sunday school's enrollment increased dramatically, reaching 150 in the late 1930s. The church was short of space, and classes were forced to meet in the church kitchen, the minister's office, and the balcony, stage and basement.

Still, the young people were asking for more, so Miss Pratt formed weeknight study groups. They proved so successful that she was invited to neighboring churches to conduct similar groups. She traveled regularly by bus to Seattle and Portland to teach classes in Buddhism. For her services, she received little or no financial compensation, because conservative church elders still did not understand or value her contributions. Masuyama, however, continued to support her. In 1936, the bishop ordained her as a lay minister and conferred on her the Buddhist name "Sunya."

By the late 1930s, the church had become a lively center for community activities of all kinds —from movies and Japanese dramas for the Issei to sports and socials for the young people. In 1937, the young people achieved a major victory when they persuaded the church elders to allow ballroom dancing in the church gym. More important, Tacoma's young Buddhists received a solid grounding in Buddhist thought while becoming active leaders in regional church activities.

World War II shattered the harmony of the church. The congregation's Issei minister, Rev. Gikan Nishinaga, was arrested by the

FBI and sent to a Department of Justice camp in Montana. Church members living outside of Tacoma were interned at the Puyallup Fairgrounds, while Tacoma residents were sent to Camp Pinedale outside of Fresno, California. The church closed its doors for the duration in May 1942. Reverend Pratt obtained permission from the WRA to continue a Sunday school program at Puyallup until the internees were relocated. By the fall, church members had been scattered far and wide, to permanent internment camps at Heart Mountain, Wyoming; Minidoka, Idaho; Tule Lake, California; Poston, Arizona; and Rohwer, Arkansas.

Reverend Pratt remained in Tacoma and kept watch over the church and the internees' belongings stored in the church basement. The church reopened as a hostel for returnees in March 1945, and Reverend Pratt held the first postwar service in her home—a memorial service for a Nisei killed in action in the South Pacific. Not until May of the following year was Gikan Nishinaga able to return to Tacoma to restore the church to a regular footing.

Sunya Pratt was vital to the postwar resurgence of the church. She developed Buddhist education materials and programs that were used throughout the Northwest District, and in some cases by the BCA as a whole.

After serving the church for twenty-five years, through the tenures of five ministers, Reverend Pratt was honored at a testimonial dinner in 1959. In 1969, she was officially appointed as a minister of the Buddhist Churches of America by the Nishi Hongwanji, the head temple in Kyoto, Japan. In 1985, she was awarded the Order of the Sacred Treasure, Sixth Class, by the Japanese government. She died at the age of eighty-eight after five decades of service to the church and to the community.

Conclusion: How We Chose the Stories and What We Learned

Choosing the stories. By June 2004 the Kansha Project had compiled a database of over 300 names, along with a brief description of what they did, the nominator's name, and sources for further information. Given limitations in time, money and access, we cannot claim that the database is comprehensive. Sixty-three years have passed since Pearl Harbor, and many stories have died with the people who lived them. Memories are subjective and inexact at best, and vital details have been lost in the shadows of time. Yet, to draw meaningful lessons from these stories, it was necessary to go beyond a simple cataloguing and bring these stories to life by asking: "Who were these people? What did they do, and why? What price did they pay?"

We decided it was neither necessary nor possible to rank one deed against another or compare one person with another. Some will argue that an act is truly selfless only if made at risk of life or liberty, or at the very least without compensation, but we found that kindness and courage came in many forms. To consider only unpaid supporters would be to ignore teachers and social workers who walked away from good jobs to work in isolated internment camps, church workers who sacrificed their health or family life to give far beyond the call of duty, and those who cared for farms or nurseries for a fair and honest fee.

Researching each name in the database, we looked for surviving supporters and/or their families, as well as beneficiaries, who were willing to be interviewed. We also sought published or unpublished memoirs, oral histories, letters, newspaper clippings, articles, books and photographs that could bring representative individuals to life. These sources provided fresh perspectives on various aspects of the internment—not so much from the victims' view as from that of people who could have chosen not to get involved.

We briefly acknowledged about 100 other supporters in the appendices and in boxes scattered through the text. Unfortunately, time and resources did not permit us to do justice to many significant individuals, such as Protestant missionaries Frank Herron Smith and Gordon Chapman, the lawyers who challenged the internment, and many who helped the student relocation movement.

Individuals and organizations. The political complexities of organizational history are beyond the scope of this book. The Kansha Project was generated by individuals nominating individuals. Those who supported the Japanese Americans were not always well supported by the institutions with which they were associated. Prior to the internment, many groups took a wait-and-see attitude, and then were caught unprepared when pressure for internment suddenly snowballed. Even the American Friends Service Committee, which did so much to assist Japanese Americans, did not officially oppose the internment but sought to work with the government to mitigate its impact. Other groups, including the Committee on National Security and Fair Play, the American Civil Liberties Union and national church groups, were internally divided about the internment. In groups such as the pacifist Fellowship for Reconciliation or the Young Men's Christian Association and the Young Women's Christian Association, some individuals or local chapters actively supported the internees, while others did not.

ABOUT THE NOMINATORS. The stories are skewed toward those who are still alive to tell them. Many of those who helped the Issei and older Nisei preserve their property are long gone, and so are detailed memories of the business arrangements needed to preserve assets. Fewer former internees than we expected came forward with stories of people who had impacted them personally. When queried directly, the vast majority of former internees recalled loss, disappointment or betrayal rather than support. Several people nominated individuals like Herbert Nicholson or Josephine Duveneck, whom they had read about, even though they had not benefited directly from them.

On the other hand, in the heaving chaos of the internment, some Nisei were deeply moved by the smallest gestures of support. When Touru Yenari was a junior high school student incarcerated at the Santa Anita "Assembly Center," his Jewish American classmate and neighbor Joe Portney bicycled ten miles from Boyle Heights to visit him and deliver a load of fresh laundry. Sox Kitashima recalled that her family's landlady, Evelyn Stevenson Perkins, served them a farewell breakfast on her finest china. Hanae Yamada Matsuda kept a tiny baby dress in her trunk for decades, part of a layette sent by the American Friends Service Committee after she gave birth at Minidoka. Her baby was a boy, but to Mrs. Matsuda the tiny dress remained a potent symbol of compassion.

A number of beneficiaries went on to highly successful careers, but here again, time and access may have skewed our perceptions. For instance, the most successful of Elizabeth Humbargar's beneficiaries were quotable, articulate and easy to find, while a working-class Nisei, found by chance, could only mumble a heartfelt "She was good to us." Many who believed they had received crucial assistance during a significant period of their lives felt an almost sacred duty to keep alive the memory of their benefactors. They were delighted to send us many pages of material.

At the other end of the spectrum, one camp high school alumna said, "We find that a lot of people...'kiss white ass' and do not give enough credit to the Japanese American teaching staff." She was suspicious of stated motives for working in the camps: "In retrospect, many of these Caucasian teachers from the outside said they were incensed at the way the government treated Japanese Americans during World War II and that was the reason for signing up to work in the...camps. Some of us smile and let it go at that."

WHY DID THEY DO IT? Most supporters were modest and matter-of-fact about their contributions, stating that their actions arose naturally out of a strong core of belief—in religious values and/or in the Constitution of the United States. Their Christianity was less interested in saving souls than in supporting the goodness inherent in all people. Love of God meant helping end war, poverty and discrimination, and love of country meant striving to bring about freedom, equality and justice for all people. For many, these deeply held beliefs fueled a transcendent power that sustained them through the most challenging of times.

Many supporters had previous associations with people of Japanese ancestry, but those who did not quickly came to love and respect them, extolling their honesty, intelligence, hard work and appreciativeness. Most felt that they received far more than they gave and learned as much as they taught. Topaz administrator Roscoe Bell wrote:

> All in all, it was a tremendous experience...working with people who had every cause to be embittered, but were not; people who were optimistic and cooperative; and people we enjoyed.... It was for us, both individually and as a family, a faith-strengthening experience.

WHO WERE THE SUPPORTERS? Within the 300 entries in the database, many supporters tended to be:
- those with preexisting relationships with Japanese Americans as teachers, neighbors or friends;
- religious people, mainly foreign and domestic missionaries and members of the peace churches, particularly Quakers;
- educators, including prewar teachers, camp teachers and those who worked with the student relocation program;
- young adults in transition—mostly recent college graduates, conscientious objectors, and those who lost their jobs as a result of the war;
- descendants of groups that were marginalized because of religion or country of origin;
- people who had experienced extreme poverty or extreme wealth;
- people from families with a history of activism, such as participation in the Underground Railroad.

A surprising number of supporters went on to do remarkable things later in life. Almost twenty years after running errands for internees at Tanforan Assembly Center, Gerda Isenberg established what is now California's oldest native plant nursery. Thirty years after operating a resettlement hostel in Chicago, Ralph Smeltzer worked to end the Vietnam War. Forty years after teaching at Manzanar, Helen Ely Brill cofounded a local chapter of Parents and Friends of Lesbians and Gays. Although several individuals reported that the people and ideas they encountered during the internment period were inspiring and transformative, it cannot be definitively determined whether these individuals were remarkable to begin with, or whether their internment experiences convinced them that they could make a difference in the world.

WHAT WERE THEIR LIMITATIONS? The supporters were the products of an age when most people knew little or nothing about Japanese Americans and when "Americanization" and assimilation were unquestioningly espoused. Some praised the internees in Christian terms. One or two even believed that Japanese American Christians had higher character than Buddhists, even though the values they applauded, such as *giri* (duty), *gaman* (the ability to endure or tolerate difficult circumstances), *shikita ga nai* (the ability to make the best of things because "it can't be helped"), *ganbare* (perseverance) and *kansha* (gratitude, appreciation), are deeply rooted in Japanese culture.

Certainly more Christians benefited from assistance than Buddhists, largely because of access. Private individuals tended to help those they knew, often through church, and many religious organizations directed aid to members of their own denominations. "The Baptists are taking care of their own, so that leaves us to take care of the Buddhists," a Quaker complained during the eviction from Terminal Island.

Students who were academically or creatively gifted tended to receive more support than average students, and those who went to college were expected to excel not only for their own sake, but to pave the way for others to follow in their footsteps. This focus on the "best and the brightest" forced the Nisei into "model minority" roles and left little room to dissent, or even to be ordinary. The climate of the times was so overwhelmingly negative that supporters tended to curry public sympathy for the "deserving." Although all Japanese Americans were deprived of their constitutional rights, the UC Berkeley gold medal scholar wasting his talent behind barbed wire made more compelling copy than the average Joes no longer able to hang around a Japantown soda fountain.

Even those who worked closely with the Issei usually chose in their public statements to focus on Nisei civil rights. By choosing their battles and focusing on the civil rights of the American-born Nisei, they kept their message simple, but largely sidestepped the unjust immigration laws that condemned Asian immigrants to an "alien" limbo where their rights were easily contravened.

The subjects of this book may seem naive or paternalistic at times, and the good that they were able to accomplish pales in comparison to the massive injustices of the internment. But injustice thrives on cynicism and apathy, and if there is one lesson to be learned from these stories, it is that no act of compassion is too small. We cannot all be Harriet Beecher Stowes or Otto Schindlers. There is, in fact, a danger in expecting heroism to be outsized. By thinking we have to make a big difference, we may end up doing nothing. Tides are turned not only by the words and deeds of historic figures, but by the quiet and enduring heroism of ordinary people acting in good conscience.

ACKNOWLEDGMENTS

We thank the following donors for their generous contributions:

Victor Abe
Cecilia Adaniya
Mitsue and David Aka
Raymond and Shizu Aka
Yoshinori Aka
Saige Aramaki
Marge Arnold
Denise and Joseph Ast
Nobuyoshi Azebu
Hans Baerwald
William and Heidi Black
E. Keith Brown
Linda and Brad Brown
Stefanie and Joseph Browning
Kevin Chapas
Charles and Jean Chapman
Ursula Coates
Anne and Arthur Colwell
Bruce Davis
A. Dean and Helen Looney
Peg and Don Dillon
Misa Egami
Evelyn J. Elster
Takeshi and Takako Endo
Orlando Epp
Carolsue Fenwick
Harold Fudenna
Tom and Annie Fujimoto
Alice Fujinari
James Fujitani
Kazuko and Wayne Fujito
Brian Fukuhara
Harry and Terry Fukuhara
Toshie and Nobuo Furuiye
Monte and Jean Furuya
Yasuko Furuya
Howard and Andrea Gabbert
Stanley and Tomoko Gillette
Jeanne Gosho
George Hachiya
Richard and Setsuko Hamasaki
Ben Hamilton
Ralph and Monique Hampton
Yuriko and Asa Hanamoto
Frank Handa
Lil and Akira Hara

Janet and Raymond Harada
Jim Hashimoto
Haruo Hayashi
Thomas (Yukio) and Frances Hayashi
Janice and George Higashi
Kiyoshi and Masae Higashi
Beatrice and Thomas Hikida
William Himel
Grant Hirabayashi
John and Mamie Hirasawa
Chris Hirohama
Leo Hosoda
Bill Hosokawa
Virginia Hotta
Flosada Huff
Stan and Rosalea Hyman
Mildred and Grant Ichikawa
Roy Idehara
Hideo Ihara
Tetsuo (Jane) Imagawa
Masaji Inoshita
Masato Inouye
Roy and Bette Inui
George Iseri
Helen Ishida
Mas and Barbara Ishikawa
Moffet and Thelma Ishikawa
Paul and Shizue Ito
Susan and Clyde Ito
Kenneth Iwagaki
Michio Iwahashi
Shoji Iwahiro
Bert and Marion Iwai
Sadame and Thomas Iwasaki
Nami Iwataki
Tetsuro Kajiya
Alice and Kin Kanagaki
Kay and Patsy Kaneda
Arthur Kaneko
Wayne Kanemoto
Mas Kasahara
Mitsugi Kasai
Louise (Misako) Kashiki
Guadalupe and Ken Kashiwahara
Stella Kato
Tak Kato

Larry Katsuyama
Mas and Ida Kawaguchi
Sadie (Sadako) Kawaguchi
Laverne and Ed Kelley
Bette and Akio Kikuchi
Hiroko and Ralph Kimoto
Shari Kimoto
Rusty (Robert) Kimura
Fukiko Kitagawa
John Kitagawa
Dorothy and Fred Kitajima
Roy Ko
George Koshi
Alice S. and Tony Koura
Spady and Miya Koyama
Ardaven Kozono
Arthur Kumada
Tomoye and Samuel Kumagai
Joseph Kurata
Bette (Michiko) and Tomoyoshi Kurokawa
Tom (Tomoyoshi) Kurokawa
Arnold and Lillian Lam
Robert Leigh
Naomi and James Maci
Henry and Tomoko Maki
Akihiko Maruya
Nori Masuda
Sophie (Takako) Masuda
George Matsumoto
Bill and Ellen McGarry
Bob and Joann Menke
Allen H. Meyer
Robert Midzuno
Nancy Mihara
Yaichiro Minami
Jane and Jim Mita
Michiko and Norio Mitsuoka
Hisao Miyamoto
Toshiko and Yukio Mochizuki
Mary Momii
Jun Mori
Misao and Frank Mori
Yoko and Tadashi Mori
Takashi Morita
Charles Moriyama

John Morozumi
Yuri and Fred Murakami
Hugh Muranaka
Mary and Bismarck Muraoka
Jean Nagaei
Pat Nagano
Elaine Nagasako
Satoshi Nagase
Alice and Don Nakahata
Ben and Hisako Nakamoto
Masaye Nakamura
Ed M. Nakasone
Chie and Craig Nakata
Clara and Francis Nishioka
Kazuko Nishita
Yvonne Noguchi
Joanne Obata
William Oda
William Odom
Helen Ogawa
Teresa and Haruji Ogawa
John and Diane Oji
May Oji
Sukeo and Tey Oji
Norio and Toshiko Okada
Peter and Mutsuko Okada
Fumie Okamoto
Shig Okimura
Don Okubo
Janice and George (Tokio) Okudara
Muneo Okusa
Sadayoshi Omoto
Edward and Miyuki Otake
Hiroshi Oto
Wesley Ouye
Sharon and Lynda Ozaki
Lois and Isamu Ozasa
Koji Ozawa
Robert and Lydia Payne
Richard Perry
Frank Sackton
Irene Y. Saiki and Sathya Seigel
Yuriko and Barry Saiki
Cherry Sakakida
George Sakanari
Hitoshi Sameshima

Ko and Sumie Sameshima
Fred Sanbongi
Anita and George Sankey
Kei K. Sasaki
Haruo Sazaki
Howard Schrecengost
Shizue Seigel
Kaoru and Mariko Shibata
Shigeru Shimazu
George Shimizu
John Shimoda

Brian and Jane Shiroyama
Sierra Nisei Post 8499 Veterans
    of Foreign War
Rinjiro Sodei
Mary Soyeshima
Robert Sugimoto
George Suzuki
Thelma and Clarence Suzuki
Kan Tagami
Mary and Roy Takai
Sojiro Takamura

Sachiko and Bob Takata
Tadao Takayanagi
Susie Takeda
Ben Takeshita
Frank Tanaka
King and Heija Tanaka
Shizuo Tanaka
Walter and Kasumi Tanaka
Harry Toda
Albert and Yoshiye Tokuno
Shiro and Asako Tokuno

Toshiko Tsudama
Ted Tsukiyama
Warren and Betty Tsuneishi
Toshi Uesato
Dick and Ruby Uno
Mary and James Uno
Marvin and Miyo Uratsu
Kiyoko Uyehata
Geraldine and Donald Wakida
Rosey and Ronald Watanabe
Donald Yabe

George and Sato Yamamoto
Naomi Yamamoto
Steve Yamamoto
Kanashi Stanley Yamashita
Peter Yamazaki
Miwako Yanamoto
Mas Yonemura
Shigeko Yoshiwara
Theodore T. Yenari and Tong
    Ha

We are indebted to the following people for providing us with nominations, information or other assistance.

Margaret Abe
Rev. Paul D. Aita
Rev. Brooks Andrews
James Arima
Hans Baerwald
Louise Barsotti
Earnest Bell
Gladys K. Bell
Paul E. Bell
Gordon and Manetta Bennett
William Manchester Boddy
Tom Bodine
Kimberly D. Bowden,
    Librarian Archivist,
    The Haggin Museum
Louise Brill
Michael Bryant, Sonoma
    County JACL
Sandra Loomis Cabassi
Charles Chapman
Philip Chin, Masanori Hongo
    and Leonard D. Chan,
    AACP, Inc.
Karleen Chinen, *Hawaii Herald*
Donald Clinton
Susanne Norton Coffey
Joey Conzevoy
Robert W. Coombs
Florence Dobashi
Robert Dockhorn, Senior Editor,
    Friends Journal
Jim Doi
Dennis Dougherty, University of
    Southern California, USC
    Specialized Libraries and
    Archival Collections

Cheryl Dulas and the JACL-
    Twin Cities Day of
    Remembrance 2000
    Planning Committee
Gerald Elfendahl
Carolyn McHenry Elwess, '71,
    University Archivist,
    Fishburn Archives, Park
    University
Arleen Andrews Engle
Dave Fawns
Tom Fujimoto
Marjorie Fujioka
Kiku Funabiki
Howard Gabbert
Stephanie George, Collection
    Curator, Center for Oral and
    Public History, California
    State University, Fullerton
Ted and John Goertzel
Junichi Gondai
Lysbeth, John and Molly
    Goodman
Deborah Guest, Descanso
    Gardens
Judy Yoko Hamaguchi
Mas Hashimoto and the –Santa
    Cruz JACL
Susan Hayase
Haruo Hayashi
Vernon Hayashida
David M. Hays, Archivist,
    University Libraries,
    University of Colorado,
    Boulder
Aiko Yoshinaga Herzig

Rose Asoo Hironaka
Jack Hirose
Fran Homer, American Baptist
    Churches USA
Dana Hoshide, Densho Project
Bill Hosokawa
Grant Ichikawa
Kazuo Ikeda
Tom Ikeda, Executive Director,
    Densho Project
Kinji Imada
Joanne Iritani
George Iseri
Jean Ishibashi
Roy Yoneo Ishihara
Harvey Itano
Ken Iwagaki, Japanese American
    Museum/San Jose
Kazue Sekiya Iwatsubo
Mary Johnson
Frank Kami
Marion Kanemoto and Joanne
    Iritani, Florin JACL Oral
    History Project
Emiko Katsumoto
Isao Kikuchi
Yuriko Amemiya Kikuchi
Pearl Kurokawa Kimura
Fujiko Kitagawa
Tsuyako "Sox" Kitashima
Nancy Klemm, Managing
    Editor, Brethren Press
Ken Kobara
Yuri Kochiyama
Cindy Kumagawa
Glenn Kumekawa

Pearl Kurokawa
John Loomis
Nadine Low
Yoshi Asaba Mamiya
Helen Amerman Manning
Anthony Manousos
Carolyn Marr, Librarian,
    Museum of History &
    Industry
Marie Masumoto and Susan
    Fukushima, the Hirasaki
    National Resource Center,
    Japanese American National
    Museum
Hanae Yamada Matsuda
Mas Matsumoto
Yayoe Matsushita Matsuura
Eunice Matthews
Marcia Mau
Dan McLaughlin, Pasadena
    Public Library
Stephen McNeil, Assistant
    Regional Director for
    Peacebuilding & Relief,
    American Friends Service
    Committee
Patricia Merritt
Ralph P. Merritt III
Allen H. Meyer
Claire Mitani, Archivist, 442nd
    Veterans Club Archives
Gail Miyasaki, Operations
    Manager, *The Rafu Shimpo*
Alan and Archie Miyatake,
    Archie Miyatake Studio
Kim Mizuhara

Phyllis Mizuhara
Yukio Mochizuki
Ronald Morimoto
Kay Murakami
Mollie Wilson Murphy
Ann Muto
Nelson Nagai
Joe Nagano
Rev. Paul Nagano
Kerry Yo Nakagawa
Yosh Nakagawa
Masaye Nagao Nakamura
Nellie Nakamura
Miyo Nakanishi
Annie Nakao
Edwin M. "Bud" Nakasone
Seiji and Jane Naya
Samuel O. Nicholson
Judy Niizawa
Alice and Flora Ninomiya
Calvin Ninomiya
Norine Nishimura
Grace Imamoto Noda
Jessie Nunn, K. Ross Toole
    Archives, The University of
    Montana—Missoula
Dorothy Harada Oda
Meredith Oda
Paul Ohtaki
George Oiye
Sukeo Oji
Chizu Omori
Rachel Onuf and Daniel N.
    Rolph, PhD, Reference
    Services, Historical Society
    of Pennsylvania

John Ortega
Fred Oshima
Helen Hannan Parra
Lian Partlow, Pasadena
    Museum of History
Cris Paschild, Archivist,
    Japanese American
    National Museum
Richard Potashin, Manzanar
    National Historic Site
Mary Calista Woodward Pratt
Kim Richards
Donald and Talbot Richardson
Greg Robinson
John Ross
Irma Roth
Robert Rusky
Barry Saiki
Eiichi Sakauye
Saren Sakurai, Oregon Nikkei
    Legacy Center
Mark Santoki
Dale Ann Sato

Dasiy Satoda
Kiyo Sato-Nunneley
Lorraine Scott, Curator,
    Bainbridge Island
    Historical Society
Eleanor Gerard Sekerak
Mari Yamamoto Siegel
Ken Shaffer Jr., Director,
    Church of the Brethren
    Archives
Hiroshi Shimizu
Francis Sogi
Mary Blocher Smeltzer
Susan Snyder, Library
    Representative, The
    Bancroft Library,
    University of California,
    Berkeley
Jared Stanley
Jack Sutters, American Friends
    Field Service Archives
George Suzuki
Seda Suzuki

Tami Suzuki
Laurel Brill Swan
Kenji Taguma, *Nichi Bei Times*
Tomoye Takahashi
Alice Imamoto Takemoto
Rev. Arthur Takemoto
Yuzuru John Takeshita
James Tanabe
Catherine Fukui Tanaka
Edith Itano Tanaka
Vivian Candy Tanamachi
Paul Tani
John Tateishi, Executive
    Director, National JACL
Dave Tatsuno
Rev. Paul Tellström, Mount
    Hollywood Church
Terminal Island Oral History
    Project
Jeanne Thevierge, Local
    History Specialist,
    Redwood City Main
    Library

Julie Thomas, Special
    Collections & Manuscripts
    Librarian, California State
    University, Sacramento
Mary Tomita
Minoru Tonai
Rosalyn Tonai, Executive
    Director, National Japanese
    American Historical
    Society
Ted Tsukiyama
Warren M. Tsuneishi
Barbara Uchiyama
Marvin Uratsu
Grayce Kaneda Uyehara
Joyce Uyehara
Eugene Uyeki
Rev. Lloyd Wake
Christine Wakeem, Mount
    Hollywood Congregational
    Church
Patricia Wakida
George Wakiji

Hannah Maggiora Wallstrum
Stephen Yale, Archives of the
    California-Nevada
    Conference of the United
    Methodist Church
Tom Yamada
Jimi Yamaichi, Japanese
    American Museum/
    San Jose
Eriko Yamamoto, PhD
J. K. Yamamoto, *Hokubei
    Mainichi*
Dr. William S. Yamamoto
Jean Yamasaki
Martha Yamasaki
Harry Yasumoto
Joe Yasutake, Japanese
    American Museum/
    San Jose
Midori Yenari
Mas Yonemura
Rev. Michael Yoshi

WHY THE MAINLAND AND NOT HAWAII: DECISIONS LEADING TO MASS INCARCERATION

During World War II, not one act was ever substantiated of espionage or sabotage by citizen or noncitizen Japanese Americans on the West Coast. Military intelligence and the Federal Bureau of Investigation (FBI) had been investigating Japanese Americans since 1939 and had concluded that the overwhelming majority were loyal. Three days after Pearl Harbor, FBI director J. Edgar Hoover reported that he had "practically all" potentially dangerous alien Japanese in custody—some 1300 persons on the West Coast and in Hawaii.[1]

And yet, within the succeeding six months, 120,000 Japanese Americans would be forcibly evicted from the West Coast and incarcerated in concentration camps and detention camps in the name of national security. About thirty percent were immigrants, who lacked the constitutional protections of U.S. citizens. In a crucial difference between Japanese immigrants and their German and Italian counterparts, the Japanese were not permitted to become U.S. citizens, no matter how long they lived in the United States. The Naturalization Act of 1790 limited naturalized citizenship to "free white persons." The 1908 "Gentlemen's Agreement" severely limited immigration from Japan, and the Immigration Act of 1924 ended it completely. Most Issei internees had lived in the United States for at least twenty-five years.

As for the seventy percent of incarcerees who were second-generation Nisei, they may have acquired U.S. citizenship by being born on American soil, but many Caucasians agreed with Secretary of War Henry L. Stimson, who noted in his diary that "their racial characteristics are such that we cannot understand or even trust even the citizen Japanese."[2]

Militarily, the threat of attack would appear far greater in the territory of Hawaii than on the mainland. The devastation at Pearl Harbor clearly demonstrated that the Islands were vulnerable to attack. They were located 2300 miles closer to Japan, and more than thrity-seven percent of the population was of Japanese ancestry—almost 160,000 residents, compared to the mainland's 127,000. Yet of the 120,000 persons of Japanese ancestry incarcerated during the war, just 1,446 were from Hawaii.

Clearly, decisions on who should be taken into custody were driven not by military necessity, but by racial, economic and political considerations. In Hawaii, the Island Japanese represented such a large percentage of the workforce that the economy would have collapsed without them, and the local power structure acted quickly and publicly to affirm their loyalty. On the mainland, racial discrimination against Japanese Americans was long standing, and agricultural interests bent on eliminating economic competition seized the opportunity to drive them from the West Coast. Public hysteria, fanned by ambitious politicians and the media, generated intense pressure for internment, especially in California.

IN HAWAII. After Pearl Harbor was attacked, Hawaii's army commander, Gen. Walter C. Short, was relieved of his duties, and Gen. Delos C. Emmons was brought in to replace him. With the declaration of martial law, Emmons also became the military governor of the Islands. He was determined to proceed justly and calmly.

The attack on Pearl Harbor had given rise to rumors that treacherous "Island Japanese" had aided the enemy. Arrows were allegedly slashed in the cane fields to direct enemy pilots; a deliberately created traffic jam snarled access roads to Pearl Harbor; and Hickham Field personnel were machine-gunned by a truckload of Nisei. These allegations were investigated and found to be false. The truth was, thousands of Nisei serving in the military had rushed to the defense of the Islands, and Issei civilians had lined up to donate blood. In his first official broadcast on December 21, Emmons told the public:

> [T]here have been very few cases of actual sabotage.... [T]here is no intention or desire on the part of the federal author-
> ities to operate mass concentration camps.... While we have been subjected to a serious attack by a ruthless and treach-
> erous enemy, we must remember that this is America and we must do things the American Way. We must distinguish
> between loyalty and disloyalty among our people.[3]

Emmons's statements never received wide circulation on the mainland, however, because of the censorship imposed by martial law. Instead, mainland newspapers focused on sensationalistic and unsubstantiated allegations made several days earlier by Secretary of the Navy Frank Knox.

Knox was the first Washington official sent to inquire into the catastrophe at Pearl Harbor, leaving for Hawaii just three days after the attack. When he returned to the mainland on December 15, he immediately called a press conference to declare that "the most effective fifth column work of the entire war was done in Hawaii, with the possible exception of Norway."[4] Knox was not a career military man. He was a Republican newspaper publisher, and a former general manager of the Hearst press. Since his tenure at Hearst had coincided with virulent campaigns against the "yellow peril," Knox could hardly be considered naive about the impact of his press conference. His written report, issued the following day, made no mention of espionage or sabotage by Island Japanese, but his press conference had already generated sensationalistic headlines and planted fears of what Japanese Americans might do if Japan attacked again.

At a December 19 cabinet meeting, Knox again asserted that "there was a great deal of very active fifth column work going on both from the shores and from the sampans" in Hawaii.[5] He urged Secretary of War Stimson to round up Hawaii's 35,000 Issei and intern them on an isolated island.

When the War Department asked Emmons what he thought about Knox's proposal, Emmons called it dangerous and impractical. Putting his career at risk, he resisted repeated calls for mass internment over the next few months. He told Washington that building the camps, transporting internees and guarding them would deplete resources badly needed for Island defenses. He felt confident that adequate security could be maintained by martial law regulations that included a curfew, censorship of the media and the mail, mandatory registration and identity cards, restrictions on bank withdrawals, and the replacement of civil courts by military courts.

In early February, the War Department again raised the question of mass internment. Shrewdly, Emmons did not directly oppose the idea; he merely transformed it into a logistical nightmare. Hawaii lacked the resources to house and feed internees, he insisted, so they needed to be transported to the mainland. Since the number of potentially disloyal Island Japanese could reach 100,000, and ships were in short supply, such an undertaking was not practical. Besides, he suggested, priority should be given to evacuating 20,000 Caucasian women and children from Hawaii to the mainland for their safety. Not long afterward, Emmons fended off a War Department order to fire all civilians of Japanese ancestry working for the army, calling them absolutely essential to the war effort. By March 1942, Emmons's foot-dragging had induced the War Department to reduce its estimate of the "potentially dangerous" to 20,000. In the end, less than two percent of Island Japanese were ever transported to mainland detention camps.

Emmons did not arrive at his decisions in a vacuum. Since he had only recently arrived in Hawaii, he listened carefully to the opinions of those around him. Lt. Gen. Charles D. Herron, Hawaii's army commander from 1937 to 1941, advised against internment, saying, "[The Island Japanese] are loyal to the soil and not the blood."[6]

Col. Kendall J. Fielder, Emmons's chief intelligence officer, concurred, stating that the Island Japanese were "as American as you are, or I."[7] Fielder had developed a thorough knowledge of the Islands through his service in the Hawaii National Guard, and subsequently, as a U.S. Army intelligence officer. His support of the Island Japanese was firm and consistent. When Emmons ordered Fielder to intern at least fifty Hawaiian Japanese a week from the area bordering Pearl Harbor, he ignored the quota at the risk of his career, detaining only individuals he determined to be a genuine security risk. In January 1942, when Nisei in the military were side-lined into noncombatant service, Fielder was sent to Washington, D.C., to propose that the Nisei be organized into a combat unit for the European theater, thereby planting the seed for the 100th Battalion. In 1943, Fielder and Emmons were instrumental in helping lift the ban against Nisei enlistments.

Fielder had an ally in FBI agent Robert L. Shivers, who had been sent to Hawaii in 1939 to assess the loyalty of the Island Japanese. Shivers had been initially suspicious, but by 1941 he was convinced that neither the Islands's Issei nor its Nisei posed a threat. He repeatedly declared that there was no fifth column activity in Hawaii before, during or after the attack on Pearl Harbor.

On the political front, Samuel Wilder King, the territory's delegate to the U.S. Congress since 1934, opposed mass internment. King, who was part Hawaiian, understood that mainland opposition to statehood was at least partially based on fear and mistrust of Hawaii's racially diverse society. Before World War II, he had assured Congress that the Island Japanese were "without a shadow of a doubt, as loyal as any other Americans," and he continued to vouch for them after Pearl Harbor.[8]

After the attack, Honolulu police officer John Anthony Burns was named head of the Contact Group, an intelligence unit charged with curbing espionage in the Island Japanese community. Burns was a fervent Democrat who had been organizing Japanese and Filipino workers along his police beat since 1934. He drew many young Island Japanese into the Democratic Party by advocating equal opportunity for the marginalized, and by opposing the powerful sugar companies that controlled Hawaii politics through the Republican Party. He withstood hysteria-driven pressures for drastic measures against the Island Japanese, and encouraged them to demonstrate their loyalty by actively supporting the war effort. (After the war, Burns invited returning Nisei vets to participate actively in the Democratic Party, and built a multiracial alliance that earned him three terms as Hawaii's governor, from 1962 to 1974. He was succeeded from 1974 to 1986 by his Nisei protégé George Ariyoshi.)

The majority of Hawaii's business community also opposed mass internment. Charles R. Hemenway, president of the Hawaiian Trust Company and a regent at the University of Hawaii, was an influential advocate for Hawaii Nisei. FBI agent Shivers later credited him with providing invaluable insights into Hawaii's complex racial conditions. Through his university ties, Hemenway put Shivers in contact with Hung Wai Ching, an Island Chinese YWCA worker who introduced Shivers to a group of young, loyal Nisei who helped Shivers and other authorities develop reasonable wartime policies toward the Japanese in Hawaii.

Other Leaders in Hawaii Who Opposed Mass Internment

RILEY H. ALLEN, the editor of the *Honolulu Star-Bulletin* from 1912 to 1960, envisioned the integration of Hawaii's ethnically diverse population into a "thoroughly American community." He banned the word "Jap" from his newspaper, even after the attack on Pearl Harbor, and he continued to publish the positive accomplishments of ethnic minorities, including the Island Japanese. Throughout his career, he supported many young people of color with counseling and financial help and pushed vigorously and tirelessly for statehood.

MILES E. CARY, principal of McKinley High School in Honolulu from 1924 to 1948, championed progressive education and democratic ideals. He raised and widened the horizons of his student body, which was forty percent Island Japanese, and urged them to become creative and flexible problem-solvers. Students included two future US senators, and a State Supreme Court justice. In 1942, he took a leave of absence and worked for the WRA to set up the public school system at the Poston internment camp.

JACK HALL, ILWU labor leader, arrived in Hawaii in 1934 and quickly saw that the exclusionary, anti-immigrant posture of mainland unions would not work in Hawaii's multiracial society. Hall actively recruited longshoremen, and sugar and pineapple workers, the majority of them Island Japanese, and built the union into a powerful political and economic force.

HUNG WAI CHING, secretary of the University of Hawaii's campus YMCA, helped organize the Committee for Inter-Racial Unity prior to Pearl Harbor. The group urged military and community leaders to develop a plan to preserve harmony among Hawaii's many ethnic groups in the event of war with Japan. After the war began, he served on the governor's Morale Committee as a crucial liaison between the military and the Island Japanese community. Working directly with Kendall J. Fielder, the army chief of intelligence, he was instrumental in maintaining a harmonious atmosphere on both sides.

Through his duties with the YMCA, Ching was well-acquainted with many Japanese American youths. He encouraged those who had been discharged from the Territorial Guard to demonstrate their patriotism by enlisting in the Varsity Victory Volunteers, a labor battalion. The success of the VVV opened the way for the creation of the all-Nisei 442nd Regimental Combat Team in 1943. When Nisei troops were sent to the mainland for training, Ching preceded them with a public relations campaign to defuse hostility. He made two trips to Hattiesburg, Mississippi, where soldiers of the 100th/442nd were training—once to help start the Aloha USO and again to investigate unfounded rumors that local philanthropist Earl Finch was feigning friendship in order to take advantage of the Nisei soldiers. Ching's complaints of discrimination against Nisei soldiers in training gained the ear of Eleanor Roosevelt, and he was asked to report directly to President Roosevelt on the loyalty and fighting spirit of Nisei troops. Back on the Islands, Ching played a vital role in bridging the gap between Island Japanese and other groups throughout the war. Later, as the vets returned from battle, he helped many obtain scholarships and employment.

Nominated by the Governor's Coordinating Committee for the 100th Anniversary of Japanese Immigration to Hawaii, 1885–1985, and by Yuri Kochiyama.

Other leaders in Hawaii who supported Japanese Americans included Leslie J. Hicks, the president of the Honolulu Chamber of Commerce and of the Hawaiian Electric Company, who condemned mass internment in a February 1942 speech, saying that Hawaii Japanese "have woven themselves into our community fabric...in such intimate fashion as to be an integral part of it."[9] Leaders in the rural plantations also opposed internment. Plantation managers John Midkoff of Waialua, Hans L'Orange of Waipahu and T. G. S. Walker of Kahuku are especially remembered for helping plantation families.

Thus, in Hawaii, the mass incarceration of Island Japanese was avoided because of strong and united opposition from both the public and private sectors.

ON THE WEST COAST. While Japanese Americans were a large and integral part of Hawaii's multiracial, multicultural society, on the mainland they were a tiny, little-known minority whose population had never reached more than three percent in any state. On the West Coast, particularly in California, many occupations were barred to them, and in 1913 and 1920, California and other states passed Alien Land Laws that prohibited "aliens ineligible for citizenship" from owning or leasing land.

Despite intense discrimination, there were 127,000 Japanese Americans living on the U.S. mainland by 1940, the vast majority in California, Washington and Oregon. Finding ways to work within or around the Alien Land Laws, they had gained a foothold in agriculture by reclaiming marginal land and focusing on labor-intensive vegetables and flowers. By 1940, two-thirds were employed in agriculture-related jobs, and Japanese Americans controlled $72 million in farmland. They produced thirty to forty percent of California's vegetable crop and dominated the wholesale produce and flower markets in Southern California. The Issei had reason to look hopefully to the future: their American-born children, citizens by right of birth, were coming of age. At an average age of twenty-one, they were finally old enough to hold title to family property.

But in the months that followed Pearl Harbor, the Japanese Americans of the West Coast would see virtually everything they had worked for swept away. Immediately after the attack, the Japanese branch banks were closed, outstanding loans were called in, and the bank deposits of any Japanese American who had had dealings with Japan prior to the war were frozen. An Alien Property Custodian appointed to the Department of Justice on December 12 took control of over $27 million in Issei-owned businesses and property. Collectively, these measures paralyzed the finances of a large proportion of the Japanese American community.

The community was further weakened by the arrests of many business, community and religious leaders. About 850 West Coast

Issei were taken into custody by the FBI in the first three days after Pearl Harbor. In the coming months, the total would climb to over 3,000. Though not one detainee was subsequently found guilty of disloyal acts, many were held without trial for months, and even years, in detention camps run by the Justice, Immigration and War departments.

The FBI had been able to make the arrests quickly because it had been compiling lists of potentially dangerous aliens to be kept under surveillance and arrested in case of war. In a joint operation, the FBI, the Office of Naval Intelligence (ONI) and army intelligence (G-2) had been collecting names since 1939. ONI had gathered the bulk of the military intelligence, with G-2 playing a very minor role. Lt. Cmdr. Kenneth D. Ringle, one of only twelve members of the U.S. Navy who could speak Japanese at the time, developed an ONI intelligence network headquartered in Los Angeles, with five branch offices and seventy-five men. After his group broke up an espionage ring operated by an officer of the Japanese navy, Ringle estimated that, by the broadest measure, there were no more than 3500 potentially disloyal residents of Japanese ancestry in the entire United States.

On February 3, Hoover told Attorney General Francis Biddle, "The necessity for mass evacuation is based primarily upon public and political pressures rather than factual data."[10] Neither he nor Ringle saw any necessity for the mass internment of either alien or citizen Japanese Americans. Nor did John Franklin Carter, a newspaper columnist whom FDR had commissioned in fall 1941 to build an informal personal intelligence network. Exactly one month before Pearl Harbor, Carter's aide, Curtis B. Munson, wrote that in the event of war:

> There will be no armed uprising of Japanese.... In each Naval District there are about 250 to 300 suspects under surveillance. It is easy to get on the suspect list, merely a speech in favor of Japan at some banquet being sufficient to land one there. The Intelligence Services are generous with the word suspect and are taking no chances. Privately, they believe that only 50 or 60 in each district can be classified as really dangerous.[11]

Unfortunately, the assessments of intelligence professionals were not made public knowledge. In late December 1941, after Knox's fifth column allegations triggered widespread mistrust of Japanese Americans, Carter urged Roosevelt to issue a statement of reassurance, but Roosevelt did not. Carter then sent the president a "program for Loyal West Coast Japanese." The Munson-Ringle plan proposed to encourage the Nisei to demonstrate their loyalty by serving in the Red Cross and civil defense, and to make Nisei groups such as the Japanese American Citizens League responsible for the loyalty of the Issei. Roosevelt seemed intrigued by the Munson-Ringle plan, but he was distracted by the war in Europe and took no action. In mid-January, Eleanor Roosevelt made a radio speech in support of Japanese Americans, and urged her husband to do the same, but again he took no action.

The Munson-Ringle plan was also sent to Gen. John L. DeWitt, who, as head of the Western Defense Command, was charged with the defense of the West Coast. On December 26, DeWitt seemed to agree with the proposal, stating, "I'm very doubtful that it would be common sense procedure to try and intern 117,000 Japanese.... An American citizen, after all, is an American citizen.... I think we can weed the disloyal out of the loyal and lock them up if necessary."[12] But DeWitt, who had a long-standing aversion to Asians and blacks, would soon change his mind.

The general fully expected a Japanese invasion of the lightly defended West Coast, and he was anxious to avoid the disgrace of another Pearl Harbor. In a state of hypervigilance, he repeatedly relayed false alarms to the War Department: power lines were sabotaged (accidental damage caused by cows); 20,000 Japanese Americans in San Francisco were planning an uprising (a falsehood from a disgruntled FBI agent); Japanese-language radio signals were being sent from California to Japanese ships (FCC experts determined that the signals were being sent from one Japanese ship to another). DeWitt's G-2 intelligence division had ceded pre-war intelligence gathering to the ONI, and J. Edgar Hoover dismissed G-2 as untrained, disorganized and susceptible to hysteria.

Nevertheless, as the press reported many false alarms on the West Coast and a steady succession of Japanese victories in the Far East, public opinion began to turn against Japanese Americans. In early January, the Native Sons and Daughters of the Golden West launched a vituperative campaign calling for the eviction of all persons of Japanese ancestry from the West Coast. By late January and early February 1942, the American Legion, the Western Growers Protective Association, the White American Nurserymen of Los Angeles, and other groups joined in. In a statement to *The Saturday Evening Post,* the Grower-Shipper Vegetable Association was frank about its motivations:

> We're charged with wanting to get rid of the Jap for selfish reasons. We might as well be honest. We do. It's a question of whether the white man lives on the Pacific Coast or the brown man. They came into this valley to work, and they stayed to take it over.[13]

On January 23, tensions skyrocketed after the results of the first official inquiry into Pearl Harbor, led by Supreme Court Justice Owen Roberts, were made public. Roberts privately told Stimson (and possibly Roosevelt) that he personally viewed the Island Japanese as "a great menace."[14] The Roberts Report itself was much less inflammatory, stating only that prior to the attack, Japan had gained knowledge of strategic targets through "Japanese consular agents and...persons having no open relations with the Japanese foreign service."[15] The harm was done by omitting to mention that the "persons having no open relations" had been Caucasian spies hired by the consulate. Since many assumed the culprits had to be of Japanese ancestry, public anger and fear against Japanese Americans exploded.

Los Angeles congressman Leland Ford, a conservative Republican facing a tough reelection campaign, became the first representative to support mass eviction. On January 16, even before the Roberts Report was issued, he wrote Stimson, Knox and Hoover to demand that "all Japanese, whether citizens or not, be placed in concentration camps."[16] On January 27, California governor Culbert Olson told DeWitt that since the Roberts Report, Californians felt "they were living in the midst of enemies. They don't trust the Japanese, none of them." On January 29, syndicated Hearst columnist Harry McLemore urged the eviction of all Japanese Americans from the West Coast, saying, "Herd 'em up, pack 'em off and give 'em the inside room in the badlands. Let them be pinched, hurt, hungry and dead up against it.... Personally, I hate the Japanese, and that goes for all of them."[17] On the same day, California's attorney general, Earl Warren (who would defeat Olson in the next gubernatorial election, and much later would become Chief Justice of the U.S. Supreme Court), announced his support for mass eviction.

After talking with Olson and Warren, DeWitt told Maj. Karl Bendetsen that "there will have to be an evacuation on the West Coast, not only of aliens, but of Japanese [American] citizens." Bendetsen, an ambitious 35-year-old lawyer from Washington State, headed the War Department's Aliens Division under the command of Army Provost Marshal Gen. Allen W. Gullion, the army's chief law enforcement officer. Gullion was the War Department's most vigorous advocate for mass internment, and Bendetsen would be its major architect. On February 4, Bendetsen handed Gullion a sweeping proposal that would become the foundation of internment policy. Without any supporting evidence, Bendetsen asserted that "a substantial majority of Nisei bear allegiance to Japan, are well controlled and disciplined by the enemy, and at the proper time will engage in organized sabotage...should a raid along the Pacific Coast be attempted by the Japanese."[18] The "safest course to follow" was to remove all Japanese Americans from the West Coast to the uninhabited areas in the interior, where they could be kept under guard.

Bendetsen's plan for wholesale removal was a radical escalation of DeWitt's earlier request that Japanese Americans be excluded from eighty-five areas—most of them no larger than a few city blocks—around airports, dams, harbors and other strategic targets. J. Edgar Hoover warned Attorney General Francis Biddle that the push for mass eviction arose from political pressure and was not supported by actual evidence. Hoover blamed the media for fanning public hysteria. Other Justice Department officials, including James Rowe, Biddle's deputy, and Edward Ennis, head of the Justice Department's Alien Control Unit, also opposed the eviction, but at a January 30 cabinet meeting, Biddle himself began to backpedal. Earlier he had maintained that while the Issei could be legally interned as enemy aliens, the Nisei were American citizens who could not be imprisoned without just cause. Now Biddle suggested that the president could use emergency war powers to suspend the writ of habeas corpus. Despite the urging of Rowe and Ennis, Biddle failed to warn the president that interning American citizens without individual investigation raised serious constitutional questions that could go all the way to the Supreme Court.

Debate continued within the War Department as well, with Bendetsen and Gullion pressing for large-scale eviction of citizens and aliens, while Stimson leaned toward the exclusion of aliens from limited areas. Aware that any justification for mass eviction had to be based on military necessity and not merely on racial assumptions or political pressure, Stimson asked DeWitt to write a report on the military rationale.

Meanwhile, the federal Office of Facts and Figures released an opinion poll indicating that the majority of California residents believed the FBI had the situation under control. Only twenty-three to forty-three percent, mostly in lower-income, less educated groups, thought that further action against Japanese Americans was required. But political pressure continued to escalate. Almost without exception, the West Coast congressional delegation clamored for internment. On February 2, under the leadership of Earl Warren, a statewide meeting of 150 law enforcement officials issued a warning that widespread violence would ensue unless the Issei were moved out of California. On the same day, Governor Olson made a speech charging that Japanese Americans had signaled Japanese ships. The following day, Los Angeles mayor Fletcher Bowron went on the radio to advocate mass eviction. The Los Angeles County Board of Supervisors fired all its Nisei employees. The California State Personnel Board soon followed suit. Los Angeles County passed a resolution asking the federal government to remove Japanese Americans, and so did sixteen other counties.

The sudden rise of hostility against Japanese Americans caught many moderates and liberals by surprise. A few religious groups and civil libertarians scrambled to release statements opposing internment, but their voices were feeble and scattered. Many groups were internally divided about internment, or were reluctant to be seen as undermining the war effort.

Meanwhile, Gullion received a report that DeWitt's support of mass internment was weakening. As a result, Bendetsen was sent to San Francisco to assist DeWitt. For his role in the eviction debate, the ambitious major was promoted to lieutenant colonel on February 4, and to full colonel ten days later.

On February 10, Stimson sent a memo to Roosevelt asking for a meeting to discuss whether Japanese Americans should be evicted (1) from the entire Pacific Coast, (2) only from the major coastal cities, or (3) only from the immediate vicinity of strategic targets. Preoccupied with the fall of Singapore and the imminent loss of the Philippines, Roosevelt declined to meet with Stimson or to express an opinion, telling him by phone to do what he thought best. Roosevelt had no qualms about placing U.S. citizens in concentration camps, however. He had raised the issue himself in a 1936 memo to the chief of naval operations about Hawaii:

> [E]very Japanese citizen or non-citizen on the island of Oahu who meets these Japanese ships or has any connection with their officers or men should be secretly...identified and...placed on a special list of those who would be the first to be placed in a concentration camp in the event of trouble.[19]

McCloy telephoned Bendetsen and told him, "[W]e have carte blanche to do what we want to as far as the president's concerned."[20] On February 14, 1942, DeWitt delivered his *Final Recommendation of the Evacuation of Japanese and Other Subversive Persons from the Pacific Coast.* The report, written largely by Bendetsen, stated:

> The Japanese race is an enemy race and while many second and third generation Japanese born on United States soil, possessed of United States citizenship, have become "Americanized," the racial strains are undiluted.... [There] is no ground for assuming that any Japanese...though born and raised in the United States, will not turn against this nation when the final test of loyalty comes. It, therefore, follows that along the vital Pacific Coast over 112,000 potential enemies, of Japanese extraction, are at large today."[21]

The report provided no concrete evidence that Japanese Americans posed a threat to national security, but declared with twisted logic that "the very fact that no sabotage has taken place to date is a disturbing and confirming indication that such action will be taken." DeWitt later explained to a congressional committee that "a Jap's a Jap.... There is no way to determine their loyalty.... It makes no difference whether he is an American citizen; theoretically he is still a Japanese and you can't change him."[22]

On February 17, Roosevelt approved eviction plans drafted by the War Department. The same day, Biddle, who had been kept out of the loop, sent the president a memo reiterating his opposition to mass eviction. When Biddle learned of Roosevelt's approval, however, he abandoned his objections and called a meeting of War and Justice Department officials to fine-tune an executive order drafted by Bendetsen.

Two days later, on February 19, 1942, Roosevelt signed E.O. 9066, which authorized the Secretary of War and his military commanders to designate military areas and impose whatever restriction they thought necessary on "the right of any person to enter, remain in or leave" these areas. Although the document did not explicitly mention Japanese Americans, it was the basis of the race-based evictions and incarcerations that followed.

IMPLEMENTING THE ORDER. Before Congress passed legislation to support E.O. 9066, California Congressman John H. Tolan's House Select Committee held a series of hearings on the West Coast. Pleas for reason were overshadowed by testimony that inflamed fearful imaginations, such as Earl Warren's speculations on how easy it would be for Japanese Americans to attack bridges, utilities and other strategic targets. The Nisei who testified were forced to choose between asserting their rights as American citizens and demonstrating their loyalty. When pressed, they said that if the eviction was for reasons of national security, they would cooperate. A few Caucasian supporters, mainly educational, religious and labor leaders, spoke against the internment, but many, believing it to be a done deed, simply pleaded that the "evacuation" be implemented humanely. Congressional legislation authorizing the internment was passed on March 21.

Bendetsen was sent back to San Francisco on February 23 to help DeWitt develop detailed eviction plans. On March 2, Public Proclamation No. 1 designated the states of Washington, Oregon, California and Arizona as military areas. A press release announced that all Japanese Americans, aliens and citizens, would soon be required to leave Military Area No. 1: the western halves of Washington, Oregon and California, and southern Arizona. Those who removed out of the area voluntarily, the press release stated, "in all probability will not again be disturbed."[23]

The idea of "voluntary relocation" did not sit well with the governors of neighboring states. On February 21, Nevada's Governor Carville fired off a letter to DeWitt stating "I do not desire that Nevada be made a dumping ground for enemy aliens to be going anywhere they might see fit to travel."[24] Carville and the governors of Utah, Wyoming and Montana opposed unsupervised resettlement of Japanese Americans in their states, and the governors of Arizona, Arkansas and Idaho thought they all should be placed in concentration camps.[25] Colorado's Ralph Carr was the only mountain state governor who did not vehemently oppose voluntary relocation. On February 28, 1942, just nine days after E.O. 9066 was signed, Carr had stated in a radio address, "If any enemy aliens must be transferred [to this state] as a war measure, then we of Colorado are big enough and patriotic enough to do our duty."[26] He did not exactly extend a warm welcome, adding, "This statement must not be construed as an invitation, however. Only because the needs of our Nation dictate it, do we even consider such an arrangement." Carr's moderate stance may well have cost him a Senate seat in the next election. The opposition of the interior states to voluntary relocation was a major factor in the program's quick demise. Few Japanese Americans were able to take advantage of the program anyway. Less than 5,000 were able to relocate voluntarily.

Meanwhile, the navy demanded the removal of Japanese Americans from Terminal Island in Los Angeles Harbor, which was surrounded by sensitive military and civil installations. Residents were forced from their homes on February 28, and the government made no attempt to provide them with alternative housing. During the following month, the army began to plan for the wholesale internment of tens of thousands of Japanese Americans.

On March 11, 1942, DeWitt appointed Bendetsen as director of the newly created Wartime Civil Control Administration (WCCA). Bendetsen was under instructions to encourage voluntary migration, but within days of his appointment, he had site selection teams looking for locations suitable for housing 100,000 people. Under his direction, temporary "assembly centers" were improvised within the exclusion zone, mostly at fairgrounds or racetracks close to major Japanese American population centers.

Once the Japanese Americans were incarcerated, the army wanted to turn jurisdiction over to a civilian agency, so Roosevelt authorized the creation of the War Relocation Authority (WRA) on March 18 and appointed Milton Eisenhower as director. An Agriculture Department official with little knowledge of Japanese Americans, Eisenhower initially hoped that Japanese Americans could be voluntarily relocated inland to work on farms. He was soon to discover that he had little real power.

On March 24, Bendetsen prepared, for DeWitt's signature, Public Proclamation No. 3, which imposed a curfew on all enemy aliens and Japanese American citizens, and restricted them to within a five-mile radius of homes and workplaces. On the same day, Civilian Exclusion Order No. 1, the first of 108, instructed the Japanese Americans of Bainbridge Island to prepare to be interned en masse, with only the luggage they could carry by hand.

On March 27, Public Proclamation No. 4 ended the "voluntary relocation" program. By June 6, all Japanese American residents of Military Area No. 1 were behind barbed wire. Shortly thereafter, DeWitt ordered them to be removed from the eastern half of California as well. Persons who had relocated from the coast in hopes of avoiding internment had moved in vain.

By August 18, Japanese Americans from the entire state of California, western Oregon and Washington, and southern Arizona were incarcerated in "assembly centers," temporary internment camps administered by the army through the WCCA. Seventy percent were American citizens. About 92,000 people were held in the "assembly centers" for an average of 100 days. By November 1, 1942, they had been transferred to ten WRA internment camps scattered in remote parts of six Western states and Arkansas. Many would stay for three years or more. Thousands more were incarcerated in detention camps operated by the Department of Justice.

Even as internees were still being transferred from "assembly centers" to permanent camps, some were permitted to resettle outside the exclusion area. In the summer of 1942, college students were permitted to enroll in schools outside the exclusion zone. Ten thousand internees were temporarily released to harvest sugar beets and other crops. By the end of 1942, the WRA decided to develop questionnaires intended to distinguish the "loyal" from the "disloyal." "Loyal" internees were encouraged to resettle outside the exclusion zone or enlist in the military. The "disloyal" were segregated at the Tule Lake Segregation Center in July 1943.

On December 17, 1944, anticipating a Supreme Court decision that the government had no just cause to hold loyal U.S. citizens, Public Proclamation No. 21 rescinded the mass exclusion orders and reopened the West Coast to Japanese Americans as of January 2, 1945. The last camp, Tule Lake Segregation Center, closed on March 20, 1946.

For more information on the internment:

Commission on Wartime Relocation and Internment of Civilians. *Personal Justice Denied: Report on Wartime Relocation and Internment of Civilians.* Seattle: University of Washington Press, 1997.

Daniels, Roger. *Prisoners with Trial: Japanese Americans in World War II.* 1st rev. ed. New York: Hill and Wang, 2004.

Irons, Peter. *Justice at War: The Story of the Japanese American Internment Cases.* New York: Oxford University Press, 1983.

Niiya, Brian, ed. *Encyclopedia of Japanese American History: An A-to-Z Reference from 1868 to the Present.* Rev. ed. New York: Checkmark Press, 2001.

Robinson, Greg. *By the Order of the President: FDR and the Internment of Japanese Americans.* Cambridge, MA: Harvard University Press, 2001.

Weglyn, Michi. *Years of Infamy: The Untold Story of America's Concentration Camps.* New York: Morrow Quill, 1976.

Additional Nominees

There are many who deserve to be acknowledged for their courage and compassion in supporting Japanese Americans during the internment. Briefly described below, alphabetically by category, are a few of them.

Politicians

Gov. Ralph L. Carr of Colorado was the only mountain state governor who did not vehemently oppose the voluntary relocation of Japanese Americans to his state. On February 28, 1942, just nine days after E.O. 9066 was signed, Carr stated in a radio address, "If any enemy aliens must be transferred [to this state] as a war measure, then we of Colorado are big enough and patriotic enough to do our duty." He did not extend a warm welcome, adding, "This statement must not be construed as an invitation, however. Only because the needs of our Nation dictate it, do we even consider such an arrangement." But his position was moderate compared to Nevada's Governor Carville, who wrote to Gen. DeWitt on February 21, 1942, "I do not desire that Nevada be made a dumping ground for enemy aliens to be going anywhere they might see fit to travel."

The opposition of the interior states to voluntary relocation was a major factor in the program's quick demise and the subsequent forced internment. Carville and the governors of Utah, Wyoming and Idaho wanted all evictees from the West Coast placed in concentration camps. Idaho governor Chase Clark went a step further by suggesting that Japanese Americans who had already entered the state be interned as well. Carr's moderate stance may well have cost him a Senate seat in the subsequent election. *Nominated by Harry Fukuhara.*

Ralph C. Dills (1910–2002), representing Gardena in the California Assembly, was one of only two California legislators to oppose the internment. Because of their action, Dills and state senator Jack Shelley were targeted for expulsion from state government. The effort failed and Dills survived to become the state's second-longest-serving lawmaker. He was honored by the legislature in 2001 for his wartime stand. Dills was a former teacher who was elected to the state assembly in 1938 as a New Deal Democrat. In 1949, he left the legislature to serve as municipal court judge in Compton. In 1966, he ran for the state senate, where he remained until 1998. During his lengthy legislative tenure, Dills was noted for his consistent support of education and the environment. Upon his death, State Attorney General Bill Lockyer lauded him for helping those who lacked a voice in the political process, and for not backing away from publicly unpopular positions. *Nominated by Harry Fukuhara.*

Hubert Humphrey, mayor of Minneapolis from 1945 to 1948, was generally supportive of Japanese Americans resettling in the area. He appointed Rev. Daisuke Kitagawa to the Mayor's Council of Human Relations. Humphrey served in the U.S. Senate from 1948 until 1964, when he was elected vice president under Lyndon Johnson. After an unsuccessful run for the U.S. presidency, he returned to the Senate until his death. *Nominated by Fujiko Kitagawa.*

John F. Shelley was one of two legislators in the state to oppose the internment. An Irish Catholic Democrat, he served as California state senator from 1939 to 1947, ran unsuccessfully for lieutenant governor in 1947, served as representative to the U.S. Congress from 1949 to 1964 and mayor of San Francisco from 1964 to 1968.

Elmo Everett Smith, publisher of the *Oregon Observer,* was also the mayor of Ontario, a small Oregon town near the Idaho border. He welcomed Japanese Americans, declaring, "If the Japs, both alien and nationals, are a menace to the Pacific Coast safety unless they are moved inland, it appears downright cowardly to take any other stand than to put out the call, 'Send them along; we'll cooperate to the fullest possible extent in taking care of them.'" Smith resigned as mayor in 1943 to serve for two years in the navy and was reelected mayor after his return. By war's end, over 800 Japanese Americans had been recruited to work in Malheur County's sugar-beet, onion and potato fields. Smith served in Oregon's senate from 1948 to 1955, and as interim governor in 1955 and 1956. *Nominated by George Iseri.*

Gov. Charles A. Sprague, publisher of *The Oregon Statesman* from 1929 to 1968, served as the progressive Republican governor of Oregon from 1939 to 1943. He was one of the earliest to express concern about Japanese American civil liberties. On December 7, 1942, he sent a wire to FDR cautioning against anti-Japanese hysteria, saying, "We must not rest until the menace of Japanese aggression in the Pacific is definitely ended...[but] let there be no hysteria among our people.... There is a considerable number of residents here of Japanese origin...but these Japanese-Americans who are citizens must not be molested." In early 1942, however, as public opinion swung in favor of internment, he swung with it. He became an early advocate for resettlement, however, and wrote editorials and speeches urging the reopening of the exclusion zone to Japanese Americans. *Nominated by Harry Honda.*

Norman Thomas was one of the few U.S. leftists to strongly oppose the internment. He was a perennial Socialist candidate for president, running in every race from 1928 to 1964. Espousing a Christian socialism that opposed both war and capitalism, he was a secretary of the pacifist Fellowship of Reconciliation in 1918 and a cofounder of the ACLU in 1920. In 1940, he cofounded the America First Committee, a powerful isolationist group that attracted over 800,000 members during its one-year existence. Pearl Harbor ended the group, and convinced Thomas and others to support U.S. entry into World War II. *Nominated by Chizu Omori and Greg Robinson.*

Law

Roger Baldwin, national director of the ACLU since its formation in 1920, had a significant impact on civil liberties issues from World War I through Vietnam. Scion of a wealthy Boston family, and a conscientious objector during World War I, he had considerable influence in Washington. In late March 1942, despite opposition from within the ACLU board, he sent a letter to FDR questioning the constitutionality of mass internment. He also encouraged the Los Angeles and San Francisco offices to look for test cases. However, as ACLU director, he was forced to implement the directives of the board, which refused to challenge government assertions that the internment was a military necessity. Instead, the board restricted ACLU arguments in the test cases to racial discrimination. Baldwin then suggested to the Hirabayashi and Korematsu defense teams that they dissociate themselves from the ACLU in order to have a freer hand. Although Baldwin was cited by the JACL as a supporter of Japanese American civil liberties, others feel that he did not take a strong-enough stand. Later in life, he supported redress, and was quoted as saying that the biggest mistake the ACLU ever made was in not opposing the internment more vigorously.

Arthur Barnett, Gordon Hirabayashi's first lawyer, was a fellow Quaker. He accompanied Hirabayashi on May 16, 1942, when the young Nisei refused to register for the eviction. Barnett felt he lacked the experience to take the case to trial, so he quickly enlisted the help of Frank L. Walters. However, Barnett remained part of Hirabayashi's legal team through Coram Nobis. He received the William O. Douglas Award from the ACLU of Washington in 1983, and, with Hirabayashi, the Washington State Trial Lawyers Association Courage Award in 1993. During the eviction, Barnett also served as chair of the Japanese-American Emergency Committee of the Seattle Council of Churches, and chair of the Seattle AFSC. He died in 2003 at ninety-six. *Nominated by Paul Ohtaki.*

Ernest Besig (1904–1998), director of the ACLU's San Francisco office from 1934 to 1971, doggedly opposed the internment. He faced opposition first from within his own Northern California chapter and then from the national headquarters. When Fred Korematsu was arrested for violating curfew, Besig enlisted Wayne Collins to represent Korematsu. The two lawyers disagreed on legal strategy, but Besig gave Collins a free hand in developing the case. When the national ACLU board tried to interfere with the case, Besig ignored them. He also investigated conditions at Tule Lake and Manzanar, and supported freedom of speech for camp dissidents.

During his long tenure, the ACLU of Northern California was involved in landmark cases in labor, racial justice and free speech, including defending labor leaders Billings and Mooney, helping to overturn the "anti-Okie" law, fighting McCarthyism, and defending publisher Lawrence Ferlinghetti and poet Allen Ginsberg in the "Howl" obscenity case.

Guy C. Calden was associated with the firm of Elliot & Calden prior to World War II. Located in the Flood building in San Francisco, Elliot & Calden served as a consultant for the Japanese Consulate on issues of anti-Japanese discrimination, and helped about 140 Issei (including Kyutaro Abiko) set up trusts and corporations to circumvent the Alien Land Laws. They were involved in many key California court cases that challenged the constitutionality of the Alien Land Laws.

Calden also helped Mrs. Yonako Abiko set up the trust for the Japanese YWCA building in San Francisco's Japantown. Mrs. Abiko's diaries documented that the building and land had been paid for by Issei women and held in trust by the YWCA because of the Alien Land Laws. Her records helped the Japanese American community recover the building from the YWCA in 2002, after years of litigation. *Nominated by Tami Suzuki.*

Wayne Collins was a young man when Ernest Besig asked him to take on the Korematsu case. Intense, impatient and something of a lone wolf, Collins ruffled many feathers with his scattershot strategies and impassioned speech, but there was no denying his passionate and lifelong commitment to Japanese American civil liberties. He smuggled photos out of Tule Lake to expose inhumane conditions inside its stockade. He worked for fourteen years to help internees who had renounced their citizenship regain it. He defended Iva Toguri D'Aquino ("Tokyo Rose") without fee, and after her conviction worked for the next twenty-five years to clear her name. Collins died in 1974, three years before D'Aquino was pardoned by Pres. Gerald Ford. At the time of his death, Collins also supported the cause of the Japanese Latin Americans, who had been kidnapped by the US. government from Peru, Brazil and other countries during World War II and secretly held in U.S. custody as a hostage-exchange pool. The Civil Liberties Act of 1988 did not recognize the Japanese Latin Americans, and redress for these little-known victims of the internment remains elusive. In *Years of Infamy*, Michi Weglyn wrote that Wayne Collins "did more to correct a democracy's mistake than any other one person."

Fred Okrand joined the law firm of Gallagher & Wirin in 1940 and immediately began working on ACLU cases. In 1942, when the partnership dissolved, Okrand stayed with A. L. Wirin and worked with him on Japanese American civil liberties cases. Okrand was drafted in late 1942 and fought in Europe. After the war, he rejoined Wirin's office as a full partner and took on Japanese American cases involving property, commercial fishing rights and the restoration of citizenship. Over the next forty years, he served as ACLU counsel on a wide range of issues, including school desegregation, fair housing, immigration rights, capital punishment, nuclear-arms testing, obscenity, unlawful search and seizure, and opposition to the House Un-American Activities Committee and the Vietnam War. *Nominated by Harry Fukuhara.*

James Purcell was a third-generation Irish American who had had only casual contacts with Japanese Americans until February 1942, when Nisei employed in state civil service in Sacramento were being threatened with discharge. Some of them appealed to Saburo Kido, then president of the JACL, for help. He enlisted the help of Purcell, a 36-year-old San Francisco attorney. By agreeing to look into the situation, Purcell assured himself a place in the history books.

He drove to Sacramento to meet with scores of Nisei civil servants who reported that they had been required to fill out a lengthy and invasive loyalty questionnaire. Purcell agreed to try to help them, but before he could do anything about it, some 200 Nisei were suspended from employment. Just weeks later, they were interned at assembly centers. When he went to visit some of his clients at the Tanforan Racetrack in San Bruno, Purcell was outraged. He decided to file for a writ of habeas corpus, which would force the government to show just cause for holding the Nisei. Mitsuye Endo agreed to let him file a petition on her behalf, which he did in July 1942 at the federal court in San Francisco. When the petition was denied, Purcell appealed and carried the case all the way to the Supreme Court. The court decided on December 18, 1944, that Miss Endo should be released from custody. *Ex parte Endo* was a profoundly significant decision that led to the end of the internment camps. It was also a personal victory for a stubborn Irishman, who had essentially pursued the case on his own. "Nobody paid me a cent," Purcell told journalist Bill Hosokawa. "I figure the whole thing cost me about $5000, not counting my time. There were printing bills, travel expenses to Washington and for interviews, stenographic expenses and the like, but the outcome was worth every bit of the time and effort." He pursued the case with determination, he said, because "I was mad—about how my client was treated and how I was treated...and an important principle was at stake."

Ex parte Endo was a landmark decision that affected all internees, but Purcell didn't forget his original clients, the Nisei civil servants dismissed in Sacramento. After they were released from the camps, they wanted their jobs back. Eighty of them engaged Purcell to represent them. In April 1946, the state personnel board announced that the dual citizenship charges against them would be dropped. Only the individuals actually involved in the suit were reinstated, however. Over 100 others who did not participate in the appeal did not regain their jobs.

A. L. Wirin was a part-time staff attorney for the Southern California chapter of the ACLU at the outbreak of World War II. He represented Ernest and Toki Wayakama in their legal challenge to the eviction. Adhering to the national ACLU's policy not to challenge the military necessity of the internment, Wirin filed habeas corpus petitions in August 1942 on the basis of race. His major non-ACLU client, the Congress of Industrial Organizations (CIO), supported the internment and objected to his work on the Wakayama case. Wirin resigned the CIO account and continued with the Wakayama case for more than a year in spite of lack of support from the national ACLU. Finally, an embittered Wakayama requested repatriation to Japan and insisted the case be dropped. Determined to be involved in Supreme Court challenges to the internment, Wirin approached the national JACL. He prepared friend-of-the-court briefs for it in the *Regan v. King* voter registration case and in the Hirabayashi case. He argued before the Supreme Court in both the Yasui and Hirabayashi cases and was involved in helping Tule Lake renunciates regain their citizenship. Wirin was a figure of some controversy. Although he was not a Communist, his representation of the Communist Party and its members annoyed some members of the national ACLU board. On the other hand, his adherence to the national ACLU's strategy on the internment cases did not sit well with Besig and Collins, who favored a more aggressive approach.

QUAKERS

American Friends Service Committee (AFSC), a Quaker service organization, did not oppose internment but sought to mitigate its effects. Prior to the eviction, Clarence Pickett of the Philadelphia headquarters office assigned two seasoned missionaries to Japan, Esther Rhoads and Herbert Nicholson, and conscientious objector Tom Bodine to work with the internees. In May 1942, Milton Eisenhower invited the AFSC to play a major role in resettlement efforts, fearing that the WRA would be criticized for "coddling" Japanese Americans if public funds were spent on hostels, student placement or housing and employment services for the internees. Instead, Eisenhower asked the AFSC to manage student relocation efforts

and to coordinate efforts by religious institutions, the YMCA and YWCA, charitable foundations and other groups to provide hostels and other services to resettlers in Des Moines, Cincinnati, Cleveland, Philadelphia and other cities. When the West Coast was reopened, the AFSC managed some hostels for returnees.

Clarence Evan Pickett, executive secretary of the AFSC from 1929 to 1950, authorized AFSC services for Japanese American internees and resettlers, and arranged for the AFSC to manage the Student Relocation Council, later known as the National Japanese American Student Relocation Council. He was awarded the Nobel Peace Prize in 1947 for the AFSC's worldwide work with persons displaced by war.

Walter and Marydel Balderston worked with Japanese Americans throughout the war. As a staff member of the AFSC during the eviction, Walter helped prepare the Forsythe Hostel for the families suddenly evicted from Terminal Island. He enrolled the children in the local schools and assisted the evictees in settling their business affairs. In October 1942, he and Marydel went to Poston, where he developed a Community Activities program that was funded by the AFSC, not by the WRA. He recruited internees to teach classes in calligraphy, woodcarving, flower arrangement, dressmaking, language and other skills. He lobbied for an outdoor stage where internees could perform Japanese drama and dance. His programs gave much pleasure, especially to hard-working Issei who had leisure for the first time in their lives to pursue arts and crafts. Marydel worked as a substitute teacher, and raised their first child, who was born during their three-and-a-half years at Poston.

Raymond and Gracia Booth worked for the AFSC's Pasadena office during the eviction— Raymond had been pastor of a West Coast Friends meeting, and had resigned to help the Japanese Americans. When Raymond was appointed as WRA representative for Cincinnati, Ohio, he and Gracia established a hostel in there and persuaded prospective employers to hire resettlers. Gracia was a vivid and moving writer whose touching account of the eviction from Terminal Island helped gather support for the evictees. *Nominated by Stephen McNeil.*

Josephine (1891–1978) and **Frank Duveneck** (1887–1985) shared a lifelong commitment to progressive education, peace, the environment and multicultural social justice. During World War II, Mrs. Duveneck was extremely active in the AFSC, helping Jewish refugees from Europe as well as Japanese Americans. She assisted evictees leaving San Francisco, visited Tanforan weekly, arranged for the AFSC to use the YWCA building for refugee services during the eviction, helped with the student relocation program, visited internment camps, worked with local Fair Play Committees to make the way easier for returnees, and cosponsored the resettlement hostel at the Buddhist Church of San Francisco.

The Duvenecks established the first youth hostel on the West Coast in 1937 (the oldest still in operation) at their 1600-acre Hidden Villa Ranch in the Los Altos Hills. The ranch sheltered Jewish refugees and Japanese American returnees, and nurtured such groups as the Native American Intertribal Council and Cesar Chavez's United Farmworkers of America. Hidden Villa became a nonprofit in 1960, and on Frank's death in 1985 the Duvenck family gave the ranch property to the organization, so that its youth hostel, multicultural summer camp, environmental education program, organic farm and hiking trails could continue to be vibrant community assets. *Nominated by George Oiye and Harry Honda.*

Winifred Hemingway (Thomforde) and family extended much kindness to Martha Ito (Yamasaki) during the internment. Winifred Hemingway, Ernest Hemingway's cousin, was a Quaker who taught at Poston internment camp. She arranged for her family to sponsor Miss Ito when she left Poston to resettle in Chicago. Once Miss Ito arrived in the Midwest, Winifred's sister Isabel, as well as her mother and aunt, were very helpful to her. *Nominated by Jean Yamasaki.*

Gerda Isenberg (1901–1997), along with Josephine Duveneck, was a member of the Palo Alto Friends Meeting. During World War II she and Duveneck were mainstays of AFSC activities in the San Francisco Bay Area. They organized a hostel in San Francisco for Jewish refugees who had fled the Nazis. When Mrs. Isenberg learned of plans to intern the Japanese Americans, she made arrangements for two young Nisei employees to avoid incarceration by resettling in Philadelphia. When the order came for Mountain View residents to report to the train station to be transported to "assembly centers," she was part of the committee that served food and beverages to the departing families. She helped drive people to the station, then retrieved forgotten items—false teeth, a briefcase, a lost key. She shopped once a week for internees at Tanforan, frequently hauling lumber requested for packing crates across the busy highway from the parking area to the "assembly center."

In 1945, she served as the first chair of the Fair Play Council, which helped pave the way for internees to return to their homes by promoting positive public opinion and helping find housing and employment. After two years of assisting returnees, the council broadened its mission to include all victims of racial or religious discrimination. Mrs. Isenberg remained an active member until 1965. During that time, she ran unsuccessfully for the State Assembly on the Democratic ticket.

Mrs. Isenberg was born on a farm in Holstein, Germany. She immigrated to the United States after marrying her cousin Roulf in 1921. The couple lived in Carmel and then Los Altos until 1941, when they purchased a 3,000-acre cattle ranch off Skyline Boulevard south of Woodside. Mrs. Isenberg had studied gardening in Germany as a young woman, but it was the native plants of the coastal California hills that really sparked her passion for growing things. By the late 1950s, she was known as "the fern lady" who sold ferns and mimulus out of the back of her station wagon to nurseries along El Camino Real. In 1960, she established the 40-acre Yerba Buena Nursery, which is now the oldest native-plant nursery in California. At the time, the cultivation of drought-hardy native plants was a radical idea, which Mrs. Isenberg promoted with a two-acre demonstration garden. She operated the nursery until she retired at ninety-three. She died in 1997, leaving a lasting legacy in social and environmental activism. *Nominated by Mary Tomita.*

Bayard Rustin, an influential African American civil rights leader, was born a Pennsylvania Quaker in 1912. The nonviolent activism he learned in his childhood informed his entire life.

He moved to Harlem in 1937 after completing an AFSC activist training program. He took a job as a youth organizer with the Young Communist League because he was attracted by its positions on peace and racial equality. He parted ways with the Communist Party in 1941 after the Germans invaded Russia, and the party reversed its antiwar stance.

The early 1940s were powerfully formative years for Rustin. During this time, he worked with A. Philip Randolph, president of the Brotherhood of Sleeping Car Porters and an influential mentor, to reduce discrimination in the defense industries. He became the first field secretary of the Congress of Racial Equality (CORE). He became a democratic socialist after meeting Norman Thomas, and he remained one for the rest of his life. At the same time, he joined the pacifist Fellowship of Reconciliation (FOR) as its race relations secretary and traveled the country teaching interracial communication strategies. In 1942, FOR and AFSC sent him to California to help protect the property of Japanese Americans being sent to internment camps. In 1943, Rustin's whirlwind of activity was abruptly suspended by a three-year prison sentence for refusing both the draft and alternative service in Civilian Public Service.

In 1947, Rustin helped FOR and CORE plan the first "freedom ride" in the South. The effort, which landed him on a South Carolina chain gang, inspired the Freedom Rides of the early 1960s. He was forced to leave FOR in 1953 after his arrest as a gay man on a "morals charge." Rustin's expertise in nonviolent action made him a key strategist for the civil rights movement. He was the chief organizer of the 1963 March on Washington for Jobs and Freedom, then the largest demonstration in the nation's history. He was a brilliant strategist and leader who was often forced to work behind the scenes because of homophobia. Throughout his life, he worked on issues such voter registration drives; minority participation in the labor unions; Vietnamese, Cambodian and Haitian refugee services; and African struggles for human rights. He died in 1987.

OTHER CHURCH WORKERS

Time and space did not permit us to adequately explore the contributions of many religious workers, including Gordon Kimball Chapman, a returned Presbyterian missionary who served as executive secretary of the Protestant Commission for Wartime Japanese Service; Frank Herron Smith, district superintendent of the Methodist Japanese Provisional Conference; Clarence Gillette, a returned missionary who served on the Congregational Church's Committee for War Victims and Services; Maryknoll priests and nuns; and many missionaries to Japan and Korea who spent the war years in the United States.

MEDIA AND PUBLIC OPINION

Charlotta Bass owned and edited *The California Eagle,* the oldest black-owned newspaper in Los Angeles, from 1912 to 1951. When George Knox Roth asked her to speak on his radio program in February 1942 in support of Japanese Americans, she readily agreed. Although nominally a Republican at the time, Ms. Bass helped found the Progressive Party in the late 1940s. After an unsuccessful run at Congress in 1950, she became the first black woman to run for vice president, on the Progressive ticket. *Nominated by Irma Roth.*

Lou Dondelet, a Quaker photographer who documented the removal of Japanese Americans from the Los Angeles area at the request of the AFSC, lives in Marin County, California.

Lucius W. Lomax was the editor of the *Los Angeles Tribune,* an African American weekly founded in 1940. In 1945, he advertised for a Nisei reporter and hired Hasaye Yamamoto, 23, former editor of Poston's camp newspaper.

Carey McWilliams, the son of a prosperous Colorado cattle rancher and state legislator who went bankrupt, could have lived a life of privilege. He began his career as a lawyer, but was drawn to progressive politics and journalism, especially after learning of the exploitation of migrant laborers and the brutal repression of their attempts to organize labor unions. He was appointed State Commissioner of Immigration and Housing by Gov. Culbert Olson, but McWilliams's efforts to improve working conditions for farmworkers drew the ire of the Associated Farmers, and he was fired by newly elected Gov. Earl Warren in 1942.

After writing two books on migrant workers, McWilliams turned his attention to racial and religious discrimination. During World War II, he worked with the Committee for the Foreign-Born to protect the rights of "enemy aliens," and championed Chicano rights in the Sleepy Lagoon case. His book *Brothers Under the Skin* (1943) chronicled the history of racism in America. *Prejudice: The Japanese American, Symbol of Racial Intolerance* (1944), published when most Japanese American internees were still in internment camps, was one of the first books to be sympathetic to the internees, along with Ansel Adams's *Born Free and Equal.* The influential and respected editor of *The Nation* magazine from 1955 until 1975, he died in 1980.

EDUCATORS

Clara Breed, a San Diego librarian, became attached to the Japanese American children who frequented the library, and she went to the train station to bid farewell as they were being interned. She gave each of them stamped and addressed postcards, asking them to write about their camp experiences. Miss Breed's correspondence with the children provided them with hope and compassion. Some of the resulting 250 letters and postcards were displayed by the National Postal Museum in Washington, D.C., and on the Japanese American National Museum (JANM) Web site. *Nominated by Harry Fukuhara.*

Ralph Burnight was principal of Excelsior Union High School in Norwalk, a small farming community in Southern California. According to Ruth Asawa, he made a special trip to Manzanar to confer high school diplomas on his interned students. He encouraged and mentored Nisei students. Alice Imamoto (Takemoto) knew him personally because she was very active in the school's music program. Immediately after December 7, Burnight called a special assembly and cautioned the student body not to retaliate against Japanese Americans for Japan's actions. Mrs. Takemoto recalled, "I was forever grateful to him for removing some of the anxiety that all the Nisei students felt."

Burnight and Dr. William Bruff, a Quaker physician, gave special support to the Imamoto family. Both parents taught at a Japanese-language school. When they were arrested by the FBI, Alice and her sisters were left to fend for themselves amid the turmoil of the evic-

tion. Burnight visited them at home and later at Santa Anita to offer support, even retrieving their musical instruments from storage for use at Santa Anita and returning them to safekeeping when the Imamotos were transferred to Jerome. Burnight kept in touch with the family throughout the internment and visited the Imamoto parents after they were released from detention and resettled in Washington, D.C. Even after the parents returned to California, Burnight continued to send them cards and books, and when he invited them to his fiftieth wedding anniversary, the Imamotos traveled hundreds of miles to pay tribute. *Nominated by Alice Imamoto Takemoto.*

Mary Catherine Durkin, who had a passion for social justice, served as teaching principal of two elementary schools at Tule Lake from 1942 to 1946. Later, at the Contra Costa County Office of Education, she and Dr. Hilda Taba developed groundbreaking strategies for teaching critical and creative thinking to elementary and middle-school students. *Nominated by Elizabeth Rosenberg and Nobuo Bob Watanabe.*

Helen Amerman (Manning) taught high school at Minidoka and continues to attend regularly student reunions in Seattle. She resides in Fremont, California. *(See chapter: Robert Coombs.) Nominated by Robert Coombs.*

Grace Nichols (Pearson) tried to get permission for a church group to serve refreshments to departing evictees in Santa Rosa, California, but a military policeman assumed that they wished to make a profit by selling sandwiches. He had a difficult time understanding that they planned to give them away. Deeply concerned about the civil rights of the internees, Miss Nichols applied to the WRA for a teaching position. When friends at Poston told her that the administration tended to hire people who showed up, ready to work, she made her way to the Arizona camp and was hired as a first-grade teacher.

Otis D. Richardson, prewar chair of the English department at Los Angeles City College, agreed to act as faculty sponsor for the newly formed Nisei Club in 1939 or 1940. He first became interested in the Japanese culture and then grew committed to the Nisei students, whose intelligence impressed him. In September 1942, he published "Nisei Evacuees—Their Challenge to Education," an article in the *Junior College Journal* about the impact of internment on Nisei students.

During the internment, according to Richardson's son Talbot, "He didn't think we could assume that everyone was innocent, but he advocated for people he knew." He made two trips to Manzanar to visit interned friends. Talbot recalled, "I was 12, 13 years old, I hadn't realized what was happening to people close to us. My father took me because he wanted me to see. With gas rationing, I don't know how he got the fuel to make the long trip." One Nisei friend, who became almost like an adopted sister, lived with the Richardson family for years after the war. Richardson taught the Japanese language to both of his sons, and Donald made a career as a military language instructor. *Nominated by Allen H. Meyer and Donald Richardson.*

Georgia Day Robertson finally saw the publication of her internment novel, *The Harvest of Hate,* just after her 100th birthday in 1986. Forty years before, after finishing a three-year stint at internment camp high schools, Mrs. Robertson had visited the Midwest and had been appalled by the general population's ignorance of and indifference to the internment of Japanese Americans. Indignantly deciding that "someone has to write a book," she sat down and wrote a fictionalized account of one family's painful experience. The heartfelt, richly detailed book is noteworthy for its compassionate but uncompromising insights into the various ways in which young people responded to the psychological stresses of upheaval and loss.

Mrs. Robertson was born in Iowa in 1886. After putting herself through college, she went to China as an educational Methodist missionary. During her five years overseas, she married a Canadian mining engineer. She was widowed at age 36 and left to raise two young boys. Far from feeling victimized, Mrs. Robertson managed to alternate teaching with studying, and acquired two master's degrees while raising her two sons. During the 1930s, the resourceful mother earned her living by writing short stories, teaching at a night school, and raising chickens and selling their eggs.

After her sons were grown, she was job-hunting in August 1942, when she learned about the internment camps and applied to school principal Miles Cary for a job at Poston. She was fifty-six years old when she was hired to head the math department for the high schools in Poston camps I, II and III. In Arizona, she endured the same isolation and searing desert heat as the internees, and rose to the challenge of teaching demoralized and angry children with no equipment or books. The school was short-staffed, and she was pressed into service as a social studies teacher when school began.

Mrs. Robertson had many heart-to-heart conversations with the young Nisei teachers whom she supervised, and she was also appointed by the social services director to counsel young men who were under special stress because their fathers were held in Justice Department camps. Because of these experiences, she was able to write accurately and sympathetically about the varied emotional states of the Nisei internees. All the frustration she felt, and the compassion and insight she gained from her years at Poston were poured into her novel. She wrote it quickly, but because of its controversial subject matter, it was not published for forty years.

STUDENT RELOCATION

Columbia Foundation. Madeline Haas Russell (1915–1999) was a great grandniece of jeans manufacturer Levi Strauss and heiress to a large fortune. She cofounded the Columbia Foundation with her brother William Haas in 1940. The foundation gave grants to the National Japanese American Student Relocation Council in 1943 and 1944. It was by far the largest donor to the program that enabled more than 3600 students to leave camp and attend college, although the AFSC received contributions from the John Hazen Foundation, the Carnegie Foundation, and the national YMCA and YWCA as well. *Nominated by Glenn Kumekawa.*

Joseph Conard was the first executive secretary of the Student Relocation Council, which was organized in Berkeley on March 21, 1942. The organization was later redubbed the National Japanese American Student Relocation Council and relocated to Philadelphia. *Nominated by Stephen McNeil.*

Monroe Deutsch, provost of the University of California, Berkeley, was an early advocate of student relocation and a founding member of the Northern California Committee on Fair Play for Citizens and Aliens of Japanese Ancestry.

Virginia Heck (1915–2004), a Quaker activist living in Berkeley in 1941, worked through the Student Relocation Council to place Nisei students evicted from the West Coast into colleges and universities in the Midwest and on the East Coast. *Nominated by J. K. Yamamoto.*

Trudy King was a key member of the National Japanese American Student Relocation Council in Berkeley and later in Philadelphia. *Nominated by Stephen McNeil.*

John W. Nason (1905–2001), chair of the National Japanese American Student Relocation Council, was instrumental in helping more than 3600 Japanese American students leave the internment camps to enroll in 680 educational institutions outside the exclusion zone. He considered his three years as chair of the National Japanese American Student Relocation Council the most important and satisfying work in a long and distinguished career. Nason was a brilliant scholar who was born in St. Paul, Minnesota, and studied at Carleton College, Oxford, Yale Divinity School and Harvard before teaching philosophy in the 1930s at Swarthmore College, a distinguished Pennsylvania school with Quaker roots. A Quaker convert, Nason was a lifelong advocate of "academic rigor, inclusion and humanity," who served as president of Swarthmore from 1940 to 1952, fought McCarthyism as head of the Foreign Policy Association, and served as a trustee of the United Negro College Fund. While president of his alma mater, Carleton College, he instituted an Asian studies program and encouraged the recruitment of minority students. *Nominated by Harry Fukuhara and Glenn Kumekawa.*

Robert O'Brien, a Quaker and a pacifist, was advisor to the the University of Washington's Japanese Student Club prior to the war. He was one of the early organizers of the Student Relocation Council, and was asked by Nason to serve as the council's second executive secretary, a position he accepted without pay. In 1949, he wrote *The College Nisei,* a book about student relocation.

Dr. Lee Paul Sieg, president of the University of Washington, was an early opponent of the internment. He wrote letters to college presidents outside the exclusion zones seeking placements for Nisei students, and ensured that students at the University of Washington, who were interned shortly before graduation, received their diplomas. When anti-Nisei elements demanded that Robert O'Brien be fired for his student relocation work, Sieg stood up for him.

Dr. Robert Gordon Sproul, chancellor of the University of California, Berkeley, for twenty-eight years, was an early advocate of student relocation and a founding member of the Northern California Committee on Fair Play for Citizens and Aliens of Japanese Ancestry. In March 1942, he and others established the Japanese Student Relocation Committee to facilitate the transfer of college students to schools outside the exclusion zone.

William P. Tolley, who had been newly appointed chancellor of Syracuse University in 1941, was asked by the AFSC to accept Nisei students from the internment camps. He offered scholarships for up to 100 students. Sixty-five students enrolled. The American Legion and Veterans of Foreign Wars protested, but the students arrived on campus anyway. Surprisingly, the military did not object, although Syracuse was also training 3800 air cadets, WACs and specialized training program recruits. A few weeks after the Nisei arrived, one of them defused the tension by winning the top prize in an American Legion art competition and donating the $100 savings bond to the Red Cross. *Nominated by Warren Tsuneishi.*

Alba Pichetto Witkin received her master's degree in public personnel administration from Stanford in the summer of 1942. She had a few months free before starting work at the state personnel board, so Margaret Cosgrave, a mentor from Fresno State College, suggested that she work for the Student Relocation Council. Having experienced discrimination as the daughter of an Italian immigrant, Miss Pichetto said in an AFSC oral history that she was glad to have "this wonderful opportunity to serve in an area where I thought our government really had done wrong, done something illegal." She worked at the student relocation office for four or five months, helping collect the documents that internees needed to obtain approval to leave the camps. It was her first exposure to Quakerism. She was profoundly affected by an "atmosphere that looked for righteousness, for correctness, for morality, for goodness.... I've always said that if I were good enough, I'd be a Quaker, because I think so highly of their spiritual content and...their behavior...their modes of living." Miss Pichetto later became a community organizer and an activist with the League of Women Voters. *Nominated by Emiko Katsumoto.*

YMCA/YWCA

Nell Finely, according to Herbert Nicholson's oral history, "was a YWCA secretary from Honolulu who did the same thing [as Miles Cary]. She was head of the social service work at Poston. Two wonderful people! You know, the WRA had many wonderful people like that. They had some 'roughnecks,' but they had a lot of good folks, too, and they did a great deal of good.... I just couldn't work with the outfit because I didn't believe in it. But those people [chose to go there], and every camp had people like that. They were really worthwhile."

Henry and Ruth Kingman were both extremely concerned about the rights of Japanese Americans. Henry Kingman was director of the campus YMCA at UC Berkeley's Stiles Hall. He and his wife Ruth recruited students to help with student relocation efforts. Ruth Kingman was also the executive secretary of the Pacific Coast Committee on American Principles and Fair Play, which was organized in January 1943 to safeguard the constitutional rights of Japanese Americans. The group coordinated about 300 groups working on race relations on the West Coast. The group was an outgrowth of the Northern California Committee for Fair Play for Citizens and Aliens of Japanese Ancestry, which was formed in early October of 1941. Mrs. Kingman was a founding member of this committee, along with Robert Gordon Sproul, chancellor of the University of California, Berkeley; Ray Lyman Wilbur, president of Stanford University; Robert Milliken, president of the California Institute of Technology;

Galen Fisher, former missionary to Japan and secretary of the Committee on National Security and Fair Play in San Francisco; economist and diplomat Henry Francis Grady, secretary of the Pacific Coast Committee on National Security and Fair Play, San Francisco; Chester Rowell, a political commentator for the *San Francisco Chronicle;* Monroe Deutsch, provost of the University of California, Berkeley; Josephine Duveneck of the AFSC; and sociologist Paul Taylor.

In 1942, the Committee on National Security and Fair Play attempted to mount opposition to the internment, but because various members disagreed on what position to take, various fair play committees were formed under different names in different communities, such as William Carr's Friends of the American Way in Pasadena, the Fair Play Council in Palo Alto, the Council for Civic Unity in San Jose, and other groups in areas such as Fresno, Los Angeles, Santa Barbara, Portland and Seattle. *Nominated by Mas Yonemura, Harry Honda and Hans Baerwald.*

BOY SCOUTS

Sam Fusco, a wholesale fruit dealer and trained musician who lived on the edge of San Francisco's Japantown, volunteered to train the drum and bugle corps of Boy Scout Troop 12, which was sponsored by the Japanese American churches. By 1940, the award-winning marching band was 100 strong and was invited to perform at many parades, including at the World's Fair on Treasure Island. When the scouts were interned, they entrusted their instruments to Fusco. When he tried to take the drums and cymbals to the boys at Tanforan, he was not allowed entry.

The young Sicilian American's scouting activities and his membership in the Japanese Episcopal Church came to the attention of the FBI. Because of his Italian American ancestry, he was classified as a potentially dangerous alien and was ordered to leave the West Coast. He relocated to Salt Lake City but was forbidden to contact his friends at Topaz. He worked as a carpenter and a laborer, but had trouble keeping jobs because the FBI often visited his employers, and he would subsequently be laid off. The young man's hair went prematurely gray from the harassment. Eventually, he entered law school in Salt Lake City, then returned to San Francisco to develop a successful law career. He helped returnees recover their lost property and returned to the scout troop the instruments that he had kept safe in a San Francisco warehouse. *Nominated by George Fukui and Hisaji Q. Sakai, MD.*

Milton Goldberg, who grew up with Japanese Americans in the multiethnic, working-class Los Angeles neighborhood called Boyle Heights, was familiar with the three Japanese American troops in Little Tokyo: Troops 79, 145 and 365, sponsored by the Buddhist, Catholic (Maryknoll) and Methodist churches. Goldberg was an official of the Boy Scouts of America from 1937 to 1945, with multicounty responsibilities in Southern California. During the internment period, he considered it part of his normal duties to treat the interned scouts as equal to any other scout troop.

He took the initiative to ask the administrator at Santa Anita if the interned scouts could be kept together and bring their uniforms, bugles and flags. After the internees were transferred to Manzanar, he arranged to visit them when he made his quarterly visits to the other scout troops in Inyo County. He considered it the "right thing to do" to make certain the Manzanar scouts were included, even though it would have been easy to ignore them. Maryknoll's Brother Theodore and Goldberg's wife, Harriet, often accompanied him to Manzanar. Goldberg called his wife a "born social worker" who befriended young internee mothers and brought them layettes and other necessities."

Goldberg heard about an incident in which the Manzanar scouts surrounded the American flag to protect it from a group of protesters who threatened to rip it down. To reward the scouts for their courageous and patriotic action, Goldberg persuaded project director Ralph Merritt to let him take them on a weeklong backpack trip in the High Sierra. The majestic mountains loomed directly over the camp, but it was highly unusual at that time for internees to be permitted to leave camp and visit them. Since Merritt was an outdoorsman and a Sierra Club activist, he was receptive to Goldberg's idea, and after the scouts' first successful outing, allowed a Sierra backpack to became an annual tradition. *Nominated by Richard Potashin.*

GOVERNMENT EMPLOYEES

Elizabeth Baumgarten, director of the Stockton Assembly Center and later Granada (Amache) internment camp in Colorado, was an "able and highly sympathetic camp director who did much to ameliorate the conditions in camp and encouraged Nisei to go to college," according to Eric Saul. *Nominated by Eric Saul.*

IN PREWAR SANTA MONICA, JACK HIROSE PLAYED FOOTBALL WITH MICKEY ROONEY BECAUSE ROONEY'S MOTHER MADE AN EFFORT FOR THE CHILD STAR TO HAVE FRIENDS OUTSIDE THE MOVIE INDUSTRY. IN RECENT YEARS, HIROSE REINTRODUCED HIMSELF TO ROONEY AFTER A PERFORMANCE, AND WAS DELIGHTED THAT THE VETERAN ACTOR REMEMBERED THEIR FOOTBALL DAYS. COURTESY OF JACK HIROSE.

Thomas Willard Holland, employment officer for the WRA, was charged with locating jobs outside the exclusion zone for resettlers leaving the internment camps. In early 1943, he visited all the internment camps to set up leave-clearance offices. On a tour of Manzanar, he met young Jack Hirose, who headed the sign shop in Manzanar. Hirose and his four colleagues in the shop were art students whose college careers had been cut short by the internment. The crew finished their camp assignments in the morning and taught each other art techniques in the afternoon. The resulting artworks turned the sign shop into a mini gallery, which became a popular stop for visitors. Holland took personal interest in

Hirose, and offered him a standing invitation to go live with Holland's family in Chevy Chase, Maryland, with "no strings attached." When Hirose arrived, Holland and his family made him welcome. He roomed with 12-year-old Nicholas Holland and introduced him to the delights of oceanography. The pair was soon building aquariums together, and the delighted Hollands "adopted" Hirose as "Jack Hirose Holland."

Hirose soon landed a job as staff artist at *The Washington Post*, helping prove Holland's case that Nisei could adjust well to life outside camp. By December 1943, Hirose was able to send for his fiancée, Kinu Hirashima. The couple was married a month later, with Wade Beach, a colleague and mentor at the *Post*, serving as best man. After several years at the newspaper, Hirose left to freelance, and eventually established his own highly successful exhibit design firm.

Holland later served as an official of the national Labor Relations Board, the Labor Department and other federal agencies, as well as a professor at George Washington University. Nicholas Holland later became an oceanographer who once met fellow ichthyologist Emperor Hirohito. The Hiroses visited Tom and Marian Holland every Christmas until they died. *Nominated by M. Jack Hirose.*

William Tuttle was teaching at UC Berkeley's school of social work in early 1942 when he volunteered to help interview Japanese Americans applying for military clearance to resettle voluntarily outside the exclusion area. The experience was deeply disturbing to him, and in November 1942, he resigned his teaching position and went to Arizona to work at the Gila River internment camp as director of welfare. In January 1945, he returned to the San Francisco Bay Area as a WRA employee assisting returnees in Oakland. In 1998, Tuttle was still going strong, with "Over Sixty Sunnyside Up," a weekly radio program for seniors at an all-volunteer radio station in Nevada City. *With thanks to the Florin JACL Oral History Program.*

YOUTH

Ralph Lazo (1924–1992) was a friendly kid of Mexican and Irish descent who had many Japanese American classmates at Belmont High School in Los Angeles. When he learned that his friends were to be interned, he was furious. "These people hadn't done anything that I hadn't done except to go to Japanese-language school," he later said. Telling his father and sister that he was going to summer camp, he voluntarily interned himself at Manzanar. He lived among his friends and finished his schooling at Manzanar High School. After graduation, he was drafted into the army and earned a Bronze Star in the Philippines. He later attended UCLA and became a teacher. He maintained ties with former internees and spoke out in support of the redress movement. He rarely spoke about his own internment experiences, preferring to focus on the unjust treatment of Japanese Americans. *Nominated by Yuri Kochiyama and Aiko Yoshinaga Herzig.*

Mollie Wilson (Murphy), an African American who grew up in Los Angeles in the multicultural neighborhood of Boyle Heights, had many Japanese American friends. She and her brother Atoy maintained friendships with their high school classmates after they were interned. Mollie was a faithful letter writer who kept up regular correspondence with June Yoshigai, Sandie Saito, Tomoko Ikeda, Mary Murakami and other Nisei while they were incarcerated, and later kept in touch as they resettled in the Midwest. Her letters, cards and gifts of stationery and candy extended a sense of stability and normality to her friends when their world was turned upside down. Her correspondents shared their fears and worries with her, as well as the small happinesses they managed to find amidst the turmoil. Mollie kept her friends' and classmates' photos in an album and saved all their letters. Decades later, she gave them to her friend June Yoshigai, who donated them to the Japanese American National Museum (JANM). Both she and her brother Atoy appear briefly in the JAMN video *Crossroads: Boyle Heights. Nominated by Norine Nishimura.*

The Sebastopol Congregational Church Youth Group protected the Buddhist church in Sebastopol, California, from vandalism and arson in 1945. The ornate and beautiful Enmanji Buddhist Temple features traditional roof structure dating back to the eleventh century. It is the only construction of its kind in the United States. The building was originally built as part of the Manchurian Railroad Exhibition Hall at the 1933 World's Fair in Chicago. After the fair closed, the Buddhists of Sonoma County purchased part of the building and had it disassembled, shipped to Sebastopol and reassembled by Japanese artisans based in San Francisco. Enmanji was dedicated on the Buddha's birthday in April 1934.

The congregation was forced to abandon their beloved temple when they were interned in May 1942. They fenced the grounds and secured the door with chains and padlocks, but in 1945, unknown elements opposed to the return of Japanese Americans to Sonoma County hacked the temple pillars with axes and attempted to burn the building down. Scars can still be seen on the structure today.

A group of young people organized to guard the temple and save it from further harm. Fourteen-year-old Sara Garrison and her future husband Jack Gerboth, then sixteen, were members of that plucky band. They belonged to a youth group for high school students that met at the Congregational Church. When their minister, Rev. Jim Center, told them about the attempted arson, Sara recalled, they were very upset and and decided to do something about it. Most determined was Jack, who pushed forward a plan for the students to stand guard over the building.

Although Reverend Center did not initiate the idea, he was supportive. But some of the townspeople didn't like it, and neither did their parents. In *Giri: The Sonoma County JACL Oral History Project,* Sara recalled, "[W]e were pretty insistent, and pretty convinced that this is what we needed to do, so they ended up letting us do it."

The students were dismayed by their first glimpse of the temple. "It had always been such a neat and beautiful place and when we came, there was chain-link fence all the way around it and a big heavy chain on the door and padlocks hanging down and weeds growing up along the link fence.... [I]t just made me feel so sad that this place was neglected," said Sara.

There were only eight to twelve students involved, not nearly enough to join hands to form a protective circle around the building. But they made a symbolic circle as far as they

could reach and made a solemn vow to protect the building. Sara and Jack, and Clayton Boughman, Bob and Peggy Marks, Ann and Dave Williams and a few others committed to stand guard over the building every weekend from sundown until 6 a.m., in two-hour shifts.

Sara recalled, "It was scary because we knew that people had been here trying to burn [the temple] down.... [W]e didn't know if people would react against us and come and try to harm us...that was always on our minds, but fortunately, nobody did.... I know there was reaction towards the church from some people, but they didn't react to us directly." The students obtained police whistles to blow if trouble began, and made arrangements for someone to call the police if they heard the whistle. But they never found out if the police would have responded because they never had reason to blow the whistle.

The group was too short-handed to post a guard on weeknights, and their parents would not have let them out on a school night anyway. But for the next three months, they guarded the temple every weekend, until the Japanese Americans were able to return and watch over the temple themselves. "I don't know that we prevented [the temple] from being burned down," Sara said, "because there were a lot of times that we weren't there, but the fact is, it didn't get burned down, so we felt successful...like we had done what we had set out to do."

For Sara, the experience was not entirely a hardship. "I was fourteen, I was in love and I would have done a lot of things in order to go spend a couple of hours in the middle of the night with my true love, so it wasn't all altruistic...[but] I do remember how much we were convinced that this was what we had to do."

FRIENDS, ASSOCIATES AND OTHERS

Roy F. Barsotti worked for his uncles' company, Ghiselli Bros., a wholesale produce business located at 230 Washington Street in San Francisco. According to a letter from his daughter Louise Barsotti, he became acquainted with many Japanese farmers on his trips "down the Valley" to contract for produce. When the farmers had to leave for camp, Barsotti took care of some of their belongings. Miss Barsotti was a child at the time, so she does not know any of the farmers' names. She does remember playing in the basement of their San Francisco house and being told that certain large trunks were "off limits" to her and her sister. "The trunks were there for some years," she wrote. "I know this is only a small thing, but I wanted you to know of it." *Nominated by Louise Barsotti.*

Estelle Peck Ishigo (1899–1990), one of the very few Caucasian internees, was the wife of Nisei Arthur Shigeharu Ishigo. As the daughter of a concert singer and a fine artist, she grew up surrounded by music and art. She met Arthur, an aspiring actor, while attending Otis Art School in Southern California. In 1928, it was illegal for people of color to marry Caucasians, so they crossed the border to be married in Mexico. Afterward, they lived in the Japanese American community because they were shunned by her family and other whites.

When Arthur was interned, Estelle accompanied him to the Pomona "Assembly Center" and then to Heart Mountain, Wyoming, where she worked as a WRA illustrator. After their three-and-a-half-year incarceration, they returned to Southern California, where they lived in a trailer camp and worked in the San Pedro fish canneries. Arthur died of cancer in 1957, and

Estelle lived in obscure poverty until her paintings were displayed at the California Historical Society. In 1972, she published *Lone Heart Mountain,* a book of writings and artwork she had created in camp. In 1988, filmmaker Steven Okazaki released *Days of Waiting,* a poignant video documentary about her life.

Alice Newman Hays kept a scrapbook of internment headlines and saved 116 letters written to her by five families interned at Heart Mountain, Wyoming. She donated her papers to the Hoover Institution.

Paul Low was a stockbroker living in Carmel-by-the-Sea in 1942. He read that Japanese American fishermen were having difficulty getting fair prices for their fishing boats as they prepared for internment. Believing this to be unfair, he used his contacts to find trustees to hold and maintain the boats until they could be sold for a decent price.

Low was born and raised in the United States, the son of wealthy German Jews who had emigrated from Germany in the 1800s. After the Depression, he and his wife moved to Paris, where their two sons were born—and raised Episcopalian. The Lows regularly visited their relatives in Germany. Interestingly, while German gentiles identified the rest of the family as German Jews, Paul Low's family was viewed simply as "American." About a year before Germany invaded France, Low moved his wife and two sons back to the United States. Their relatives, who had not been concerned about Hitler until it was too late, remained in Germany. Once the true extent of the *Fuhrer's* virulent anti-Semitism was understood, Paul Low did not have the resources to pay the ransoms that the Nazis extorted from the foreign relatives of Jews applying for exit visas. Low's German relatives perished in the Holocaust, as did many of the family's Jewish friends in Paris. In light of the heroic few who helped hide European Jews from Hitler, Low's son Peter is very modest about his father's support of the Japanese American fishermen, saying that he and his family were never at physical or social risk—in fact, their circle of friends believed that he was doing the right thing. Nevertheless, Paul Low extended help when many looked the other way. *Nominated by Midori Yenari. Information courtesy of Nadine Low.*

Dr. Helen Mackler, according to Tomoye Takahashi, "was an intern at Children's Hospital in San Francisco when my mother, Masano Nozawa, was hospitalized for osteomyelitis. I was in my last year as a student at UC Berkeley. I went frequently to be with my mother and met Dr. Mackler. After June of 1937 when I graduated, I was able to be at my mother's bedside daily, sometimes staying overnight on the cot in her room. Penicillin had not been yet widely used and her condition was a losing battle. Dr. Mackler became concerned about my physical and emotional condition as well, and she became a compassionate friend and advisor. After my mother passed away, she kept in close touch, checking on my condition. She invited me to her home for lunch, and became my closest friend during the ensuing period of grieving, adjusting, and regaining my health.

"In 1939, when I was selected to become one of the Nisei staff for the Japan Pavilion of the Golden Gate International Exposition on Treasure Island, she had become a resident physician at Children's Hospital and then established a practice. Although her professional and personal life was a busy one, she enthusiastically supported my relationship with the Japan Pavilion and my new public exposure as guide and docent of the arts and crafts of Japan being presented live by artisans from Japan. She participated in a contest held by the Japan Pavilion and won one of the ten trips to Japan by submitting a paper on the study of *tsutsugamushi* in the treatment of ailments.

"In 1941, when I was married, she gave me advice and caring guidance. After her Japan visit, she became even more interested in American Japanese like myself, and spread her concern about the Evacuation among her friends to help and sympathize with Nisei victims of the military edict. She visited our family at Tanforan, bringing food and toilet tissue, which were in short supply. We were in constant correspondence throughout our confinement in the Central Utah Project, also called Topaz. She kept all my letters describing life in Tanforan Assembly Center and Topaz. I wrote about our friendship with Victor and Mildred Goertzel, conscientious objectors who were assigned to Topaz; my husband Henri's work as English editor of *Topaz Times,* the camp's daily newsletter; my work as the director of adult education; my contributions as a staff writer on the camp paper; and other personal observations and family news. Dr. Mackler contacted a literary magazine with my bundle of letters in an attempt to expand information about the evacuation and confinement of American Japanese, but the subject was rejected as being too sensitive for the times.

"She continued to help us during the years of rehabilitation in experimenting with a new career by buying us equipment for Henri's attempt to start in photography, his hobby at the time. This was abandoned as we started Takahashi Trading Company, sending care packages to Japan." The Takahashis eventually lost touch with Dr. Mackler after she moved to Bakersfield. *Nominated by Tomoye Takahashi.*

Evelyn Stevenson Perkins was the neighbor and landlady of Tsuyako "Sox" Kitashima's family in prewar Centerville (now Fremont, California). Descended from a pioneer ranch family, Mrs. Perkins was "one of the few people around town who wasn't afraid of being called a 'Jap lover.'" She served the family a farewell breakfast on her best china on the morning of their eviction, and then drove them to the assembly site. She visited them numerous times at Tanforan Assembly Center, bringing food and clothing, and even linoleum to cover the splintery floor. *Nominated by Tsuyako "Sox" Kitashima.*

RESETTLEMENT

Martha Graham, world-renowned modern dancer, recognized the talent of a young Kibei dancer and welcomed her into her dance studio and into her company at the height of World War II, when feelings against Japanese Americans still ran high. Yuriko Amamiya (Kikuchi) was born in San Jose, California, and raised in Japan, where she studied classical Japanese dance. She returned to the United States after high school to study dance, but was soon interned at Gila River in Arizona. In 1943, she obtained leave clearance to move to New York City. She took classes at Martha Graham's studio, and the dance legend soon recognized Yuriko's bright, charismatic talent. Within four months, Miss Graham offered the young dancer a scholarship, and three months later invited her to join the prestigious dance company. Company members were asked whether they had any objections to Yuriko's presence, but everyone made her welcome. It was the beginning of a long and successful career. Yuriko, who is now in her mid-eighties, continues to work professionally. In tribute to the woman who gave her a start when she left the internment camp, she now teaches Martha Graham's works to dance companies around the country without charge. "It's my way of saying thank you to Martha Graham personally and to the dance world in American that gave me such a wonderful life," she said. *Nominated by Warren Tsuneishi.*

RETURNEES

The Council for Civic Unity of San Jose established a resettlement hostel after Anne Peabody raised the question in late 1944 of what could be done to help returnees to the area. Marjorie Pitman volunteered to lead a survey of the housing situation in the former Japantown, where many African Americans, Filipinos and Latinos had moved. A group of black and white women undertook the survey and also began to educate the residents regarding the returnees. By the time the first large trainload of returnees arrived, the council had enlisted forty-four hostel sponsors, many of whom met the returnees at the train station with transportation and hot food.

Mrs. Peabody gathered information from the AFSC and other groups on how to set up a hostel, and conferred with Heart Mountain internees regarding the most suitable place for a hostel. It was decided to use the Japanese-language school near the Buddhist church. Toranike Kawakami served as the first hostel manager. The San Jose hostel was the only one that began without financial backing, and when the hostel opened on April 6, 1945, Kawakami and others provided furniture and paid initial expenses out of their own pockets.

By the end of April, the local WRA officer, James Edmiston, obtained beds and other government equipment for fifty people.

At first, the WRA imposed a three-week limit on hostel stays, but the order was rescinded because of an acute housing shortage. By the the fall of 1945, San Jose's hostel operation occupied four buildings and housed up to 370 people at time in buildings that lacked adequate plumbing and heat. According to a 1946 report by Evelyn B. Settles, chair of the Civic Unity Hostel Committee, "We tried to call a halt to the number of people coming in. It just seemed inhumane to accept any more, but the Relocation Centers were getting ready to close [and]...people were being forcibly put on trains.... We just had to accept them and do the best that could be done for them."

By January 1946, hostel registration had dropped below 100, and the WRA issued a directive that hostels using government surplus equipment must close by March 31. On that date, with fifty people still in residence, the council handed hostel operations over to the Buddhist church. In almost a year of operation, the hostel had served 1,423 guests, and expended almost $25,000. A profit of $3400 was donated to the Japanese American churches and to the JACL. *Nominated by Eiichi Sakauye and Barbara Uchiyama.*

A San Francisco landlady was willling to rent a room near Japantown to Pearl Kurokawa when she returned to the West Coast and enrolled in the graduate program in public health nursing at San Francisco State College. Nevertheless, the Caucasian landlady feared that racists might cause problems for one or both of them, so she suggested that Miss Kurokawa list her name on the mailbox as "Kurokowski." *Nominated by Pearl Kurokawa Kimura.*

National Japanese American Citizens League Sponsors 1941–1950

Compiled and annotated by Harry K. Honda, editor emeritus, Pacific Citizen.

The reverse side of the National JACL's stationery from 1942 to 1950 listed 76 prominent Americans known as "National JACL Sponsors." They were among the few who raised their voices in opposition to the mass denial of civil rights to Japanese Americans by the U.S. government. They came from all walks of life—business, labor, professions, education, churches—befriending and defending the Nisei when it was most needed.

Upon advice of numerous friends, the National JACL Headquarters began recruiting these sponsors after the attack on Pearl Harbor in 1941, because the general public could not distinguish between Americans of Japanese ancestry and the "enemy" Japanese. Within a month's time, 25 nationally prominent leaders lent their names, support and cooperation to the JACL. And the list grew. The gathering of support began at both ends of the continent—with Saburo Kido, Teiko Ishida, Dr. Thomas Yatabe, Jimmie Sakamoto and Mike Masaoka working on the West Coast; and Peter Aoki and T. Scott Miyakawa on the East Coast.

In 1944, four sponsors—author Pearl S. Buck, Bishop James E. Walsh of the Maryknoll Fathers, ACLU founder Roger Baldwin, and John W. Thomas of the American Baptist Home Mission Society[1]—cosigned a letter, which the JACL circulated to raise funds. It resulted in enough money to launch the JACL's educational and public relations campaign in the Midwest and East, where Japanese Americans were virtually unknown. The sponsors were kept up-to-date on problems confronting persons of Japanese ancestry through the JACL's weekly publication, the *Pacific Citizen.*

Upon the deaths of two National JACL Sponsors, Dr. Reinhold Niebuhr (1971) and Dr. David de Sola Pool (1970), former national JACL president (1958–60) Shig Wakamatsu of Chicago said: "(They) were known to most of us only as famous names. Yet, it comes as a reassuring wave of feeling to us and, we hope, to the Sansei, to know that these great men exhibited their faith in us. To remember them is to reaffirm our faith in the pure central core of democracy, which in this day seems encrusted with bitterness, doubt and divisiveness."

Below is a list of the National JACL Sponsors, along with biographical information where available.

Ackerman, Dr. Carl W. (1890–1970) New York, New York. Educator, journalist; dean, Columbia Graduate School of Journalism (1931–56), administered Pulitzer Prize program, a champion of civil liberties and freedom of information; lectured on the value of "public opinion" at Tokyo Imperial University (1935). National JACL Sponsor, 1944–45.

Agar, William Macdonough (1884–1972) New York, New York. Geologist, winner of French Croix de Guerre (1918); chairman, Freedom House. National JACL Sponsor, 1944–45.

Alexander, Mrs. Wallace B. Orinda, California. National JACL Sponsor, 1944–45.

Alexander, Dr. Will Winton (1884–1956) Chicago, Illinois. Authority on race relations; director, Interracial Commission (1930s); administrator, Farm Security Administration (1936–1940); vice president, Rosenwald Fund (1940–1948); special assistant, War Manpower

Commission. National JACL Sponsor, 1944–45.

Baldwin, Roger N. (1884–1981) New York, New York. Lifelong pacifist, founding director, American Civil Liberties Union (1920), established with such liberals as Helen Keller, Norman Thomas, Felix Frankfurter and Clarence Darrow to defend rights of Negroes, labor and women; among the trusted advisors of National JACL during the war years. On October 12, 1942, when the ACLU national board objected to the court cases of Minoru Yasui, Gordon Hirabayashi, Fred Korematsu and the Tule Lake stockade incident because it appeared the ACLU was interfering with the war effort, Baldwin expressed his personal commitment by contributing $500 of his own money to help meet court costs. During the Occupation, Baldwin worked in Japan for several months with Gen. Douglas MacArthur on civil liberties issues. In 1950, when the ACLU national board was again on the opposite side of the JACL on the Walter–McCarran bill that provided for Issei naturalization, Baldwin privately expressed his regrets to JACL leaders Saburo Kido and Mike Masaoka. National JACL Sponsor, 1942–45.

Barnett, Eugene Epperson (1888–1970) New York, New York. General secretary, YMCA International Committee (1937–41); began "Y" work at University of North Carolina in 1908, served in China (1910–37). National JACL Sponsor, 1942–45.

Benjamin, Robert N. (1910–xxxx) New York, New York. Cochair, Greater New York Committee for Japanese Americans; advised and assisted with problems faced in jobs, housing and welfare for persons of Japanese ancestry at the outbreak of World War II. National JACL honoree, New York City, 1959.

Binsse, Harry Lorin. New York, New York. Managing editor, *The Commonweal.* National JACL Sponsor, 1944–45.

Black, Benjamin W., M.D. (d. 1945) Oakland, California. Physician, medical administrator, Alameda County General Hospital. National JACL Sponsor, 1944–45.

Buck, Pearl Sydenstricker (1892–1973) Perkasie, Pennsylvania. Author of the Pulitzer Prize-winning novel *The Good Earth* (1931) and many other titles, she was the first American woman to win the Nobel Prize in Literature, in 1938. She recorded her anxiety about the plight of Japanese Americans in her book, *American Unity and Asia,* but expressed confidence that they would not lose faith in American democracy. The child of Presbyterian missionaries, she was born and raised for seventeen years in China. After graduating from Randolph-Macon College in Virginia, she married agricultural missionary Dr. John L. Buck in 1917 and returned to China to teach English literature until 1930. In 1949 she founded Welcome House, an adoption agency for mixed-heritage Asian children and mentally retarded children. National JACL Sponsor, 1941–45 (among the very first National JACL Sponsors soon after Pearl Harbor).

Bynner, Witter (1882–1968) Santa Fe, New Mexico. Writer, playwright, translator of Chinese and Native American poems, introduced Japanese poems to Americans (1916). National JACL Sponsor, 1944–45.

Cary, Miles E., PhD (1895–1959) Honolulu, Hawaii. Educator, Honolulu McKinley High principal (1924–48), hailed as "Tokyo High" because of its predominantly Hawaiian Japanese student body. He volunteered during World War II to establish a public school system and was principal of the high school in Poston, Arizona, which was named after him in gratitude. His students learned values of self-reliance, individuality, initiative, leadership, citizenship—"the American dream." In addition to the three Rs, they learned to think for themselves and solve new problems. Two McKinley High School graduates, Hiram Fong and Daniel Inouye, sat in the U.S. Senate at the same time (1963–1976), making McKinley the only American high school so represented. National JACL Sponsor, 1944–45.

Chase, Dr. Harry Woodburn (1883–1955) New York, New York. Educator, University of North Carolina (1910–30), University of Illinois president (1930–33), New York University chancellor (1933–51) who strengthened its school of medicine, doubled NYU's student enrollment to 70,000, faculty of 4,000 with a $18 million budget in 1950. National JACL Sponsor, 1944–45.

Colby, Mrs. Ruth Gage (1923–xxxx) St. Paul, Minnesota. As a volunteer, she operated an office which helped resettlers find jobs and housing in the Minneapolis/St. Paul area, according to Yuri Kochiyama. National JACL Sponsor, 1944–45.

De Sola Pool, Rabbi David (1895–1970) New York, New York. Rabbi at America's oldest Jewish congregation, Shearith Israel, the Spanish/Portuguese synagogue (1907–70), world leader in Judaism, president of the Union of Sephardic Congregations (1928–67). National JACL Sponsor, 1942–45.

Deutsch, Monroe Emanuel, PhD (1879–1955) Berkeley, California. University of California, Berkeley provost (1931–47). National JACL Sponsor, 1944–45.

Embree, Dr. Edwin R. (1883–1950) Chicago, Illinois. Anthropologist, educator; president-director, Rosenwald Fund (1928–48), specializing in Far East, race and cultural anthropology of blacks and Asians. He engaged in extensive medical research, public health and teaching in China; member, Chicago Mayor's Commission on Race Relations (1943–48). National JACL Sponsor, 1944–45.

Fisher, Dorothea Frances Canfield (1879–1958) Arlington, Virginia. A novelist whose magazine by-line was "Dorothy Canfield." She was awarded honorary Doctor of Literature degrees from nine major colleges and universities. National JACL Sponsor, 1944–45.

Fleming, Dr. Dena Frank. Nashville, Tennessee. National JACL Sponsor, 1944–45.

Forster, Clifford. New York, New York. ACLU counsel in New York who fought discrimination against Japanese Americans prior to the ACLU's official decision to do so in 1944. National JACL honoree, New York City, 1959.

Fosdick, Rev. Dr. Harry Emerson (1878–1969) New York, New York. Author, clergyman, Baptist preacher since 1903, Union Theological Seminary (from 1915), professor of practical theology, ardent pacifist in the 1930s, pastor, Riverside Church. National JACL Sponsor, 1944–45. (His younger brother Raymond was affiliated with the Rockefeller Foundation, serving as its president from 1935 to 1946.)

Gaeth, Arthur. Salt Lake City, Utah. Vice president, Intermountain Radio Network, an outspoken radio newscaster remembered for his favorable treatment of the all-Japanese American 442nd Regimental Combat Team. National JACL Sponsor, 1944–45.

Goldblatt, Louis. San Francisco, California. Secretary general, West Coast Longshoremen's Union. National JACL Sponsor, 1944–45.

Graham, Dr. Frank P. (1886–1972) Chapel Hill, North Carolina. President, University of North Carolina (1930–49), appointed to U.S. Senate (D, 1949–50), United Nations official (1950–67). National JACL Sponsor, 1944–45.

Hammaker, Bishop Wilbur E. (1876–1968) Denver, Colorado. Missionary bishop of Nanking, China (1936–39), Methodist bishop in Colorado, Iliff School of Theology (1940–48). National JACL Sponsor, 1944–45.

Harlow, Dr. S. Ralph (1885–1972) Northampton, Massachusetts. Educator, Smith College (from 1923); United Nations Refugee Relief Agency director in Greece (1945–46). National JACL Sponsor, 1944–45.

Holt, Dr. Hamilton B. (1872–1951) Winter Park, Florida. Educator, editor-owner *New York Independent* (1897–1921); Rollins College president (1925–49), initiated "conference format" where teachers and students studied together for two hours. National JACL Sponsor, 1944–45.

Kizer, Benjamin H. Spokane, Washington. Attorney; chairman, Washington State Planning Commission; advisor to the founders of the Spokane JACL in 1940. National JACL Sponsor, 1944–45.

Lewis, Read. New York, New York. Executive director, American Council for Nationalities Service since 1928; founded Common Council for American Unity (CCAU), comprised of over 30 member agencies from Boston to Honolulu working with problems faced by newcomers to the United States as well as struggles of immigrant groups to maintain their identity and attempt to be assimilated; was cited by CCAU in 1969 for his many years of service. National JACL Sponsor, 1943–45; served on the JACL committee to solicit other National JACL Sponsors.

Marshall, Rev. Dr. J. W. Bill. Richmond, Virginia. Foreign Mission Board, Southern Baptist Convention. National JACL Sponsor, 1944–45.

Matthew, Dr. Rufus (1863–1948) Haverford, Pennsylvania. Philosopher, educator; professor in philosophy at Haverford College (1904–34), in Yenching University, China (1931–32). National JACL Sponsor, 1944–45.

McNaughton, E. B. Portland, Oregon. President, First National Bank; Reed College president and trustee (1948–1952). National JACL Sponsor, 1944–45.

Mitchell, Rt. Rev. Walter Mitchell (d. 1977) Phoenix, Arizona. Episcopal bishop. National JACL Sponsor, 1944–45.

Morley, Dr. Felix W. (1894–xxxx) Haverford, Pennsylvania. Educator, journalist; Rhodes scholar (1919–21), *Baltimore Sun* journalist (1922–29), *Washington Post* editor (1933–40), Haverford College president (1940–45). National JACL Sponsor, 1944–45.

Morrison, Charles Clayton. Chicago, Illinois. Editor, *Christian Century*. National JACL Sponsor, 1944–45.

Musser, Mrs. Burton W. (d. 1968) Salt Lake City, Utah. Volunteer social worker, National YWCA board member, among the early women elected to the Utah Senate, credited for founding day care centers and the Neighborhood House for underprivileged children, Salt Lake JACL's first advisor in 1930s, President Franklin D. Roosevelt's representative to Pan-American Conference. National JACL Sponsor, 1944–45.

Nason, Dr. John W. (1905–2001) Swarthmore, Pennsylvania. Educator, Quaker and a Rhodes scholar from Minnesota (1928); was the youngest professor on the faculty at age 35 when chosen president, Swarthmore College in 1940; chaired the National Japanese American Student Relocation Council, enabling Nisei in wartime relocation centers to leave and continue their college education; president, Foreign Policy Association, New York (1952). National JACL Sponsor, 1944–45.

Neilson, Dr. William Allen (1869–1946) Falls Village, Connecticut. Writer, educator; associate editor of 50-volume Harvard Classics (1910–1911); president, Smith College (1917–39), condemned ethnic quotas at major colleges; editor-in-chief, *Merriam's International Dictionary*, unabridged 2nd edition (1934). National JACL Sponsor, 1944–45.

Niebuhr, Rev. Dr. Reinhold (1892–1971) New York, New York. Conspicuous American Protestant theologian at Union Theological Seminary since 1929; political observer and activist with the Socialist, Liberal, Democratic parties prior to World War II. Worked to end totalitarianism and aggression and bring about world peace and order." National JACL Sponsor, 1941–45 (among the very first National JACL Sponsors soon after Pearl Harbor).[2]

Odum, Dr. Howard Washington (1884–1954) Chapel Hill, North Carolina. Sociologist, Kennan professor of sociology (1920–54); director, Institute for Research in Social Science (1922–44), University of North Carolina; President Roosevelt's Commission on Interracial Cooperation (1934). National JACL Sponsor, 1944–45.

O'Hara, Most Rev. Edwin V. (1881–1956) Kansas City, Missouri. Roman Catholic bishop of Kansas City, archbishop (1954); was ordained priest in 1905, established Catholic Rural Life

Conference (1923), bishop of Great Falls, Montana (1930). National JACL Sponsor, 1944–45.

Page, Kirby (1890–1951) La Habra, California. Author, Quaker, social evangelist, YMCA worker from the 1910s. National JACL Sponsor, 1944–45.

Palmer, Rev. Dr. Albert W. (1879–1954) Chicago, Illinois. Clergyman, president, Chicago Theological Seminary (1930–46); author, *Orientals in America* (1934); radio ministry, Congregational Church of Los Angeles (1934); radio ministry, Congregational Church of Los Angeles (from 1946). National JACL Sponsor, 1944–45.

Parsons, Rt. Rev. Edward L. (1868–1960) San Francisco-based Episcopal Bishop of California (1919–1940), champion of civil rights and civic concerns during his Episcopate; chairman, ACLU California (1941–1956), an early West Coast voice opposing Evacuation, retired 1947. National JACL Sponsor, 1944–45.

Patton, James George (1902–1966) Denver, Colorado. Agricultural leader of the family-type (in contrast with corporate) farms; president. National Farmers' Union founded in 1902, one of four major farmers' groups during World War II, advocated draft deferment for skilled farmers, restored crop insurance; appointed by FDR to Economic Stabilization Board (1942); to the War Mobilization and Reconstruction Advisory Board (1944); NFU was branded by House Un-American Activities Committee as a Communist-front organization fighting for liberal causes (1944); conceived Peace Corps idea in 1945 to send farm technicians to live abroad and teach their skills in undeveloped countries; cofounder with Clarence Pickett of American Council of Race Relations (1947), lost his left eye in operation (1947) and wore a black patch; cited in 1957 by JACL for his wartime efforts. National JACL Sponsor, 1944–45.

Paxton Jr., James L. Omaha, Nebraska. Businessman, community leader, president and board chairman of Paxton–Mitchell Steel Co. National JACL Sponsor, 1944–45.

Perry, Jennings. Nashville, Tennessee. Editor, *The Tennessean*. National JACL Sponsor, 1944–45.

Perry, Dr. Ralph Barton (1876–1957) Cambridge, Massachusetts. Prolific writer (24 books), Harvard University professor of philosophy (since 1902, emeritus in 1946); Pulitzer Prize winner in Literature on William James (1935); chair, Committee on American Defense, Harvard Group. National JACL Sponsor, 1944–45.

Pickett, Clarence Evan (1884–1965) Philadelphia, Pennsylvania. Executive Secretary, American Friends Service Committee (1929–50), especially known with Dr. John Nason for organizing the National Student Relocation Council to assist Nisei in the World War II relocation centers, be they Christian or Buddhist, to pursue higher education in the Midwest and on the East Coast; his wartime and postwar refugee relief work worldwide led to the Nobel Peace Prize in 1947 and shared jointly by AFSC and British Friends Service Council; president of American Council of Race Relations (1944) to work on problems affecting African American, Mexican, Japanese and other minorities. National JACL Sponsor, 1944–45.

Poteat, Rev. Dr. Edwin McNeill (1892–1955) Rochester, New York. President, Colgate University Theological Seminary. National JACL Sponsor, 1944–45.

Rainey, Dr. Homer P. (1896–1985) Austin, Texas. Educator, college president, and ordained Baptist minister who turned down a baseball contract from the St. Louis Cardinals in 1919 to teach at Oregon (1924–26). He was president of Bucknell Baptist College (1931–35) and directed the American Youth Council in 1935 to survey and develop youth, recreation and health programs with the Rockefeller Foundation. As president of the University of Texas, beginning in 1939, he became embroiled in controversy in 1941 when several members of the board of regents pressured him to fire four economics professors who espoused New Deal views. The single issue that divided the regents and Rainey was the board's repression of John Dos Passos' *USA* on the sophomore English reading list; he was fired by the regents in 1944. Though students protested and defended him for promoting "academic freedom and free speech," they failed to have him reinstated. Rainey (D) finished second in 1946 primaries in bid for Texas governorship, returned to education as president of Stephens College for Women, Columbia, Missouri (1949). National JACL Sponsor, 1944–45.

Reichert, Rev. Dr. Irving F. San Francisco, California. National JACL Sponsor, 1944–45.

Reifsnider, Rt. Rev. Charles S. (1875–1958) Pasadena, California. Retired Episcopal churchman-missionary in Japan (1901–41), presided as bishop of Japanese American Episcopal congregations in World War II internment camps, retired in 1947, decorated by Emperor with 4th Class Order of Sacred Treasure, National JACL Sponsor, 1944–45.

Rundquist, George. Chair, Federal Council of Churches of Christ, which aided resettlers through various denominations and social agencies throughout the United States. National JACL honoree, New York City, 1959.

Scarlett, Rt. Rev. William (1881–1973) St. Louis, Missouri. Episcopal bishop of Missouri (1935–53), dean of Grace Cathedral (1920–30); member, ACLU, American Council Race Relations (1930); member, ACLU, American Council Race Relations (1930–55). National JACL Sponsor, 1944–45.

Scholle, August (1887–1979) Detroit, Michigan. President, Michigan State CIO. National JACL Sponsor, 1944–45.

Schuyler, George S. (1895–1977) New York. Essayist and chief editorialist, *Pittsburgh Courier* (1926–65), most widely read African American columnist in the 1930s to 1940s; criticized FDR and other government officials for allowing segregation and discrimination to continue in the armed services. "Indeed, one sometimes asks whether they are not fighting the Negro harder than they are fighting the Germans and Japanese. Certainly many German and Japanese prisoners are being treated better than some of the Negros wearing the uniform of Uncle Sam,"[3] autobiography *Black and Conservative* (1966). National JACL Sponsor, 1944–45.

Sibley, Mrs. Georgianna Farr (1887–1985) New York, New York. Wife of Harper Sibley, pre-war member of Laymen's Foreign Missions Inquiry (Japan/Asia), YWCA national board, Episcopal Church leader and champion of civil rights and racial justice. National JACL Sponsor, 1944–45.

Sibley, Harper (1885–1959) New York, New York. Agriculturalist. National president of U.S. Chamber of Commerce, one of the few businessmen who stood openly for Japanese Americans in early 1942. National JACL Sponsor, 1944–45.

Sprague, Hon. Charles A. (1887–1969) Salem, Oregon. Editor-publisher of the *Oregon Statesman*, Salem (1929–68), governor of Oregon who focused national attention on war in Europe and alerted America to threat of Japan (1939–43). When Evacuation began in early 1942, he convinced Americans to stiffen their attitude to protect the constitutional guarantees for all minorities. He denounced wartime internment of Japanese Americans in his daily newspaper column, "Seems to Me." After the war, he personally appeared at meetings to speak on behalf of returning evacuees. National JACL Sponsor, 1944–45.

Steiner, Dr. Jesse F. Seattle, Washington. Educator, University of Washington. National JACL Sponsor, 1944–45.

Stenzel, Henry O. (1884–1963) Milwaukee, Wisconsin. National JACL Sponsor, 1944–45.

Stevens, Rt. Rev. W. Bertrand. Los Angeles, California. Prewar and wartime Episcopal bishop of Los Angeles. National JACL Sponsor, 1944–45.

Sweetland, Monroe (1910–xxxx) Portland, Oregon. President-editor of *Milwaukie Review*, Oregon state legislator, with American Red Cross (Washington, D.C.), postwar Western representative of the National Education Association; a Palo Alto, California, resident who predicted in 1972 that Norman Mineta would be elected mayor of San Jose. National JACL Sponsor, 1944–45.

Swing, Raymond E. (Gram) (1887–1969) Washington, D.C. Foreign correspondent, journalist, radio reporter; *Chicago Daily News* (1912–15), *New York Herald* (1919–20), *Wall Street Journal* (1920–24), *New York Post* (1924–29), *The Nation* (1934–36). Network commentator on CBS, NBC and ABC; political commentator on American affairs (1935–45, 1959–64) on BBC. National JACL Sponsor, 1944–45.

Taft, Charles Phelps, 2nd (1897–1983) Cincinnati, Ohio. Lawyer, son of President William Howard Taft, family spent the summers in Yokohama when his father was head of the U.S.–Philippine Commission and first civil governor of the Philippines (1900–04); served on Cincinnati city council (1938–42, 1955–77); director, War Relief Control Board, Washington (1941–43), State Department Office of Wartime Economic Affairs (1944); first lay president, Federal Council of Churches of Christ (1947–48), returned to city politics, Cincinnati mayor (1955–57); his wife, Eleanor K. Chase (of Ingersoll Watch Co.), both National JACL Sponsors, 1944–45.

Thomas, Dr. John W. (1902–1994) New York, New York. YMCA Work secretary (1918), graduated Crozer Theological Seminary (1930), served Baptist Union of Philadelphia, master's degree in psychology from University of Pennsylvania (1933), pastor in New Jersey until 1936 when he became Cities Department secretary, American Baptist Home Mission Society. After Pearl Harbor he led efforts with focus on Japanese Baptists and in coalition with other Christians, helped organize Committee on Resettlement of Japanese Americans (September, 1942), resigned Home Missions to teach pastoral theology at Crozer in March 1945. (In 1995, the American Baptist Churches national board of ministries received a generous bequest from the estate of Mari Sabusawa Michener to create a scholarship fund in memory of John W. Thomas, who continually opened his home to Nisei resettlers en route to college or employment. The scholarships were to assist those who could afford to attend church workshops, seminars and other educational opportunities. Sabusawa had stayed at the Thomas home and received help in relocating to Antioch College.) National JACL Sponsor, 1941–45 (among the very first National JACL Sponsors soon after Pearl Harbor).

Thomas, Norman Mattoon (1884–1968) New York, New York. Reformer, onetime Socialist; Presbyterian minister who joined the Socialist Party in 1918, six-time candidate for President on the Socialist ticket (1928–48), protested 1942 internment of Japanese during the 1944 presidential campaign; recognized as national treasure of U.S. politics, successfully led efforts to oust Communists from important posts in ACLU, strongly denounced atomic bombing of Hiroshima and Nagasaki. National JACL Sponsor, 1941–45.

Thompson, Joseph S. (1878–1970) San Francisco, California. Executive, founder of Pacific Electric Manufacturing Co. (1906–54). National JACL Sponsor, 1944–45.

Townsend, Willard S. Jr. (1895–1957) Chicago, Illinois. African American labor leader, began as a "red cap" at Union Station, Cincinnati (1914–16), dining car waiter (1921–25), Urban League executive; president, United Transport Service Employees of America-CIO (from 1940). Author, Trade Union Practices (for Japan in 1950). National JACL Sponsor, 1944–45.

Trumble, George T. Cleveland, Ohio. National JACL Sponsor, 1944–45.

Tucker, Rt. Rev. Bishop Henry St. George (1874–1959) Washington, D.C. Prewar Episcopal missionary to Japan, fluent in Japanese language, president St. Paul's (Rikkyo) College, Tokyo; elected presiding bishop of Episcopal Church of the United States (1937–1946), publicly deplored Japan's aggression against China, but also noted Western nations, including the U.S., had provided bad examples to Japan and to most of the world governments for not paying attention to Christian principles in their activities; called for retention of Emperor of Japan after the war as a "stationary factor" (1945); headed Federal Council of Churches in Christ in

America (1949); a great-grandnephew of the first president, George Washington. National JACL Sponsor, 1944–45.

Vollmer, August (1876–1958) Berkeley, California. Criminologist, Berkeley chief of police (1905–32), associate professor, UC Berkeley (1932–48). National JACL Sponsor, 1944–45.

Walsh, Richard John. Perkasic, Pennsylvania. President, John Day Publishing Co. (New York), publisher, *Asia Magazine* (1941–46); second husband of Pearl Buck. National JACL Sponsor, 1944–45.

Walsh, Most Rev. James E. (1891–1981) Maryknoll, New York. Prewar missionary in South China. As superior general of the Maryknoll Society (1936–46), he protested 1942 internment of Japanese Americans. He returned to China in 1948 to coordinate a missionary bureau in Shanghai. Upon closure by Communist officials, he decided to stay, and was arrested in 1958 for "espionage under guise of religion." He was sentenced to 20 years imprisonment and released in 1970, as China relations thawed prior to President Nixon's visit in 1972. National JACL Sponsor, 1941–45 (among the very first National JACL Sponsors soon after Pearl Harbor).[4]

Walton, Dr. O. M. Cleveland, Ohio. National JACL Sponsor, 1944–45.

Watson, Annie Clo (1892–1960) San Francisco, California. Executive director, International Institute (1933–57), cofounder (with Rev. Galen Fisher, San Francisco) of Pacific Coast Committee for American Principles and Fair Play (1942, Berkeley); provided space for JACL office in 1945. JACL Leader Mike Masaoka recalled that prior to the eviction, "We depended upon her advice and counsel more than any other individual to provide what leadership we could to a frightened and disorganized society."[5] National JACL Sponsor, 1941–45.

White, William Allen (1868–1944) Emporia, Kansas. Journalist, author, owner of the *Emporia Gazette* (from 1895), known as the most distinguished small newspaper in U.S. because of its editorials in a lively conversational style. National JACL Sponsor, 1943–44.

Wilbur, Ray Lyman, MD (1875–1949) Stanford, California. Physician (1899). He met Herbert Hoover at Stanford in the 1890s and their careers entwined into the 1930s. Wilbur headed Cooper (later Stanford University) Medical School (1910–16), promoting research aspects in medicine; president, Stanford University (1916–27). Developed major study of Asian American/Pacific race relations (1923–25), which opposed exclusion laws and supported full equality and assimilation; Secretary of Interior in Hoover Administration (1928–29); honorary chancellor, Stanford University (1943). National JACL Sponsor, 1944–45.

SOURCE NOTES

1. WALT AND MILLY WOODWARD

Walter Woodward's writings quoted by permission of *The Bainbridge Review* and Mary Calista Woodward Pratt. *The Seattle Times* quoted by permission of *The Seattle Times*. Paul Ohtaki's writings reprinted by permission of Paul Ohtaki.

1. Don Hannula, "The lonely voice against internment," *The Seattle Times,* September 14, 1981.
2. Walter Woodward, "Plain talk," editorial, *The Bainbridge Review,* December 8, 1941.
3. Walter Woodward, "The Japanese evacuation—could it happen again?" *The Seattle Times,* December 7, 1969.
4. Gerald Elfendahl (speech, Freedom's Light Award ceremony, September 17, 1998).
5. Walter Woodward, oral history, interviewed by Eric Saul, November 23, 1986, 2. National Japanese American Historical Society Oral History Project, Go For Broke, Inc. Quoted by permission of the National Japanese American Historical Society.
6. Paul Ohtaki, telephone conversation with author, November 8, 2004. Quoted by permission of Paul Ohtaki.
7. Woodward, oral history by Eric Saul, 2.
8. Woodward, "The Japanese evacuation."
9. Ohtaki, telephone conversation with author.
10. Walter Woodward, editorial, *The Bainbridge Review*, March 26, 1942.
11. Woodward, oral history by Eric Saul, 3.
12. Ibid, 4.
13. Tom Welch, "Evacuation order brutal, says Woodward," *The Bainbridge Review,* September 16, 1981. Quoted by permission of *The Seattle Times.*
14. Woodward, oral history by Eric Saul, 4.
15. Paul Ohtaki, "Camp Correspondents," *It Was the Right Thing to Do!: Walt and Mildred Woodward* (San Francisco: self-published, 2005), 12. Quoted by permission of Paul Ohtaki.
16. Walter Woodward, editorial, "We'll tell, sometime," *The Bainbridge Review,* April 2, 1942.
17. Woodward, "The Japanese evacuation."
18. Ohtaki, "Camp Correspondents," 12.
19. Open Forum, *The Bainbridge Review,* April 2, 1942.
20. Paul Ohtaki, "What I Remember About the First Few Days," *It Was the Right Thing to Do!: Walt and Mildred Woodward* (San Francisco: self-published, 2005), 10.
21. Ibid.
22. Paul Ohtaki, "Evacuees sing on trip," *The Bainbridge Review,* April 2, 1942.
23. Paul Ohtaki, telephone conversation with author, May 7, 2004.
24. Paul Ohtaki, "What I remember," 11.
25. Walter Woodward, letter to Paul Ohtaki, April 24, 1942.
26. Ohtaki, "Camp Correspondents," 12.
27. Walter Woodward, letter to Paul Ohtaki, June 28, 1942.
28. Open Forum, *The Bainbridge Review,* November 27, 1942.
29. Walter Woodward, "You shouldn't pack apples with lemons," *The Bainbridge Review,* December 17, 1942.
30. Walter Woodward, "Nisei get a break," *The Bainbridge Review,* February 4, 1943.
31. Walter Woodward, letter to Sachiko Koura, July 8, 1944.
32. Art Koura, Open Forum, *The Bainbridge Review,* August 25, 1944.
33. Walter Woodward, letter to Sachiko Koura, November 20, 1944.
34. Open Forum, *The Bainbridge Review,* February 18, 1944.
35. Open Forum, *The Bainbridge Review,* November 10, 1944.
36. Open Forum, *The Bainbridge Review,* November 24, 1944.
37. Open Forum, *The Bainbridge Review,* November 11, 1944.
38. Open Forum, *The Bainbridge Review,* December 1, 1944.
39. "Schuyler charges 'smear' as *Review* is hit again," *The Bainbridge Review,* December 1, 1944.
40. Open Forum, *The Bainbridge Review,* December 22, 1944.
41. Open Forum, *The Bainbridge Review,* January 12, 1945.
42. Open Forum, *The Bainbridge Review,* January 19, 1945.
43. Welch, "Evacuation order brutal."
44. Florangela Davila, "Debate lingers over internment of Japanese Americans," *The Seattle Times,* September 6, 2004.
45. Woodward, oral history by Eric Saul, 9.
46. *Civil Liberties Act of 1988,* Public Law 100–383, August 10, 1988, 102 Stat. 903. http://www.access.gpo.gov/uscode/title50a/50a_69_1_.html (May 5, 2005).

2. VIRGINIA SWANSON YAMAMOTO

The oral histories of the Terminal Island Life History Project quoted by permission of the Japanese American National Museum. "Terminal Island Days" quoted by permission of the Japanese American Internment Project. Rev. Paul Nagano's writings quoted by permission of Paul Nagano and the *American Baptist Quarterly.*

1. Virginia Swanson Yamamoto, "Terminal Island Days," *Triumphs of Faith: Stories of Japanese-American Christians during World War II,* ed. Victor Okada (Los Angeles: Japanese-American Internment Project, 1998), 165. Courtesy of Paul Nagano.
2. Virginia Swanson Yamamoto, letter to Rev. Paul Nagano, June 1994, 1. Courtesy of Paul Nagano.
3. Rev. Paul M. Nagano, "Leading to Executive Order 9066," *American Baptist Quarterly* 16, no. 2 (June 1998): 109.
4. Teruko Miyoshi Okimoto, oral history, Terminal Island Life History Project, 1994, Japanese American National Museum, Teruko Miyoshi Okimoto.
5. Charlie O. Hamasaki, oral history, Terminal Island Life History Project, 1994, Japanese American National Museum, Charlie O. Hamasaki.
6. Yamamoto, letter to Paul Nagano, June 1994.
7. Yutaka Dave Nakagawa, oral history, Terminal Island Life History Project, 1994, Japanese American National Museum, Yutaka Dave Nakagawa.
8. Rev. Paul M. Nagano, "Dr. Ralph L. Mayberry: A Hero Without Headlines," *American Baptist Quarterly* 16, no. 2 (June 1998): 129–144.
9. George D. Younger, "Dr. John W. Thomas: American Baptist Servant and Advocate," *American Baptist Quarterly* 16, no. 3 (September 1998): 182–191.
10. Fusaye Hashimoto, oral history, Terminal Island Life History Project, 1994, Japanese American National Museum, Fusaye Hashimoto.
11. Yamamoto, "Terminal Island Days," 163.
12. Hashimoto, oral history.
13. Yamamoto, "Terminal Island Days," 164.
14. Rev. Paul M. Nagano, "Leading to Executive Order 9066," *American Baptist Quarterly* 16, no. 2 (June 1998): 110–111. First published in Earl O'Day, "Terminal Isle Japanese in muddle over their status," *Los Angeles Daily News,* February 10, 1942. Reprinted by permission of William Manchester Boddy.
15. Yamamoto, letter to Paul Nagano, 3.
16. Ibid., 5.
17. Ibid., 6.
18. Yamamoto, "Terminal Island Days," 164–165.
19. Ibid.

20. Yamamoto, letter to Paul Nagano, 2.
21. Rev. Paul M. Nagano, e-mail message to author, Jan 19, 2004.

3. GEORGE KNOX ROTH

The writings of George Knox Roth and Irma Brubaker Roth are courtesy of Irma Brubaker Roth, and are quoted by her permission. The *Los Angeles Times* quoted by permission of the *Los Angeles Times*. The *Rafu Shimpo* quoted by permission of *The Rafu Shimpo*.

1. Dwight Chuman, "George Roth: Man JAs forgot to thank," *The Rafu Shimpo*, July 15, 1977.
2. George Knox Roth, written testimony, Commission on Wartime Relocation and Internment of Civilians, Los Angeles, August 6, 1981. Courtesy of Irma Brubaker Roth.
3. Irma Brubaker Roth, interviewed by author, Pasadena, California, February 20, 2004. Quoted by permission of Irma Brubaker Roth.
4. Masamori Kojima, letter to George Roth, July 29, 1977. Courtesy of Irma Brubaker Roth. Quoted by permission of Joyce Uyehara.
5. *Personal Justice Denied: Report of the Commission on Wartime Relocation and Internment of Civilians* (Washington, DC: The Civil Liberties Public Education Fund/Seattle: University of Washington Press, 1997), 69.
6. George Knox Roth, letter to Los Angeles City Council, July 13, 1967. Courtesy of Irma Brubaker Roth.
7. Irma Roth, interview.
8. Chuman, "Man JAs forgot to thank."
9. "Subversive acts here described," *Los Angeles Times*, March 25, 1942.
10. "Reds accused of plan to dupe mayor," *Los Angeles Times*, March 27, 1942.
11. Ibid.
12. "Tenney tells inquiry goal: Legal action will be taken against Roth, chairman asserts," *Los Angeles Times*, March 28, 1942.
13. Irma Roth, interview.
14. "Roth convicted of contempt," *Los Angeles Times*, April 5, 1942.
15. "Ruling due today in contempt case," *Los Angeles Times*, June 4, 1942.
16. Irma Roth, interview.
17. George Knox Roth, letter to Lillian C. Kimura, October 18, 1977. Courtesy of Irma Brubaker Roth.
18. Irma Roth, interview.
19. Ibid.
20. Clifton's Cafeteria, www.cliftonscafeteria.com.
21. Irma Roth, interview.
22. Ibid.
23. Ibid.
24. Irma Brubaker Roth, letter to Henry S. Sakai, January 12, 1977. Courtesy of the Japanese American National Museum.
25. Chuman, "Man JAs forgot to thank."
26. "Community to fete Roth for war camp stand," *The Rafu Shimpo*, July 15, 1977.
27. Dwight Chuman, "Hot Metal," *The Rafu Shimpo*, August 12, 1977.
28. Henry S. Sakai, letter to the editor, *The Rafu Shimpo*, August 18, 1977.
29. Y. Shiroma, letter to George Roth, July 29, 1977. Courtesy of Irma Brubaker Roth.
30. Irma Brubaker Roth, oral testimony, Commission on Wartime Relocation and Internment of Civilians, Los Angeles, California, August 4, 1981. Courtesy of the William Hohri Collection, Japanese American National Museum.
31. George Knox Roth, oral testimony, Commission on Wartime Relocation and Internment of Civilians, Los Angeles, California, August 6, 1981. Courtesy of the William Hohri Collection, Japanese American National Museum.

4. HERBERT AND MADELINE NICHOLSON

Herbert Nicholson's writings quoted by permission of Samuel O. Nicholson. *Voices Long Silent: An Oral Inquiry into the Japanese American Evacuation* quoted by permission of the Center for Oral and Public History, California State University, Fullerton.

1. Herbert Nicholson, "A Friend of the American Way: An Interview with Herbert Nicholson," *Voices Long Silent: An Oral Inquiry into the Japanese American Evacuation*, eds. Arthur Hansen and Betty Mitson (Fullerton, CA: California State University, Fullerton, 1974), 116.
2. Ibid.
3. Betty E. Mitson, "Looking Back in Anguish: Oral History and Japanese American Evacuation," *Voices Long Silent: An Oral Inquiry into the Japanese American Evacuation*, eds. Arthur Hansen and Betty Mitson (Fullerton, CA: California State University, Fullerton; 1974), 27.
4. Herbert Nicholson, *Treasure in Earthen Vessels* (Upland, CA: privately printed, J. Irvin Brunk, printer, 1972), 79.
5. Nicholson, *Treasure in Earthen Vessels*, 10.
6. Ibid., 11.
7. Ibid., preface.
8. Ibid., 37.
9. Nicholson, "A Friend of the American Way," 111.
10. Ibid., 112.
11. Nicholson, *Treasure in Earthen Vessels*, 39.
12. Samuel Nicholson, telephone conversation with author, February 26, 2004. Quoted by permission of Samuel O. Nicholson.
13. Nicholson, "A Friend of the American Way," 117.
14. Ibid., 118.
15. Ibid.
16. Ibid., 124.
17. Ibid., 125.
18. Ibid., 122.
19. Ibid., 124.
20. Ibid., 123.
21. Ibid., 122.
22. Ibid.
23. Ibid., 123.
24. Herbert Nicholson, oral testimony, Commission on Wartime Relocation and Internment of Civilians, Los Angeles, California, August 6, 1981. Courtesy of the William Hohri Collection, Japanese American National Museum. Originally from the National Archives, Record Group 220, Records of the Commission on Wartime Relocation and Internment of Civilians, 1981–1983, NC3-220-83-4, Hearings, Box 75, Folder Los Angeles, August 6, 1981.
25. Nicholson, "A Friend of the American Way," 127
26. Ibid., 126.
27. Ibid., 129.
28. Samuel Nicholson, "Truck-Driving Missionary," *Friends Journal*, November 1992: 18. Quoted from an article by Samuel Nicholson that was first published in *Friends Journal*, November 1992. ©1992 Friends Publishing Corporation. Reprinted with permission. www.friendsjournal.org.
29. Nicholson, *Treasure in Earthen Vessels*, 45.
30. Samuel Nicholson, "Truck-Driving Missionary."
31. Audrie Girdner and Anne Loftis, *The Great Betrayal: The Evacuation of the Japanese Americans During World War II* (New York: The MacMillan Company, 1970), 305.
32. Samuel Nicholson, telephone conversation with author.
33. Nicholson, "A Friend of the American Way," 118.

34. Nicholson, *Treasure in Earthen Vessels,* 53.

35. Nicholson, "A Friend of the American Way," 131.

36. Clifford Uyeda, "Shot Dead: Killed by Sentries in America's Concentration Camps," *Nikkei Heritage,* Spring 2000: 5.

37. Nicholson, "A Friend of the American Way," 135.

38. Ibid., 138–139.

39. Nicholson, *Treasure in Earthen Vessels,* 62.

40. Ibid., preface.

41. Sources for E. Stanley Jones:

Christian Ashram Web site: http://www.christianashram.org/jones.htm (June 27, 2004).

Jones, E. Stanley. "Barbed Wire Christians" (speech, Topaz internment camp, Utah, October 24–29, 1943). Courtesy of Paul Nagano. Quoted by permission of Eunice Matthews.

Nicholson, Herbert. *Treasure in Earthen Vessels* (Privately printed. J. Irvin Brunk, printer, Upland, CA: 1972), 52.

Suzuki, Lester E. *Ministry in the Assembly and Relocation Centers of World War II* (Berkeley, CA: Yardbird Publishing, 1979), 74, 117–118, 173, 186–188, 260–261, 261–271, 289–290, 303–304.

5. Elizabeth and Catherine Humbargar

The *Sacramento Bee* quoted by permission of the *Sacramento Bee.* The *Stockton Record* quoted by permission of the *Stockton Record.* Quotations from the *Hokubei Mainichi* reprinted with permission of the *Hokubei Mainichi.*

1. Max Norris, "Standing by her friends: Former teacher recalls internment-camp classroom," *Sacramento Bee,* August 11, 1984. Courtesy of Barry Saiki.

2. Helen Flynn, "City sets 'Elizabeth Humbargar Day': Ex-teacher aided Japanese," *Stockton Record,* February 20, 1970. Courtesy of Barry Saiki.

3. "Award from Japan for local teacher," *Stockton Record,* October 15, 1976. Courtesy of Barry Saiki.

4. Ibid.

5. Richard Hayashi, "A remembrance of a saintly lady," *Hokubei Mainichi,* July 28, 1989. Courtesy of Barry Saiki.

6. Grayce Kaneda Uyehara, telephone interview by author, September 30, 2004. Quoted by permission of Grayce Kaneda Uyehara.

7. James Doi, telephone interview by author, January 29, 2004. Quoted by permission of James Doi.

8. Ibid.

9. Ibid.

10. "A Person in Time: Elizabeth Humbargar," Blue Bear Books, 1996. Courtesy of Barry Saiki.

11. Marjorie Flaherty, "Japan Americans and her other friends mourn a tough 'saint,'" *Senior Spectrum,* July 24, 1989. Courtesy of Barry Saiki.

12. Barry Saiki, telephone interview by author, September 30, 2004. Quoted by permission of Barry Saiki.

13. Flaherty, "Friends mourn a tough 'saint.'"

14. Uyeda interview.

15. Norris, "Standing by her friends."

16. "Award from Japan."

17. Norris, "Standing by her friends."

18. Hayashi, "$15,000 scholarship fund in Stockton set," *Pacific Citizen,* date unknown. Courtesy of Barry Saiki.

19. "Award from Japan."

20. Norris, "Standing by her friends."

21. "A Person in Time."

22. Grayce Kaneda Uyehara, letter to author, December 20, 2004.

23. Ibid.

6. Prewar Relationships

1. Nellie Nakamura, *A Century of Change: The Memoirs of Nellie Yae Sumiye Nakamura, 1902–2002* (Fremont, CA: David Nakamura, 2000). Quoted by permission of Nellie Nakamura.

2. Reprinted by permission of Phyllis Mizuhara and the California State Library.

3. Harry Fukuhara, unpublished essay, 2005. Published by permission of Harry Fukuhara.

7. Good Neighbors

1. Dan and Liz Krieger, "Baseball and the Good Neighbor Policy," *War Comes to the Middle Kingdom: Vol. 1: 1939–1942,* eds. Stan Harth, Liz Krieger and Dan Krieger (San Luis Obispo, CA: EZ Nature Books, 1991), 161–163. First published in *San Luis Obispo County Telegram-Tribune,* September 28, 1991. Quoted by permission of Dan Krieger.

2. Kazuo Ikeda, telephone interview by author, September 13, 2004. Quoted by permission of Kazuo Ikeda.

3. John Loomis and Gordon Bennett, *John and Gordon: The Old Days, 1932–1944 in Arroyo Grande, California* (Arroyo Grande: Boococks of America Press, 2002), 56–57. Courtesy of Gordon and Manetta Bennett. Quoted by permission of John Loomis and Gordon Bennett.

4. Kreiger, "Baseball and the Good Neighbor Policy."

5. Sandra Loomis Cabassi, telephone conversation with author, April 4, 2005. Quoted by permission of Sandra Loomis Cabassi.

6. Kreiger, "Baseball and the Good Neighbor Policy."

7. John Loomis, telephone conversation with author, September 15, 2004. Quoted by permission of John Loomis.

8. Ikeda, telephone interview by author, September 15, 2004. Quoted by permission of Kazuo Ikeda.

9. Ibid.

10. John Loomis, telephone conversation.

11. Haruo Hayashi, telephone interview by author, September 15, 2004. Quoted by permission of Haruo Hayashi.

12. Kreiger, "Baseball and the Good Neighbor Policy."

13. Ken Kobara, telephone interview by author, September 15, 2004. Quoted by permission of Ken Kobara.

14. Hayashi, telephone interview.

15. Ikeda, telephone interview.

16. Kreiger, "Baseball and the Good Neighbor Policy."

17. Hayashi, telephone interview.

18. Ikeda, telephone interview.

19. John Sherrill, "Neighbors," *Readers' Digest,* November 1992, 141–143. First published in *Guideposts,* April 1992. Courtesy of Harry Fukuhara.

20. Materials courtesy of Jean Thevierge, Local History Specialist, Redwood City Public Library.

Daily News, "Banker aided Japanese prisoners held in WWII internment camps," October 28, 2002.

Hokubei Mainichi, "Banker Who Helped Internees Honored Posthumously," November 5, 2003.

Hokubei Mainichi, "Researcher to discuss JA History in Redwood City," February 9, 2005.

Kansha: Honoring J. Elmer Morrish, September 27, 2003 (Redwood City: Redwood City Public Library, 2003. Commemorative brochure.

Reed, Dan. "Banker honored for deeds in W.W. II," *San Jose Mercury News,* September 28, 2003.

21. Materials courtesy of Judy Niizawa and Harry Fukuhara:

Dillon, Pat. "One light in darkness," *San Jose Mercury News,* November 1991.

Kumada, Art. "History of the San Jose Buddhist Church Betsuin" http://www.sjbetsuin.com/who%20pages/history.html (May 21, 2005).

Mineta, Norman Y. U.S. Congress. House. Extension of remarks introducing a bill to designate the federal building in San Jose, CA, as the Robert F. Peckham Courthouse and Federal Building, HR 1346, 103rd Congress, March 16, 1993. http://thomas.loc.gov/cgi-bin/query/D?r103:7:./ temp/~r103TEFTN6:: (May 21, 2005).

Neuman, Johanna. "What Moves Him? Cars, Trucks, Trains and Planes," *Los Angeles Times,* April 25, 2005.

Nichi Bei Times, "How San Josean Aided World War II Internees," August 13, 1987.

22. "Liberty Lost...Lessons in Loyalty," commemorative program for the Re-enactment of the 1942 Evacuation on April 27, 2002, in Watsonville, CA. Courtesy of Mas Hashimoto.

23. "What of the West Coast Japanese?" *Watsonville Register-Pajaronian,* January 13, 1943.

24. "Defense Council Raps Freeing of Interned Japs," *Watsonville Register-Pajaronian,* February 24, 1943.

25. John L. McCarthy, letter to the editor, *Watsonville Register-Pajaronian,* March 9, 1943.

26. "Flare Thrown at Buddhist Temple Here," *Watsonville Register-Pajaronian,* September 24, 1945.

8. HELEN ELY (BRILL)

The writings of Helen Ely Brill, Robert Brill and Laurel Brill Swan quoted by permission of Laurel Brill Swan.

1. Helen Ely Brill, oral history, University of Connecticut, interviewed by Karen Will, November 18, 1999, 1. Quoted by permission of the University of Connecticut.
2. Laurel Brill Swan, unpublished essay on Quaker activism.
3. Helen Ely Brill, oral history, American Friends Service Committee, interviewed by Antonio Leal, August 17, 1991, 4. Courtesy of Stephen McNeil. Quoted by permission of the American Friends Service Committee.
4. Brill, University of Connecticut, 3.
5. Ibid., 1.
6. Brill, American Friends Service Committee, 1.
7. Brill, University of Connecticut, 3.
8. Ibid.
9. Brill, American Friends Service Committee, 4.
10. Brill, University of Connecticut, 6.
11. Ibid.
12. Ibid., 8.
13. Ibid.
14. Ibid., 9.
15. Ibid.
16. Ibid., 8.
17. Ibid.
18. Brill, American Friends Service Committee, 5.
19. Ibid., 6.
20. Ibid., 2.
21. Brill, University of Connecticut, 11.
22. Brill, American Friends Service Committee, 6.
23. Helen Ely, "On Manzanar," 1942, unpublished essay. Courtesy of Laurel Brill Swan.
24. Brill, University of Connecticut, 11.
25. Brill, American Friends Service Committee, 7.
26. Helen Ely, "Christmas at Manzanar," 1942, unpublished essay. Courtesy of Laurel Brill Swan.
27. Ibid.
28. Brill, University of Connecticut, 12.
29. Brill, American Friends Service Committee, 6.
30. Ibid., 4.
31. Ibid., 7.
32. Helen Ely Brill and Robert Brill, "The Manzanar Yearbook," unpublished oral history by Laurel Brill Swan. Courtesy of Laurel Brill Swan.
33. Ibid.
34. Ibid.
35. Helen Ely, "Ansel Adams at Manzanar," unpublished essay. Courtesy of Laurel Brill Swan.
36. Brill, University of Connecticut, 13.
37. Susan Campbell, "Her pledge was 'Justice for all,'" *The Hartford Courant,* April 27, 2003.
38. Brill, University of Connecticut, 14.
39. Jane Gordon, "When America imprisoned the innocent," *The Hartford Courant,* December 9, 1996.
40. Campbell, "Her pledge was 'Justice for all.'"
41. Joe Nagano, letter to editor, *The Rafu Shimpo,* May 27, 2003. Quoted by permission of Joe Nagano.

9. MARGARET MATTHEW D'ILLE (GLEASON)

1. Susanne Norton Coffey, "Relocation camp is scene of family's holiday," *Lake County Record-Bee,* January 3, 2004. Quoted by permission of Susanne Norton Coffey and the *Lake County Record-Bee.*
2. *Memorial Service: Margaret Matthew Gleason* (Los Angeles: Mount Hollywood Church, May 1954). Courtesy of Susanne Norton Coffey. Quoted by permission of Susanne Norton Coffey.
3. Ralph P. Merritt III, telephone conversation with author, May 9, 2005. Quoted by permission of Ralph P. Merritt III.
4. Ralph P. Merritt, *Memorial Service: Margaret Matthew Gleason.* Quoted by permission of Ralph P. Merritt III.
5. Ibid.
6. Ibid.
7. Miya Sannomiya Kikuchi, *Memorial Service: Margaret Matthew Gleason.* Quoted by permission of Isao Kikuchi.
8. Ibid.
9. Ibid.
10. Ibid.
11. Mildred Magruder, *Allan Armstrong Hunter: A Biography* (Los Angeles: Mount Hollywood Church, 1974).
12. *A History of Mount Hollywood Congregational Church, 75th Anniversary Edition, 1906–1981* (Los Angeles: Mount Hollywood Church, 1981).

10. THE BELL FAMILY

Bell family writings courtesy of Paul and Earnest Bell.

1. Gladys K. Bell, "Memories of Topaz: Japanese War Relocation Center, 1942–1945," 1981, 1. Originally published in the *Hokubei Mainichi.* Quoted by permission of Gladys K. Bell and the *Hokubei Mainichi.*
2. Ibid.
3. Ibid., 2.
4. Roscoe E. Bell, "Relocation Center Life: Topaz, Utah, 1942–1945," unpublished memoir, 1982, 1–2. Quoted by permission of Gladys K. Bell.
5. Roscoe Bell, "Relocation Center Life," 1–2.
6. Gladys Bell, "Memories of Topaz," 2.
7. Paul Bell, oral history, *Blossoms in the Desert: Topaz High School Class of 1945,* ed. Darrell Y. Hamamoto (San Francisco: Topaz High School Class of 1945, 2003), 4–9. Quoted by permission of Paul Bell.
8. Gladys Bell, "Memories of Topaz," 15.

9. Ibid., 9.
10. Roscoe Bell, "Relocation Center Life," 13.
11. Ibid., 14–15.
12. Ibid., 16.
13. Ibid., 17.
14. Ibid., 25.
15. Ibid., 27.
16. Ibid., 28.
17. Ibid., 30.
18. Ibid., 34.
19. Gladys Bell, "Memories of Topaz," 6.
20. Roscoe Bell, "Relocation Center Life," 36.
21. Gladys Bell, "Memories of Topaz," 6.
22. Ibid., 12–13.
23. Ibid., 14.
24. Ibid.
25. Paul Bell, *Blossoms in the Desert*, 5–6.
26. Ibid., 8.
27. Ibid., 4–5.
28. Ibid., 9.
29. Roscoe Bell, "Relocation Center Life," 39.

11. Dr. Joseph Goodman

1. Joseph Goodman, "Topaz," unpublished memoir, February 1991, 1. Courtesy of Glenn Kumekawa and Paul Tani. Quoted by permission of Lysbeth Goodman.
2. "Topaz," 4.
3. Glenn Kumekawa, "Dr. Joseph R. Goodman: A Tribute to His Memory," in e-mail message to author, May 19, 2004. Quoted by permission of Glenn Kumekawa.
4. Goodman, "Topaz," 1.
5. Goodman, "Topaz," 2.
6. Goodman, "Topaz," 3.
7. Lysbeth Goodman, telephone conversation with author, December 2, 2004. Quoted by permission of Lysbeth Goodman.
8. Goodman, "Topaz," 5.
9. Goodman, "Topaz," 22.
10. Paul Tani, e-mail message to author, June 2, 2004. Quoted by permission of Paul Tani.
11. Goodman, "Topaz," 11.
12. Goodman, "Topaz," 15.
13. Goodman, "Topaz," 17.
14. Goodman, "Topaz," 22.
15. Goodman, "Topaz," 22–23.
16. Alan Gathright, "Joseph Goodman: UCSF professor," *San Francisco Chronicle*, April 22, 2004.
17. Glenn Kumekawa, e-mail message to author, May 19, 2004. Quoted by permission of Glenn Kumekawa.
18. Ibid.
19. Eleanor Gerard Sekerak, "A Teacher at Topaz," *Only What We Could Carry: The Japanese American Internment Experience,* ed. Lawson Fusao Inada (Berkeley: Heyday Books/California Historical Society, 2000), 126–137.
20. Paul Tani, untitled (address written for the 2000 Topaz High School Reunion, Classes of 1943 and 1944). Courtesy of Paul Tani. Quoted by permission of Paul Tani.

21. Eleanor Gerard Sekerak, telephone conversation with author, April 2, 2005. Quoted by permission of Eleanor Sekerak.
22. Tani, untitled address.
23. Victor Goertzel, "Recollections," unpublished essay, August 1989. Quoted by permission of Ted Goertzel.
24. Ibid.
25. Ted Goertzel, biography of Mildred Goertzel, http:///www.crab.rutgers.edu/~goertzel/mildred goertzel.htm (January 17, 2004).
26. Tomoye Takahashi, e-mail message to author. Quoted by permission of Tomoye Takahashi.
27. Victor Goertzel (draft of speech delivered at the ACLU Civil Libertarian Award Ceremony, Seattle, 1993). Courtesy of John Goertzel. Quoted by permission of Ted Goertzel.
28. Ibid.
29. Glenn Kumekawa, letter to Mrs. Milton J. Shapp, née Muriel Matzkin, August 25, 1976. Courtesy of Glenn Kumekawa. Quoted by permission of Glenn Kumekawa.
30. Muriel Matzkin, rough transcript of conversation with Joe Anderson, March 2, 1991. Courtesy of the Historical Society of Pennsylvania. Quoted by permission of the Historical Society of Pennsylvania.
31. Ritsuko Nakahira Iwasa, oral history, *Blossoms in the Desert: Topaz High School Class of 1945,* ed. Darrell Y. Hamamoto (San Francisco: Topaz High School Class of 1945, 2003), 79.
32. Matzkin, conversation with Joe Anderson.
33. "Governor Milton J. Shapp," *Pennsylvania Governors Past and Present,* Pennsylvania Historical and Museum Commission, http://www.phmc.state.pa.us/bah/dam/governors/shapp.asp?secid=31 (April 10, 2005).
34. Eleanor Sekerak, telephone conversation with author.
35. Hannah Maggiora Wallstrum, telephone conversation with author, April 25, 2005. Quoted by permission of Hannah Maggiora Wallstrum.
36. Ibid.
37. Ibid.

12. Rev. Emery Andrews

Quotations from the writings of Rev. Emery Andrews and Rev. Brooks Andrews by permission of Rev. Brooks Andrews.

1. Yukio Mochizuki, letter to Harry Fukuhara, July 30, 2003. Courtesy of Harry Fukuhara. Quoted by permission of Yukio Mochizuki.
2. Rev. Paul M. Nagano, "Reverend Emery E. Andrews: Northwest's 'Man for Others,'" *American Baptist Quarterly* 16, no. 3 (September 1998): 194. Quoted by permission of Rev. Paul M. Nagano and the *American Baptist Quarterly.*
3. Ibid., 194.
4. Rev. Brooks Andrews, oral history, Densho Project, interviewed by Tom Ikeda, Seattle, Washington, March 24, 2004. Densho Visual Histories, Densho ID: denshovh-aemery-01, segment 5. Quoted by permission of the Densho Project.
5. Ibid.
6. Arleen Andrews Engle, e-mail message to author, September 29, 2004. Quoted by permission of Arleen Engle.
7. Rev. Brooks Andrews, e-mail message to author, September 19, 2004. Quoted by permission of Rev. Brooks Andrews.
8. Rev. Paul M. Nagano, e-mail message to author, October 26, 2004. Quoted by permission of Rev. Paul M. Nagano.
9. *An Evening of Fellowship with Mrs. K.* (Seattle: Japanese Baptist Church, 1977).
10. Andrews, Densho interview, segment 7.
11. Archie Satterfield, "Looking back on Minidoka," *Seattle Post-Intelligencer,* Northwest edition, July 24,

1977. Quoted by permission of the *Seattle Post-Intelligencer.*
12. Nagano, "Andrews," 193.
13. Robert Shaffer, "Opposition to Internment: Defending Japanese American Rights during World War II," *Historian,* Spring 1999.
14. Teresa Watanabe, "Deja vu," *Los Angeles Times,* June 8, 2003. Quoted by permission of the *Los Angeles Times.*
15. Andrews, Densho interview, segment 9.
16. Rev. Brooks Andrews, "The American Exile Experience" (speech, Minidoka reunion, Seattle, WA, August 2–3, 2003).
17. Andrews, Densho interview, segment 9.
18. Washington Council of Churches and Religious Education, "Japanese Assembly Center at Puyallup," Council of Churches, Seattle, Box 15. Manuscripts and University Archives, University of Washington Libraries.
19. Andrews, e-mail message to author, June 4, 2004.
20. Satterfield, "Looking back on Minidoka."
21. Engle, e-mail message to author, September 27, 2004.
22. Rev. Brooks Andrews, e-mail message to author, September 19, 2004.
23. Engle, e-mail message to author, September 29, 2004.
24. Nagano, "Andrews," 194.
25. Andrews, "Exile."
26. Andrews, e-mail message to author, June 4, 2004.
27. Satterfeld, "Looking back on Minidoka."
28. Ibid.
29. Nagano, "Andrews," 192.
30. Satterfeld, "Looking Back."
31. Andrews, Densho interview, segment 17.
32. Andrews, Densho interview, segment 20.
33. Satterfeld, "Looking back on Minidoka."
34. Engle, e-mail message to author, September 27, 2004.
35. Andrews, Densho interview, segment 22.
36. Andrews, Densho interview, segment 23.
37. Nagano, "Andrews," 196.
38. Andrews, Densho interview, segment 22.
39. Andrews, e-mail message to author, June 7, 2004.
40. Andrews, e-mail message to author, June 4, 2004.

13. ROBERT COOMBS

1. Robert Coombs, telephone interview by author, January 15, 2004, 5. Quoted by permission of Robert Coombs.
2. Robert Coombs, oral history, Densho Project, interviewed by Alice Ito, Seattle, Washington, March 24, 2004. Densho Visual Histories, segment 4. Quoted by permission of the Densho Project.
3. Coombs, Densho interview, segment 3.
4. Robert W. Coombs, *Oral History Interview with Robert W. Coombs* (Sacramento, CA: Florin Japanese-American Citizens League and Oral History Program, California State University, Sacramento; 1995), 4. (Special-order book that includes an oral history interview with Robert Coombs conducted by Henry Yui on June 3, 1993, for the Florin Japanese American Citizens League and Oral History Program, California State University, Sacramento.) Quoted by permission of the Florin JACL.
5. Coombs, Densho interview, segment 8.
6. Ibid., segment 11.
7. Ibid., segment 13.

8. Coombs, *Oral History Interview,* 17.
9. Ibid., 28.
10. Robert W. Coombs, "A Unique Experience," appendix to *Oral History Interview with Robert W. Coombs* (Sacramento, CA: Florin Japanese American Citizens League and Oral History Program, California State University, Sacramento, 1995), 4. (Special-order book.)
11. Coombs, *Oral History Interview,* 5.
12. Ibid., 6.
13. Ibid., 8.
14. Coombs, Densho interview, segment 16.
15. Coombs, "A Unique Experience," 6.
16. Ibid., 11.
17. Ibid., 8.
18. Ibid., 7.
19. Calvin Ninomiya, "Remembering Robert W. (Bob) Coombs," unpublished essay, February 8, 2004.
20. Coombs, Densho interview, segment 17.
21. Coombs, telephone interview, 3.
22. Eugene Uyeki, letter to author, January 20, 2004.
23. Coombs, telephone interview, 2.
24. Coombs, Densho interview, segment 18.
25. Coombs, *Oral History Interview,* 30.
26. Coombs, "A Unique Experience."
27. Coombs, Densho interview, segment 24.
28. Ibid.
29. Uyeki, letter to author.
30. Coombs, Densho interview, segment 20.
31. Uyeki, letter to author.
32. Coombs, "A Unique Experience," 10.
33. Ibid., 8.
34. Calvin Ninomiya, e-mail message to author, February 8, 2004.
35. Coombs, *Oral History Interview,* 11.
36. Ninomiya, "Remembering."
37. Coombs, *Oral History Interview,* 13–14.
38. Coombs, Densho interview, segment 22.
39. Ibid., segment 23.
40. Coombs, *Oral History Interview,* 12–13.
41. Coombs, "A Unique Experience," 7.
42. Coombs, *Oral History Interview,* 28.
43. Coombs, telephone interview, 5.
44. Uyeki, e-mail message to author.
45. Coombs, *Oral History Interview,* 29.
46. Ibid., 17.
47. Ibid., 22.
48. Ninomiya, "Remembering."
49. Jean Bilodeaux, "Teacher at World War II internment camp tells about his experiences," appendix to *Oral History Interview with Robert W. Coombs* (Sacramento, CA: Florin Japanese American Citizens League and Oral History Program, California State University, 1995). (Special-order book.)
50. Ninomiya, "Remembering."

14. REV. RALPH AND MARY SMELTZER

Quotations from the Brethren Archives by permission of the Brethren Historical Library and Archives.

304

Courtesy of the Brethren Historical Library and Archives, with thanks to Kenneth M. Shaffer Jr., Director.

1. Togo Tanaka, "How to Survive Racism in America's Free Society," lecture dated April 3, 1973, published in *Voices Long Silent: An Oral Inquiry into the Japanese American Evacuation*, eds. Arthur Hansen and Betty Mitson (Fullerton, CA: California State University, Fullerton, 1974), 98. Unattributed quotation, probably from Joe Kurihara's oral history.
2. "What Is Our History?" http:///www.brethren.org/anotherway/archive/sroots.htm (March 10, 2004).
3. Mary Blocher Smeltzer, interviewed by author, La Verne, California, February 12, 2004, 5. Quoted by permission of Mary Blocher Smeltzer.
4. Mary Blocher Smeltzer, *My Odyssey*, self-published, limited edition, 2004, 27–28. Quoted by permission of Mary Blocher Smeltzer.
5. Stephen L. Longenecker, *Selma's Peacemaker: Ralph Smeltzer and Civil Rights Mediation* (Philadelphia: Temple University Press, 1987), 3.
6. Mary Smeltzer interview, 8.
7. Ibid., 2.
8. Ibid., 7.
9. Mary Smeltzer, *My Odyssey*, 27.
10. Ralph Smeltzer, letter, March 4, 1942, Church of the Brethren Archives, Box 1, File 7.
11. Letter to Franklin D. Roosevelt, June 23, 1942, Church of the Brethren Archives, JR - Problems, Box 1, File 2.
12. Mary Blocher Smeltzer, "Japanese-American Resettlement Work," *To Serve the Present Age*, ed. Donald F. Durnbaugh (Elgin, IL: Brethren Press, 1975), 124. Quoted by permission of the Brethren Press.
13. Ibid., 125–126.
14. Ibid., 126.
15. Ibid.
16. Mary Smeltzer interview, 11.
17. Tanaka, "How to Survive Racism," 100.
18. Leland E. Brubaker, letter to Mr. and Mrs. Ralph Smeltzer, November 19, 1942, Church of the Brethren Archives, BC - Box 1, File 7.
19. Ralph Smeltzer, letter to Leland E. Brubaker, November 28, 1942, Church of the Brethren Archives, BC - Box 1, File 7.
20. Charles C. Ellis, letter to Ralph Smeltzer, January 26, 1943, Church of the Brethren Archives, BC - Box 1, File 7.
21. Ralph and Mary Smeltzer, undated script for slide presentation.
22. Ralph Smeltzer, letter to Charles C. Ellis, February 18, 1943, Church of the Brethren Archives, BC - Box 1, File 7.
23. Anetta Mow, letter to Mr. and Mrs. Ralph Smeltzer, November 18, 1943, Church of the Brethren Archives, BC - Box 1, File 7.
24. Ralph Smeltzer, letter to Anetta Mow, December 21, 1942, Church of the Brethren Archives, BC - Box 1, File 7.
25. Anetta Mow, letter to Mr. and Mrs. Ralph Smeltzer, December 17, 1943, Church of the Brethren Archives, BC - Box 1, File 7.
26. Ralph Smeltzer, letter to Anetta Mow, December 21, 1942.
27. Mary Smeltzer, "Japanese-American Resettlement Work," 127.
28. Thomas Temple, letter to Ralph and Mary Smeltzer, January 21, 1943, Church of the Brethren Archives, Bethany, Box 1, File 9.
29. Ralph Smeltzer, letter to Thomas Temple, February 3, 1943, Church of the Brethren Archives, Bethany, Box 1, File 9.
30. Thomas Temple, letter to Ralph and Mary Smeltzer, February 5, 1943, Church of the Brethren Archives, Bethany, Box 1, File 9.
31. Leland E. Brubaker, letter to Ralph Smeltzer, February 4, 1943, Church of the Brethren Archives, Bethany, Box 1, File 9.
32. Leland E. Brubaker, letter to Ralph Smeltzer, February 13, 1943, Church of the Brethren Archives, Bethany, Box 1, File 9.
33. Mary Smeltzer, "Japanese-American Resettlement Work," 127.
34. Longenecker, *Selma's Peacemaker*, 7.
35. Mary Smeltzer, "Japanese-American Resettlement Work," 128.
36. Mary Smeltzer, interview, 14.
37. Mary Smeltzer, "Japanese-American Resettlement Work," 128.
38. "Relocation Through the Brethren Hostel," undated brochure published by the Brethren Service Committee. Courtesy of Mary Smeltzer.
39. Longenecker, *Selma's Peacemaker*, 7.

15. Ross and Libby Wilbur

1. Marvin Uratsu, press release, National Japanese American Historical Society, March 6, 2003. Courtesy of Marvin Uratsu.
2. Tom Walsh, "An Open Door for the Wronged of a War," *Friends Journal*, November 1992.
3. Hikaru Iwasaki, photo captions, War Relocation Authority Photographs of Japanese-American Evacuation and Resettlement, 1942–1945, Series 12–13: Relocating Evacuees. Various cities and states, 1942–1945. Courtesy of The Bancroft Library, University of California, Berkeley.
4. Ibid.
5. Ibid.
6. Walsh, "An Open Door."

16. Dr. William Lindsay Young

Historical information and photographs courtesy of Fishburn Archives, Park University, Parkville, Missouri. Carolyn McHenry Elwess, '71, University Archivist. Quoted by permission of Park University.

1. "Dr. William Lindsay Young, President, Park College, Parkville, Missouri," biographical sketch. Courtesy of Fishburn Archives, Park University.
2. Ibid.
3. William Lindsay Young, letter to Dr. Jerzy Hauptmann, March 28, 1952. Courtesy of Fishburn Archives, Park University.
4. William Lindsay Young, "The Growing Edge: Some Reflections on Eight Years at Park College," November 26, 1956. Courtesy of Fishburn Archives, Park University.
5. Ibid.
6. *In Appreciation of a Great Year by a Great Leader*, commemorative booklet, Board of Trustees of Park College, May 22, 1941. Courtesy of Fishburn Archives, Park University.
7. Gary Y. Okihiro, *Storied Lives: Japanese American Students and World War II* (Seattle: University of Washington, 1999), 30–31.
8. Okihiro, *Storied Lives*, 32.
9. David M. Hays, "'A Quiet Campaign of Education': Equal Rights at the University of Colorado, 1930–1945," unpublished manuscript. Courtesy of David M. Hays.
10. Andrea Wood Cranford, "Not an Enemy," *University of Nebraska—Lincoln Nisei Reunion, November 4–5, 1994, A Commemorative Album* (Lincoln, NE: UNL Alumni Association, 1994). First published in *Nebraska*, Summer 1994.
11. Okihiro, *Storied Lives*, 43–44.
12. Harold F. Smith, "The Battle of Parkville: Resistance to Japanese-American Students at Park College," *The Journal of Presbyterian History* 82, no. 1 (Spring 2004): 46–51. Courtesy of Fishburn Archives, Park University.
13. Kazue Sekiya Iwatsubo, telephone conversation with author, April 19, 2005. Quoted by permission of Kazue Sekiya Iwatsubo.

14. Okihiro, *Storied Lives*, 43.
15. Smith, "The Battle of Parkville."
16. Ibid.
17. William Lindsay Young, "Cool Heads for Hot Times," opening address at Park College, September 11, 1942. Courtesy of Fishburn Archives, Park University.
18. Eleanor Roosevelt, letter to William Lindsay Young, September 10, 1942. Courtesy of Fishburn Archives, Park University.
19. William S. Yamamoto, MD, letter to Dr. Tim Westcott, August 18, 2002. Courtesy of Fishburn Archives, Park University.
20. Masaye Nagao Nakamura, telephone interview with the author, April 22, 2005. Quoted by permission of Masaye Nagao Nakamura.
21. Carolyn Elwess, letter to Masaye Nakamura, April 4, 2004. Courtesy of Fishburn Archives, Park University.
22. Young, "The Growing Edge."
23. Young, "Cool Heads for Hot Times."
24. Tom Bodine, "The Story of Harvey Itano," *Friends Journal*, November 1992. Reprinted by permission of the *Friends Journal.* Excerpted from an article by Tom Bodine that was first published in *Friends Journal*, November 1992. ©1992 Friends Publishing Corporation. Reprinted with permission. www.friendsjournal.org.

17. Student Relocation and Resettlement
1. Esther Torii Suzuki, unpublished response to JACL Twin Cities Day of Remembrance questionnaire, February 19, 2000. Quoted by permission of George Suzuki.
2. Esther Torii Suzuki, "The Good Lives On," *Friends Journal: Quaker Life and Thought Today,* November 1992. Excerpted from an article by Esther Torii Suzuki that was first published in *Friends Journal*, November 1992. ©1992 Friends Publishing Corporation. Reprinted with permission. www.friendsjournal.org.
3. Daisuke Kitagawa, *Issei and Nisei: The Internment Years* (New York: Seabury Press, 1967), 163.
4. Fujiko Sugimoto Kitagawa, letter to author, February 18, 2004. Edited by author with permission of Fujiko Sugimoto Kitagawa.

18. Earl Finch
Based on a series of articles by Mark Santoki originally published in the *Hawaii Herald* on September 17, October 1, October 15, and November 5, 1999. Quoted by permission of the *Hawaii Herald.*
1. Sen. Daniel K. Inouye, telegram read at Earl Finch's funeral service, August 29, 1965. Reprinted by permission of Sen. Daniel K. Inouye.
2. Mark Santoki, "One-Man U.S.O.: The Earl Finch Story," Part I, *Hawaii Herald*, September 17, 1999.
3. Masayo Umezawa Duus, *Unlikely Liberators: The Men of the 100th and the 442nd* (Honolulu: University of Hawaii Press, 1987), 144.
4. Lyn Crost, *Honor by Fire: Japanese Americans at War in Europe and the Pacific* (Novato, CA: Presidio, 1994), 65.
5. Duus, *Unlikely Liberators*, 144.
6. Santoki, "One-Man U.S.O.," Part I.
7. Mark Santoki, e-mail message to author, March 17, 2005. Quoted by permission of Mark Santoki.
8. Earl Finch, letter to the editor, *Honolulu Star-Bulletin*. Quoted by permission of the *Honolulu Star-Bulletin.*
9. Santoki, "One-Man U.S.O.," Part II, October 1, 1999.
10. Ibid.
11. Santoki, "One-Man U.S.O.," Part III, October 15, 1999.
12. Ibid.

13. *Go For Broke Official Carnival Program,* June 7–11, 1947, p. 12–13. Courtesy of Junichi Gondai. Quoted by permission of the 442nd Veterans Club Archives.
14. Santoki, "One Man U.S.O.," Part III, October 15, 1999.
15. Ibid.
16. Ibid.
17. Ibid.
18. Ibid.
19. Santoki, "One Man U.S.O.," Part IV, November 5, 1999.
20. Ibid.
21. Ibid.
22. Ibid.

19. Hannan Family
Hannan family papers courtesy of Helen Hannan Parra and Mary Johnson. Quoted with permission of Helen Hannan Parra and Mary Johnson. Quotes have been edited slightly at their request.
1. Helen Hannan Parra, telephone interview by author, December 12, 2003, 19. Quoted with permission of Helen Hannan Parra.
2. Ibid.
3. Helen Hannan Parra, "Family History," unpublished essay.
4. Helen Hannan Parra, untitled, unpublished essay.
5. Ibid.
6. Parra, telephone interview, 4.
7. Helen "Nell" Duffy Hannan, letter from Amache, August 2, 1945.
8. Parra, telephone interview, 4.
9. Helen Hannan Parra, "The Odyssey," unpublished, 17.
10. Parra, telephone interview, 6.
11. Ibid.
12. Nell Hannan, letter, August 2, 1945.
13. Ibid.
14. Helen "Nell" Duffy Hannan, letter from Amache internment camp, August 30, 1945.
15. Parra, "The Odyssey," 17.
16. Jeffrey F. Burton, Mary Farrell, Florence B. Lord and Richard W. Lord, *Confinement and Ethnicity: An Overview of World War II Japanese American Relocation Sites*, 2nd ed. (Tucson, AZ: Western Archeological and Conservation Center, National Park Service, 2000), 282.
17. Ibid., 283.
18. Brian Niiya, ed., *Encyclopedia of Japanese American History*, rev. ed. (Los Angeles: Japanese American National Museum, 2001), 347.
19. *Kinenhi: Reflections on Tule Lake*, 2nd ed. (San Francisco, CA: Tule Lake Committee, 2000), 101.
20. Nell Hannan, undated letter fragment, numbered "21."
21. Nell Hannan, letter, dated "Winter 1945."
22. Nell Hannan, letter to "Dearest Pop," Winter 1945.
23. Nell Hannan, letter, Jan 15, 1946.
24. Parra, telephone interview, 19.
25. Ibid., 9.
26. Ibid.
27. Nell Hannan, letter, January 10, 1946.
28. Nell Hannan, undated letter.
29. Parra, telephone interview, 6.
30. Nell Hannan, undated letter.
31. Nell Hannan, letter to "Dearest Pop," January 1946.

32. Ibid.
33. Ibid.
34. Ibid.
35. Nell Hannan, letter numbered "19."
36. Parra, telephone interview, 10.
37. Ibid.
38. Parra, telephone interview, 17–18.
39. Helen Hannan Parra, untitled notes about Mari's photographs, May 20, 1994.
40. Margaret Mary "Mari"Hannan, "The Closing of Tule Lake," unpublished.
41. Parra, telephone interview, 8.
42. Ibid.
43. Parra, telephone interview, 9.
44. Parra, telephone interview, 16.

20. DEVOTED TO THE DHARMA

1. National Japanese American Historical Society, press release on Rev. Ernest Shinkaku Hunt. Courtesy of the National Japanese American Historical Society.
2. Kansha—In Appreciation: The 100th Anniversary of Japanese in Hawaii, 1885–1985 (Honolulu: Kansha Committee), 1985. Courtesy of Ted Tsukiyama.
3. Newton Ishiura, "Rev. Ernest Shinkaku Hunt." Courtesy of the National Japanese American Historical Society.
4. "Rev. Goldwater, who helped JAs during WWII, Dies at 93," Hokubei Mainichi, June 27, 2001.
5. Elaine Woo, "Rev. Julius Goldwater: convert to Buddhism aided WWII internees," Los Angeles Times, June 22, 2001.
6. Rev. Arthur Takemoto, "Julius A. Goldwater, Subhadra (Kinsui)." (Excerpts published in Betsuin Jiho, March 1990.) Courtesy of the Buddhist Churches of America Archives, Japanese American National Museum.
7. Rev. Arthur Takemoto, telephone conversation with author, May 24, 2004. Quoted by permission of Rev. Arthur Takemoto.
8. Buddhist Churches of America, Vol. 1, 75th Year History, 1899–1974. Chicago: Nobart, Inc., 1974, 62–63.
9. Newton Ishiura, "Hillcrest Sanitarium—wartime home for the Nikkei," Nichi Bei Times, December 16, 1995.
10. Takemoto, telephone conversation.
11. "Rev. Goldwater," Hokubei Mainichi.
12. Joyce Nako, "Rev. Goldwater, Buddhist priest who aided Japanese Americans during World War II passes," Pacific Citizen, July 6, 2001.
13. "Rev. Julius Goldwater helped AJA internees," Los Angeles Times, undated.
14. "Prominent Buddhist leader Julius Goldwater dies," The Rafu Shimpo, June 17, 2001.
15. Takemoto, telephone conversation.
16. Woo, "Goldwater: convert to Buddhism."
17. Tacoma Buddhist Temple History, http://www.tacomabt.org/history.htm.

WHY THE MAINLAND AND NOT HAWAII

1. Commission on Wartime Relocation and Internment of Civilians, Personal Justice Denied: Report on Wartime Relocation and Internment of Civilians (Seattle: University of Washington Press, 1997), 55.
2. Ibid., 79.
3. Ibid., 265.
4. Greg Robinson, By the Order of the President: FDR and the Internment of Japanese Americans (Cambridge, MA: Harvard University Press, 2001), 77.
5. Ibid.
6. Kansha—In Appreciation: The 100th Anniversary of Japanese in Hawaii, 1885-1985 (Honolulu: Governor's Coordinating Committee for the 1985 Japanese 100th Anniversary Celebration, 1985).
7. Ibid.
8. Ibid.
9. Ibid.
10. Commission on Wartime Relocation, Personal Justice Denied, 73.
11. Ibid., 52.
12. Roger Daniels, Prisoners with Trial: Japanese Americans in World War II, 1st rev. ed. (New York: Hill and Wang, 2004), 32.
13. Commission on Wartime Relocation, Personal Justice Denied, 69.
14. Robinson, By the Order of the President, 95.
15. Ibid.
16. Commission on Wartime Relocation, Personal Justice Denied, 70.
17. Ibid., 72.
18. Peter Irons, Justice at War: The Story of the Japanese American Internment Cases (New York: Oxford University Press, 1983), 58.
19. Robinson, By the Order of the President, 56.
20. Irons, Justice at War, 58.
21. Commission on Wartime Relocation, Personal Justice Denied, 66.
22. Brian Niiya, ed. Encyclopedia of Japanese American History: An A-to-Z Reference from 1868 to the Present, rev. ed. (New York: Checkmark Press, 2001), 151.
23. Irons, Justice at War, 66.
24. Commission on Wartime Relocation, Personal Justice Denied, 102.
25. Audrie Girdner and Anne Loftis, The Great Betrayal: The Evacuation of the Japanese Americans During World War II (Toronto: The Macmillan Company, 1969), 115–116.
26. Commission on Wartime Relocation, Personal Justice Denied, 102.

NATIONAL JACL SPONSORS

Source notes by Harry Honda.
1. According to T. Scott Miyakawa (1906–1981), Boston University sociology professor and East Coast solicitor for National JACL Sponsors.
2. Ibid.
3. George S. Schuyler, Black and Conservative (Arlington House, 1966), quoted in Patrick Washburn, J. Edgar Hoover and the Black Press in World War II.
4. According to T. Scott Miyakawa.
5. Mike Masaoka, Pacific Citizen, January 15, 1960.
Other Sources:
Biographical Dictionary of U.S. Congress, Bicentennial Edition, 1774–1989.
Biography Index (H. H.Wilson, No. 11: September 1976/August 1989, 1980).
Current Biography, 1961–70, 1971–80, 1981–90.
Dictionary of American Biography, 1957; supplements to Volume 8, 2000.
Encyclopedia of American Biography, 2nd ed., 1996.
Negro Almanac, 5th ed. (Detroit: Gale Research, 1989).
Webster's New Biographical Dictionary, 1988, 1st ed., 1969.
Who Was Who in America (Chicago: Marquis, Inc.), Vol. I: 1897–1942, II: 1943–1950, III: 1957–1960, IV: 1961–1968, V: 1969–1973.
Who's Who in America (Chicago: Marquis, Inc.).
Paul M. Nagano, "Serious Injustices I, II," American Baptist Quarterly, June and September 1998.
Ted Tsukiyama, "Hawaii Kansha Honor Roll," 1995.

INDEX